≈≈ Battling the Inland Sea ≈≈

Battling the Inland Sea

Floods, Public Policy, and the Sacramento Valley

by

ROBERT · KELLEY

Foreword by David N. Kennedy

University of California Press
BERKELEY • LOS ANGELES • LONDON

University of California Press
Berkeley and Los Angeles, California

University of California Press, Ltd.
London, England

First Paperback Printing 1998

Library of Congress Cataloging-in-Publication Data

Kelley, Robert Lloyd, 1925–1993.
Battling the inland sea: Floods, public policy, and the Sacramento Valley, 1850–1986 / by Robert Kelley.
p. cm.
Bibliography: p.
Includes index.
ISBN 978-0-520-21428-6 (pbk; alk. paper)
1. Flood control—Economic aspects—California—Sacramento River Valley. 2. Sacramento River Valley (Calif.)—History. I. Title.
HD1676.U6513 1989 333.91′009794′5—dc19 88–20912

Printed in the United States of America

15 14 13 12 11 10
10 9 8 7 6 5 4 3

The paper used in this publication meets the minimum requirements of American National Standard for Information Sciences—Permanence of Paper for Printed Library Materials, ANSI Z39.48-1984. ♾

FRONTISPIECE: *In the midst of the monster northern California flood season of mid-February, 1986, during which the Sacramento River and its tributaries produced raging, unprecedented outflows, Todd Bimstock, 16, and his dog were caught in a small aluminum boat on the Feather River's surging waters, where for hours he hung on until local authorities could get a team out to rescue him. Photo: David Parker, in the* Appeal-Democrat, *Marysville-Yuba City, Feb. 17, 1986.*

to

Berta Lee Winniford Kelley
(1898–1985)
&
Loyd Amos Kelley
(1899–   )

≈ Contents ≈

≈ Foreword ≈

The suggestion to publish a new edition of Robert Kelley's classic book on Sacramento Valley flood control came to me at a legislative hearing a few weeks after the great flood of January 1997. The largest Sacramento River flows in the State's history had resulted in two major levee breaks in the Sacramento River system, with massive flooding of farmland and several hundred homes. Farther south, the San Joaquin River and several of its tributaries overwhelmed both natural and manmade channels, causing widespread damage. California news was dominated by these events. Legislators gathered in a special meeting to hear reports from flood control officials on all aspects of what had happened.

Amid these intense discussions, one Sacramento Valley legislator mentioned that a good way to begin understanding this flood experience would be to read Professor Kelley's book. I was pleased to respond that, as a great admirer of the book, I very much agreed. Indeed, there is no better description of the flood control problem Californians face with their largest river than this unique and fascinating history. Shortly after the hearing, we approached the University of California Press to inquire about the book's current availability. Those discussions led to this edition.

Critics of California agriculture like to describe the Central Valley as a natural desert, which man has transformed into a vast garden with massive irrigation schemes. Actually, as described by Professor Kelley, prior to development the Valley floor more nearly resembled a swamp than a desert. Every winter and spring, rainfall and melting snow resulted in often destructive stream flows coming off the mountains into the Sacramento River and its tributaries. Typically, vast ponds would form on much of the Valley floor, taking months to drain into San Francisco Bay. The struggle of farmers and towns was, as often as not, with too much water rather than too little.

Written late in Professor Kelley's career, this book culminated a lifelong interest in Sacramento Valley flood problems. His first book, *Gold vs. Grain*, based on his doctoral dissertation, chronicled the conflict between hydraulic miners and farmers. For more than half a century, debris from hydraulic mining washed down the Sacramento River tributaries, choking channels, and inundating farms and communities. The ensuing debate was not only about how to control the debris, but also, from the miners' point of view, whether they had any obligation to control it.

Over his career, Professor Kelley came to view the miners-farmers conflict in a larger context of competing political theories about how the young State and nation should be governed. One of the most interesting contributions of this book is Kelley's description of the changing political climate surrounding the search for flood control. For instance, to what extent should the State and federal governments step in and control the activities of one interest to protect the property of another interest? And, to what extent should individual groups of farmers be allowed to organize governmental agencies such as reclamation districts to build levees and protect their lands?

Indeed, the history of Sacramento River flood control is a story of raging, prolonged debate—neighbor against neighbor, upstream vs. downstream, farmer against miner, one political party against another. The debates were not merely among competing economic and political interests but between renowned technical experts and self-educated lay people, with the latter eventually proved right on a key issue. For more than fifty years the State legislature and at times the U.S. Congress were the forums for the debates.

One of the central issues in the Sacramento Valley, not resolved until the first decade of this century, was whether large flows coming down the Sacramento River should be controlled entirely within levees bordering the natural channel, or, rather, be allowed to spill into a defined bypass system. For a long time, engineers proclaimed that there always would be enough hydraulic capacity within the levees of the river for even the largest flows. They based this belief on studies of the flatter, slower-moving Mississippi River. Their theory, proven incorrect, was that high velocities in a constricted river would scour the channel bottom deep enough to carry all the water.

A competing theory, first advanced in the 1860s by Will Green, a newspaper editor from Colusa, held that a defined bypass system would more nearly mimic the Sacramento River's natural condition in which high flows spilled out of the channels and ponded onto adjacent lands. Green realized that mountain runoff meant swift flooding that could overtop levees. He recognized that his proposed bypasses would require dedication of large tracts of farm land to occasional flooding. He worked hard to make the bypass system a reality, but it did not happen during Green's lifetime.

The great flood of 1907 ended this particular debate. In one fell swoop, the huge amount of water flowing through and out from the channels made it clear that a bypass system was essential. To the extent that any "doubters" remained after the 1907 flood, they were silenced by the nearly-equal 1909 flood. The engineering experts gave up their long-held views and what we now call the Sutter and Yolo Bypasses gained broad acceptance.

A latter-day version of the bypass debate is now unfolding on the San Joaquin River, after the 1997 flood. In this most recent event, the San Joaquin River and several of its tributaries overwhelmed the channel capacity, inundating farmland and some communities. In contrast to the two major Sacramento Valley levee breaks in 1997, in which flows did not exceed channel capacity but rather seeped in some way through the levees to cause blow-outs, the San Joaquin channels were not large enough for the size of the flows. Recognizing the futility of simply raising the levees, flood control experts will now evaluate the feasibility of removing levees in some locations and letting future flood flows pond onto adjacent lands. Further, consideration is being given to opening up some form of bypass through the south Delta to relieve pressure on the levees as the San Joaquin River flows into the Delta. It is hoped these issues will be resolved and changes will be made before the next major flood.

On two crucial issues, the early flood control debates that produced the present channel-bypass system in the Sacramento Valley were essentially silent. First, there was little discussion about the use or value of flood control dams. While small dams to hold back mining debris were envisioned and attempted early on, the first reservoir to allocate a specific portion of its storage space to flood control was not created until Shasta Dam and Reservoir were built by the U.S. Bureau of Reclamation in the early 1940s. Today, there are six reservoirs in the Sacramento River Basin with flood control storage paid for by the federal government. It is estimated that without this storage at least $10 billion of additional damage would have occurred in the Sacramento Valley in the 1997 flood.

A second significant fact given scant consideration many years ago is that levees constructed adjacent to natural river channels are inherently not as reliable and safe as dams. In design of dams, whether of earth or concrete, the practice is to dig out and replace the alluvial material that exists in any river channel. Sometimes this involves very deep excavations to ensure that potential seepage paths are eliminated. However, with levees it was the practice simply to build on top of the adjacent ground without much regard to an old meander layer of sand or gravel that might lie underneath. It was recognized that some seepage would occur through or underneath levees but it was assumed that the brief time in which high water stood against a levee would not lead to failure.

This defect in many levees was recognized in recent years. Remedial steps like grout-cutoff walls and seepage control systems are being retrofitted into existing levees. However, given the more than 1,000 miles of levees in the Sacramento Valley, this is a time consuming and costly process. Even when levees are upgraded, they are not designed to the same safety standards as dams. The public would probably not be willing to pay for levees constructed to the same standards as dams. Thus, while actions must be taken to make levees safer than when they were first constructed, levees by their nature are the weak link in the flood control system.

In the last two chapters of his book, Professor Kelley brings the story up to 1987 by, first, assessing how the flood control system performed in the 1986 flood, and, then, summarizing the historical political forces that brought California to that point. The 1986 flood was the flood-of-record for the Sacramento Valley, producing record flows throughout much of the system. Afterwards, if one were to take statistical probability as a guide, there was every reason to believe we would not see another flood of that magnitude for many years. And yet, only eleven years later, the January 1997 flood produced flows on several major streams, such as the Feather and Yuba rivers, some 20 percent greater than 1986.

Professor Kelley quotes California's first State engineer, William Hammond Hall, as saying that there will always be a larger storm to face. He feared that people might become complacent and think we had finished providing flood control, when in fact we should always remember that most Sacramento Valley urban and agricultural development is in the historical floodplain. To the extent we can afford it, we should improve our flood control system to guard against what we haven't yet seen but most certainly can expect.

A current pitfall is to think the federal standard of protecting against the one-in-a-hundred year storm is adequate. That standard is merely a statistical approach to administer a flood-insurance program. It has little to do with ensuring protection for the hundreds of thousands of people living and working behind the levee system. It is worth remembering that the Dutch, who have lived with flood threats much longer than Californians, aim for a minimum protection of 1200 years, going up to 3,000 years on their major rivers.

Should we even be living behind the levees? This question has been raised frequently in somewhat abstract terms following the 1997 floods. It is certainly a legitimate issue for discussion, particularly in areas where there is presently little or no urban development. For most of the Sacramento Valley, however, the horse is a long time gone from the barn. Significant numbers of people live and work in the historical floodplain. The cost of moving or of stopping further development would be far, far greater than the cost of providing adequate flood protection.

The real challenge lies in preparing for California's inevitable future floods by accommodating natural river flows where possible and by improving flood control systems to protect existing urban areas.

As the communities of the Sacramento Valley, together with State and federal government agencies, wrestle with these and other flood control issues we can be thankful that Professor Robert Kelley wrote this fascinating history.

David N. Kennedy, Director
Department of Water Resources
State of California
Sacramento
1997

≈ Preface ≈

The rain came down, the floods rose, the wind blew, and beat upon that house; down it fell with a great crash.

Matthew 7:27–29

"Nature in California," . . . the San Francisco journalist Carl Nolte observed . . . "is a smiling killer that can turn on you at any time."

Quoted by Herbert Michelson in Sacramento Bee, March 3, 1986

Soon after the Gold Rush which exploded in the late 1840s, thousands of the people who came to Central California followed a brief fling at the mines by moving down from the mountains to settle in the fertile Sacramento Valley. Here they shortly encountered a gravely threatening natural phenomenon. They discovered that during the annual winter cycle of torrential storms that for millennia have swept in from the Pacific, or in the season of the spring snow melt in the northern Sierra Nevada, the Sacramento River and its tributaries rose like a vast taking in of breath to flow out over their banks onto the wide Valley floor, there to produce terrifying floods. On that remarkably level expanse the spreading waters then stilled and ponded to form an immense, quiet inland sea a hundred miles long, with its dense flocks of birds rising abruptly to wheel in the sky and its still masses of tule rushes stretching from the delta to the Sutter Buttes and beyond. Not until the late spring and summer months would it drain away downstream.

For the better part of the next several generations, embattled

Wild waters in the lower Sacramento Valley during the great flood season of mid-February, 1986, released as Deer Creek rushes south at an overflow point near Galt, produce a scene of austere beauty. It tells compellingly, too, of the huge force the Valley's flood control system, put together painfully over many generations, seeks, sometimes unsuccessfully, to control.
Photo: Char Crail, Elk Grove Citizen, *February 20, 1986.*

farmers and townspeople struggled to get control of their great river system so they might live in safety on the Valley floor and put its rich soils to the plow. In our time, after that long labor, we observe in the Sacramento Valley a literally remade environment, a creation of artifice, a produced object shaped into disciplined and rational form after many fumbles and misdirections, and decades of humbling trials and errors. Where wide floodwaters regularly swept freely over the countryside and the great silent inland sea held dominion for months on end with its half-million acres of swamplands running far beyond vision's reach, there is presently an ordered, carefully drained and cultivated garden, carrying on its face a populous network of protected farms and towns, including California's swarming capital city.

Thin stands of tules rise in the drainage ditches by the roads, living fossils of the huge matted tule forests that, in the Valley's natural condition, blocked almost all cross-Valley travel. Even the natural grasses have almost disappeared, for the seeds that arrived with the immigrants from the Eastern states produced a new flora of grasses in California's grazing lands.[1] Rice and alfalfa fields occupy hundreds of square miles of the Valley floor, and deep-plowed fruit orchards mass in closely packed ranks beside the rivers. The Sacramento and its tributaries are hidden behind a thousand miles of high levees, massive in their bulk, which have made a Holland of the Sacramento Valley. In high water times the rivers are allowed carefully to overflow at controlled locations into a leveed bypass channel, the excess waters then moving within these walls down-valley through the lowlands to pass unimpeded out a straightened and gigantically widened river mouth. No more the long tarrying of floodwaters on the Valley floor for months on end, forming the inland sea; it is a brisk and disciplined passage now to Suisun Bay.

The struggle to remake the Sacramento Valley and create this carefully planned environment, and the argument that raged year in and year out over how best to do it, is the central theme of my story. The remaking of the Sacramento Valley was born and carried forward in an intensely personal struggle that for many years spawned an embittered and relentless guerrilla warfare of neighbor against neighbor, with injunctions serving as artillery cannonades and levees as fortifications, all waged amid a war of words focused on clashing theories of flood control, which echoed on year after year.

In following the Valley's story, we watch small communities of villagers and farmers gathering together their meager local funds, hooking up their horses and rudimentary scrapers, and piling up long mounds of earth to make levees along their stretches of the river high enough to force floodwaters over onto the other side, in order to safeguard their own. In prompt riposte, those who live behind the opposite river bank then step forward to do the same, so that levees mount higher and higher, and all without overall plan or guidance in an absolute wilderness of classic American laissez-faire and localism. Ironically, the Valley at these times seems like a lilliputian version of the European landscape of centuries before, with its walled towns in a permanent state of each against all, everyone looking out for themselves in a situation in which damage to someone else—pushing the floodwaters over to the other side—would in this case be an advantage to the home folks.

In the presence of this internecine conflict, at one point we follow a masked party rowing to a disputed high embankment to overpower guards and cut the embankment open, allowing the river once more to pour out through its normal overflow channel and thereby save riverfront lands downstream. And after the embankment is rebuilt, we see its enemies mounting another naval assault to rip it open again. Eventually a complicated patchwork of what are in effect small city-states takes form on the Valley floor, in the shape of many locally financed and locally controlled reclamation districts, each with its own levees and more or less in permanent rivalry with its neighboring principalities.

In the search to create some order out of this anarchy, which made effective flood control impossible, the battle against the inland sea quickly surfaced in the state legislature, and it periodically sounded back and forth in that chamber for half a century and more into the future. In one bitterly conflicted session in the early 1880s the flood control controversy brought the legislature's proceedings entirely to a halt, so that not even an appropriation bill was enacted.

In the midst of it all was the large, puzzling, obstinate question:

how, in fact, did the great plexus of streams and rivers in the Valley behave, in floodtime? How big were the flows, where did they go and why? What mental picture of the rivers and their performance best fit that immense and, for decades, largely unknown reality? And what kind of plan for controlling its floods would work? A difficult, painfully slow, and frustrating learning process had to be worked through by the whole community, ordinary citizens and civil engineers alike. The people of the Valley had gone to school with the Sacramento River, and they would still be trying to decipher its lessons well into the twentieth century.

From the 1880s onward, Californians began looking to higher levels of authority for assistance by mounting appeals to Washington, D.C., which in the 1890s started producing significant results. In the post-1900 Progressive Era, all of this came to fruition in an extraordinary burst of public discussion and policy making, in California and in Washington, reaching its peak during the whirlwind years of Governor Hiram Johnson and President Woodrow Wilson (1910–1920). The campaign achieved lasting success in the building of a still actively functioning state and federal partnership, embodied in California's Reclamation Board and in the U.S. Army Corps of Engineers' Sacramento Flood Control Project. The construction of this partnership, and the adoption and building of a centrally regulated valley-wide system of integrated levees, weirs, and bypasses, put in place what policy scholars call a "standing policy decision" that endures to this day.

Its appearance, which led in time to the transforming of a stagnant, flood-ravaged province into one of the world's most fruitful food-growing regions, forms the concluding point for this book. An epilogue in chapter 14 brings the story of the Sacramento Flood Control Project to our own time, with a brief look at the enormous, unprecedented flows and flood season of 1986 to see how the Project currently works. Chapter 15 presents an overview analysis of what the whole story reveals about American political culture and policy making.

This long encounter in the Sacramento Valley makes an absorbingly human story, especially at the level of local conflicts and arguments. It has been a fascinating one to dig out in researches that began more than a quarter of a century ago into bodies of private and public documents scattered all over the Valley. History in its truest and most ancient form, as we see in the writings of Herodotus, is a human tale, a narrative of a particular group of people whom we come to know as persons and follow, step by step, as they confront and seek to master a large and life-absorbing challenge, mobilizing such mother wit and gifts of character as they may possess. In the pages that follow, telling this kind of story has occupied center stage.

Thucydides, the other of the great Greek founders of the discipline, thought of history as having another purpose as well: it should tell us large truths about public affairs. In that spirit, this book is intended as a case study that reveals and illuminates larger national public policy themes and dynamics. As another great historian, Edward Augustus Freeman, put the matter, "the real . . . problem is how to make a universal statement through a specific example." Thus, the subtheme in my work has been to use it as an opportunity to tease out general understandings of how public policy has been made in this country and how that activity is shaped by the encompassing political culture. Policy making, after all, is the oldest and most central task in human society; we can find no people, however primitive, without some arrangement at their core for making and carrying out joint decisions, painfully devised as solutions to their shared problems. The gathered elders seated in an arguing circle: this is the archetypical scene among scattered tribal peoples in the deserts and remote jungle dwellers in their hutments in the rain forests.

In this sense, it has always seemed to me that nothing could be more important, more revealing of us at our most universally human and also at our most distinctively American, than to study historically—that is, over time—how we do these things.[2] To watch the policy-making process, however, is to observe an untidy and complicated scene filled with movement, personalities, multiple encounters, and powerful crisscrossing human urges and needs. How to explain it all with some system and order? Within my discipline there is not much guidance. Historians have traditionally been fascinated by public affairs, and in describing them they have long developed a skilled touch in managing their primary commodity, the time dimension, but they generally pay little attention to thinking systematically about how to explain the policy process and its outcomes.

I have found wise advice on this score in a humane and sensitive book written by two distinguished and richly experienced policy analysts, Garry D. Brewer and Peter deLeon, *The Foundations of Policy Analysis* (Homewood, Ill., The Dorsey Press, 1983). Focusing on the human equation as the central influence in any situation and not simply on economic motives—they deplore the traditional one-factor, cost-benefit, "economic man" approach—they urge those who set out to understand and explain a policy controversy to work out: who the players are, and especially their values and ideas; their definitions of the specific situation at hand (always a fertile source of differences); how the various participants image each other; the role of the time dimension, which introduces a continual flow of shifts and changes in the total scene; how the information system is working (what do people know, in a factual sense, about the issue?); and the specific structures of governing that are in operation, the particular ways in which formal decisions are reached and implemented.

The personal element, ever powerful, ever elusive—in short, the unique qualities and contributions of key individuals—and even the impact of sovereign chance: both of these are anathema to the numbers-oriented, yet these elements are given an important place in this pluralistic "policy sciences" approach. We must closely examine, too, the emotions, the affective influences, for people are rarely simply logical or rational in the things they do. They are driven by hopes and fears, by optimism and anxiety, by preexisting hostilities between ethnic and religious groups, even by paranoia. Most of all, the policy sciences approach insists that we must understand the *context* of the situation, its overall setting. Context is powerful, probably primary, in the policy process. In an important sense, my book is an essay on that theme. "Contextuality," Brewer and deLeon write, "means understanding the relationship between the parts and whole of a problem . . . we urge comprehensiveness by giving preference to the whole."[3]

≈≈≈

Preface

My California studies are a segment of my research and teaching interests as a whole, which over many years have been aimed at exploring and seeking to understand the entire sweep of American politics and public policy—and especially the public mind in this country—from the time of origins to the present. Thus, keeping context steadily in mind has for me meant putting California affairs within the larger setting of what was going on, contemporaneously, in the nation at large. Indeed, if the task were to understand a current state problem, I would do no less. This book is built around that core principle: that local experience gains its full meaning for us only when we see it within the framework of national experience; that to treat California's history in isolation, as is too much the custom, is to deny ourselves the soundest insights into its nature.

Putting California in its national context allows us to learn how powerfully what happened in the state was shaped by American political culture nationwide. To this interplay, I pay a great deal of attention. It might be asked, what is "political culture"? It is not, for one thing, the simple story of event following event in everyday politics. A useful analogy could be the difference between reporting the flow of play in a particular sporting event and describing the larger framework that sets up its overall nature: the rules of the game; the contrasting ideas about it, even its purpose in the larger scheme of things, believed in by the opposing coaches; the kinds of people the two teams tend to recruit, their values, and their consequent style of play; who their traditional "enemy" is, toward whom they orient themselves; and their sense of identity, of cohesion.

We cannot say that these influences are the "cause" of the teams' season-long performance, since causation is ever elusive, indeed if the philosopher David Hume was correct, out of reach. Rather, with William Dray in *Laws and Explanation in History* (London, Oxford University Press, 1957), we may instead say that when these underlying factors are brought into the analysis, we are enabled to understand the situation more deeply. That is, what actually happened is more clearly seen as reasonable and appropriate, which is as far as we can expect explanation, in any mode, to take us.

The decades-long struggle to get control of the Sacramento

River illustrates, too, how a society originally built almost exclusively around individualism and localism was slowly but irresistibly pushed on to construct, out of necessity, strong regulatory central authorities. In this sense, *Battling the Inland Sea* is a study in the history of American federalism. The people of the Valley pursued their long learning process within the framework of a Madisonian constitutional system. In that arrangement, unique to the American republic, power, conceived by the American people to be the common enemy, was broken up, dispersed, coop'd and cabined in by bills of rights, and fettered by divided and competing powers between branches of government, as well as by a triumphant national faith in laissez-faire. As Harry N. Scheiber and Donald J. Pisani have written, its effect, through its quite extraordinary dispersal of power, was to stimulate the swift development of the continent's vast resources.[4]

This it achieved by freeing entrepreneurs to do pretty much as they pleased, and by leaving the states in possession of such large, potent powers that they were able to plunge into ambitious programs of state-aided local economic development, from the Erie Canal of the 1820s onward. A theme in this study, therefore, has been to illustrate how local conflicts created by this system pushed the process, almost against its will, to the national level, bringing more potent authorities into play and creating a complex federal–state partnership.

≈≈≈

That all of this ended in the destroying of a large natural environment is of course the background to this story. As a person who shares the environmentalist and naturalist impulses of our time, the disappearance of all that natural beauty—one of America's largest fresh-water wetlands—is not something I am able to contemplate in bland indifference. That in our own time we possess in the Valley a chemicals-driven, soils-exploitive corporate agriculture empire that has given us grave ecological problems is without question. However, it is impossible to conceive of a historical situation in which the regular outbreak of ravaging floods, and the periodic reappearance in the Valley of a vast inland sea, would have been simply passively accepted. There are now hundreds of thousands of people living on a million acres of protected land in the Valley who could never have taken up residence there were affairs still in their natural condition; immense volumes of food are being produced for which the world apparently has need, though market forces are eternally erratic. To say that the Sacramento Flood Control Project should never have been brought into being seems beyond any reasonable calculus in responsible public policy or scholarship.

Before the turn of the twentieth century the classic debate took place on this issue. Lord Acton argued that the historian's task is to sit in moral judgment on the past; his mentor, the distinguished German historian Father Johan Döllinger, responded that our responsibility is rather to search for an understanding of the past, so that we may explain it soundly to readers and thereby enable them to make their own judgments.[5] History can never be entirely indifferent; we must care about the issues at hand in our books or we will never properly penetrate their reality; and there are occasions when judgment cannot be escaped, as when writing of Adolf Hitler and his crimes. As a general rule, however, my stance is Father Döllinger's, and so it is in this book.

≈≈≈

Battling the Inland Sea, which brings to completion studies of the Sacramento Valley which I began in the 1950s, can be thought of as a companion volume to my first book on American politics and public policy, *Gold vs. Grain: The Hydraulic Mining Controversy in California's Sacramento Valley* (Glendale, Calif., Arthur H. Clark Co., 1959). Its subject was an intense political struggle set in motion by the depredations of hydraulic gold mining in the northern Sierra Nevada, whose operations deposited enormous volumes of mud, sand, and gravel in the rivers and greatly exaggerated the Valley's natural flooding habits. As it happened, writing *Gold vs. Grain* made me the only historian to know about flooding in the Sacramento Valley and the efforts to deal with that problem. In 1963, due to a recent change in judicial doctrine which required the state to justify its design of public works when challenged, the state Attorney General's office asked me to serve as a consultant on the history of flooding and flood control planning and public works in the Valley, and as an expert witness in a pending case. The basic need was to find out how the intricate flood control system in the Valley, constructed over more than a hundred years, had come into being in particular locales and also valleywide, more or less flood by flood and project by project. So far as the deputy attorney generals who worked with me were able to find out, this was the first time an historian had been asked to do more than testify in court as to a particular document, that is, to take the stand and present a lengthy narrative history that would be admissible as evidence.

On eleven occasions over the next twenty years it was my responsibility to serve in the capacity of historical consultant, in each case conducting lengthy research to work out the local story in different parts of the Valley. In all but one case, in which the Department of Water Resources was my client, my task was to prepare documented histories in the form of unpublished consultant papers, which are listed in the bibliography of sources cited and are on file in the Water Resources Archive, University of California, Berkeley. In seven cases, my role was also that of expert witness, on occasion for as long as three days on the stand.[6]

The writing of this book, then, has in a number of its chapters been in good part based in the research carried forward in these many consultantships. It always seemed to me that in my crowded file drawers of notes there lay the core of another book on the Sacramento Valley which, if appropriately fleshed out by further research to take in larger dimensions, would tell an important chapter in environmental history as well as offer valuable insights into policy making in this country. My first effort in this direction was in an article entitled "Taming the Sacramento: Hamiltonianism in Action," in the *Pacific Historical Review* 34 (Feb., 1965), 21–49.

The following years were occupied by the writing of other books, by the usual heavy schedule of academic obligations in a busy university, and by more quite instructive consultantships, which deepened my knowledge of the Sacramento Valley. In 1979, while serving as a

Fulbright lecturer on American political history in the United States history program at Moscow University in the Soviet Union, where requests from geographers came periodically to me to lecture on the history of water in California, I was able, in the quiet afforded by being thousands of miles from committee meetings and other distractions at the University of California, Santa Barbara, to get started on the present book. Subsequently, after my return, the project could be periodically addressed, and in 1986 a time of steady research and writing could resume, the manuscript being completed in early 1988.

Unfortunately, too many people have aided me in many ways over the past several decades for me to recognize all of them here individually. However, I wish to record my special gratitude for their companionship and tutelage to the attorneys who from 1963 to 1985 retained me as historical consultant and, on occasion, expert witness. By doing so they afforded me the opportunity for some of the most intensive, probing research tasks and, in effect, seminar discussions and lecture presentations I have ever conducted or participated in. Nowhere else but in litigation support and in courtroom testimony does the historian encounter such demands for exactness and careful procedure. Though some have since gone into private practice, most were then deputy attorney generals in California's Department of Justice: Robert Burton, who first had the highly original idea to turn to an historian; and the others who worked with me in particular cases: Lloyd Hinkelman, Hugh Bowers, Seward Andrews, and Richard M. Frank, as well as Edward Connors, an attorney for the Department of Water Resources when we labored together. Rick Frank, a published scholar in the field, gave me especially crucial guidance in the knotty issue of constitutional law and the rivers.

Three civil engineers, the late Frank Kochis, long of the U.S. Army Corps of Engineers in Sacramento, and Joseph I. Burns and the late Jerry Elliot, both of the distinguished firm of Murray, Burns, and Kienlen, Consulting Civil Engineers, were keen guides to engineering lore and warm companions in those years. More recently, Joseph Burns kindly read through the final manuscript and gave me his valuable reactions, while he and his colleague Joseph D. Countryman, who for many years was an engineer with the U.S. Army Corps of Engineers in the Sacramento region, helped bring me up to date on the operations of the Sacramento Flood Control Project.

To the remarkable William Kahrl, who in 1977 as director of research in the governor's office brought me into the planning and writing of *The California Water Atlas* (State of California, 1979), and who then and later urged the writing of this book, I offer my special thanks for his encouragement and for his example of important public service.

My students in the history of American politics and public policy, graduate and undergraduate, have over the years given me stimulation and challenge in learning how best to understand and to explain these matters. Professor Donald J. Pisani of Texas A & M University, upon whose remarkable work I have much relied, carefully read the manuscript in its final form and gave me his valuable advice, as did my friend and brother-in-law, the planning engineer Dion B. C. Sutton. My thanks, too, to Dr. Martin Reuss, senior historian for the U.S. Army Corps of Engineers, for his aid and support; and to Professor Donald Critchlow of the University of Notre Dame, who is coeditor of the *Journal of Policy History*, for encouraging submission of an essay on the theme of this book which has appeared in that journal's first issue under the title: "The Interplay of American Political Culture and Public Policy: The Sacramento River as a Case Study." During the referee process, I received the major benefit of important suggestions and commentary which helped shape the eventual form of this book's argument and narrative. The Research Committee of the Santa Barbara Division of the Academic Senate has periodically provided some research support funds; Linda Moore, doctoral student at UCSB, and Alan Bloom, a senior in the History of Public Policy major, searched out important information for me.

I am especially grateful to the Board of Editors of the University of California Press; and to the team in the Los Angeles office of the Press who responded so warmly to the manuscript and with enthusiasm gathered round to turn it into such a handsome, skillfully produced book: Stanley Holwitz, assistant director of the Press; David

Lunn, gifted designer; Shirley L. Warren, managing editor, and Diana Feinberg, assistant editor; and Paula Cizmar, sensitive copy editor.

My partner in this as in every other endeavor, Madge Louise Kelley, not only read chapters as they were being written and gave me a steady flow of considered, skilled, and crucial advice, she brought her gifts as a calligrapher to the exacting enterprise of cartography and produced *Battling the Inland Sea*'s splendid maps. For all of this, and for the boon and strength of her companionship, I am her continuing beneficiary.

Robert Kelley

Mission Canyon Heights
Santa Barbara, California
June 1988

C H A P T E R

The Sacramento Valley: Eden Invaded

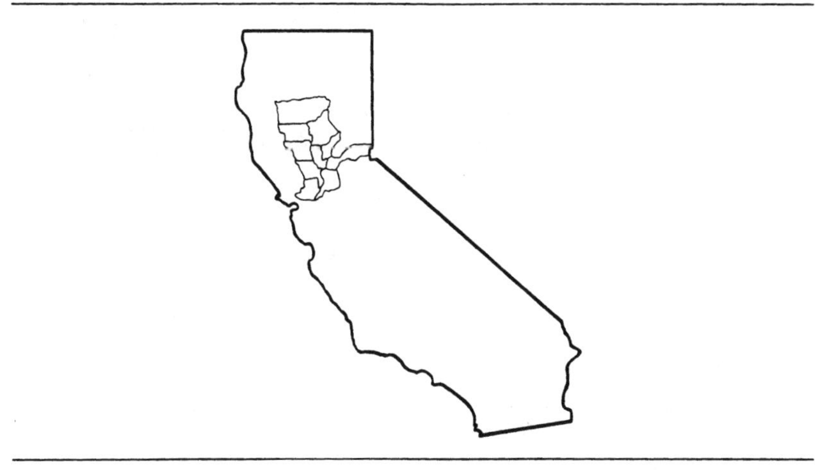

What is this strange quality in humans that makes them court disaster? They build their homes on flood-plains and riverbanks, cliff edges, slipping hillsides, brush-choked canyons and on the slopes of volcanoes. . . . All over this planet we (defy) the eternal forces of nature. Then we try to coerce those forces into doing our bidding.

> *Arthur Hoppe,* San Francisco Chronicle. *Quoted in* Rivers of Fear, *p. 34.*

In Alta California, a quiet and remote province in a far northwestern corner of the Spanish Empire, in the year 1808, a young officer of the Crown, Ensign Gabriel Moraga, led a small exploring party through the maze of bays, islands, and channels which lie easterly of San Francisco Bay, working his way into what was clearly a great delta. He was searching for the source of a heavy flow of water which poured in among the delta islands from the north. In time he came to it, a deep, clear, strongly moving river, many hundreds of feet across, which in honor of his church's holiest sacrament, the eucharist, he named the Sacramento.

Ascending the wide stream, he entered the Sacramento Valley, a warm and abundant natural environment rich in wild game. Thousands of antelope, tule elk, and deer grazed the Valley floor in drifting bands; grizzly bears hunted the thickets near the rivers; and the Valley's many small and larger watercourses were full of fish. The Indian peoples of the Valley clustered near the watercourses, living in villages made of tule-reed hutments. Walled off from each other by language barriers in their separate enclaves of flatland and rough hill country, they called themselves by such names as the Co'lus and the Maidu and the Yana.

A contemporary sketch of the city of Sacramento during the high water of the winter of 1849–1850. On January 10, 1850 the new American town was under water for a mile back from the embarcadero. Shortly, the town was launching its first of many levee construction projects.
Courtesy: California State Library.

The Indians conducted their lives in synchrony with the Valley's resources and rhythms, living in relative abundance in their golden valley by gathering grass seeds and acorns, occasionally by killing large game animals or netting wild geese—great sport for the young men—and often by catching fish with nets of wild hemp cast into the streams. They did little more to violate the Valley's nature than to wade out into the watercourses each spring, and drive poles vertically into stream beds to form crude dams as, yearly, the salmon in a swelling tide returned from the sea to swarm upstream to their spawning grounds; they even formed such dams across the Sacramento itself where it was sufficiently shallow, and thereby created salmon-catching ponds. Through much of the year, drying salmon strung up by the Indians' tule-reed houses gave their villages a reddish aspect.

Indeed, as Theodora Kroeber's tale of Ishi tells us, even among his remote people, the Yahi, who dwelled far inland by one of the smaller streams of the Mt. Lassen foothills, the annual advent of the salmon crowding into upland waters was for them a wondrous time of the renewal of nature's abundance, of sport and carnival and feasting. And it was no less for the Co'lus of the Valley floor or the Yurok peoples living along the large rivers of the north California coast.[1]

The Valley itself, which forms the northern third of California's 400-mile-long Central Valley, is a broad flat amphitheater lying open to the south. Its floor, most of which is essentially a floodplain, rises so slowly and imperceptibly from the bay that eighty miles in a direct line north of the Sacramento's mouth, it lies but sixty feet above sea level. Running a hundred and fifty miles north to south, the Valley attains a width of roughly forty miles through most of this distance. (The Sacramento River is actually 370 miles long from its headwaters in the Trinity Mountains to the delta, but local usage restricts the term "Sacramento Valley" to the flatlands downstream from Red Bluff, which is 247 river-miles, including bends and switchbacks, from the river's mouth.) About midway in its length, a compact group of small volcanic mountains, the Sutter Buttes, rears up steeply from the Valley floor, offering the only visual break in the level plains. In Moraga's time, birds of all descriptions swept overhead in flocks that could darken the sky, making the air clamorous with the sound of their wings and their loud cries.

The flatlands of the Valley were studded with oaks—high, stately trees with broad spreading crowns. The deep flowing Sacramento dominated the scene, its banks lined by a tangled riverine growth of tall oaks, sycamore, cottonwood, willow, and ash, about a mile in width. Men traveling horseback across the Valley floor in the late 1840s rode through open seas of wild oats and other grasses standing six feet high, stretching as far as the eye could see, and so thickly grown that their horses could only make their way with difficulty.

In normal flow the Sacramento is a big river, carrying about 5,000 cubic feet per second, but in flood times it can on occasion swell gigantically to such immense flows as 600,000 cubic feet per second. Indeed, the river's channel could never contain within its natural banks the huge flows of water that almost annually poured out of the canyons of the northern Sierra Nevada. Signs of yearly flooding were everywhere apparent to Ensign Gabriel Moraga, reaching out, he estimated, to cover a band of territory perhaps five miles across on the eastern side and three miles on the west.

In effect, each watercourse on the flat Sacramento Valley floor, from small stream to great river, flowed on an elevated platform, built up by the silt the streams deposited in their own beds. As floodwaters periodically rose to overtop the stream banks and spread out over the Valley floor, natural levees were also built up, for as the overflowing waters lost velocity they dropped their remaining burden of silt most heavily on the land immediately bordering the rivers. From these more elevated locations paralleling the watercourses, floodwaters flowed down to pond in wide shallow basins lying between the streams, the broad expanse of these flood-created lakes often leaving nothing dry but the natural levees bordering the rivers and the higher lands next to them. Together, the ponds in the basins annually created a vast inland sea a hundred miles long occupying the centerline of the Sacramento Valley which slowly drained back into the river channels and down through the delta during the spring months. In their lowest elevations, where the water ponded longest, these basins contained immense swamps of tules (that is, large bulrushes), standing ten to fifteen feet high. The Indians built not only their homes but their boats and sleeping mats of these tall, woody reeds.[2]

For thirty years after Moraga's explorations, the Valley saw little further intrusion from the European settlements along the coast, where the Spaniards had planted missions and royal presidios since their arrival in the 1760s. The Latin American wars of independence began within two years of Moraga's journey, and they continued into the 1820s, after which California was placed within the newly created Republic of Mexico. By the 1830s the authorities in Mexico City had decided to begin a rapid development of their country's frontier regions, such as the distant state of Alta California, by the granting of rancho lands to enterprisers willing to stock them with cattle and raise crops.

In 1829 a Swiss adventurer, John Sutter, arrived on the California scene to secure a large grant from the authorities in Monterey, Alta California's capital. He was the first of the grantees to locate his rancho in the Sacramento Valley, placing it along a Sacramento tributary that in later years would be called the American River. Knowing of the Sacramento's habit of annual flooding, he placed his New Helvetia fort and settlement some two miles back from that stream and immediately launched his many ambitious undertakings.

The British and American governments were much interested in California. Periodic local revolts against Mexico City authorities led to increasing talk that the state might become a British protectorate or part of the American Union. Therefore, naval officers from these two nations were sent to explore the region. On his entry into the Sacramento Valley, Sir Edward Belcher observed flood marks on the trees which demonstrated, to his amazement, that the great river rose at least ten feet in high water, producing floods that ran not simply the few miles out onto the plains as Moraga had estimated, but instead created "one immense sea, leaving only scattered eminences which art or nature have produced, as so many islets or spots of refuge."[3]

Lieutenant Charles Wilkes of the United States Navy arrived in 1841 to learn from the Indians that the whole country, for a hundred miles up the Valley, was almost annually under water. He was even able to discover the general outlines of the river's performance in floodtimes, observing that, as is indeed the case, the first major outflows over the Sacramento's banks occur as it passes by the Sutter Buttes, "and [they submerge] the whole of the Sacramento Valley as far down as the San Joachim [*sic*]."

Wilkes also reported that the Sacramento would be an excellent stream for navigation by large vessels. It was so flat in its gradient that in the Sacramento's lower 247 river-miles from Red Bluff to the delta, it drops an average of only a foot a mile. The daily tides, pouring in the Golden Gate of San Francisco Bay, reached inland to flow far up the Sacramento, producing rises of two to three feet some sixty river-miles upstream at the present site of the city of Sacramento.

The river, therefore, could carry to that point vessels drawing up to twelve feet of water, even when it was at a low water stage. "The banks of the river," Wilkes went on to remark, "are bordered with marshes, which extend for miles back . . . [forming] the proper Tula [sic] district of which so much has been said." Eight years later, after the American acquisition of California in the Mexican War, another American naval officer making a systematic survey said that the tule swamp ran as far northward as the Buttes, observing that it was "impassable for six months out of the year."[4]

In 1848 John Sutter resolved to make a large-scale industrial use of water power, a largely unprecedented undertaking in California. He caused a sawmill to be constructed on the upper reaches of the American River, where it could get power from the swiftly flowing stream. When his foreman found gold in the mill's tailrace, California was utterly transformed. To this moment, there had been perhaps 10,000 people of European descent in the state. Within a relatively few months there were 100,000, drawn from Europe, the Eastern American states, Latin America, and Australia, as well as, eventually, many thousands from the Orient. The mountains, the Sierra Nevada, hitherto ignored by all but the Indians, were engulfed by a rush of gold seekers. San Francisco exploded into a large American city, and thousands of people were shortly living in the new city of Sacramento, built at the juncture of the American and Sacramento rivers. Now a civilization had descended on California which would make heavy and complex demands upon its land and waterscape.

Ranchers and farmers were soon moving out onto the plains of the Sacramento Valley. Their herds of sheep and cattle took the place of the tule elk and antelope, which were quickly hunted to virtual extinction (some few of the former survive in protected sites), while at the same time the Indians of the Valley were dwindling rapidly in numbers and their villages were disappearing. In a tragic local reenactment of the slaughter that had begun centuries ago when Europeans had first arrived along the eastern coasts of the Americas, at least since the 1840s the Valley Indians had been dying of European diseases as if struck down en masse by a great scythe.[5] Settling on the now-vacated flatlands, American farmers planted that wide spectrum of crops, almost bewildering in its variety, which was thereafter to be the distinctive mark of California agriculture.

The Sacramento Valley had abundant water, a long warm growing season such as American farmers had rarely before seen, rich soils, and highly profitable nearby markets, since from the time of the Gold Rush California would be one of the most urban states in the Union. Great herds of cattle were soon in the Valley, quickly followed by sheep. As they grazed, the high thick virgin grasses of the plains were cropped down. Fruit, wine, grains, and dairy products were produced in great volumes from thousands of acres of orchards, vineyards, and pasture lands. Smoke filled the Valley as the cutting down and burning of the great forest of valley oaks, to clear the land for agriculture, began. As the tall wild grasses and valley oaks disappeared, the long, clear vistas now characteristic of the Valley opened out. Will S. Green, a young Kentuckian who helped found the mid-Valley town of Colusa in July 1850, tells us that the thick forests lining the Sacramento's banks were quickly put to the axe and saw to feed the fire boxes of the many steamboats plying the rivers, as well as the fireplaces, stoves, and industries of Sacramento and San Francisco.[6]

Farmers taking up Valley lands avoided the immense tule marshes that occupied the lowest portions of the basins paralleling the Sacramento River, since no one knew yet how to drain them, or had the necessary resources to do so. There was, however, ample land to farm on the higher lands that immediately bordered the rivers themselves and tilted imperceptibly down into the tule swamps, or rose slowly upward from their outer fringes to the foothills.

Sutter County, lying in the heart of the Sacramento Valley, where it is cupped between the converging Feather and Sacramento rivers, offered a typical Valley scene in the years after the Gold Rush. Census figures reveal that there were almost 3,400 people in the county in 1860, and that in the next ten years they grew in numbers more than fifty percent to 5,030. Of 109,063 acres of land which by 1866 Sutter County farmers had succeeded in enclosing within fences, 45,424 were cultivated: 15,732 acres in wheat, 18,655 in barley. In that year the Sutter County farmers produced 83,506 pounds of butter, 1,600 pounds of cheese, and cared for almost 11,000 apple trees, as well as some 15,000 peach trees, more than 3,000 pear trees, 1,377 growing plums, and even 323 cherry trees. From 163,663 grape vines came 26,290 gallons of wine, in addition to which there was much wool, honey, corn, peanuts, beans, potatoes, turnips, pumpkins, squashes, and the like produced.[7]

Sacramento Valley farmers could easily ship their crops to market by river vessels. As early as May of 1849 a seagoing vessel, the bark *Whiton,* arrived at the waterfront of the city of Sacramento after a voyage of 140 days from New York. A square-rigged vessel drawing almost ten feet of water, the *Whiton* arrived "with her royal yards crossed." Before the year was out, the Sacramento River was alive with vessels. Two large steamers, each carrying hundreds of passengers, journeyed regularly between Sacramento and San Francisco, following a deep channel through the Sacramento-San Joaquin delta which still bears the name Steamboat Slough. The sails of commercial vessels stood up prominently across the flatlands downstream from the city of Sacramento, moving slowly back and forth as they navigated through the delta and the winding river above that point, maneuvering to catch the winds. In the month of September 1857, a typical harbormaster's report in Sacramento recorded the arrivals and departures of twenty-three schooners, twenty-seven sloops, and nine steamboats—the latter vessels making seventy appearances in that month in their busy comings and goings.[8]

North of Sacramento, other towns quickly sprang up on the Valley floor. The mid-Valley towns of Colusa and Marysville, some fifty miles north of Sacramento, came into being almost as soon as the Gold Rush began. Colusa was laid out beside the Sacramento River at a point roughly opposite to and due west of Sutter Buttes, while Marysville appeared on the opposite, easterly side of the Buttes on the Sacramento's largest tributary, the Feather River, which flows in a north-south line down the Valley. Marysville was sited where the Yuba River, flowing swiftly out of the northern Sierra Nevada to run southeasterly across the plains, joins the Feather. It was a much more important town than Colusa, for as the effective head of navigation on the Feather it served as the principal market town and *entrepot* for the northern mines. Within days of its appearance in January 1850, two steamers were making regular runs between Marysville and Sacramento. In the mid-1850s the town of Oroville made its appearance thirty miles further north from Marysville on the Feather, at the point where that stream emerges from its mountain canyon to flow out on the Valley floor. In the year 1857 steamboats even called regularly at its waterfront, though this difficult navigation did not survive beyond a few weeks.[9]

≈≈≈

During the night of the 7th of January 1850, a great storm swept in from the west over the Sacramento Valley and the Sierra Nevada. Soon the thousands who had newly arrived in California were learning surprising facts: the Sacramento River was not only a means of transport and a source of water, it could almost overnight become a grave threat to life and property. Within two days of the storm's beginnings, plunging rains on the Sierra Nevada, where the downpours in such storms can reach an inch an hour, had transformed the rivers into raging torrents. As they poured their waters into the Sacramento, that stream in turn grew gigantically in volume, renewing its immemorial flooding cycle and sending its waters far out over the plains.

There was no levee protecting the new city of Sacramento,

which began right at the river's banks, and within hours the entire community, for a mile back from the river, was deep under rushing waters. Houses were toppled, businessmen watched thousands of dollars in inventory wash out of their doors, and a small steamboat navigated the town's streets, delivering freight. The local *Placer Times,* sending out an extra edition on January 15, reported that "very few houses escaped having water on their first floors, while many have been swept from their underpinnings by the strong current." Only around Sutter's fort, and at other locations similarly distant from the river, was there dry land.[10]

The town of Sacramento, as these events revealed, was built in the middle of the inland sea that the Indians had warned appeared almost annually on the Valley floor. Few in the city, however, knew or talked with the Indians. As townspeople recovered from the inundation and looked about them at the waste of waters, they were not appalled and humbled by their experience but instead confident that the problem could be promptly mastered. On the 29th of January 1850, as the floodwaters were just beginning to drain away, a meeting of citizens quickly decided on the building of a levee around the town, and launched an engineering survey. When within a few days it was completed, the *Placer Times* remarked with complete assurance that "From the . . . examination and estimates, it will be seen that Sacramento City can be easily protected against inundations, and that, too, at comparatively small expense." In this same mood, two years earlier, the editor of the *California Star* had cast his eye over the great farming potential of the Sacramento Valley and had observed complacently that the low tule lands bordering the Sacramento River "can be drained at comparatively small expense. . . . Before many years, levees will be constructed . . . and the vast tract known as the 'Tulares' will be cultivated."[11]

The levee project for the city of Sacramento, however, languished. This was, after all, not a simple public policy question. Many who lived in Sacramento had never seen a levee or understood their workings. Building such a structure would certainly be an expensive undertaking, the town was yet relatively small and its resources limited, and was a levee, people asked, entirely necessary or even practical? Would not the water simply percolate right on through such a structure and inundate the town anyway? The speculators who had sold Sacramento's town lots had assured everyone that the city's site was safe from all inundations. This was now seen to be clearly not so, but nonetheless a lingering doubt remained. Had they just witnessed a flood that would be repeated only occasionally?

Those who had arrived in California from the Southern states, where the sight of local authorities in low-country regions leveeing flood-prone rivers was doubtless a relatively familiar one, appear to have been the leaders in urging action. Northerners, however, held back. They could only decide this question on the basis of their past experiences, and in their part of the Eastern United States flooding occurred infrequently and then not with such suddenness and overwhelming impact as in the Sacramento Valley. As it happened, they were now living in one of the nation's most flood-ravaged valleys, though as yet they were ignorant of this fact. Three quarters of a century later, after generations of a painfully slow learning process, a U.S. Army Corps of Engineers officer would tell a congressional committee that the intensity of flood conditions in the Sacramento Valley was greater than in any other American river system. The river rose in flash fashion, unlike the slow-rising Mississippi. In the wide valley of that stream and its tributaries, the ratio of water to square foot of land available to take run-off was about 1.5, whereas in the Sacramento Valley it was 22.[12]

In 1850, however, this informed state of mind was far in the future, and in the new town of Sacramento, "Such . . . was the infatuated determination to believe the reiterations of the speculators [as to the town's safety]," wrote a local resident, John F. Morse, ". . . that a few weeks only [of drying out] were required to induce a confidence of future security, almost as great as that which had been manifested prior to the flood. . . . With Northern men," Morse caustically observed, "and those from the Atlantic seaboard, a levee was a species of fortifications of which they knew nothing, and nothing could exceed the unpopularity of the subject."[13]

Natural events, as so often in later years, then burst in to resolve the policy debate. Under the impact of spring rains the immense snow pack in the Sierra Nevada began, in its customary fashion, to melt, and in March 1850, the rivers began rising again. Now one of the men who had been active in the earlier levee meetings, an individual of energy and personal force who carried a Southern-sounding name and a Southerner's habit of command, Hardin Bigelow, gathered

> a handful of men . . . [and] commenced damming out the waters at every low point . . . finally [extending] his temporary levee almost to its present limits. Night and day he was in the saddle, going from point to point, stimulating his men to exertion. For a few days he met tide and torrent, mud and darkness, and croaking discouragements which but few men could have endured, and, to the astonishment of all, saved the town from a second inundation. As a natural consequence, everybody praised him, and on the first Monday of April he was elected Mayor of the city.[14]

In this spontaneous event, this personal triumph in the life of a man otherwise unknown to history, the basic form of the Valley's response to the Sacramento River, from that time to the present, was set. Bigelow had correctly forecast that flooding would be a recurrent danger, but in a crucially important decision he and those agreeing with him did not define the situation as one calling for the town of Sacramento to get out of nature's way, that is, to move back to higher land, as John Sutter had earlier done, and thereby leave a clear passageway for flood waters. Rather, without apparent thought to an alternative, they urged the people of Sacramento to dig in where they were and fight off the water, clearing out a dry space in the middle of the inland sea for themselves and their town.

The decisive fact in all of this hurried policy making was the circumstance that, in reality, Hardin and the townspeople of Sacramento knew almost nothing about the Sacramento River and its tributaries, save that they sent floods over the nearby flatlands. How big, actually, were the rivers of the Sacramento Valley in floodtime? How much water did they produce? Where was it determined to go? How deep could their inundations potentially be? If floodwaters were denied overflow at one point, where would they then burst out? How high did levees have to be to keep out the water not just in one, but in all, flood seasons?

None of this fundamental information about the environmental problem the people of the Sacramento Valley faced—information that was absolutely essential if an enduringly effective policy were to be fashioned—was yet known, nor would it be in more than a fragmentary way for decades into the future. The inescapable result was that the flood control history of the next half-century in the Sacramento Valley would be filled, as we shall see, not only with lofty plans and bold projects, it would be a long experience of costly failure and apparently endless frustration. The people of the Valley were trying to understand the Sacramento River, and the learning process they now had to undergo, both about the river and about the complications cast up before them by their own values and ways of doing things, would be long, surprising, and unforgiving of error.

We will observe the people of the Valley, therefore, making mistake after mistake, and yet continuing to make decisions about the river for all the world as if they knew what they were doing. In truth, given their nature, given the inner state of American political culture—which had now been transported bodily across thousands of miles and planted firmly in California—nothing else was actually possible. Midnineteenth century Americans were shaped in their most basic outlooks by the ebullient, burstingly expansive years from the 1820s through the 1840s, the already mythical Age of Jackson, which they had just passed through. They were confident, impatient, entrepreneurial, defiant of life's limitations, and determined actively to possess and develop the enormous continental expanse that had now opened before them.

Those who had arrived in California were people who had been sufficiently courageous and risk-taking abruptly to leave their homes in the Eastern states and stream westward through a host of dangers to reach their goal. Their instinctively activist impulse was to solve (as they believed they were doing) such difficulties as they now faced in the flood-endangered city of Sacramento by some simple practical step that would force nature to behave as they wished it to. Rather than making an adjustment to the environment and its realities, they resolved to transform it by pushing the river back, hardly entertaining the thought that they might fail.

Soon after Bigelow was elected mayor, the citizens of Sacramento on April 29, 1850 voted overwhelmingly (543–15) in favor of raising $250,000 by taxation—a princely sum for so small a community—to proceed with constructing a levee entirely around the town. The embankment that they built over the rest of the year was in reality, however, a laboriously constructed physical statement of how little they understood the problem they faced. Only three feet high and twelve feet across at its base, this first levee in the Sacramento Valley was a diminutive ancestor of the more than a thousand miles of immense levees up to twenty-five feet in height that now line the banks of the Sacramento and its tributaries. It could not do what they hoped for it. Two years later, in the high water season of 1852, it failed, to the accompaniment of bitter recriminations on all sides.[15]

Over the long span of years that lay before them in their adventure with the Sacramento River, the people of the city of Sacramento and of the Valley at large would eventually find out that everything said about the river being easily controlled was simply fantasy. However, they persistently avoided this reality. They were the most reluctant and laggard of learners. So optimistic were nineteenth-century Californians, so assured were they that the environment could be manipulated as they wished, that they went on proclaiming their confidence to themselves decade after decade, despite the repeated failure of their plans and projects. The city of Sacramento would have to build its levees ever higher as the years passed and at ever greater cost. Well into the twentieth century it would be still taxing itself to pay for increasingly expensive and elaborate flood control measures. At one point the city even had to bring in millions of tons of dirt to fill in its own streets, raising them to the second floor of business houses. In this fashion Sacramento lifted itself bodily, for a considerable distance back from the river, to put its daily life above the flood level.

Periods of high water in the Valley continued to recur with disquieting frequency after the flood of 1850. The people of Marysville, like those in Sacramento, had also built to the water's edge—in this case, to the banks of the Feather River—and in March 1852, during the same flood that breached the city of Sacramento's first levee, they found that their town was under water. (The community would eventually withdraw from the Feather River's banks, abandoning a number of streets.) In the countryside surrounding Marysville, "crops were flooded and a large number of cattle and horses drowned."

In December of that year, 1852, the Sacramento Valley was again inundated, the tule lands filling even more deeply than they had in the high water of 1850. "There was no place on the west bank of the Sacramento," a local history later observed, "between the . . . [delta] and Colusa, except the Indian mounds, that was not under water. . . . Thousands of cattle were caught in the lowlands and drowned." A few months later, in March of 1853, a disastrous outrush of waters on the flatlands was so sweeping and violent in its effects that for years afterward the flood of 1853 was a landmark event in local memories. At Marysville the Yuba River was almost three feet higher than it had been during the previous December. The town was a lake, boats were in the streets, and the water did not drain away for two weeks. In the bottom lands next to the rivers where the soil was especially dark and fertile, where farmers had settled earliest and agriculture was the most productive, almost every farmer suffered heavy losses.[16]

≈≈≈

In the very month of the 1853 flood, enterprising miners in the mountains were discovering and putting to use a new mining technique that would drastically change the physical context of life in the Sacramento Valley for generations into the future, complicating beyond anyone's imaginings the environmental problems that townspeople and farmers on the flatlands faced. These transformations had their origins several years before, in the spring of 1850. In that year, while the city of Sacramento was debating whether or not to build a levee, miners in and around Nevada City, which lies in a steep mountain canyon along a tributary of the Yuba River, were encountering discouraging news. As elsewhere in the Gold Rush, they had been working the stream placers by loosening the dirt and gravels in the streambeds with their picks and then shoveling it into long toms (short lengths of sluice box) for washing and gold extraction. They were finding to their dismay that the stream placers were quickly exhausted, that hours of labor in the streaming waters and hot sun were now producing few gold flakes in their long toms. Casting about for other mining ground to excavate, they discovered that they need not dig simply in the stream beds, rather, that they could sink their picks into the red gravelly hillsides that reared up around them and still find paydirt.

These new diggings were not nearly so rich as those in the bed of the streams, where the running water had for millennia been washing and concentrating the gold flakes, but nonetheless they still yielded precious metal. Miners tore up the entire hillside above Nevada City, eventually sinking many small shafts far down into the lower strata of the hill to get at richer gravels, which seemed to be buried at some depth. In time, a remarkable geological fact was learned: they were digging into a broad and deep river bed, dry for millions of years and lifted upward as the Sierra Nevada range itself rose, in the gravels of which thinly scattered flakes of gold were lodged. It had been, in fact, from these Tertiary-era gravel beds that the modern streams now flowing out of the Sierra had gotten their gold, washing it out of the ancient gravels as they cut down through them.

The miners faced, however, a heavy task as they dug into the gravel hillsides. Since the gold was so thinly distributed in them, many hours of pick and shovel labor were necessary to yield a living wage. A search was soon on among the more enterprising miners for a means of speeding up the process. In the spring of 1852, a tolerably effective procedure emerged. Miners would run a stream of water onto the surface of their claims and feed paydirt into it by breaking the ground on either side and shoveling it into the current. Periodically, they would shut off the flow of water and shovel the now more-concentrated paydirt into a long tom. Ground-sluicing, as this process was called, spread rapidly in the mines.

It was still an inefficient procedure, however. Interest flared quickly, therefore, when in March of 1853 an imaginative New Englander at work in the Nevada City mines, Edward E. Matteson, hit on the solution. He arranged to have water delivered to his claim at a point sufficiently elevated above the working face of his mine so that by means of a long hose it would drop into the pit with considerable force, or, as the miners called it, head. Attaching a nozzle to this water source, he directed the jet thus produced on the hillside bluff he and his partners had been working.

The results were gratifying. Under the impact of the hurtling water, the bank dissolved into a flowing, muddy gruel, the entire mass running downslope, where it was caught in a long sluice box that had been so placed that it lay in the path of the turbid mixture. In the bottom of the sluice box, which could be made as long as convenient in order to extract as much of the metal as possible, was the usual arrangement for capturing gold: a series of riffles set crossways to the current. The gold, being much heavier than the gravel and dirt, settled behind the riffles just as, in natural conditions, it had lodged behind rocks and other obstructions in existing stream beds. Periodically, the water would be shut off and the gold recovered by scooping it out from in front of each riffle. Thus was the momentous new process of hydraulic gold mining—as it was soon termed—brought forth.[17]

If a miner had water, mining ground, drainage into a nearby stream bed, and the proper equipment, with a minimum of labor he could do in a day what many men could hardly do with pick and shovel in weeks. Consequently, hydraulic gold mining, an environmentally revolutionary process, swept the California placer mining industry (and eventually spread worldwide). It was a process that expanded rapidly in conditions of absolute and complete laissez-faire—it was under no public supervision or regulation whatever, not even an ordinary business license had to be secured. Ancient Tertiary gravel beds that could be mined in this way were found to lie in a long band of territory in the Sierra Nevada, running generally north and south, which crossed the watersheds of the Feather, Yuba, Bear, and American rivers and occurred also in a few more southerly locations. As miners began work in each setting, they quickly diverted water from nearby watercourses to feed their operations. Claims were fitted with hoses and nozzles, and the characteristic hissing roar of hydraulic mining began widely to be heard in the mountains.

Contemporaries found the sight of a hydraulic mine in operation an arresting spectacle.[18] Standing at the large North Bloomfield mine in 1879, when after a quarter of a century the industry had reached full technical development, a reporter for the *San Francisco Bulletin* recorded his amazement:

> There is a real pleasure, very distinct, but hard to describe, about this gigantic force [issuing from the nozzles]. . . . one might easily believe that it comes out with not merely the force of much gravity, but also with a wicked, vicious, unutterable indignation. The black pipe, three feet in diameter, leads down the cliff, and across the mine. It becomes smaller, and ends in a jointed, elbow-like pipe, with a movable nozzle. . . . large rocks two feet in diameter fly like chaff when struck by the stream. The actual work of tearing down the cliff is hard to see, for there is a cloud of red foam hanging over the spot. You hear little rattling and slipping noises through the incessant roar, and a stream which seems ten times greater than could come out of the pipe, flows down the dripping pile, and so into the rock-channels which lead to the tunnel [which carried the mine tailings off to a nearby river canyon for deposit].[19]

Since the process used incredible volumes of water, as soon as the industry got going in the mid-1850s the miners began demanding more and more of it. In response, the first large-scale engineering projects in the history of California were begun. Their purpose, again through the application of entirely private enterprise and capital and innocent of any public supervision, was to gather water from far up in the mountains and deliver it to the hydraulic nozzles. The most spectacular mining and water-gathering enterprises were constructed within the watershed of the Yuba River, in Nevada County, where the largest Tertiary gravel deposits lay. As early as 1857 the busy miners had dug 700 miles of ditches in that single county. The ditches snaked upwards along the long, broad, slowly rising east-west ridges of the northern Sierra Nevada, reaching from the mines ever higher to tap larger water supplies. Long flumes were sometimes suspended from sheer cliff-faces above the rivers. Most of these early ditch and flume systems were relatively short, but one was already forty-five miles long.

Millions of dollars were invested in these projects, which as the years went by evolved into an immense interlinked complex of lakes and artificial reservoirs spread over a number of mountain counties. The rise of this huge water system was fueled by such demands as those of the North Bloomfield mine in Nevada County, which in the 1870s consumed a hundred million gallons of water a day. By 1879, when the hydraulic mining industry was at its apex of development, Nevada County was crisscrossed by more than a thousand miles of ditches and flumes.

Most of the gravel deposits lay on the high broad ridges between the deep river canyons in the northern Sierra Nevada, and many small hydraulic mining towns soon appeared on them. Far up on the north fork of the American River were, among others, the communities of Yankee Jim's, Iowa Hill, Gold Run, and Forest Hill. The mud, sand, and gravel which washed out of their mines into the tributaries of the American River eventually flowed downstream to settle out in the river channels around the city of Sacramento and below. In the upper basin of the Bear River, a considerably shorter stream next northerly from the American, there were the towns of Dutch Flat, You Bet, Red Dog, Little York, and Gouge-Eye. Along the upper Feather River, above and below the point where it emerged from the mountains onto the Valley floor at Oroville, a number of mines that clustered around the town tailed directly into that stream.

In the wide watershed of the Yuba, however, with its many large gravel deposits, was the busiest center of the hydraulic mining industry. The Nevada City mines drained into the Yuba through one of its tributaries, as did those of Blue Tent, Omega, and Washington. The highlands between the south and middle forks of the Yuba River, locally called the San Juan Ridge, held a long east-west string of hydraulic towns that followed one of the major Tertiary gravel channels: French Corral, Birchville, Sweetland, North San Juan, Columbia Hill, Lake City, Relief Hill, Moore's Flat, and North

Bloomfield—now the site, with its adjoining Malakoff pit, of a state historical park. In the upper reaches of the north fork of the Yuba were the mines of Camptonville and Downieville. Far downstream from all of these operations, near the point where the Yuba flows out of the Sierran foothills into the flatlands, were the hydraulic mining towns of Smartville and Timbuctoo and their large operations. All of these mines along the Yuba, like those along the Feather, sent their tailings downstream toward Marysville and Yuba City, sited where the Feather and Yuba join.

Turning their powerful jets on the hillsides, the hydraulic miners soon excavated great pits in the flanks of the Sierra Nevada, their red-dirt interiors gleaming through the dark green forest. Out of these broad cavities stretched long lines of sluice boxes, three feet wide, through which rushed torrents of brownish-red muddy waters. The nearby air echoed to the steady deep rumbling of the gravel and rocks rolling along the bottoms of the sluices. Out of their mouths shot spraying catapults of debris-laden waters that tumbled on down the hillsides into adjacent creeks. Much of the debris lodged there, where it permanently remains—wide glaring white deposits of sand and gravel. Great volumes of tailings, however, also washed on down these upland creeks to flow into the deep river canyons. In 1879 a young state engineer, Marsden Manson, looked in awe at the discharges coming from Nevada County's Sailor Flat and Blue Tent mines. The material, he later wrote,

> seems . . . to descend the face of the canon, in a series of cascades, the water dashing wildly from one series of "undercurrents" and "riffles" to another, forming a spectacle which might be considered beautiful, but for the muddiness of the water and the ceaseless grinding and pounding of the rocks swept along by the current. . . . For three-fourths of a mile down the dumps the water is backed up by the dam they create, and fine quicksands, dangerous to traverse, are deposited over the entire bed of the canon. Occasionally the dam partially breaks away, releasing the confined waters, which rush down the canon with great violence, imperiling [all] . . . who may chance to be in its way.[20]

C H A P T E R

The Interplay of American Political Culture and Reclamation Policy: *The 1850s*

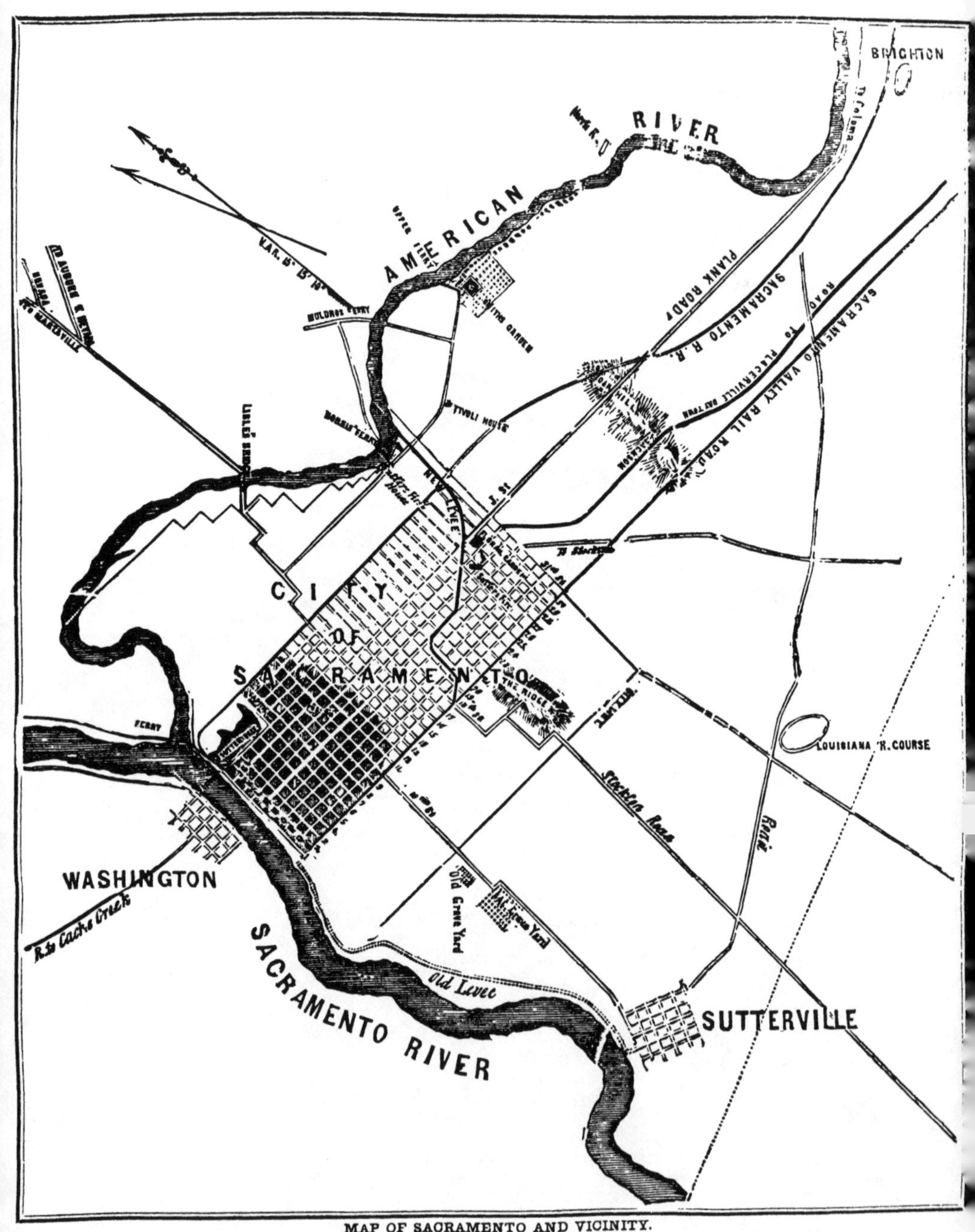

MAP OF SACRAMENTO AND VICINITY.

The breach in the levee . . . grew continuously until it reached 180 feet. The Yuba River was pushing its way through the hole. Water 12 feet high was flowing through the gap at such a rate that half an acre of peach trees . . . were sucked through. . . . When dawn came . . . water stood as high as 10 to 15 feet in some areas. About 600 homes built in a low-lying area . . . were inundated to the eaves.

> *Chuck Smith,* Marysville Appeal-Democrat, *March 6, 1986. Quoted in* Rivers of Fear, *pp. 42–47.*

In early 1856 a letter appeared in the *Marysville Herald* from French Corral, a hydraulic mining town whose operations tailed into the Yuba River about twenty miles upstream from Marysville, warning the townsfolk: "You will perhaps be surprised to learn that in a single day no less than ten thousand tons of earth are run through the long sluices at the lower end of this ditch."[1] The spectacle of hydraulic mining did not need to be looked at long before such cautions began to be uttered. It was obvious that a new industrial process was roaring along, entirely without check, which could not help but have disastrous consequences for the Valley's rivers. In many locations in the mountains, long plumes of muddy water and its burden of debris flowed down from the mines into nearby creeks, then commingled as those streams, washing the tailings along in their beds, joined, and together poured in a swollen flood into the deep river canyons.

Here these streams of sand and gravel flowed together to bury the canyon bottoms under an immense moving deposit of debris which in time would reach depths of more than a hundred feet. It

An 1855 map of Sacramento and vicinity, from the contemporary Sacramento Illustrated History. *It shows a "New Levee," Sutter's Fort on higher land outside of it, and the streets actually built on (shaded), with an "Old Levee" running downriver. Two railroads headed eastward from the waterfront to the mines.*
Courtesy: California State Library.

was a massive flood rising in the mountain canyons which during the high water periods of winter and spring moved in pulses downstream toward the flatlands below. The finest silts, or "slickens" as they were called, made their appearance in the flatland rivers right away. They floated down the watercourses more or less continually, turning the rivers a soft brown all the way to the Sacramento-San Joaquin delta as soon as hydraulic mining operations began each spring. Ship captains in the lower Sacramento began noticing mud in the water as early as 1854.[2]

In 1856, three years after the invention of hydraulic mining, the first flurry of commentary on the problem surfaced in local newspapers.

> For ourselves [observed the editor of a Nevada County newspaper, the *Nevada Democrat*], we candidly believe that the Sacramento River will not be a navigable stream five years from today. . . . The fact that the navigation of the Yuba [at Marysville] has already been impeded by the filling up of the bed of that stream strengthens this opinion. . . . [The] Sacramento must become such a receptacle of mud as to fill up the river bed nearly on a level with her banks.[3]

Two months later, in March 1856, the *California Farmer* remarked: "Much fear has been expressed in many sections of our country relative to the condition of the Sacramento, Yuba, Feather, and other rivers opening into the Sacramento. . . . [The] constant rush of muddy water from the streams above will continually fill them up, so long as the mining operations continue."[4]

The lightest hydraulic mining silts, floating toward the mouth of the Sacramento River, settled rapidly to the bed of that stream where it levels out in the sixty river-miles below the city of Sacramento and assumes an almost-flat gradient. We have noted that passenger steamboats more than two hundred feet in length traveled this relatively level route regularly between Sacramento and San Francisco, following the shortest and deepest channel through the delta, Steamboat Slough. As they pushed along upstream under their long plumes of steam, their engines heaving, the dining rooms busy, and their saloons crowded, a short distance after entering the slough they passed through the first reach of shallower water, over a series of shoals called the Hog's Back, a feature boatmen had known of since the earliest naval explorations in the 1840s.[5] Located where the slough widened and the current slackened, the Hog's Back Shoals—the first of them several hundred yards long—together encompassed a distance of three and a half miles. The bottom, in this location, was in its natural condition composed of hard pan (densely compacted soil almost rock-like in consistency).

However, a steady inflowing deposition of fine hydraulic mining slickens on the bed of Steamboat Slough had been silently taking place since 1853, the slough's deeper and more rapid current having pulled silt into its channel more copiously than the other longer and more slow-moving delta channels. By 1856, therefore, the Hog's Back was rising. In the fall of that year, when after many months of dry weather the Sacramento's flow was slackening and shallowing, during low tide hours steamers suddenly began finding themselves catching fast in this muck in the Slough's bed and remaining lodged there, however impatient their passengers might be, until floated off in the next high tide. The San Francisco press was filled with outcries of complaint. Something, it was said, must be done.[6]

We have seen that, some years before, the Sacramento's habit of annual flooding had impelled the people of the city of Sacramento to begin trying to push the river back by building a levee system around their town. Now, the river's role as drain for the hydraulic mines had cast up a new problem: the streams that received mining debris were shallowing. Their beds were rising, though their banks were not, so that the Valley's drainage channels were becoming increasingly less able than before to carry floodwaters without overflowing. Shallower streams also created another problem: they gravely hampered river navigation. What would now be done, in this circumstance, about the Hog's Back Shoal?

It was not so simple to make a public decision on this matter as it had been to begin building levees around the city of Sacramento. There was no community of people living around the shoal to be stung into action and assume jurisdiction. Furthermore, puzzling constitutional questions presented themselves. Ever since Chief Justice

John Marshall's U.S. Supreme Court decision in 1824, in what legal historian Lawrence M. Friedman refers to as "the mighty case of *Gibbons* v. *Ogden*," it had been fundamental constitutional doctrine that the federal government was in control of the country's navigable rivers. Marshall derived this principle from the historically crucial commerce clause, in Section 8 of the federal Constitution, which declares that "The Congress shall have power . . . To regulate Commerce . . . among the several states."[7]

This was not a dry technical ruling based on logic alone. Marshall as a Federalist was determined to insure that the United States would be *one* national market, not a market divided up into as many segments as there were states. *Gibbons* v. *Ogden*, which involved that new piece of technology, the steamboat, and a monopoly over Hudson River steam transportation granted by New York State in a charter given to its original entrepreneur, Robert Livingston, offered Marshall his historic opportunity. As the distinguished authority Archibald Cox, professor of law at Harvard and former solicitor general, writes:

> For the steamboat to bring economic unity to the North American continent, the Commerce Clause would have to be made into a vehicle for barring the State from granting such monopolies, and also from erecting the customs barriers, imposts, diverse local regulations, and like instruments of economic rivalry that hampered the Old World.[8]

And in Marshall's ruling, so it was decreed. The monopoly, adjudged a hindrance to interstate commerce, was quashed. Within eighteen months, there were not six steamboats calling at New York City's wharves, but forty-three. All the nation's rivers were opened to free passage, an event of immense national importance.

The significance of this matter for the story being recounted in this book is that in his great decision Marshall had introduced a persistent, knotty complication into American government. California, like all the other states, certainly *owned* the rivers within its borders, as an attribute of its sovereignty; that much was certain. But if any of them proved to be navigable, that is, useful for commerce, then

Gibbons v. *Ogden* meant that Washington, D.C., had paramount authority over how such portions of the rivers were *used*, so as to ensure that they remained free to interstate and foreign commerce.[9] In other words, since this narrative deals with navigable streams, it is inescapably a study of the operation of American federalism, for California and Washington were bound together, whether they wished to be or not, in anything that was decided concerning the Sacramento.

California was not denied the right to govern and perhaps by public works modify its rivers; the authority given the federal government in *Gibbons* v. *Ogden* was not exclusive, it was merely (!) supreme. Thus, the American system of federalism had produced a complex and subtle relationship of shared responsibility, and therefore shared authority, to be worked out situation by situation. Eventually, *Gibbons* v. *Ogden* would get the far-distant federal government deeply involved in the affairs of the Sacramento Valley by bringing in the United States Army Corps of Engineers; and it would shape events so that their concluding outcome would be a complicated partnership arrangement between Sacramento and Washington as the final solution to the problem of the Sacramento Valley.

If, then, it were wished in the late 1850s to find someone to clean out the Hog's Back, the federal authorities would be the proper people to approach. However, that government was 3000 miles away, and a civil war and twenty years would pass before the U.S. Army Corps of Engineers would begin its first limited operations in the Sacramento River system. In the immediate circumstance, the only public agency that might be turned to was the government of the new state of California, which might be prevailed on to spend its funds on the river, subject to approval from Washington.

After all, it was steamboats full of people heading for the state capital that were being detained and the state's business that was being interfered with, by the Hog's Back Shoal. However, was the political climate a friendly one for such proposals? What was the nature, in the 1850s, of California's political culture? Was a project of this sort the kind of thing which might reasonably be thought of as Sacramento's business, given the existing state of people's minds as to what they conceived government to be for? Was this project something Sacramento could properly take under its wing?

≈≈≈

Answering these questions requires us for a moment to stand back from the California scene itself and consider American political culture in general, nationwide, for the way the American people as a whole did things in public, their accustomed ways of thinking about their common government and its activities, would ultimately shape everything that, henceforth, Californians would do with the Sacramento River.

From the 1830s on, when the idea of "party" as something legitimate and important took hold of the national mind, practically every white male American citizen participated in American public life eagerly and almost continuously. Party politics became the country's folk theater, a continuing patriotic drama with a cast involving tens of thousands of ordinary citizens. European observers, who lived in monarchical and elite-governed societies in which the masses were usually passive, were fascinated—and usually appalled. Many came to America, arriving in an almost annual contingent, to gaze on the spectacle. They returned home to publish a stream of widely read books about the armies of voters that in America marched and counter-marched, turning out in orderly ranks for frequent elections.[10]

From their beginnings, Americans have also been almost peculiarly, in the world, an individualistic people.[11] This national trait, proudly, repeatedly, and volubly declaimed by Americans both to themselves on all available public occasions, and to all observers from abroad who could be got to stand still to listen, has produced as a fundamental element in American political culture a distrust of government so profound, and a dispersion of authority so complete, that to foreign observers the governing system in the United States has always had an air of near-anarchy. Power, Americans believed, is always at war with liberty, and they built their constitution around the belief that those who govern must be kept in check by dividing and scattering authority and putting the various powers in government at war with each other.[12]

This basically Madisonian constitution—so-called for its principal author, James Madison—was universally accepted in its essential nature, if debated in its parts. However, within that consensus, from the beginning there was no agreement as to how far this distrust of government and its humbling and weakening should go. From the first rumblings and declamations of American public life, one of the obsessive issues has been: how strong should government, at all levels, be? What are its legitimate uses? When does it step beyond the pale and threaten to create tyranny?

Those who were disciples of Thomas Jefferson and Andrew Jackson and who, from the early 1830s, called themselves *Democrats,* were the fundamentalists on the issue. They inherited Jefferson's and Jackson's brooding distrust of the monied, regarded capitalists skeptically and worried about what entrepreneurs were doing to the country. They insisted that strong and active government was the greatest threat to liberty that Americans faced; that it was usually the instrument by which the wealthy got, through corrupt means, special economic privileges (tariffs, land grants, financial and taxing advantages) that enabled them to exploit the community at large. Democrats worried particularly about monopoly, which in these years governments themselves seemed to be creating, by means of special banking and incorporation charters and such devices as grants of the power of eminent domain (for railroad and canal companies). Arguments over these issues agitated state as well as national politics throughout the nineteenth century; and at the state level the distinctions between Whigs and Democrats were identical to those to be observed on the national level.[13]

Thus in the national as well as in the state capitals Democrats condemned all proposals for governments to aid businessmen, including publicly funded internal improvements (roads, canals, and river and harbor projects) as unfair measures that took money from all to benefit a few, as government subsidies for wealthy entrepreneurs. Andrew Jackson's Maysville Road Veto (1830) was a famous event of historic political proportions, and in the mid-1840s Jackson's protege in the White House, the Democrat James K. Polk, struck down one of the nation's earliest "rivers and harbors" bills with a ringing veto.[14]

Let everyone solve their problems on their own, Democrats insisted, and make their own way without government-provided aids or special privileges. There was a good deal more to this argument. The world was still a place where governments freely interfered with and sought to dictate how people lived their private moral lives. Democrats, who spoke for minorities with unusual ways of life that others frowned on, such as Catholicism, saloonkeeping, and German beer gardens, insisted that America was the place where a new way of life, a new era of personal liberty, was being created. They demanded that every (white) American be left free to live his private life as he saw fit. That is, no one should try to use government to deny a citizen drink if he wanted it, to maintain a parochial school and not send his children to the public one, or to recreate on a Sunday (Sabbatarian, "blue law" crusades went on year after year)—or to own slaves.

Thus, white Southerners should not be condemned for their slaveholding, or Roman Catholic Irishmen harrassed for their saloons. "Personal liberty" was a constant cry of Democrats, who angrily battled against the liquor-prohibition crusades that erupted in state after state from the 1820s through the 1850s. They seemed, in short, to prefer a style of life that was free-swinging, individualistic, and unbuttoned. *Cultural and economic laissez-faire*: this, Democrats insisted over and over again, had to be in all matters the fundamental public policy doctrine for America, at the national, state, and local levels, if its people wished to live in a truly democratic and freedom-loving country. To insure this, government should be kept small, localized, cheap, and inactive. Southerners of the Democratic persuasion preached this doctrine with passionate force, for they were convinced that the principle of activist government, once admitted, would lead to assaults on their peculiar institution: slavery.[15]

Who opposed the Democrats in all of this, who was their enemy? They were opposed by a great bloc of Americans, the people who from colonial times were called Yankees. With their homeland in New England, these devout, thrifty, and hardworking people who deplored slavery, Catholicism, and immorality (especially the use of alcohol) had migrated far westward into the region around the Great Lakes and beyond. Most Yankees, who liked to see trade and industry flourish, looked back in time admiringly to those prophets of active government aid to economic development, Alexander Hamilton and Henry Clay. Accordingly, they lined up nationally, in California as well as in the Eastern states, behind what was called the *Whig* party, Clay's creation. It was the Whigs who enthusiastically cheered economic development and urged it on; who, far from thinking of businessmen with sour distrust, admired and encouraged them. They insisted that government should be actively used to aid the opening of the continent's resources and to establish an expansive, flourishing climate for investment and risk-taking by imaginative (usually Whig) entrepreneurs.[16]

The Whigs did not, however, have only economic goals and economic policies in mind. At the core of the Whig party was a pious puritanism that made them view everything in public life as charged with a religious significance. Whigs believed that the national way of life must be shaped to their image of what God wanted humanity to be. In this sense, government must have a *moral* as well as an *economic* plan for society, just as God's providence, Whigs would say, is the divine plan for humankind. Government, as God's agent on this earth, must be put actively to use in many ways, cultural as well as economic. It must promote virtue, moral purity, hard work, and schooling, as well as enterprise and investment. The goal: building industry and cities, which for Whigs meant a civilized, progressive national life.

Those who called themselves Whigs also believed that they were a more educated people, more inclined to look to books, learning, and science for guidance in public issues. They also had a much stronger sense that society is ultimately not simply a collection of isolated individuals, each looking out in solitary fashion for himself, but rather it is an organic, corporate body in which team spirit and cooperation in joint public enterprises must be the unifying theme. Whigs, therefore, put much greater stress than did Democrats on the idea that the community was superior to the individual; that the nation at large should be thought of in the model of the legendary New England village itself, doing things jointly through the vehicle of its shared governing institutions.

In the pre–Civil War decades the Whigs were usually denied much authority in Washington, D.C., where Southern Democrats were dominant. Thus, they turned inward to put their own state governments, primarily in the North, to work at carrying out their agenda, their plan, for America. They got state governments launched on the task of founding schools to create an educated and skillful citizenry; building canals and road systems to open the country, often by granting the power of eminent domain to private companies; and passing laws to put down drunkenness and immorality, not only as an affront to God but as sources of idleness and social wastage.

As disciples of Henry Clay, in the national Congress Whigs argued, usually fruitlessly, for the adoption of a national plan for economic development. It called for the building of a unified "American System" of public policy which would include a strong national bank to mobilize the nation's capital and turn it to industrial development, protective tariffs to encourage the rise of industry, and internal improvements (roads, canals, dredged rivers and ports, and railroads) to open the country's resources and bind the nation together.

≈≈≈

All of this was meat and drink in California politics in the 1850s, where the classic American political culture of Democrats and Whigs and their endless policy arguments swept into the state as part of the Gold Rush and flourished luxuriantly. It was the Whigs in California who chanted an almost ecstatic chorus of delight in the state's potential economic future: if people were only confident enough and worked hard enough and took risks and invested and were enterprising and *developed* the country. We listen to an aggressively Whig newspaper in Marysville, California, exulting in 1854, five years after the great rush to California began, that the gold in the mountains would never give out, and that, if that were not enough, the Sacramento Valley

> present[s] a theatre for agriculture worth all the gold of our mountains. California is the last spot . . . in which a croaker should show his despicable face. This is the land of enterprise, of energy, of hope, of high-tensioned nerves; not the land of mewling, pewling, fearful, tearful croakers. Our watchwords are "EXCELSIOR!" and "GO AHEAD WITH A RUSH!" and the croaker, who essays to throw cold water upon the glorious fame of enterprise, deserves death by the common hangman.[17]

California began its political existence, however, with a strong Democratic majority. People from the South and ethnic minorities from the Northern working classes made up most of its citizens. The Whigs, while active in state politics and especially strong in the state's few urban centers where Yankee businessmen congregated, watched the Democrats running the state government and winning the presidential elections. In the state's first decade, therefore, California politics were dominated by Southerners and by Irishmen from great Northern cities like New York, each of these groups struggling for supremacy within the Democratic party. Given the cultural style of the rivals, this led to turbulent Democratic state conventions, savage infighting, and tragic duels, for both groups resorted quickly to violence, on occasion, to get their way.[18]

For our purposes, however, more important than the often-told story of California's disorderly state politics in the 1850s was what Democratic ascendancy in Sacramento meant for the management of the state's natural resources. This question came up as soon as California was admitted as a state, for in the Arkansas Act of September 28, 1850, Congress gave to the states all the public land (that is, federal land as yet unsold) within their borders that was swamp and overflowed. It made this astonishing bequest subject to one condition: that the states use the funds they realized from the sale of these lands to insure that they would be drained, reclaimed, and put to productive agriculture.[19]

For California, this was legislation of very great importance. We are aware that an immense region in the trough of the Sacramento Valley was occupied by swamplands. There were also vast areas of such lands in the Sacramento-San Joaquin delta (almost entirely swamp and overflowed), and in the San Joaquin and other California valleys, especially around San Francisco Bay. The total eventually arrived at, statewide, was 2,192,506 acres of land. Of this, some 500,000 acres were in the Sacramento-San Joaquin delta, and 549,540 in the Sacramento Valley itself.[20]

As California undertook to decide what to do with the swamplands it expected to receive, and thus to take advantage of the great promise held out by the Arkansas Act, it had before it a large opportunity for centralized planning. The draining and reclamation of large basins in regions sharing a common geography, as in a single valley, would seem on its face to call for an overall plan for supervision and coordination. Such was not, however, the state's reaction. With Democrats in charge in the 1850s, the state's initial swampland policies, enacted by the Legislature in 1855 and 1858, took quite a different direction. Of course, it was not that the Democrats went about proclaiming "we do this because our Democratic creed dictates it"; political ideology and public policy are rarely so baldly interlinked. Rather, intellectual history's method is to put broad ideologies side by side with specific stands on particular issues to gain a deeper understanding of what happened by noting how closely they fit each other. Policy choices are usually so instinctive and natural to people of particular partisan mentalities, which are well known to contemporaries, that their origins in party creed normally need and receive no explicit remark.

First, we will remember that Democrats were by ancient doctrine philosophically in favor of doing everything locally. Jefferson had said that if we must have government, let us keep it small, and right under our own eyes, so that we may keep it disciplined. Furthermore, on principle Democrats would reject the idea of an activist state government in public works aimed at helping private investors.

First, then, Democratic legislators turned over the most important task in this enterprise to local authorities: to the counties. They were called on to appoint surveyors to establish which lands were swamp and overflow properties, which were then to be sold through a state Land Office where the funds would be gathered in a Swamp Land Fund. Second, they defined the issue in another characteristic way: unlike the Whigs, who would have been centrally concerned with efficient management, the chief purpose of public policy as the Democrats clearly saw it in this matter was to ward off special privilege and monopoly. They worried that the swamplands would be bought up in large holdings by wealthy speculators, who would then hold them off the market awaiting a rise in prices. To insure against this, purchases were limited in size to 320 acres at $1 per acre (in 1859, this was raised to 640 acres).

Whatever happened, under a Democratic regime the central government in Sacramento would not get into the business of building public works to dry out the swamplands. Those buying such property from the state were simply asked to certify, by affidavit, that they intended to drain their holdings and settle on them (another anti-speculator device). For the rest of it, the Democrats relied entirely on their core Jeffersonian concept: laissez-faire. They threw the swamplands open to all comers without system or plan. Flood control was left entirely in the hands of each individual farmer, to be solved by his own good sense and initiative. He could erect levees around his property without any form of public supervision.[21]

≈≈≈

However, the national context was soon beginning to change drastically and explosively. In the mid-1850s a great national uproar was erupting in the Eastern states: the growing North-South controversy over slavery. As angry arguments flared over whether or not the institution should be allowed to expand into the territories, America's politics broke into fragments, several political parties competing where formerly there had been but two. At the same time, this already boiling pot was thrown into an even greater state of agitation by the addition to it of a new and explosively complicating element: in these years a massive and unprecedented immigration of Catholics from Ireland and Germany brought millions of intensely disliked people into the overwhelmingly Protestant United States of America. Their arrival set off near-hysterical jeremiads of anti-Catholic oratory and soon resulted in the forming of a short-lived but extraordinarily powerful political organization, the American ("Know-Nothing") party, which tore into and dominated the politics of many states in the mid-1850s.

This complex sequence of events, the details of which do not concern us here, utterly transformed the policy-making context in the United States, both nationally and within the several states, including California. In the midst of this confusion the once-mighty Whig party, always the party of moderation and compromise, fell calamitously apart and died away. In its place, beginning in 1854 a new and much more aggressively anti-Southern (and anti-Catholic) party, the *Republicans,* who were entirely limited to the nonslave states, came swiftly into being. It was essentially a reborn Whig party, but without any Southerners in it—and therefore a party considerably more Yankee in spirit and goals than ever the Whigs had been.[22]

A Republican party in California quickly appeared, holding its first state convention in 1856. The gathering, like the Republican party nationally, was Whiggish in mood; that is, it was strongly probusiness in its attitudes, sober (no Democratic-style drinking), and orderly. The convention's deliberations were also in the classic Whig mold in being conducted in an almost church-like atmosphere of evangelical piety. The Republicans were a party of entrepreneurs, and most notably of railroad advocates. They were also firmly antislavery in the Abraham Lincoln manner; that is, they could not as yet bring themselves to call for so radical a measure as abolition, but they were rock-hard in their determination to keep slavery from expanding out of the states in which it presently existed and into the territories.[23]

As the national controversy over slavery grew more violent and divisive in the 1850s, it tore the national Democratic party wildly and angrily apart. Its pro-Southern wing argued against the antislavery stand of the Republicans, but many thousands of Northern Democrats, by now thoroughly enraged at their Southern colleagues in the party who seemed arrogantly to be thrusting slavery down Northern throats in such bitterly contested measures as the Kansas-Nebraska Act of 1854, broke away. In New York City, powerful Irish Catholic politicians supported the anti–slavery–extension position (though they were decidedly not abolitionists).

All of this was duplicated in California politics, the Democrats within the state splitting into two estranged camps. When in 1860 the national climax was reached in the presidential election of that year, California Democrats voted for two different candidates. One of them, Stephen A. Douglas, was pledged to an anti-Southern stand on the slavery expansion issue, and the other, John C. Breckinridge, was supported by die-hard pro-Southerners. Thus, against this divided opposition the Republican presidential candidate, Abraham Lincoln, by a small margin took California's electoral votes. In 1861 the Southern states seceded from the Union, and a great collapse of the Democratic party in California, hitherto dominant in state affairs, began. Its many pro-Southern members were, of course, now stigmatized as traitors to the Union, and its candidates had great difficulties winning votes. In the gubernatorial election of 1861 the Republican candidate, railroad entrepreneur Leland Stanford, was elected, and in 1863 the Republicans formally took control of the legislature.[24]

A new mood was now sweeping over California in response to the great events that were shaking the nation from top to bottom. The Civil War, and the long crisis leading up to it, was literally an earthquake in the Northern mind, swinging people strongly toward a cooperative, team-spirit outlook as they joined ranks and faced a common enemy, the militant South. This, in turn, transformed the way people thought about the institution of government itself. Now, as the common instrument of national defense and the general welfare, government was seen in Northern eyes—as Whigs had always urged people to conceive of it—as a great social mechanism to be energetically used in solving society's shared problems. For years prominent Whig, and now Republican, writers and clerics had been urging Americans to turn away from the chaotic and (as they described it) destructive confusion and anarchy of unrestrained Jeffersonian individualism. Left to ourselves, Whig-Republican writers and clerics said, we give way to selfishness; placed under the tutelary wisdom and authority of *institutions*—the family, the church, and God's divinely created instrument, government—we are able jointly to discipline our self-regarding appetites and achieve, harmoniously and with the strength of joint endeavor, great common goals.[25]

Within this emerging national mood, the notion that the larger energies of the community should be gathered together and mobilized behind government-supported enterprises had a new power. Out of Congress during the war years came a string of landmark enactments that put in place the national plan that Whigs and their successors the Republicans had been proposing for many years: protective tariffs, subsidies for internal improvements (especially a transcontinental railroad), land-grant state universities, a national currency, and a system of national banks. This "blueprint for modern America," as it has been called, was a model of energetic government for all the states to follow.[26]

≈≈≈

With this national political context before us, events in California fall into place as appropriate and understandable. In the growing North-South conflict, California took a strongly Northern, anti–slavery-extension stand, and during the Civil War it lined up on the side of the Union. At the same time, California's own internal political culture, its fundamental frame of mind, shifted in Whiggish directions, leaning toward corporate, team-spirit, and community-centered attitudes. In this climate of opinion, it was only natural that the state government would begin taking a vigorously active, interventionist role in managing the state's natural resources. Criticisms of the laissez-faire swampland policies enacted in 1855 and 1858 were widely heard in the state, and inspired by the new mentality the legislature, at the opening of the 1860s, responded to the swampland problem not by piecemeal, incremental reforms but by throwing the whole system out. In its stead it created a bold and dramatic new policy that was astonishingly innovative and, governmentally speaking, far ahead of its time.

It was absurd, opponents of the Democrats' swampland policies were by these steps saying, to allow any amount of land, however small, to be leveed. Absurd, too, were the egalitarian limitations placed on the number of acres any single purchaser could buy. San Joaquin County's surveyor, who in the Sacramento-San Joaquin delta had an immense region of swamplands to supervise, had regularly insisted that the swamplands could not be properly drained on a small-holdings basis. When great floods arrived, as they did regularly, the small works that such property owners could afford to erect were simply overwhelmed. It was essential, he said, for the system to be changed into one that would let persons of large capital buy sizable holdings and build large-scale enterprises—a proposal inherently appealing to those of a Whiggish cast of mind.[27]

As subsequent events revealed, there were many among the Whig-Republicans in California, a predominantly city-based group, who were obviously thinking of much more than this relatively minor alteration in the system. They appeared to have in mind an entirely new definition of the situation. Looking out on the vast spreading swamplands of the Sacramento Valley, running as far as the eye could see and beyond, they saw an immense natural arena potentially capable of being transformed by an energetic government if it relied on the classic elite devices of trained expertise and centralized regulation. From a wasteland (as it was then seen to be) the Valley, they believed, could be transformed into an ordered, fruitful, and profitable agricultural empire. The reclaiming of the Sacramento Valley, the Sacramento-San Joaquin delta, and hundreds of thousands of acres in other California valleys would simply not ever take place, Whig-Republicans believed, if left to local county governments and to ordinary citizens—that is, to untrained amateurs—in the populist, egalitarian style the Democrats in the mid-1850s had preferred. Rather, order and system under competent authority, exercised from the center, must replace confusion and failure.

The 1861 legislature, convened as the nation was breaking apart—the first seven seceding Southern states were in these months forming the Confederate States of America—seized energetically on the swampland problem. At the core of the new reform movement was a group of activists who, as we might anticipate, came from the precise location in the state where the learning process about river management had been most intensive: from Sacramento, one of California's urban centers where Republican voters tended to congregate. In this community and its environs the level of (presumed) knowledge about the Sacramento River was much more sophisticated than elsewhere, for the town had already mounted energetic joint efforts to protect itself from floods, mobilizing the entire community's resources and energies in this direction (in 1862, it would move ahead to create a city levee district with formal taxing powers).[28] Now, its representatives in the legislature, with the crucial assistance of colleagues from next-door El Dorado County, were ready to project their hard-earned flood control concepts valleywide.

Initially, under this leadership the state senate enacted a bill that would give the county governments a strong role. Within their borders, they would be empowered to take control of the leveeing of swamplands by appointing engineers who would develop reasonably integrated and coordinated plans. The state assembly's swampland committee, however, under the leadership of Sacramento's Amos Adams, counseled the assembly to put that proposal aside. They would soon be before the body, they said, with a much better plan. Flood control, they observed, was a unitary, valleywide task. It could never be successfully met if the task was left up to many individual counties, whose efforts would necessarily be poorly aligned with each other. Rather, the time had come for the State of California itself, by freshly created instrumentalities, to assume direction of the entire matter.

Accordingly, on May 31, 1861, with the support of legislators who came overwhelmingly from counties that in 1860 had cast their votes for the Republican candidate, Abraham Lincoln (or at least for Stephen A. Douglas, the candidate of the anti-Southern Democrats), the legislature passed Assembly Bill 54 (AB 54): "An Act to provide for the Reclamation and Segregation of Swamp and Overflowed, and Salt Marsh and Tide Lands, donated to the State of California by Act of Congress."[29] A strikingly new departure had been taken: an instrumentality had been created which would make it possible, legislators believed, to mount a valleywide reclamation program. A bold experiment in policy making, which opened the next phase in California's long struggle to get control of its flooding rivers, was ready to begin.

≈ ≈ ≈ ≈ ≈
≈ ≈ ≈ ≈
≈ ≈ ≈
≈ ≈
≈

CHAPTER

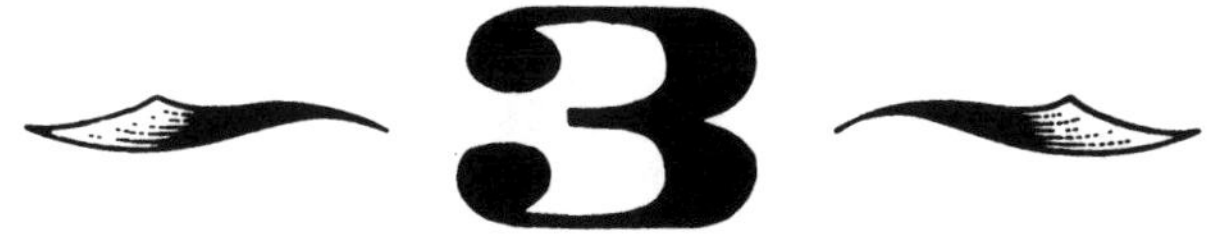

The Failed Dream:
The Swampland Commissioners Experiment
1861–1868

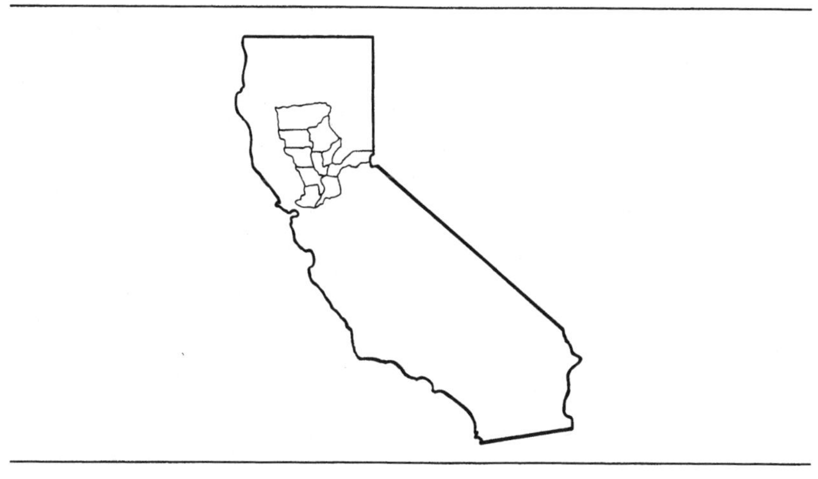

HAYES
WELCOME HAYES INVINCIBLES

"It was hell that night," said [an] . . . out-of-work computer technician. The worst part, they agreed, was the sound of dogs and cats who howled and screamed as they drowned. . . . "I couldn't take it. I went and got some cotton and stuffed it in my ears." . . . "God, [the water] just kept coming in and everything started floating. It kept coming and coming," he said.

> *Amy Chance,* Sacramento Bee, *February 23, 1986. Quoted in* Rivers of Fear, *p. 27.*

The great experiment was in place. By AB 54 the state of California, acting in its sovereign capacity, had dramatically swung over to a Whig-Republican policy base. Under presumably knowledgeable central direction, the state's resources were to be opened in a coordinated way, in the hope that this would create an encouraging climate for entrepreneurs and stimulate investment. Moved by the conviction that it had the necessary wisdom and capacity, Sacramento took the management of entire valleys into its hands. Now an independent public commission that was not under the governor's authority but stood by itself—the first such body in California's history—had been called into being: a Board of Swamp Land Commissioners, elected by the legislature, would begin responding to the problems of central management of state resources, at least so far as this affected swamplands.

The board set out to do its work in accord with sophisticated scientific principles. It brought an abrupt halt to the practice of allowing the Valley to be chopped into small uncoordinated drainage projects, each of them within borders aligned only with property owner-

The Republican party headquarters in San Francisco during the 1876 presidential campaign, meeting place of the "Hayes Invincibles." Mass politics, army-style (note the uniforms), was clearly America's folk theater, with thousands playing their parts. A black American, representing the party's special constituency, is prominently displayed in the foreground.
From Harper's Weekly, *October 21, 1876.*

ship. Henceforth, flood control works were to be aligned with, rather than run across, the Valley's natural drainage pattern. Experience had thus far shown not only that individually constructed levee enterprises failed, since farmers by themselves could not build large enough works to be effective, they actually worsened the problem because they cut off normal paths of flow.

By what mechanism would the commission carry out its tasks? With their appetite for governing, in characteristically innovative fashion in this arena the Republicans in creating the swampland commission had put to use a fresh device. The commission was empowered to create a new class of legal entity called *districts,* previously unknown in California governance, through which the actual work of reclamation in particular parts of the Valley would be carried out. This was a most fertile conception, one that would be seized on in the following generations in California to meet a wide range of basic tasks in governance. The "district," for example, would in time become California's fundamental solution to the task of creating viable irrigation systems,[1] and would eventually be put to use to create and manage public schools, fire protection systems, and many other public services. It had the genius of blending America's instinctive localism with central supervision, since legislative guidelines could tailor the districts specifically to meet particular policy objectives, primarily by establishing limits on their nature and powers. Resembling small principalities, the districts—which would be regarded by the courts as municipal corporations—had specified governing powers, to include taxation, over the territories within their borders.

A swampland district was to be created only if it encompassed an area of land "susceptible to one mode or system of reclamation," by which was meant land contained "within natural boundaries" that comprised, in drainage terms, an integrated unit. In practice, the board understood this requirement to mean that a district would usually encompass an entire basin between the main channels of the rivers. (Since the Valley's rivers were in a depositional phase, laying down silt in their beds rather than scouring it out, their beds were higher than the lands on either side.) Individual basins could encompass more than a hundred thousand acres.

When a petition came in from at least a third of the landowners in such an area, the commission would proceed to erect the district. Thereafter, it would draw on the money held in the Swamp Land Fund (created from the sales of swamplands in that district) and on such additional funds as landowners might themselves have to provide, to build a single system of levees and outfall works for the entire district. Thus, there would be no levees around individual properties; rather, the entire basin would be drained and protected from flood, so that all land would be protected in common. (In 1862, taxing powers were given to the districts for this purpose.) These works, it will be noted, were not simply to be thrown up in the traditional, amateur way, they were to be *planned,* and by engineers appointed by the Board of Swamp Land Commissioners, not by the landowners.[2]

The board quickly organized itself, holding its first meeting in Sacramento within two weeks of the founding legislation's passage. Moving ahead with what must have seemed admirable dispatch, it shortly had before it applications for the reclaiming of twenty-eight districts widely scattered in the Sacramento and San Joaquin valleys and around San Francisco Bay.

District 1 was its most ambitious project, and the one most visible to the watchful legislature, since it lay just north of Sacramento. It comprised all of what was called the American Basin, or that immense lowland area bordered on the west by the north-south line formed by the Sacramento and Feather rivers, on the north by the Bear River, and on the south by the American. In floodtimes one great sea of water, the American Basin ran northward from the city of Sacramento for more than twenty miles, holding within it some 53,000 acres of swampland.

An estimate came in from the board's appointed engineer that this entire princely domain could be reclaimed by levees which in construction would cost about $38,000. This was a sum that fell quite within the available Swamp Land Fund moneys for the district, which at the standard swampland selling price of a dollar an acre would run to more than $50,000, and the project was approved. District 1, however, was slowed in its work by the onset of the Civil War and hampered by disastrous floods. In 1863 it plunged ahead energetically to build miles of levees—until it ran out of money and ceased operations, far short of completion, so that the American Basin was still, in high water periods, regularly inundated.

District 2, also established in 1861, contained 70,000 acres of swamp and overflowed lands in the Sacramento Basin. These lowlands, which lie east of the Sacramento River and include Sacramento City, run southward for twenty miles from their northern border—the American River—to the Mokelumne River, at the edge of the delta. Hampered, too, by floods and by the exigencies of wartime, District 2 was not able to begin its construction of forty miles of riverfront levee, six feet in height, until 1864. When it completed the project, heavily in debt, it possessed a structure that, as later experience would show, would be quickly overtopped in major inundations and therefore of little real use. The other districts that had been formed, some of them designed to take in entire delta islands, all slowed and came to a halt as they faced physical challenges much more complex than they had anticipated and costs far higher than originally forecast.[3]

By the end of the Civil War, this extraordinary experiment in centralized planning and basinwide flood drainage had fallen victim to its own exaggerated confidence. For one thing, not nearly enough money was available to do the job correctly. Engineers were routinely overconfident in what they believed their planned works could achieve, estimates as to costs were never high enough, and the dollar per acre selling price did not produce enough funds. Furthermore many landowners who lived back from the rivers on land rarely overflowed refused to pay their share, while others simply could not afford such expenses. The board, therefore, was in a chronic financial crisis, and subjected to a drumfire of complaint on this ground.[4]

The swampland commission dream had its critics even before its failure was manifest. It aimed at nothing less than a wholesale transforming of the natural environment, and the task was far beyond its means. Floodwaters were going to be excluded from immense stretches of Valley floor into which for thousands of years they had regularly flowed, in order that huge areas of wetlands, then in tule swamps, could be dried out and put to agriculture. As people watched the early efforts at doing all of this, there were soon many who protested energetically. Was the Sacramento Valley in its natural condition in reality an unusable, unlivable place? Did it have to be transformed into an artificial environment in the manner of the Netherlands in Europe? Townspeople like those in Sacramento City and Marysville might have good ground to insist that nothing else could be thought of, if people were to live in the Valley in anything more than simple Indian villages. Most of those who lived out in the ranches and farmlands, where floods could bring disaster to homes, livestock herds, and crops—indeed, to human life—would agree. It usually took very few occasions of being overrun by floodwaters to produce a widespread and enduring fear of such catastrophes.

Nonetheless, others disagreed profoundly. To them, seasonal floods were thought an advantage, not a scourge to be fought off. Floodwaters were of course wonderfully fertilizing, since they regularly deposited fresh soil on the land, and it was often said that a succession of dry seasons produced overrunning populations of crop-eating rodents, which only periodic inundations could put down. More important, the floods offered a cost-free form of irrigation, which, after they had receded, allowed farmers to raise fields of hay and other crops to feed their livestock. As a Colusa County farmer, William Reynolds, would later observe to a legislative committee in the early 1870s,

> the best crops of grain ever raised upon the prairie lands . . . were after they had been overflowed by one of the heavy freshets which have occurred every few years, and without such overflow no dependence can be put upon raising a good crop of grain.[5]

Even the waterlogged tule lands were useful for this purpose. The state's surveyor-general remarked in 1856 that "It is well known the tules are extensively used in the dry season for food by cattle, and swine fatten in them better than elsewhere."[6] Perhaps, it was said, the swamplands should not be reclaimed at all.

Other critics of the program sensed accurately that in adopting what amounted to bold flood control plans for huge segments of the Valley, California was teetering on the edge of an extremely serious commitment. The first thing that the board's engineers called for and set in motion when a reclamation plan was approved for a particular district was the closing off of the sloughs—the natural overflow channels that opened out from the rivers' banks to spread floodwaters out into the paralleling basins. This meant keeping much more water in the rivers' main channel than it was used to carrying, with the inevitable result that the rivers ran at higher levels and flood stages were elevated. When high waters came and levees eventually gave way, as they usually did, the outrush of floodwaters on the Valley floor was even more violent and destructive than before, often reaching areas usually beyond the floodwaters' reach. "[Unless] means can be devised to carry off the water excluded by levees [from the basins] as rapidly as they add to the accumulation of the main waters," a letter to the *Sacramento Daily Union* remarked on February 19, 1862, "they must diffuse themselves over the rich border level lands that had never previously been subjected to inundation."[7] Did the Valley really want a flood control system, if it required closing the sloughs and putting much bigger rivers behind precarious embankments?

Most damaging of all, the Board of Swamp Land Commissioners had taken on far too big a task. They had been charged by an overconfident legislature with building a valleywide flood control system long before anything of this nature was remotely possible. Though engineers seem never to have been humbled by this fact, in reality no one knew enough to plan the projects effectively. The necessary information system was simply not yet in place, nor were the skills. Adequate knowledge, expertise, and technology were almost entirely lacking. Only the most primitive dredges and levee-building apparatus were available, and the board was in total ignorance of the kinds of things that it needed to know: detailed statistical information as to the size of flood flows and their flowage patterns.

Generations would pass before cumulative valleywide surveys by competent engineers, one building on the other, and the emplacement of stream gauges in the rivers, would finally uncover this information, that is, before the necessary learning process would approach maturity. The State of California and the U.S. Army Corps of Engineers would eventually discover to their surprise that the Sacramento River in floodtime was an enormously larger stream than anyone as yet dreamed. The state's initial natural resource management program, hurried into being in an excess of Whiggish hubris, had taken on much too large a task—and one that would be fatally injured by the continuing experience of rising costs outrunning tax resources.

≈≈≈

At the same time, by the post–Civil War years the setting for policy making in California was once again changing rapidly. The impact of national events was washing irresistibly westward to reshape California's public life and therefore its internal policies. The Republicans, who in the cause of saving the Union had during wartime drawn into their ranks hundreds of thousands of Democrats across the Northern and Western states, and in that cause had briefly taken on the name "Union" party, were soon divided into hostile factions in California after the South laid down its arms in the spring of 1865. Former Democrats now active in Republican ranks found themselves quite unable to live in peacetime with their Whiggish party colleagues, for their differences on every other kind of policy issue, now that the fighting was over and defeat of the South was not the single obsessive concern, were too sharp. In a viciously violent Republican state convention in 1865 the truculent "Short Hairs"—as former Democrats were called—burst out in chair-overturning physical attacks on the more aristocratic and genteel "Long Hairs"—as Republicans of Whig antecedents were called—sending many fleeing through the windows and out of the building.[8]

What caused the turmoil? Racism. Former Democrats flared up in angry rebellion when in the national Congress Radical Republicans led a crusade to give the vote to the black people of the Southern states, the former slaves, and insure their civil rights. Trouble on these issues flickered and flashed as early as 1866, when President Andrew Johnson bitterly attacked and vetoed proposed civil rights legislation for the former slaves—at which the citizens of Colusa, a strongly Democratic, pro-Southern town and county in the middle of the Sacramento Valley, fired a cannon salute in jubilation, while Republicans in Sacramento fumed.[9] The controversy escalated to erupt explosively in 1867, when Congress put the Southern states under military occupation to force Southern whites to give the vote to former slaves.[10]

All of this made Republicans unpopular in many Northern and Western States, and nowhere more so than in California. On anything to do with black Americans or with the Chinese and the Indians, toward all of whom the Republicans were seen as liberal in policy, most Californians were firmly racist. The Democratic party, for its part, was openly and unashamedly racist, condemning the Republicans endlessly on these questions. Henry Haight, the (successful) Democratic candidate for governor in 1867, scorned the Republican party's "coercion" of Southern whites. On this ground German and Irish voters in San Francisco, who were traditionally antiblack, supported him enthusiastically, as did a splinter group, San Francisco's Workingman's party. The Republicans were called "mongrel leaders" who wanted a racially mixed American people. In 1867, after a hard-fought campaign argued out around these noisome themes, the Democrats in California won a landslide victory, taking all statewide offices and winning control of the legislature.[11]

There was also, contemporaneously, a powerful economic push coming on board. It had been learned that California's long, warm, dry growing season and fertile unexploited soils produced a particularly high-quality grade of hard-kernel wheat that well survived long-distance transport by merchant marine vessels. Then in the mid-1860s railroads began opening the state's interior valleys to export-crop farming; a cycle of splendid rainfall years produced astonishingly bounteous crops (sixty to eighty bushels per acre, which astounded farmers used to Middle Western yields of fifteen per acre); excellent markets opened in England and the Eastern American states; and a wheat mania exploded. The new political context in California contained, therefore, growing pressure to get at all possible acreage for wheat culture, including, we must surmise, that in the as-yet unreclaimed swamplands.[12] The time for learning how to effectively implement centralizing ideas in natural resource management, built around a Republican concept of energetic state government that Democrats detested, was over.

In the midst of the postwar backlash in California against the Republicans and their activist-government philosophy, and the swift economic changes, it was open season on the swampland commission. The program clearly needed drastic reforms to overhaul it, but at this juncture that was not to be the next policy decision, for the swampland commissioners program had lost its supporting coalition. The experiment it embodied, the learning process it had begun, was not going to be continued.

In early 1866, in fact, the commission had poisoned the wells at its very policy source: the city of Sacramento. It was the Whig-Republican leadership of this busy town, where the Sacramento River and its floods had earliest been struggled with and people had first been seized with the belief that levee-building was the master solution, who in 1861 had evolved the concept of the valleywide, centrally supervised, "expert"-based swampland commissioners plan, and had guided it through the legislature. However, in their desperation over the continued failure of the huge District 2 in Sacramento Basin (which included the city of Sacramento), the swampland commissioners had put a bill in the legislature that would set up heavy taxation on Sacramento City to help District 2 pay its bills.

There was an immediate outcry. As one protestor put the matter in the March 1, 1866 issue of the *Sacramento Daily Union:*

> What does the author of this bill . . . desire? Does he wish to drive property-owners out of the city? For they certainly cannot live here under the pressure of such taxation. Or does some swamp land engineer or other party want a job? . . . if reclamation of District No. 2 is wished for, the property-owners of this city have no particular ambition to be swamped entirely in achieving it.

Now, in the Legislature the swampland commissioners were the object of attack. The conclusive facts were that the centrally directed swampland reclamation program had failed badly. On the heels of the Sacramento uproar the assembly's Swamp Land Committee launched an investigation of the whole valleywide reclamation system and, on the 22nd of March 1866, announced its death knell, reporting for passage AB 591, "An Act supplemental to and amendatory of an Act . . . approved May 18, 1861, and all Acts amendatory thereof." What did it call for? Scrapping the Board of Swamp Land Commissioners and localizing the entire effort by turning the job over to the county governments.[13]

The legislature in 1866, however, was still not yet entirely out of Republican hands. Indeed, after a long, harsh, and intensely partisan debate over President Johnson's recent veto of the Freedman's Bureau bill, a debate that dredged up the Civil War and the South's grievances for yet another angry hearing, on the 28th of February the assembly had voted almost two to one (forty-seven to twenty-six) to condemn Johnson's veto, that is, to confirm the broad Republican position toward the South and the freed slaves.[14]

So, too, the new reclamation policy kept a distinctly Republican coloration. It did not give up on the root idea of having someone in government in charge of swampland reclamation by private parties, even if it had to be at the county level. The state's swamp and overflowed lands, given to it under the Arkansas Act, and all moneys from its sale, were given to the counties not simply to throw away, but "to hold in trust for the purpose of constructing the necessary levees and drains to reclaim the same." In other words, the swampland commission was simply replaced by making each County Board of Supervisors into a miniature swampland commission for the territory within their own borders. They were given authority to approve or deny all levee-building plans presented to them, and the county surveyors were charged with being the flood control engineers for their jurisdictions. Thus, these local bodies and officials were suddenly given very large new responsibilities: they were explicitly to "have control of that portion of the work to be performed within their respective counties."[15] As the assembly Swamp Land Committee put the matter in its report, it

> was satisfied that the present Swamp Land Commission was of little value, because the Commissioners could not visit and personally

> inspect the several districts, and there was . . . no proper means of supervising the expenditures. The Supervisors of the several counties and the County Surveyors could act more intelligently and efficiently.[16]

Furthermore, though there would obviously be no more huge basinwide districts, the science-based principle that whatever levees were built should be aligned with natural drainage patterns was clung to still. When a petition came to a particular board from half of the swampland holders in an area asking authority to form a district for reclamation purposes, the land they were proposing had to be "susceptible of one system or mode of reclamation."

Thereafter, the County Board of Supervisors was to charge the county surveyor with the task of examining the tract in question and devising plans for its reclamation, a complicated fate for many ordinary men who to this point had had nothing more serious to do than survey straight lines. The legislation was explicit: county surveyors, it decreed, "shall be ex-officio engineers of reclamation, and shall superintend all works and give general directions, subject to the control of the Board of Supervisors."[17] To this threadbare base, far removed from the original concept of expert control, was the program reduced.

There were those who mourned the collapse of the ambitious swampland commissioners program into this dispersed, truncated, and far more egalitarian form. The people at large had been too impatient, one "N.N." wrote to the *Sacramento Daily Union,* a strongly Republican paper. The swampland commissioners plan had been designed to be an experiment, a learning process. Now, he said, the counties would be free to "sell, let, grant away, or otherwise dispose of" the land placed in their hands in any amount that they wished. Deeply distrustful of the kind of pliable, susceptible governing arena the rustic county boards of supervisors actually provided, N.N. warned of a coming orgy of corruption, predicting that monopolists would seize it all.[18] Though this was not the immediate outcome of the 1866 policy, N.N. was more prescient than doubtless even he could have wished.

In late 1867 the new postwar mood in California declared itself unequivocally when the Democrats swept the legislature and took the governor's office behind Henry Haight. Soon, in consequence, the revolution in swampland management that the 1866 legislation had begun was brought to a decisive conclusion. The man directly responsible for this step was one of the newly elected Democratic assemblymen, Colusa's Will S. Green. He was a man in his mid-30s who five years before, during the Civil War, had become editor and publisher of *The Colusa Sun,* making of it a lively, opinionated, widely read paper of, as Green put it, "ultra States rights doctrines."[19] During the Reconstruction years its columns were regularly filled with angry attacks on the Radical Republicans and on ideas of equality for black Americans. In a typical effusion, in early 1868 Green put his own definition of the national situation: "We have to deal with a party led by lunatics, and possessing all the destructive elements of a beast of prey. . . . They propose to destroy the Constitution; we must boldly maintain it."[20]

For all of his racism, Green was in other matters no fool; in fact, he had remarkable power of mind. A Kentucky-born person of almost no formal education, he had poured himself into book-reading as a young man; by his midtwenties he was scribbling out journal articles on public affairs, and he carefully absorbed the current manuals in technical arts, becoming a self-taught civil engineer. The consuming obsession of Green's life lay all about him: the wide-spreading lands of the Sacramento Valley and its great central river, and speculations as to how the two might be brought together to create a rich agricultural empire. In 1857 he won election to the office of surveyor in Colusa County, which in these early days of settlement was an active, honored public post, and in his decade of work in that position, which taught him in detail how the land actually lay and where natural basins and potential passageways for canals existed, he became seized with ambitious dreams of irrigation. He poured his own funds into these dreams, commissioning the running of necessary canal-route surveys. In 1866 he had taken his plans to the legislature, though without result. A visionary to the end of his long life, almost forty years into the future Green would try again to get his irrigation plans realized—as, after 1900, they were, in the building of the Glenn-Colusa Irrigation District.[21]

In six weeks of concentrated intellectual and political labors in the legislative sitting of 1868, Will Green swept up all the state's confused land laws, twenty-two in number, recast and adjusted and interwove them, and produced an integrated, systematic code. His bill, which he would ever thereafter proudly refer to as the Green Act, was a formidable document of twenty-four printed pages, testifying to a remarkable achievement in legal craftsmanship on the part of a self-educated man.[22]

From the perspective of later generations his subsequent success in getting his proposal through to enactment did not involve a heroically complicated legislative undertaking. Green's own accounts of what happened speak eloquently of the spare and simple process for the making of major public policy that existed in the California legislature of the 1860s. He simply distributed his bill widely to people he knew in the state who, he said, "were familiar with land questions"; he urged other legislators to do the same; and he got back, Green tells us, only approval from "all the holders of State lands and [lawyers] engaged in such matters." Locating agents, who profited from the existing legal confusion, attacked the bill, but "I sat down by most of the members [of the Legislature], or went to their rooms and explained it to them so thoroughly that I was enabled to kill any amendment to which I did not consent, and hence, I am responsible for the whole law, the bad with the good." For two evenings the relevant assembly committee discussed the matter, "with a room full of land owners from different parts of the State," and then sent it on to the full assembly. Here it was unanimously approved, after which the bill shortly won a similarly unanimous passage through the senate, as well as the governor's signature.[23]

It had been, in truth, a notable feat. Some months later, when the *Santa Clara Argus* was proudly toting up the achievements of the Democratic majority in the 1868 legislature, it included the new land law high among them. "To the industry and capacity of Mr. Green, Democrat from Colusa," the *Argus* remarked, "is the State mainly indebted for the revision and systemization of the land laws," which, the paper went on, had replaced great confusion with simplicity and clarity.[24]

In his new land law, Green, who was anxious to see the lands of the Sacramento Valley opened and developed, took the opportunity given him to recast entirely the state's swampland system. (He does not appear to have profited personally from this legislation; Green avoided investing in swamplands. He simply wanted to see the land developed and the Sacramento Valley turned into an agricultural paradise, his lifelong dream.[25]) The quasi-regulatory legislation of 1866 had not been followed by a burst of swamplands reclamation, possibly because of the costs imposed by the relatively close county-level supervision that the act had established, and the great swamplands on the Valley floor still lay in their natural condition. Following his hard-core Democratic impulses, Green proceeded to replace the 1866 system with one based unequivocally on Jeffersonian principles of unadorned, categorical localism and laissez-faire. At a dollar an acre, under the Green Act individuals were allowed to buy as much swampland as they could afford, subject only to the condition that title to the property would not be actually granted until it was adjudged to be reclaimed.

In his new legislation Green gave the Republicans' "district" concept a revealing Democratic twist: he radically localized it. That is, when purchasers of half or more of a tract of swamp and overflowed land "susceptible of one mode of reclamation"—in practice, now, this simply meant whatever land the group owned—wished to build protective levees, they needed only to petition their local County Board of Supervisors for creation of a swampland district (which could be limited, now, to a single piece of property), informing them of their desire "to adopt measures to reclaim the same." The board, in its turn, was to make certain that the lands to be included were properly described, after which it had no choice but to authorize formation of the district. It no longer possessed, in short, any authority to examine and approve, or disapprove, proposed levee systems around the property, their alignment or nature, or whether they interfered with the Valley's natural drainage patterns. That was left entirely, from this point on, to the Board of Trustees of each district; or, if all the land in the proposed swampland district were owned by one man, it was entirely up to him, at his discretion. No public authority could at any point intervene.

The Board of Trustees of each swampland district would thereafter report their reclamation plans to the county supervisors, together with cost estimates, upon which the supervisors would arrange to have proper tax assessments made on the property owners in the district—who might well be part of the minority in that district, that is, not among the owners who had originally petitioned for creation of the district. Such tax assessments were explicitly not even to be subject to a vote; the control of the original "half or more" of the landowners was conclusive.

The Green Act was even more generous to swampland developers. The money they had paid in for the purchase of their lands was to be placed in a special account by the Board of Supervisors, credited to the particular district. Then, if the owner or owners of the swampland parcel could prove that the land had been cultivated for three years—the proof being made to a locally appointed board of three temporary inspectors—they would receive back their dollar an acre purchase price, and the State Land Office would issue a full patent of ownership.[26]

On Saturday, the 30th of May 1868, Colusa county people picked up their copy of the *Sun* to read Will Green triumphantly reporting that "The Land Act, which, by the way, was our individual winter's work and of which we feel somewhat proud, went into effect last Thursday. . . ." He went on: "[As] it materially lessens the expense of entering State lands, there were a good many standing ready to make applications on that morning, and during the day there were applications filed, for school and swamp land, for some fifteen thousand acres."

With the impetus of the wheat boom behind it, the Green Act set off a great and historic land rush in California. Entrepreneurs in the swampland counties who were willing to risk large sums and dreamt of owning baronial estates acquired huge holdings. L. F. Moulton, a prominent farmer in Colusa County, built up an estate of more than 30,000 acres in that county, in the lowlands between the Sacramento River and Sutter Buttes. Another leading figure, W. H. Parks, acquired equally large landholdings in Sutter County, primarily in Sutter Basin. The large maps of landholdings published in the 1870s by these two counties are dotted with the names of Parks and Moulton, who were simply the most prominent, locally, of the swampland proprietors.[27]

In fact, in just three years of wild speculative scramble, from 1868 to 1871, under the laissez-faire Green Act practically all the state's millions of acres of swampland holdings passed into private hands, and in circumstances widely regarded as corrupt. Federal military scrip was purchased for a few cents on the dollar and used to buy swamplands. In one case a single holding of 250,000 acres was secured by this means. Another purchaser got 116,000 acres, and purchases running upwards to this figure were not uncommon. Historian Joseph McGowan registers a report that "the only expense incurred by the purchase of the Yolo Basin [a region encompassing over a hundred thousand acres] was that of paying witnesses to testify that the land had been reclaimed so that the owners could get a refund on the amount paid."[28] The "swampland thief" was a stock figure in California political rhetoric for many years after these events.

≈≈≈

Thus, by this route, what is now called by policy scholars a "standing policy decision" had been put in place. There was no repealing of the Green Act; for the next half-century, it was California's established public policy. In a crucial area of natural resource management involving millions of acres of land, laissez-faire was firmly in command. California's peculiar tradition of land monopoly was vastly expanded, which is certainly one of the more ironic outcomes for a Democratic piece of legislation that American history affords.

The Green Act did not simply produce another explosion of land monopoly in California, it completely atomized flood control planning and construction down to the individual reclamation district. The Jeffersonian passion for localism, and for putting people on their own, had been entirely satisfied. The result was that for most of the next half-century, the Sacramento Valley would be scissored into a crazy-quilt of small reclamation districts whose levees followed property lines, not the Valley's natural drainage pattern. Flood control anarchy, and therefore massive flood control failure, would be the result.

The Green Act system, however, was clung to doggedly. American political culture was too deeply individualistic, too powerfully dominated by a universal determination to control one's own property as one wished. It fed too much on distrust of distant government, skepticism toward publicly employed experts, indeed on the simple demonstrated fact of the state government's incompetence to do anything effective in flood control. Thus, the fundamental policies embodied in the Green Act were not to be significantly changed until many decades of a valleywide and in fact national learning process had passed. There would be much talk of reform, and in the 1880s a brief dramatic effort to achieve it, but until well beyond 1900 all such efforts would fail.

≈≈≈

While all of this was going on, the problem no one was trying to do anything about—the rise of hydraulic gold mining in the northern Sierra Nevada and the filling in by mining debris of the river system of the Sacramento Valley—continued to worsen. Since the filling of a river channel by mining debris did not at the same time raise its banks, a stream so damaged could carry much less water, and provided a shallower and more chancy navigable channel. With this in mind, many attempts were made to attack and eliminate a bar that had formed in the Sacramento River in front of the capital city, created by the plume of hydraulic mining debris that poured out of the American and into the Sacramento just above town, but to little advantage. By 1866 it was clear that large steamers could dock only intermittently at the Sacramento City landing, so severely was the river shoaled at that point. By 1879, when federal and state engineers examined the river below the community, they found that for many miles, reaching to the delta, the big stream had filled in to an average depth of more than fifteen feet.[29]

Because of the filling of channel beds by mining debris, in low water periods the steamboats continued to find it difficult to navigate through the delta islands on Steamboat Slough, although their experience varied from year to year. The problem was eased in the late 1850s, for the first surge of hydraulic mining had passed, and the industry was in decline. The initial phase of its history, when loose and easily moved gravels could be washed down by small, primitive hydraulic works, was completed, and the mines would lie fallow for a number of years while their problems were slowly solved by the invention of new technology and methods. Meanwhile, high water seasons and heavy river flows appear to have sluiced out into Suisun Bay enough of the silt lying on the Hog's Back, the shoal that occupied the lowest reaches of Steamboat Slough, to allow boats to pass through the slough without difficulty, thus quieting the loud complaints earlier heard when they had regularly grounded at this point.

During the late 1860s, however, a second hydraulic mining boom opened. Huge operations, heavily capitalized and using powerful new equipment, began pouring incredible volumes of debris into the rivers. Soon, as this new and much larger avalanche of mining debris surged down into the Valley's watercourses, new complaints about river problems began to be heard. In the very year of 1867, when the Democrats won back control of the state legislature, the *San Francisco Examiner* was beginning to grumble once more that the Hog's Back was getting troublesome, that steamers regularly grounded and had to lay over several hours waiting for higher tide. The state government, the paper went on to insist, should do something to rectify the problem.[30]

However, now that the Democrats controlled Sacramento, the window of opportunity for innovation and for the active involvement of the state government in managing natural resources was no longer open. Democratic hegemony meant a drastic shift in mood. Republican concepts of strong government were out, and now the emphasis was on laissez-faire, small and inexpensive government, everyone on their own with no help from the authorities, and full reliance on unassisted private enterprise. Thus, if anything were to be done about the Hog's Back, it would have to be without government intervention. Eventually, Steamboat Slough was so shallowed that it had to be abandoned for commercial transportation.

CHAPTER

Crisis on the Yuba and the Feather: *The 1860s*

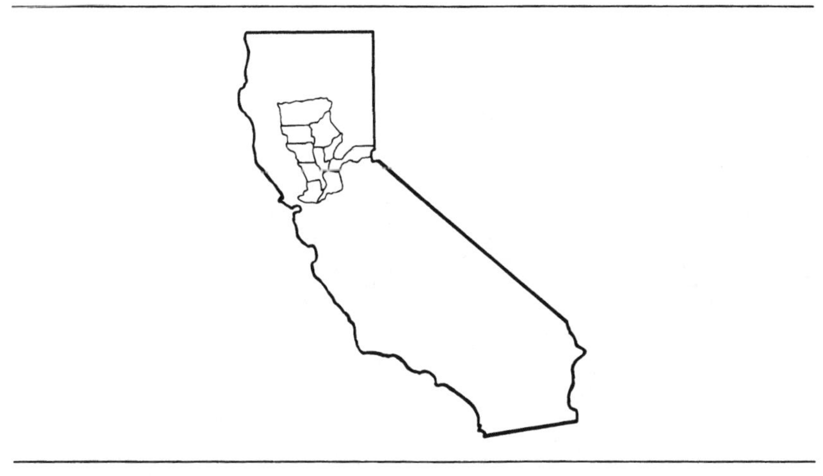

"It's such a beautiful house," she cried. ". . . last year I lost my mother, and now I've lost my home." . . . [He] talked about a squawking rooster pheasant that approached him early that day, apparently terrified by the flood, and about little mice swimming toward his boat. "Everything wants to live."

John C. Cox, Ted Bell, and Jon Engellenner, Sacramento Bee, *February 19, 1986. Quoted in* Rivers of Fear, *p. 30.*

On the 31st of March 1860, the rivers were high at Marysville and rising fast to flood levels. The "yellow Yuba . . . that turgid vehicle of sediment," the *Marysville Appeal* remarked in irritation, "takes a vulgar pride in spreading out its dirty face." The slump in hydraulic mining in the late 1850s—induced because the miners had been getting down to harder gravels in the ancient Tertiary river beds which required more force to break apart than their equipment could provide—had given way to a renewed boom in operations. Stronger hoses had been developed which could bear a more powerful head of water, and dynamite blasting became a regular procedure to loosen the more toughly bound deposits. The discharging of debris into the streams had taken up again, only now in heavier volume. The Yuba River, which drained the most active hydraulic mining region, carried an especially heavy load of mud, sand, and gravel flowing downstream either in suspension or sliding along on its bed. Emerging from the mountains at Parks Bar at an elevation of 259 feet, the Yuba was a fast-moving stream, dropping some 200 feet in

An 1880s view by Carleton E. Watkins of hydraulic mining in the North Bloomfield company's famous Malakoff Diggins, now a state historical park. It discharged a huge volume of mud, sand, and gravel into the South Fork of the Yuba River. In January 1884, the federal injunction in Edwards Woodruff *v.* North Bloomfield et al. *shut down the entire industry in America's first major environmental decision.*
Courtesy: Bancroft Library, University of California, Berkeley.

the sixteen miles of sloping Valley floor it would cross before joining the Feather at Marysville.[1]

The people of that town stood worriedly on the Yuba's banks during high water times to watch the swollen brown sinewy mass of water rushing by and to talk among themselves about what was happening below the surface. Clearly, the Yuba's bed was filling with debris and rising in elevation. By the end of the summer of 1860, while the nation at large was caught up in the climactic electioneering that would see Abraham Lincoln sent to the White House, the silent flowing sands from the mines which the Yuba carried in its bed were reaching the mouth of the Yuba and moving out into the channel of the Feather. A large sandbar had built up, forming an arc in that stream which reached its eastern bank and left "but a very narrow curving passage way for vessels of the smallest size and lightest draft." The steamboat *Governor Dana,* which had been calling at the Marysville dock for years, had in fact recently gotten stuck in the deposits.

> Steaming on Feather river during the summer season [observed the *Appeal*'s editor] has already ceased to be a covetable experience from this cause. The Yuba is not navigable, and its receptacle will soon be in the same condition. . . . Below its junction with the Yuba, it is now a channel of muddy impurity, chocolate-colored, narrow and shallow. Along its course great bars of sand are formed and forming, shifting their locality continually. In some places it is so narrow that a steamboat can barely pass.[2]

By this time, with ten years of flooding experience behind them, Valley people were awakening to the fact that high water was not just an occasional, but a chronic phenomenon. Almost a year to the day after the flood of March 1860, there was yet another great inundation. For three days in March 1861, there were heavy rains and widespread overflow in the flatlands. Between Marysville and Sacramento the Valley was again a sheet of water, and the Yuba, its channel even more filled in, reached higher levels than at any time since 1853.

The lowlands south of that stream, between Marysville and the mountains, were one vast expanse of water, thousands of acres of orchard and farmlands being covered by the yellow flood. "It seems

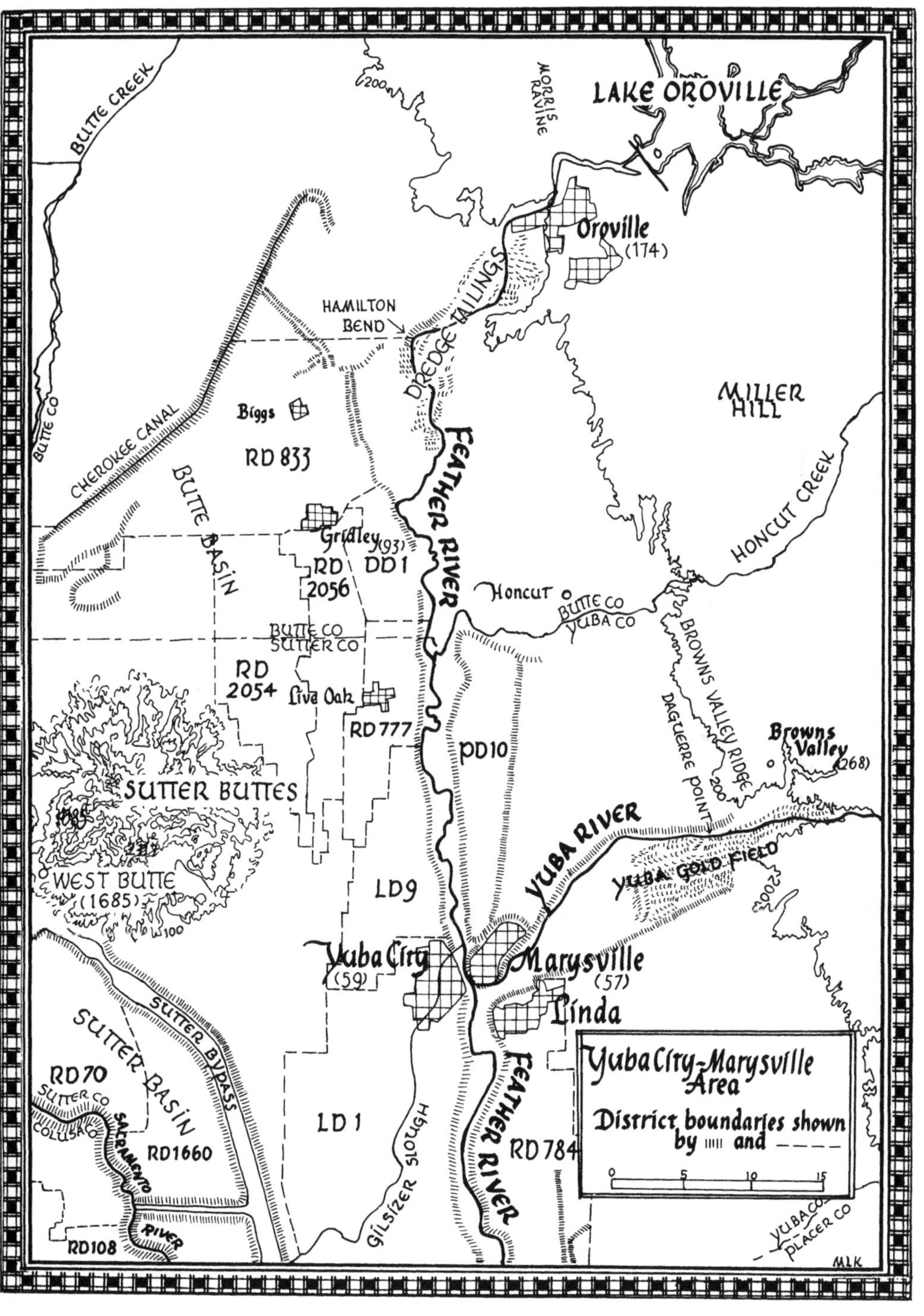

LAKE OROVILLE
BUTTE CREEK
MORRIS RAVINE
Oroville
(174)
HAMILTON BEND
DREDGE TAILINGS
CHEROKEE CANAL
Biggs
RD 833
MILLER HILL
BUTTE CO
FEATHER RIVER
BUTTE BASIN
HONCUT CREEK
Gridley (93)
RD 2056
DD1
Honcut
BUTTE CO
YUBA CO
BUTTE CO
SUTTER CO
BROWNS VALLEY RIDGE
RD 2054
Live Oak
DAGUERRE POINT
RD 777
PD10
Browns Valley
(268)
SUTTER BUTTES
YUBA RIVER
YUBA GOLD FIELD
WEST BUTTE
(1685)
LD9
Yuba City
(59)
Marysville
(57)
Linda
SUTTER BYPASS
SUTTER BASIN
RD70
SUTTER CO
COLUSA CO
SACRAMENTO RIVER
LD1
GILSIZER SLOUGH
RD784
RD1660
RD108
YUBA CO
PLACER CO
Yuba City-Marysville Area
District boundaries shown by and
0 5 10 15
MLK

certain, now," remarked the *Appeal* after the worst of the flood had passed, "that every five or six years an overflow may be apprehended, as the Indians told the first settlers." It was also becoming obvious that mining debris was no longer confined to the river channels and injuring navigation only, for the sands had filled them to the brim and were beginning to flow out over the natural levees of the Yuba to settle on the countryside on either side. Laissez-faire, luxuriating in the mountains, was producing a massive blight on the environment. At year's end, in 1861, the *Appeal*'s editor scanned the annual report of the county assessor and observed that he "might have added [in his report] that the valuation of bottom lands on the Yuba and Bear rivers is merely nominal this year . . . for the reason that the spreading deposit of sand and gravel has ruined what was, a year ago, excellent land."[3]

These words were hardly printed when an enormous flood far exceeding anything people had earlier seen swept in to bury the Sacramento Valley. It would be fixed forever, thereafter, in the Valley's memory as historically the most massive of all of its floods. Lasting for more than a month, its two peaks separated by several weeks, the double flood of 1861–1862 (December–January) spread devastation throughout the entire Valley. Cattle died in great numbers, city business districts and residential neighborhoods were buried deep in water, farm dwellings were destroyed, and many were swept away to their deaths by high waters. The inland sea had rarely ever spread so widely or had been so deep.

When the waters finally receded in the Marysville region, there was general shock at what they left behind. A large part of the hydraulic mining tailings which had been piling up in the mountain canyons since the process first began in 1853 was scoured out by the high waters to settle on the flatlands. The territory south of the Yuba was reported to be "a desolate waste . . . a thick sediment of sand destroying all hopes of vegetation, at least for some time to come." The editor of Marysville *Daily California Express* took a ride toward the mountains, crossing the plains bordering the Yuba River, and he came back to his desk to write out a sobering report:

> For miles back of the Yuba [i.e., to the easterly of it], in fact almost at the base of the foothills . . . great elevations of sand have been thrown out upon the plains, and fruit trees, which, in low water times, are many feet above the level of the Yuba, are almost entirely covered by sand deposits. A ranch owner up the Yuba . . . informed us that out of about two thousand acres of tillable land in the neighborhood, extending from the Yuba back on the plains a considerable distance, not more than two hundred acres were fit for agricultural or grazing purposes, the sand averaging on the greater part of this region of territory from two to seven feet in depth.[4]

This was an appalling sight. Particularly disturbing was the knowledge that the lands disappearing under the sands—the bottoms—were among the richest and most fertile in the Valley. The Yuba's original channel, in its natural condition, had been about three to four hundred feet wide, gravel-floored, with steep banks rising about fifteen to twenty feet on either side at low water. From the top of these banks, as a federal judge, summing up testimony in his court, would later describe the scene, there

> extended a strip of bottom-lands of rich, black, alluvial soil, on an average a mile and a half wide, upon which were situate some of the finest farms, orchards, and vineyards in the state. Beyond this first bottom was a second bottom, which extended some distance to the ridge of higher lands, the whole constituting a basin between higher lands on either side, of from a mile and a half to three miles wide.[5]

It was the fertile bottoms that the first settlers had most eagerly taken up. Though but a dozen years had passed since the Gold Rush began, in the early 1860s the bottoms along the Yuba River were already a handsome farming scene. Among an agricultural people, therefore, there was something especially saddening in the sight of a comely and abundant countryside being obliterated, and they long remembered it with a particular poignancy. "It was a kind of meadow [in its original condition]," mused J. H. Jewett, a Marysville banker, many years later during court testimony, " . . . what you would call a prairie. [It was] grass land, with some large trees skirting the river. . . a dark alluvial soil through there . . . of the best quality . . . probably, in this country; perhaps in the State. It produced very large crops."[6] The burying of the bottom lands did not in fact occur in just one flood, but rather it occurred in a lengthy but progressive process which extended over a number of years. The "encroachment from time to time was so gradual," Jewett remarked, "that is, to take a few acres more, go a little further, 2 or 3 feet higher each year, it has been so gradual. . . ." that to Valley people it was like watching a slow death, one about which they were helpless to do anything.

≈≈≈

It all posed a cruel, puzzling conflict of interests for the Valley people. As the rivers turned brown and silt settled in flatland channels, the shape of the future was obvious to all, and yet, the response was denial. For the simplest fact before the farmers and townsfolk of the flatlands was the ironic reality that they had a large economic stake in the gold mining industry, and therefore in one of its major segments, hydraulic mining. The mountain towns bought food and supplies from flatland farms and towns. As early as 1851 steamboats carrying freight to supply the miners were so numerous at the Marysville waterfront, which served as the head of navigation on the Feather, that there was not enough room to discharge cargo. In 1855 something like 200 tons of freight arrived daily at the docks, and in early 1856 a thousand teams of horses were reported to be pulling freight wagons on the long rising road from Marysville to the mining towns. "Heavily loaded teams, which creak under pressure of their accumulated burdens, fill our streets on their way to the mines," observed a local editor. "Numbers of pack trains leave the city each day, for parts as yet not reached by wagon travel. Stages, literally full to overflowing of passengers, are constantly coming and going."[7]

The people of Marysville were therefore in a deep uncertainty as to their interests in this matter, and for a number of years unable accurately to define their situation—which in turn meant that deciding on what to do, what line of policy they should adopt, was impossible. We may understand the reasoning, if not approve the foresight, in the response given by the mayor of Marysville to a visiting reporter in January of 1856. What do you think, he was asked, about the shallowing of the Yuba which has occurred since the onset of hydraulic mining? He replied that he could only view it as a good thing, since mud in the water meant that the miners were at work, and that, being prosperous, they would continue buying from the farmers.[8] An enthusiastically Whig local newspaper, the *Marysville Herald,* which, true to its political faith, optimistically boomed economic development in all directions, two months later chattered along in a similar vein. "We rejoice," the editor remarked eagerly, "that the miners have conquered [their water gathering problems]," having built a network of ditches and flumes, the editor went on to admiringly observe, "which intersects the diggings like a spider's web."[9]

Indeed, more people benefited from the mountain trade than simply the farmers. Marysville and Sacramento both provided many goods and services through their railroads, steamboat lines, staging companies, mercantile houses, banks, hotels, and small factories. The very technology that the hydraulic miners used, as in the case of the hydraulic "monitor" invented around 1870—a long cannon-like movable nozzle made of iron which could send powerful hissing streams of water in four-hundred-foot arcs to strike mining faces with great force, and thus greatly accelerate the pace and volume of hydraulic mining—was devised and fabricated in Marysville foundries.[10] San Francisco capital would eventually be heavily invested in hydraulic mining, bringing in another powerful group behind the industry. With so many predominantly Republican political and economic interests reluctant to support curtailment of mine operations, it would be difficult to carry legislation against the miners through the legislature, even if a majority in that body actually wished to enact it.

The fact of the matter was that many years would pass before people even in the badly affected regions in the Valley would begin demanding action. Finding themselves in a circumstance where drastically new policy innovations were being demanded by a steadily evolving new situation, they behaved in the classic fashion: until prodded by crisis or outside authority, they were reluctant to move. It takes a long time for a community to develop what has been called a "culture of protest"; to put new policy problems on the public agenda, come to a state of mind which insists that something must be done about them by someone; to be ready, in a concerted way, to leave quietism behind, begin mobilizing, and start taking action. As policy analysts put the matter, ordinary citizens have heavy "sunk costs," that is, substantial psychological as well as social and economic investments, in a stable and quiet life, and activism on principle is avoided.

Everything in the silently growing hydraulic mining problem encouraged this state of mind. The debris produced by the mines was gradual in its impact, and it arrived on the flatlands anonymously, as a kind of natural fact. No one could tell from which mine the mud was originating, since there were many separate operations in the mountains and their debris merged and commingled long before it issued out of the mountain canyons. Therefore, litigation was difficult even to conceive of, let alone to mount. Who could be sued, and for what?

If thoughts turned, instead, to gaining help from the legislature, the larger political and cultural context in the state would for some time quiet that impulse. Californians at large were in the wrong state of mind to respond favorably. They still conceived of the gold mines as their core industry, and of the miner, in his dangerous and exhausting work (which many in the cities and farms had themselves experienced) as benefactor to the whole community; the miner, in the eyes of Californians, was the creator of the wealth that made the state both legendary and prosperous.

Nationwide, in fact, there was a kind of heroism attached to miners, whose industry had simply exploded in the western mountains following the California Gold Rush. The miner seemed to be the ultimate, emblematic expression of the core American ideal of unrestrained, courageous individualism. Journalists poured out reams of admiring copy. "Such words as *pluck, enterprise, endurance,* and *courage* flowed from writers' pens," Duane Smith remarks, "and joined phrases such as 'heroes of the pan and spade' to characterize the miners." As more and more gold and silver flowed out of the Western mountains, from the Rockies to the Sierra Nevada, national interest and enthusiasm about the miners mounted.[11] Therefore, before an assault on the mines would gather supporters, fundamental outlooks had to change. People had to begin thinking of California as essentially a farming state and of its basic fount of wealth and prosperity as coming from the land. This cast of mind would not emerge until at least the 1880s.

In addition, midnineteenth-century Americans generally looked on the environment in ways that led them to ignore the damage the miners were causing. Since the hydraulic mining debris was carried within the natural system of streams and rivers, the sense that most Americans had of a limitless and resilient environment inclined them to an instinctive passivity on such questions. Nature, people believed, would endlessly tolerate whatever humanity did to it and still find some means of balance and absorption. Miners, for their part, were convinced that the nation's public domain held an infinity of mineral resources that would never run out. They took an almost savage pleasure in the spectacle of nature being ripped and torn, its mountains disemboweled, its treasures gouged out of their hiding places. When some critics charged them with being shockingly wasteful of nature's bounty, a miner in the Comstock lode replied by talking confidently of "the privilege of American citizens to waste the mineral resources of the public land without hindrance." And indeed, as the hydraulic miners themselves were to say in their defense, Congress in the midnineteenth-century decades enacted a continuing stream of laws giving away the nation's public lands with a lavish, unquestioning hand for the precise purpose of encouraging mining.[12]

If this were not enough, in this slowly rising argument the miners had another powerful argument on their side: ancient traditions as to private property and freedom of enterprise. Nothing was more certain in America, miners would say in absolute confidence, than their right to do what they pleased with their own property. They were literally astonished when downstream people finally began insisting that they should actually shut down their operations. The assertion that people should use their property only in ways that would not damage that of others was a principle as yet not much heard, and when it was, given little official sympathy. In a famous Pennsylvania case in 1886, which challenged a coal mine's polluting of a stream, the state's supreme court ruled that if people bought property in an area known to be profitable for mining, there was

> no great hardship, nor any violence to equity, in their accepting the inconvenience necessarily resulting from the business. . . . damages resulting to another, from the natural and lawful use of his land by the owner thereof . . . in the absence of malice or negligence [do not produce a cause for legal action]. The trifling inconvenience to particular persons must sometimes give way to the necessities of a great community. Especially is this true where the leading industrial interest of the state is involved, the prosperity of which affects every household in the Commonwealth.[13]

In any event, to do anything at all about hydraulic mining which would be effective, something genuinely large and unprecedented in the American public tradition would have to be done. Major innovations in law and government, and in the management of the natural environment, would have to be evolved. This in itself immobilized people. We have seen how strongly most people were on principle opposed to the idea of strong government, how much it required the intervention of an extraordinary event, a great civil war, to get Californians into a team-spirit frame of mind and inspire them to move in this direction in the management of natural resources. And how quickly that effort collapsed thereafter. Even Republicans, despite their Yankee-inspired ideas of vigorous government, would resist putting this concept to use in any way that would be unfriendly to large industrial operations. Thus, the use of public authority to interfere with or to shut down an entire industry was a concept that would never be enacted into law by the legislature. The courts themselves in California would only come to this position reluctantly, and then after many years of litigation and a slow crabwise sidling in this direction in case after case.

The people of the Sacramento Valley responded to their great public policy challenge, then, by simply living with their problem, year after year, and looking the other way. They seemed unable to get their minds around the inevitable. Rather, they hoped, we can only imagine, that whatever the evidence before those who cared to look, the issue was not so serious as, in their darker moments, they knew it to be.

≈≈≈

In the Marysville vicinity, no one set up an outcry against the hydraulic miners or sent to Sacramento to ask for aid. There was nothing to do, it was said, but abandon the bottoms. Farmers were advised to look again at the gravelly, less fertile but more elevated lands of the prairie which were beyond the overflowed bottoms. They have lain, said the *Appeal*'s editor, "high and green above the general waste, affording glad refuge to men and brutes. . . ." The *Marysville Express* agreed, remarking that the "higher portions of the plains, heretofore considered valueless except so far as affording grazing grounds for loose stock during the spring months, are now in demand."[14]

In San Francisco a newspaper for the mining industry, the *Mining and Scientific Press*, had been jolted out of its indifference to the Valley's problems by the immense flood of 1861–1862, and by the widespread outflowing of sands it had produced. Mud was indeed coming from the mines, the paper admitted, and filling up the river channels. This was a fact, of course, which could hardly be denied by a San Francisco newspaper, when for six years steamboats had been catching on the Hog's Back in Steamboat Slough, but the editor insisted that an inundation such as the Valley had just experienced would not come again for a lifetime. For their part the hydraulic miners themselves were reported to be pleased by the great storms, for after the powerful, boiling outflows of 1861–1862 had passed down the canyons and the rivers had subsided, they noted with pleasure how deeply the high water had scoured out the piled-up debris. From all the riverbeds in Sierra County—that is, along the north fork of the Yuba River—an average of ten feet of mining debris had been swept away.[15]

The Civil War was now raging in the Eastern states, taking attentions away to scenes far from the Sacramento Valley. At the same time, in the first years of the 1860s a severe drought seared California, almost killing off the huge cattle herds of the southern counties while at the same time it quieted the hydraulic miners' nozzles. In 1863 a great explosion of mining excitement erupted following the discovery of silver in Nevada's Comstock Lode, leading to a rush of miners away from California to Virginia City. Comstock Lode mining required heavy investments in tunneling and mining equipment, and the money had to be raised by selling stock in the San Francisco exchange. This had historic results, for it set off a stock-exchange boom out of which emerged a group of risk-taking entrepreneurs, pleased by their great profits, who now began looking afresh at the California mines.

When in late 1864 the rains began again in California, heavy and pounding, capitalists started once more searching out promising investment opportunities in the hydraulic mines of the northern Sierra Nevada. Another year of abundant water supplies came in 1865, and mining operations, widely fitted out with new equipment and more extensive water systems than they had formerly possessed, turned the rivers brown with a continuous heavy flow of sediment. In 1866 a group of San Francisco capitalists formed a large operation in Nevada County, the North Bloomfield mine, by consolidating many smaller claims on the broad high ridge that lies between the south and middle forks of the Yuba River. It became the model and pace setter for many other large operations. The North Bloomfield, however, like the other larger mines now starting work, soon found itself running out of drainage outlets into which to discharge its detritus. The sand and gravel from the mines' long sluices piled up so deeply in the relatively slow-moving creeks that meandered across the tops of the broad Sierra ridges that by 1868 many operations had had to cease for lack of outfall.

The San Francisco capitalists who were now buying up the hydraulic mining industry—men like L. L. Robinson of the city who had already conceived and constructed the West's first railroads—were a far more sophisticated group of entrepreneurs than the operators of small mines they were replacing. They quickly began bringing in another kind of highly skilled person, the mining engineer, to solve the technical problems they were encountering. These professional, college-trained experts took an activity that, on the level of the individual mine, had been small and crude, amateur in mood, and owner-operated, and transformed it into an advanced extractive industry. Drawing on the latest technology (soon they would be using electric lights, telephones, and steam-driven, diamond-pointed drills) they broke through the physical limitations that formerly had kept hydraulic mining relatively small-scale.

Using the recently invented drilling equipment they drove bedrock tunnels from locations underneath their consolidated mining claims directly to the deep river canyons, where mining debris could be freely dumped and subsequently carried downstream in periods of high water. At the same time, from the early 1870s onward new and larger mining equipment, such as the Hoskins "Little Giant" monitor, accelerated both the pace of operations in the upper Yuba River watershed and the downward flow of debris toward Marysville.[16]

In these same years the hydraulic miners in and around the town of Oroville, which sits on the south bank of the Feather where that stream emerges from the mountains, thirty miles upriver from Marysville, were also solving their technical difficulties and launching increased operations. As early as 1854 the Oroville miners had started putting "the pipe hose" to use in small hydraulic mines on both sides of the river. In 1855 the construction of the South Feather River Ditch reached Oroville, bringing in abundant water for the mines, and in 1857 the Walker & Wilson Ditch got to Thompson Flat, on the opposite, northerly side of the river. Hydraulic mining spurted, and soon Oroville was booming, with hotels, boarding houses, saloons of all kinds, and stores and private homes. Ditches to drain the mines in the bluffs behind town were cut through the city's streets to the river. A plume of hydraulic mining debris discharged by these ditches began to take form in the Feather's channel, producing a long island or "bar" in front of town. The people of Marysville, downstream, found in the 1850s that the Feather as well as the Yuba was turning brown with suspended slickens.[17]

In 1864, after seven years work, a drainage tunnel directly to the Feather was completed from the Thompson Flat mines, and the filling in of the Feather's bed from the northern side, at Oroville, quickened. Soon, in 1866, the completion of another long ditch gave Thompson Flat miners far more water, the local editor exulting that as a result "the vast extent of land on the [north] . . . bank of the Feather river [opposite Oroville] . . . will . . . be washed to bedrock, yielding good pay."[18]

In the latter 1860s the Oroville region mines purchased much more powerful equipment; smaller mines were consolidated into larger operations; more drainage ditches were excavated; and increasing volumes of debris were dumped into the Feather. At the head of steep Morris Ravine, a few miles upriver from Oroville, an "amazingly colossal" operation, the Hendricks mine, opened up in 1870, turning big monitors on the mountainside. Before their hurtling arcs of water, "the earth melts away, and even the bed-rock is torn up and thrown high in the air, shivered to atoms and whirled away down the flume by the rapid current." The water and debris streaming out of the mine was caught up by a sluice-box four feet wide and a mile long which dropped precipitously down the steep ravine to discharge the mine's mud, sand, and gravel directly into the Feather River.[19]

To look ahead briefly into the 1870s, so busy were the Oroville miners, and so massive did their operations become, that by November 1873, one of the larger mines had to shut down, at least temporarily, because the river bed at Oroville was choked and no dumping ground was left. "Mining operations have so filled the bed of the river," the *Butte Record* observed, "both at the upper and lower end of town, that it is difficult to tell where the channel will be after another such flood as that of '62."[20] And yet the pace of work continued to build. In the ensuing years ever larger mines were formed, ditches were increased in capacity, and thousands of feet of iron pipe almost two feet in diameter were installed, allowing the water to shoot out of the monitors at ever higher pressures.[21]

≈≈≈

During the latter 1860s a new cycle of floods struck the Sacramento Valley. The first of them, in the last days of December 1866, left editor Will S. Green of the *Colusa Sun* commenting that "without doubt, more water passed down the valley [during the flood] than ever before since its settlement by whites in the same length of time." One sheet of water more than twenty miles across was reported to cover the Valley floor between Marysville and Colusa. That is, the entire Sutter Basin, the region that lies south of the Sutter Buttes and is enclosed between the Feather and Sacramento rivers, was filled.[22]

Two months later, in February, there came another great flood, producing "one continuous body of water" many miles across straddling the whole course of the Sacramento River from above Colusa southward. Then in April and May the rivers rose again to high levels, staying in that condition for weeks. "Never since '49 have the Yuba and Feather rivers been known to be so full of water and continue so high so long as at present," the *Weekly Sutter Banner* in Yuba City remarked. Not for over a month, in fact, would they begin receding, so that steamboats could make the run from Sacramento to Marysville. The rivers rose yet a third time in 1867, with the *Colusa Sun* reporting in December that the town and its environs were "now an island; above, below, to the right and left is one vast sheet of water. Between town and the Coast Range the water presents the appearance of an inland sea."[23] For many weeks, the rivers remained large, steamboat captains reporting them higher than ever before. Storm after storm passed over the Sacramento Valley.

If ever anyone had thought that the Sacramento River and its tributaries would only rarely rise to threaten life and property, that delusion was thoroughly dead now. It was depressingly clear to Valley people that what they were trying to do was to live and farm on the floor of a Valley much of which in almost every year was buried under water. It was a grave fate, prompting correspondingly grave reflections.

C H A P T E R

The Struggle Begins:

Sutter County in Siege

1866–1875

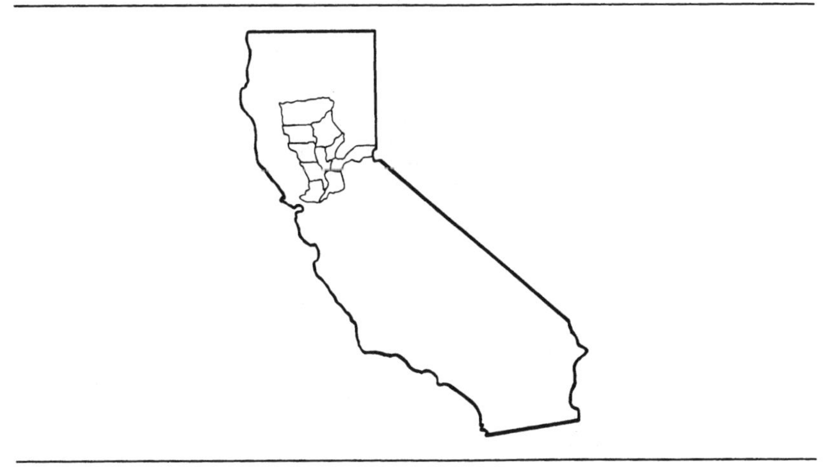

KEY TO MARYSVILLE.
BIRD'S EYE VIEW OF
MARYSVILLE
AND YUBA CITY, CAL.
AND SURROUNDING COUNTRY.
COMPLIMENTS OF THE
MARYSVILLE DAILY AND WEEKLY DEMOCRAT.

There's a body of psychiatric research that indicates some never recover from being flooded out. Forget monetarily. Emotionally. There is a sense of personal loss, much as if one has been robbed or raped. There is the feeling of having been violated. *There is the response, "Why me?" And then there is the frustration-born anger.*

> *Herbert Michelson,* Sacramento Bee, *March 3, 1986. Quoted in* Rivers of Fear, *p. 34.*

For people who lived along the middle and lower reaches of the Feather River, the limit of their stoicism had finally been reached. The river bed in their part of the Valley was filling with mining debris, which made flooding more frequent and destructive. The battering cycle of floods in the latter 1860s produced, therefore, a decisive and historic shift in mood. We had seen that those living down-valley in the city of Sacramento had already been attempting to protect themselves from floods, but now the larger task of shielding the enormous reaches of the open countryside, and its farming families, was taken up. People threw off their torpor and began actively working together, in a collective fashion hitherto alien to their spirit, to (they believed) take positive control of their environment and put an end to flooding.

There was of course no flood control governing structure in place to provide an arena for them to work within. The swampland commissioners program enacted in 1861 did not apply to the somewhat higher and, except in floodtimes, drier lands nearer the rivers where the Valley's farmers had settled and towns had sprung up, nor would the Green Act. There was no set of rules and larger social obligations

A drawing of the Marysville-Yuba City region in the late 1860s, with the Sutter Buttes in the distance. Steamboats are shown navigating the Feather River to Marysville, the head of steam navigation on that river. However, by this time hydraulic mining was making steamboating increasingly difficult, and the traffic would soon die.
Courtesy: California State Library.

for them to keep in mind or established procedures for them to follow; the people of the Valley were in a virtual state of nature in their relation to the rivers. And in this as in every other decision-making situation, structure had crucial effects. Yuba City folk, and the surrounding country people out in Sutter County, were entirely free to do, spontaneously, whatever in their judgment seemed appropriate, no matter how self-regarding it might be or, in the long run, no matter how self-destructive because harmful to valleywide flood control needs. They needed only to avoid direct violations of existing laws, almost none of which had flood control for their subject.

Whatever they did, furthermore, would take place entirely within a wilderness of local settings. Each part of the Valley was on its own. Few thought of the Valley as a single community that should work together, or as a single hydraulic unit that needed common policy making for the floods its rivers sent running over the open countryside to be effectively controlled. From the late 1860s onward, when this process of regional levee building began (as distinct from the point-protection provided by city levees), the reigning principle in Sacramento Valley flood control policy making would with rare and brief exceptions be that of each against all.

Like a group of Renaissance Italian city-states, each locality regarded every other within its particular watershed with suspicion and distrust, fortified itself behind the highest walls (levees) it could afford, and regularly sought to solve its own flooding problems by pushing the water over onto the neighbors, that is, building levees higher than those on the opposite side of the river. In this primal matter—protection of life and property against flood, a frightening specter that, once experienced, all worried about—there was no self-rising sense of community spirit at work which reached beyond the immediate small-town and rural neighborhoods within which people lived and worked.

By the latter 1860s private parties in the farming countryside had here and there begun throwing up levees against the Valley's rivers, particularly after the disastrous floods of December 1866, the turning-point year. By the spring of 1867 a seven-mile privately built structure was actually in place on the Feather River's west bank from a point about a mile above the mouth of that stream, opposite the village of Nicolaus, upriver to Starr Bend.[1] Such projects, however, could never offer lasting protection, for though they were admirably heroic achievements on the part of a few energetic individuals, they were too impromptu, too small, and too limited in support.

It was further upstream from the Starr Bend levee along the Feather River that the first stirrings of organized flood control activism of a public nature began. They had their focus in the small town of Yuba City, seat of Sutter County, which lay directly across the Feather from that considerably larger and much more prominent community, Marysville, itself the seat of a rival entity, Yuba County. The two counties both fronted on the Feather and they looked at one another across its waters, for it formed most of the boundary between them. The stream overflowed on each of them in high water times, but Sutter County people were more endangered by it than those in Yuba. A large part of Sutter County was composed of Sutter Basin, much of which was occupied by tule-filled swamp-water lowlands. In brief, most of Sutter County lay below the height of the Feather River when it was in flood stage.

Thus, the townspeople of Yuba City and the farmers in their vicinity were exceptionally vulnerable to overflow from the Feather. The surface of that stream in low water, next to Yuba City, is at about fifty feet elevation, and the Sutter County courthouse, sited about a block from the Feather in the higher lands next to it, is at sixty-two feet. However, within a few blocks to the west the elevation figures drop to the fifties and below. The flatlands of the county continue to tilt gradually to the westward (the unaided eye cannot discern the slant; the land seems level), coming eventually, at a point about nine miles southwestward of Yuba City, to what in the 1860s were the immense tule swamps of Sutter Basin, where elevations drop below thirty feet.[2]

As they began stirring to their problem, Sutter County people did not focus first on the Feather River. Rather, they were worried about the behavior of a much smaller watercourse that now, in the latter twentieth century, is considerably shrunken, dried out through much of its length, and little noted: Gilsizer Slough. Many such sloughs (small intermittent creeks) crossed the floor of the Sacramento Valley in its natural condition, and in most cases they still exist, if much reduced in size and importance. Their function was to serve as channelways through which the rivers sent their excess waters, during floodtimes, out into the tule basins. During the dry months, when the rivers had fallen back down to low levels within their regular channels, the large lakes of floodwaters which had formed in the basins would drain back into the rivers through sloughs lower down, and thence on down to the bay.

The sloughs were a constant irritant to the farmers. Each was sizable enough to carry a local name, and through much of the year they were mucky and hard to cross. Since, like the rivers, they flowed on elevated platforms laid down by their own deposited silt, the sloughs produced floods of their own. Bridges and in some locations ferries had to be provided to cross them, and the money for such projects was difficult to raise. The west bank of the Feather River, like that of the Valley's other major streams, was pierced by slough openings at intervals along its entire course on the Valley floor from Oroville down to its mouth, a distance of fifty miles.

Gilsizer Slough was the largest of these Feather River sloughs. Its mouth, which was about sixty feet wide, opened out from the west bank of the Feather River just above Yuba City.[3] The official county map of 1873 depicts it with great prominence as a large body of water issuing out of the Feather and sweeping for many miles southwestward down through the countryside to disappear into the tule swamps. It was, in short, the most important of the Feather River outlets, and since it flowed right through the town of Yuba City, its periodic swelling into a major watercourse caused much inconvenience. (Its course may still be traced through the community. In the tragic flood of 1955, which occurred after a nighttime levee break on the Feather, many living in homes built in its broad and usually dry bed were drowned.[4]) From the earliest years of settlement, a bridge had to be maintained over the slough at Yuba City so that farmers to the west could get into town.

In 1874, Gilsizer Slough's bed below Yuba City was described as in many places a quarter of a mile wide, with standing pools where the water was perhaps four feet deep. The county's most fertile, valuable, and thickly settled strip of farming land lay along both sides of the slough, presumably because its periodic overflows deposited rich soil in the vicinity. For some farmers whose land it bisected, the stream was both a menace to crops and a barrier that required a wagon journey of as much as fifteen miles, making use of the Yuba City bridge in order to cross the stream and work their acres on the opposite side.[5]

The lands in the immediate vicinity of the slough's mouth, where it opened out in the Feather's west bank just above Yuba City, were especially fertile. To that point beside the Feather in 1850 had come a contentious, outspoken German named John Gelzhaeuser, to lay out a farm, build a slaughterhouse, and establish a butcher business—and give his name, simplified in spelling, to the watercourse. In the 1860s he turned to vegetable farming, selling his crop to Marysville people. Much in the news for various reasons, he was a familiar sight riding back and forth on the bridge over the Feather to Marysville, taking his wagon of truck vegetables to market.[6]

In April 1867, the Feather River, whose surface was now more elevated because of the debris that had flowed into it from the Oroville mines, and because of the debris dam pushed across its channel by the inflowing Yuba just below Marysville, rose so high that it began overflowing Gelzhaeuser's crops, ruining an acre and a half of onions and a thousand cabbages. Once more, as so often in the past, the Feather's waters also began passing through the head of Gilsizer Slough and flowing down through the county, endangering grain crops and causing widespread anger.

Now the local gentry began to offer leadership. Judge H. W. Hurburt, who also edited and published the local Yuba City newspaper, the *Weekly Sutter Banner,* came forward in its pages with a novel (and environmentally revolutionary) proposal for solving the problem. "All this damage by overflow," he wrote, "might be prevented if all the people interested would but take the matter in hand and build a levee across the head of the slough [i.e., close its mouth at the river bank]." This undertaking, he went on, would keep Feather River water out of the slough until it got at least four feet higher than was ordinary (this being, apparently, the height of the Feather River's natural levee). Its cost, he assured county people, would "be very light in comparison with the damage done yearly by the want of it. The levee is sure to be built, and the sooner the better."[7]

It took no more than this brief suggestion, given the local state of mind, for the idea of a barrier along the river to take hold. Almost twenty years of periodic inundation had been endured; no one else was coming forth to help the people of Sutter County, certainly not the authorities in Sacramento or in Washington, D.C.; and patience had vanished. To gain wider support, within a week the plan was expanded beyond its original aim of putting a levee simply across the slough mouth. It now called for building a long embankment that would include not only that project, but would run southward along the west bank of the Feather for thirteen miles downriver and thereby protect the farm families in the countryside. The length of thirteen miles was chosen because that would be enough to allow the levee to make a juncture with the Starr Bend levee. Thus, a continuous levee twenty miles long would be created, and Sutter County, Hurburt confidently asserted, would henceforth be in "no danger from overflow."

By mid-May, at Gelzhaeuser's urging, Judge Hurburt had visited the head of the slough, had gone over the richest part of Gelzhaeuser's farm (in a boat; it was under water), and with the German had "found that there is a ridge of high ground running along the edge of the river all the way up [i.e., the natural levee] with the exception of narrow passages or cuts, through which the water [exits to flow westward]." By filling up these cuts and "building a levee three or four feet high all the water might be kept out."[8]

On the 18th of May 1867, county folks came together in a large gathering at the courthouse in Yuba City to discuss among themselves how best to go about launching the project. Speakers rose to agree that their situation had been properly defined by Judge Hurburt: they desperately needed a levee. The land was deteriorating in value without a protecting levee; 70,000 acres, said one participant, were at that time overflowed, and those living beside Gilsizer Slough were "subject to chills." Two-thirds of the present crop had been washed away by the recent floodwaters, another said, and each year the farmers lost enough in this way to pay for a levee.

Without question these arguments, given out in grave urgency before the gathered community, were sound, in light of the way of life these people shared. What was now inescapably obvious to these Americans in the Sacramento Valley was that, though the Indians had for millennia lived in harmony with the natural, unchanged environment in their simple villages and tule-rush wickiups, people like themselves, with their life expectations and their economic institutions, with their physical domiciles, their farm animals, the kinds of food crops that they raised, and their hoped-for populousness and fixity of settlement, could not live in security on an active floodplain. It was too dangerous, the floods were too destructive. Indeed, without the flood control system whose beginnings they were in this meeting helping to initiate, without in the long run the building of a carefully reshaped and quite artificial environment through the length and breadth of the Sacramento Valley, none of the towns and cities and farms now densely placed in that Valley could exist. The people of Sutter County had a forced choice to make. Either they must decide to leave so flood-ravaged a Valley, letting it return to its natural and thinly peopled state—the thought was in reality an inconceivable one—or they must take on the task of transforming their environment.

But how might they do it? No one could believe for long that the task could be left entirely to individuals living along the river to carry out by themselves. Something of a public nature had to be organized. However, though some suggested going to the state legislature for aid, it was after all the year 1867, when laissez-faire, inactive-government Democrats had got back into control in Sacramento. Little could be hoped for from that direction. Besides, most recoiled from appealing to distant authority, for they were nineteenth-century Americans and one of the idols they honored almost above everything else in their political culture was an intense localism. They had to rely on themselves, use their own county instrumentalities.

The County Board of Supervisors, it was pointed out, could

under the existing road law—created, manifestly, for quite a different purpose—grant a right of way for an embankment. Levee building, then, could grow naturally and incrementally out of road building. No dramatic new innovation in governing arrangements need be pioneered. There was not even any need for taxes, the meeting decided, for they could simply rely on public-spirited private subscriptions, that is, on an entirely informal fundraising in the form of gifts to the community.

There were, of course, other questions to consider, such as how would their levee affect the people on the other side of the Feather, in Yuba County? Had they not an obligation to consider the effects of their actions on those people, too? However, the situation of Yuba City—located in Sutter County—was too pressing, in a literal sense too dangerous, for such thoughts to linger. In a surprisingly bald pronouncement later printed verbatim in his newspaper for everyone to see, Judge Hurburt insisted that Sutter County should press on regardless, leading the way, so that "we can throw the water over to the Yuba [County] side and reclaim all the land in Sutter. . . . [There was] not energy enough [in Yuba County]," he scoffed, to build a levee. "Self-protection," he went on, "is the first law of nature."

Others immediately took up this tone of rivalry and self-regard. Yuba City had always resented the superior size and prosperity and attitudes of Marysville in Yuba County. If a levee were built, it was said, and if Sutter County grew rapidly in population and development because of its protection, then "they will come to us": that is, it would no longer be necessary for people to buy across the river. The steamboats from Sacramento would not tie up at Marysville, the larger community on the Feather's opposite side, but at Yuba City, and Sutter County would get the fees now going to Marysville. In this mood, a resolution was unanimously adopted to push on with the levee project. A committee was formed and put in charge, including in its members John Gelzhaeuser and Dr. S. R. Chandler, a local physician who had served as secretary of the meeting and whose lands comprised one of the farms cut in two by Gilsizer Slough.[9]

It must be noted that in these proceedings two crucial questions were not asked: Do we know enough to do this? Will the project as designed do the job? About this, there were apparently no doubts. The community was assured in mind that a brief survey by local notables was all that was needed to develop a fully adequate plan and that the Feather River, an immensely powerful stream in full flood flow which for millennia had been overtopping its banks in heavy volume and flooding the Sacramento Valley, could be put under control by simple and relatively inexpensive works. Indeed, the people of Yuba City and its surrounding countryside could do this, they believed, without calling upon higher authority at all for assistance. The environment could be made to do what they wished by none other than themselves, moving vigorously and with determination. And they would accomplish this through no other instrumentality than that of an informal local democratic assemblage, the American republic's germinal folk-institution, and for funding they would ultimately rely upon the unforced civic spirit of good republican citizens.

A new vision, then, had seized fast on the Sutter County mind: the possibility that they could free themselves from the fear of flood, a fear that had by repeated disasters been pushed deep into the local consciousness. The courthouse meeting, doubtless lifted in mood by the invigoration of its unanimous decision, must have dispersed with a feeling of a great public task well tended to. It had been agreed to mount a direct battle against the river; now the task remained only of putting this bold policy into effect.

Soon, however, the difficulties of implementation, a stage in policy making which is often far more complicated and filled with unsuspected obstacles than that simply of arguing out decisions, began to surface. The context in Sutter County was not what they had thought it was; the local state of mind toward the project was not nearly so unanimous as in the high emotions of the public meeting it had seemed to be. The committee found itself quickly running into a deeper and more resistant reef of reluctant holding back from the financial realities of what had been agreed to than had earlier revealed itself. The committee had estimated that the levee would cost about a thousand dollars a mile to construct, but Dr. Chandler, who had the task of raising the money for it, discovered that a simple reliance on civic spirit, that is, on people coming forward with unforced gifts of their own funds to pay for construction, was a risky foundation for such an ambitious project. Success came slowly and incompletely as the months passed and the next flood season grew nearer. Finally, in August, the *Weekly Sutter Banner* had to announce that the plan itself had had to be pruned back to conform to funding realities, for they had only enough money to build, before the next high waters came, simply a levee to close off the mouth of the slough.

During the fall's construction work, the next controversy erupted, this time over the project's specific contours. John Gelzhaeuser had been an enthusiastic advocate of the levee project from its beginnings—he may actually have been its instigator—apparently because he believed that a publicly built levee would follow the outline of his property and put a wall between his land and the river. However, Gelzhaeuser was not one of the local gentry. Rough and combative in his personal style, his occupations of slaughterer, butcher, and truck gardener were not those of a gentleman. Though as a voluble and well-known public figure who had been one of the project's earliest movers his presence on the committee in charge was a natural one, it was perhaps not altogether welcomed, and when practical details were settled on he found that his interests were going to be lightly regarded. The levee as actually laid out was to be constructed across, not around, his land in a fashion that would divide his farm, part of it being buried under the levee embankment and the rest still lying outside of it and unprotected from flood.

Angered, Gelzhaeuser asked for damages. An arbitration committee was convened which may have been more than ready to treat him peremptorily. The committee in its wisdom decided that the benefits he was receiving from the project outweighed its harm to him, and he got nothing. Construction moved along, and in mid-November 1867, the *Banner* could report enthusiastically on its progress. Though there had not been enough money to build the long levee originally projected, one across the mouth of the slough and for a distance downstream from it, protecting the front of the town of Yuba City, was shaping up. (Levees were simply built of earth, locally scraped up to form a mound.) Hurburt expansively assured the community that all "will be made safe against the floods of the coming winter."[10]

The small town of Yuba City, if it shared Hurburt's sense that all was now well, was not able to enjoy this state of mind for long. Storms were soon sweeping in over the Valley, and work on the levee had to halt. Furthermore, some $700 of the promised subscription funds had not come in, and Hurburt was fretting that the levee would be entirely lost in impending higher waters if caught uncompleted. Then on Saturday, the 21st of December 1867, torrential rains began, and they continued for four days. Both the Yuba and Feather rivers were high after the second day, their rushing waters reaching a point within inches of that attained in "the memorable flood of the winter of 1861 and 1862."

At first it looked as if the levee across the head of the slough would be quickly overtopped by the rising Feather, but Chandler and others hurried to the embankment and worked incessantly, with apparent success, to hold back the river. Then in the early morning of Thursday, the 26th, disaster came: "a crevasse was discovered in the new levee at the big slough," and shortly it gave way entirely, sending a torrent of pent-up waters, up to ten feet deep, into the Yuba City courthouse square. Floodwaters then rushed on down the slough and out over the countryside, stretching westward from town in the direction of Colusa as far as the eye could see and at a height considerably above that in 1862. High winds blew down Gelzhaeuser's barn, and about a fifth of the new Yuba City levee washed away. On New Year's Day, 1868, the rivers rose again, flooding the town once more. The project had failed. All was not "safe against the floods of the coming winter."[11]

Among Sutter County people, however, the possibility that they might win freedom from fear of flood had taken their minds too deeply for them to let it go. That this vision eventually took hold also throughout the Sacramento Valley would be, in truth, the fundamental force driving everything that in later years would occur in the seemingly interminable struggle to tame the Sacramento and its tributaries. For long stretches of years the Valley's efforts would be answered only by frustration and failure, but still the dream held on, surprisingly durable and resilient.

In most cases those who had settled down to live and farm by the Feather River did not conclude, from the renewed flooding, that their only recourse was to move off the floodplain. (Census figures tell us, however, that after 1870 the most seriously flood-ravaged counties in the Valley stagnated, while the rest of the state boomed. Sutter County grew rapidly in its first two decades of existence, 1850–1870, but it was at a plateau for thirty years thereafter, rising only 850 in population above the 5030 who lived there in 1870. Not until after the turn of the century, and especially after 1910, when the impediment of periodic flooding was greatly reduced, did its population begin to rise swiftly again.) Sutter County folk remained convinced, in the face of apparently conclusive experience to the contrary, that if they could only figure out how to do it, the environment could be pushed into the shape they wanted it to assume so that they might live in peace.

Clearly, however, Sutter County citizens had to do something much more ambitious than their initial effort at flood control, and they had to ground what they did much less on illusions. Gathering funds by private gift could not be relied on; civic spirit unaided by legal sanctions, even in an endangered community, was not strong enough. This meant reinitiating their consideration of the problem, redefining their situation, and, as they searched for a different line of policy, turning now to listen to those who at the outset had suggested a different course than the County had taken: going higher in the state's hierarchy of authority to tap more potent powers than, among themselves, local people could generate.

This recommendation forecast what would be the long-term course of flood control policy making in the Valley: a step-by-step reaching upward to ever more elevated levels of authority as it was learned that, unassisted, those lower down could not do the job. Localism, however cherished it was as a core value by nineteenth-century Americans, had slowly to be compromised and in time greatly modified as an operating principle, though never—and this is striking—would the essentially localist and therefore highly decentralized structure of water management in California actually disappear or become effectively a nullity. American political culture was too profoundly localist in its deepest heart for this deep-rooted impulse ever to fade away.[12]

Sutter County people, in short, had to accept a new understanding of their situation: levee building could not proceed as a simple extension of road building when public taxing powers were absent. And in truth, the public scene in California in the year 1868 was crowded with models of what might be done in Sutter County. Since 1861, when the concept of a special public principality, the self-governing, tax-raising swampland "district" created to achieve a particular purpose, had been first adopted, Sacramento had been awash with proposals for the forming of such bodies to deal with water management problems, and they had been popping up in numerous Valley locations. Furthermore, the policy-making context in the state capital had briefly become an open and flexible one in water matters. When Sutter County spokesmen went to the legislature in early 1868 to ask for help, they found it in these very months engaged in working through and adopting the sweeping reorientation of flood control policies which Will Green's new swampland management proposal instigated.

In this setting, Sutter County's agenda was clear. The Green Act would be of no use to Yuba City and its surrounding countryside, since that legislation applied only to swampland regions. As we have seen, it was some nine miles southwest of Yuba City before the tule swamps were reached. However, a window of opportunity had nonetheless opened, given what was then going on in Sacramento. Sutter County could argue that its higher, nonswampland sections had a need for some kind of flood control district equally as urgent as that being responded to in the swamplands. In the presence of Green's proposed new plans, surely such a local district as Yuba City was asking for would seem a modest affair and could easily win passage. For that matter, neighbor Green, from next-door Colusa County, could probably be counted on to help. And so it turned out. Three days before the Green Act's actual passage, the governor on March 25, 1868 signed a bill into law which provided, as its title stated, "for the protection of certain lands in the county of Sutter from overflow."[13]

This was in truth most remarkable legislation, which perhaps could not have been enacted at any other time than when the local-control enthusiasts of the Democratic party had just won supremacy in the legislature and water management policy was in such flux. Not only did the legislature authorize the creation, in Sutter County, of the first nonswampland levee district in the Valley and give it plenary authority over how it might align and build its embankments—that is, it could do anything it liked to water flowage patterns, to the sloughs and river banks, within its borders, no matter what damage it might do to others living elsewhere—it also gave that district highly unusual taxing powers. Never again would the legislature enact a levee district law that would have the authority not simply to tax the land, but even the personal property, of people living within the district's borders. The new law, of course, applied only within Sutter County, so it remained a special enclave in flood control policy with, as we shall see, politically explosive results some years later.

Five days after the law's enactment, Sutter County's Board of Supervisors created Levee District 1 and ordered an election to be held on whether the voters approved its establishment.[14] An intense controversy erupted. Apparently the people of Yuba City itself had lost whatever enthusiasm they had had for paying out of their own pockets what would be the larger share of the cost of a levee that would run not simply across the front of the town and protect it—there was already one there, of course, which only needed repairs—but would go on downriver for thirteen miles and offer safeguards to the farmers. The details of the argument are lost, but perhaps the earlier experience, when the farmers downriver had apparently not been forthcoming with private subscriptions, had left enduring wounds. Possibly the provision for taxing private property, which would reach more into the pockets of the town's business and professional people than into those of the farmers, created anger.

Whatever the case, "Brothers, father and children, and even partners in business are divided," reported the *Marysville Appeal* from its vantage point across the river. "Indeed, we have never known so much cross firing." When the balloting took place on April 13, 1868, Yuba City precinct voted more than two to one against establishing the district (40 for, 100 against), but heavy majorities southward along Gilsizer Slough, in Yoculumne and Slough precincts, carried the victory (119 for, 37 against).[15]

What is now the oldest continuously operating flood control district in the Sacramento Valley, Levee District 1, was by these events enabled to set about building the first publicly supported levee in the Valley outside those already built by the cities of Sacramento and Marysville, that is, the first which was aimed at regional protection. Moving quickly, Sutter's supervisors turned to their own engineer, County Surveyor John Pennington—this time, the project's design was not to be left simply to amateurs among the local gentry—and went out with him in person on the 17th of April, four days after the election, to survey the levee route along the river. During the rest of April, and through May and early June, Pennington developed specific plans and specifications. As completed, he proposed an embankment more than 17 miles long, beginning 2.5 miles north of Yuba City, with an average height of 5.5 feet, the whole to cost $36,800, a sum several times that originally thought of in the County's initial effort. Pennington offered the grotesquely incorrect forecast that the top of his levee would be 3.5 feet above the Feather's high water mark. The project of building the Sutter County levee was divided, organizationally, into many short sections so that citizens could work out their taxes by laboring on particular reaches of the project. Construction got underway in August.[16]

Unfortunate John Gelzhaeuser had by this time passed through enough tragedies to last a lifetime. In November of 1867, his arm was so badly shattered in the explosion of a cannon being fired to honor a visiting dignitary that it had to be amputated. Then the levee break at the slough mouth in December 1867 had, as we have seen, destroyed his new barn and flooded him out. In the early months of 1868 he and his wife lost three of their four children to disease, one after another. He was still disputing the question of whether he was due damages by the building of the levee through his land, and, perhaps in sympathy, a reconsideration in July 1868 awarded him $300.

He thought this quite insufficient, and when the levee builders got to his property in October 1868, he "and his women" fought them off at their fence, leading to several physical encounters. His exasperated antagonists promptly hauled him into court, but then a compromise settlement finally awarded him the price he had asked. Subsequently, he was appointed levee superintendent for the section of the levee north of the Marysville bridge crossing, and thereafter John Gelzhaeuser faded from history.[17]

Across the Feather River in Yuba County, the floods of the 1860s had also been devastating. Yuba County's Board of Supervisors took the first steps, therefore, toward providing general protection to the countryside. Marysville itself had already begun building its own levees, which would eventually encircle the town entirely. Easterly of the town, the Yuba River, which by this time was badly filled with mining debris, was in high water periods discharging flood waters not only into the growing debris-wasteland south of that stream, but had begun sending them into the farmlands northward of the Yuba as well. Through this section, as it happened, ran Marysville's main road to the mountains and gold mining towns, the Brown's Valley Road. Often under water, especially in a low swale about five miles upriver from town, where water regularly coursed through into the northern flatlands when the Yuba was high, the road's protection was essential to Yuba County's lucrative mountain trade. Coincidentally, its alignment was also essentially along the route that a levee through this section would take.

Yuba County, then, was able to do what Sutter County failed at achieving: it could move into levee building incrementally, simply as an extension of road building. The Board of Supervisors could on reasonable grounds provide public tax funds for that purpose without having to go to the legislature for a special district, since an important existing road was being protected. Accordingly, in 1866–1867 the Yuba County Board of Supervisors sent out horsedrawn scrapers and dirt-moving equipment to put up an elevated roadway that ran northeastward across the plains north of the Yuba River for a distance of about 7.5 miles, until it reached the highlands at the edge of the foothills. It was first thrown up to a height of two or three feet, on a four-foot base.

Thinking to avoid as much overflow as possible, the Brown's Valley Grade (the road's name thereafter) was laid down a mile distant from the river, enclosing exceptionally fertile land beside the river which then held fine orchards. In succeeding years flood waters would flow out regularly over these orchard lands to run on over the road—Yuba County was as expert as Sutter County in consistently underestimating its task. By 1882 Yuba's supervisors had had to pour much more money into building up the Grade, making it a formidable structure averaging ten to twelve feet in height, on a sixty-foot base. Even so, it continued to be broken through repeatedly, for hydraulic mining deposits kept flowing into the Yuba and raising it higher and higher, sending flood levels to more threatening levels each year.[18]

Meanwhile, in Sutter County the new embankment put up by Levee District 1 also was being periodically overtopped, in later flood years, and the District had had to raise ever more taxes. In December 1871, the levee broke at the mouth of Gilsizer Slough in the night; in January 1874, it threatened to go out again at that location until two train car loads of timber were taken there to strengthen the levee (to be discovered more than half a century later, in 1938, during excavations for levee strengthening); and in 1875 the levee broke in two separate places, both above and below town. By that date, the district had spent more than $112,000, an immense sum of money for so small a community, and the levee had been raised to a seven-foot height.[19] Efforts to win freedom from fear of floods were exacting a high price.

If nothing else, Sutter County was going through an expensive and lengthy learning process. This one Valley county constituted a special place where a unique set of forces was converging to teach special lessons, lessons that the rest of the Sacramento Valley would not learn for a great many years into the future. In this concentrated setting, where people faced not only a flooding river but an avalanche of mining debris, and where the Valley's first attempt at building a regional flood control system had been launched, by the mid-1870s a new understanding was dawning. To anyone who looked at what was going on in the hydraulic mining industry and to what was happening to the rivers, and who was no longer ready to look the other way, it was clear that far more and far heavier costs, and probably more disastrous failures, were yet to come.

In February 1874, Dr. S. R. Chandler, who had already devoted seven years to leading the Sutter County struggle against the rivers, sat down to write a long, worried letter to the *Weekly Sutter Banner*. The growing height of the Yuba River's bed, he said, was what the community should keep its eyes on and build higher levees against; the Feather was no longer the major problem. At a point twelve miles above Marysville, Chandler wrote, the Yuba was flowing on a bed that was raised *sixty feet higher* than its old level. Some 15,000 acres of land, he went on, were now covered by mining debris, and the Feather River itself was badly filled many feet deep with sand.[20]

Three days later another voice chimed in, this time from a farmer named George Ohleyer who would soon become the county's leading advocate, for twenty years into the future, in the struggle against floods. In his own letter to the *Banner* he offered to Sutter County a distinctly more radical definition of the situation than had Chandler. The good doctor was right, Ohleyer said, in saying that the locally built levees had helped and that more were needed, but he was wrong in believing that their small levee district could ever hold back the floods soon to be caused by the rising torrent of mining debris. Ohleyer was a militant Democrat, his political alliance traditionally distrusted the wealthy and powerful corporations, and his style was accusatory. As soon as he appeared on the scene he was using words like "evil," for he was clearly absorbed not simply by a physical problem, but by pointing to those behind it. It was an *enemy* that he thought about, and that enemy was a particular group of people: the hydraulic mining owners. In this letter he began what would for him be a long crusade taking him to Sacramento and eventually to Washington, D.C.: to shut the hydraulic mining industry down and to keep it in that condition.

It was, then, the mining industry that they must fight, Ohleyer said, not just the river. This meant that they could no longer rely on their own resources, they must turn to the legislature once more for aid. Hydraulic mining debris was "an evil only palliated by levees, but not cured; the security [they] . . . afford is delusive." Maybe levees,

Ohleyer remarked, were not at all the answer. While they kept the rivers' flow within their walls, as desired, this in turn meant that the rivers were raised even higher, in elevation, above the land on either side. Thus they became a greater danger to everyone, once the embankments broke. The floods now to come would ironically be more dangerous than those in the past, Ohleyer warned, precisely because of the partial successes of the levee idea.[21]

Editor Hurburt of the *Weekly Sutter Banner* offered his own conception of the issue. Not ready to raise the cry for a charge against the hydraulic miners, in Ohleyer's fashion, he was nonetheless ready to say that the solution could no longer be a local one, it had to be valleywide. It had to be based, in short, on the assumption that the Valley was a single natural unit, and that what affected one affected all. "What is wanted," he wrote, "is a general scheme of reclamation and protection throughout, from the bay up the Sacramento and Feather rivers and their tributaries. Local schemes of reclamation rarely provide a remedy, and only complicate the matter, besides entailing a never-ending expense, and creating dissatisfaction." The whole valley, he said, must get together on this matter and go to the legislature.[22]

In March he raised the warning again. The "amount of dirt brought down by the mining streams in the valley is . . . alarming. The bed of the Yuba at Marysville is already some sixteen feet higher than it was 20 years ago! . . . [And the] worst has not yet come. In less than two years the amount of washings will be double what it is now. It is a saying among some of the miners that they are going to cover Marysville up."[23]

≈≈≈

Hurburt was right: in the river bottoms along the Yuba River, between Marysville and the mountains, farmers felt a growing desperation. After the disastrous flood of 1862 they had tried to protect themselves from the invading flood of mining debris by erecting levees beside the increasingly high bed of the Yuba, digging new channels and drains, opening sloughs for drainage, and spending thousands of dollars trying to protect their lands. Many gave up the attempt and moved out; depopulation set in along the Yuba from the mountains to Marysville.[24] Hoping to get a protest movement started, a group of farmers called a public meeting in Marysville late in August of 1874, but few people appeared in response to the call. The river was down, and people preferred to look the other way.[25]

Then came the winter of 1875; an enormous deluge of storm waters in early January battered the Valley day after day and produced a catastrophic flood. By the morning of the nineteenth the swollen brown waters of the Yuba had broken through the Brown's Valley Grade some six miles upstream from Marysville. A wild torrent of floodwaters rushed out into the flatlands north of town, taking it, so to speak from the rear. Here Marysville's levee was only a foot and a half high. With the firehouse bell ringing in their ears, men rushed out of their homes and flung themselves into a nightmare struggle to save the city.

Near the town cemetery, despite frantic efforts, the river began slipping over the levee and pouring down into the town. By nightfall people were rushing wildly for safety; at eight o'clock the levee broke near the hospital, and a torrent of water rushed into the streets. In wild confusion women and children were rescued, barns, sheds, and frame houses began floating about, and a little boy was drowned. By the following noon Marysville had filled like a bowl, within its encircling levees. Not until the evening of the 21st of January did the cold and hungry citizens of Marysville get aid, with the steamer "Flora" breasting the flood from Sacramento.

As the stricken city recovered from the flood, with the aid of thousands of dollars sent in by surrounding communities, its people found that Marysville had become a vast dump for mining debris. Enormous quantities of sand and mud had sluiced into the town and filled streets, basements, stores, and homes. Months of backbreaking toil passed before Marysville completed the task of digging itself out of the mud.[26]

This was an electrifying event. Nothing like it had ever happened before. The tragedy of it forced people to consider at close range the problem Marysville folk had ignored for so long. The flood of 1875 had not simply inundated Marysville, it had delivered what was in effect the finishing blow to the farming of the Yuba bottom lands. The lower bottoms had been largely filled in by the floods of the 1860s, but what local people called the "second bottom" had remained in cultivation. The 1875 high water, however, covered these higher lands, and whole ranches were abandoned. In the later 1870s the land still remaining uncovered and south of the Brown's Valley Grade was progressively buried by mining sands, so that a wide bleak expanse of desert presented itself, where formerly there had been rich farms, orchards, and pasture lands.[27]

Even the militantly pro-miner editor of the *Nevada City Transcript*, L. S. Calkins, was sobered by the flood of 1875 and its results.

> What are the owners of farms to do [he asked]? It is evident mining can never be stopped. It is an industry the whole world desires to foster. The Government will encourage it, notwithstanding agriculture may suffer. Hydraulic mining is in its infancy. The very storms which are so destructive to the valleys are just what the mines require. The sediment, which has been accumulating for years in the ravines and river beds, and preventing a good fall, has all been washed away, and made a place for the deposit of other quantities unwashed. . . . Each year adds to the amount of sediment deposited in the valleys. . . . It is evident mining will have to be stopped or that country will have to be abandoned for its present purposes, unless some method can be devised to overcome the difficulty. It is certain mining will never be stopped. . . . What relief can be afforded we cannot apprehend.[28]

Unclear as the solutions might be, the time of passive acceptance in Sutter and Yuba counties had passed. In late December 1875, after more disastrous flooding, the farmers and townspeople of those two counties gathered to begin an historically crucial cycle of public meetings. It was in these closely argued gatherings that those who were receiving the heaviest and most direct onslaught of mining debris came to grips with their problem, hammered out their initial definitions of the issue, and considered often sharply diverging strategies of response. Then, convinced by George Ohleyer that they must begin a crusade against hydraulic mining, the people of Sutter and

Yuba counties launched a long, embittered, and remarkably tenacious campaign against hydraulic gold mining which over the next decade raged back and forth between the legislature and the courts and issued finally in a famous victory over the enemy in 1884: the North Bloomfield injunction, won in the federal Ninth Circuit Court in San Francisco, which shut down the entire industry.

Meanwhile, as the Valley and the mountains struggled over the fate of hydraulic gold mining—a controversy which I have elsewhere described[29]—farmers and townspeople in the Valley still had the continuing problem before them of taming the Sacramento—that is, fending off and ultimately getting control of the floods sent out upon them by the increasingly damaged Sacramento River and its tributaries. To the working out of a solution for this extraordinarily difficult problem, which consumed more than a half-century of time, we shall now return.

C H A P T E R

Colusa, the Sacramento River, and the Argument Over What to Do: *1850s–1870s*

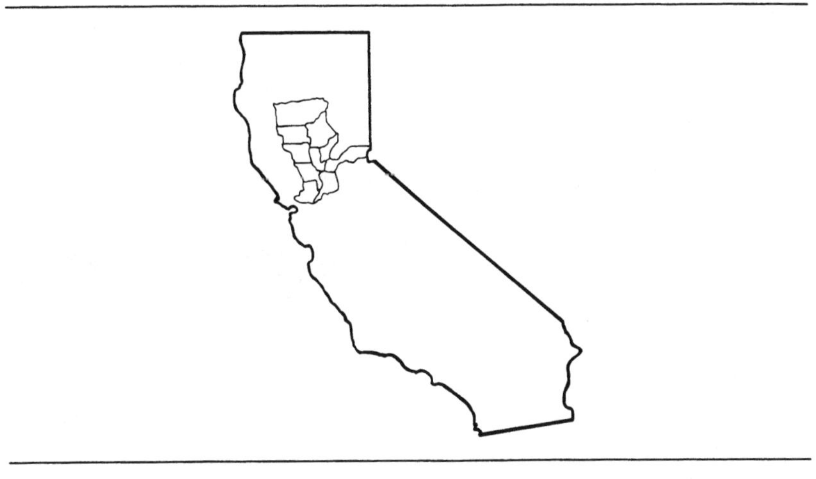

"People have to be careful," [he] said . . . "The water will chase rattlesnakes out of their burrows and they'll go anyplace where it's dry—people's yards or houses. . . . Anything that habitates in the river bottoms is bound to be out now . . . rats, skunks, possums, raccoons or rabbits."

Marysville Appeal-Democrat, *February 19, 1986. Quoted in* Rivers of Fear, *p. 48.*

The Sacramento River, a deep-running stream hundreds of feet across, flows swiftly southward out of the mountainous uplands of far northern California, passing through the last low line of hills just below Red Bluff. Here the river enters the relatively flat Sacramento Valley proper and begins its 247 river-mile meandering traverse of the Valley's floodplain, heading toward the delta, Collinsville at the opening of Suisun Bay being its official terminus. About forty miles down-valley the stream passes just to the west of the sharp vertical mass of Sutter Buttes, a clustering of small volcanic peaks in the middle of the Valley rising steeply to 2100 feet in elevation, which on clear days catches the eye for many miles in all directions. About five miles due west of the Buttes is the small farming town of Colusa, a quiet county seat of wide streets and tall leafy trees. Sitting on the west bank of the Sacramento River, it lies a few feet above that stream at an elevation of 61 feet above sea level. This makes it at the same elevation as Yuba City, twenty miles due eastward of Colusa on the other side of the Valley.

In most cases, therefore, when floodwaters were at their highest,

Will S. Green, longtime widely read editor of the Colusa Sun *(1863 to his death in 1905). Fervent Southern Democrat and brilliant self-educated flood control theorist, Green conceived the bypass system forty years before its reluctant adoption by the U.S. Army Corps of Engineers. He authored the state's 1868 Green Act, which established the Valley's basic swampland reclamation policy until well after 1900. Green was an enthusiast in the cause of irrigation all his days.*
Courtesy: California State Library.

the same vast pool of water in Sutter Basin threatened both communities, since they sat on opposite sides of it. Colusa's site, however, was sufficiently high above the Sacramento so that, unlike Yuba City and Marysville, in its history it has never itself been actually flooded. However, it has been much more likely to be entirely surrounded for long periods by flooded territory. Colusa borders a much larger river, and it sat in the midst of what then were wide tule swamps that encircled it, making the town in floodtimes an island in a sea of floodwaters.

Upstream from Colusa the Sacramento River flows with a strong current, for its bed, though relatively flat, has a significant fall: about thirty feet in elevation in the twenty river-miles above town. In this reach, therefore, the Sacramento winds tortuously back and forth within a wide bed, for the river has power enough to cut into the banks on either side, forcing them three quarters of a mile apart. Meandering between these banks, the Sacramento has actively formed loops and islands. Because this made steamboating more difficult, the original party of settlers in 1850 chose Colusa's particular site to lay out a town, and named it for the resident Indian tribe, the Co'lus.[1]

Just below town the Valley floor flattens out markedly, its fall moderating to about a foot each river-mile. The river flows more slowly, is unable so sharply to cut into its paralleling banks, and they close in, producing a narrower channel that meanders considerably less. A narrower and straighter channel makes it a better steamboating river, but one that cannot carry so much floodwater. While the Sacramento's wide bed above Colusa is able to enclose volumes that, in flood times, reach 250,000 cubic feet per second, the constricted channel below that point can hold only a flow of 70,000 feet per second. There is, in short, "a strange funnel-shape effect in the natural formation of the river that makes itself felt at Colusa. . . ," as engineer B. A. Etcheverry of the University of California described the situation to a congressional committee in 1927.[2]

For many years, therefore, Colusa County people would have to struggle with the fact that at various locations above and below the town, a great deal of water had to leave the river channel when the

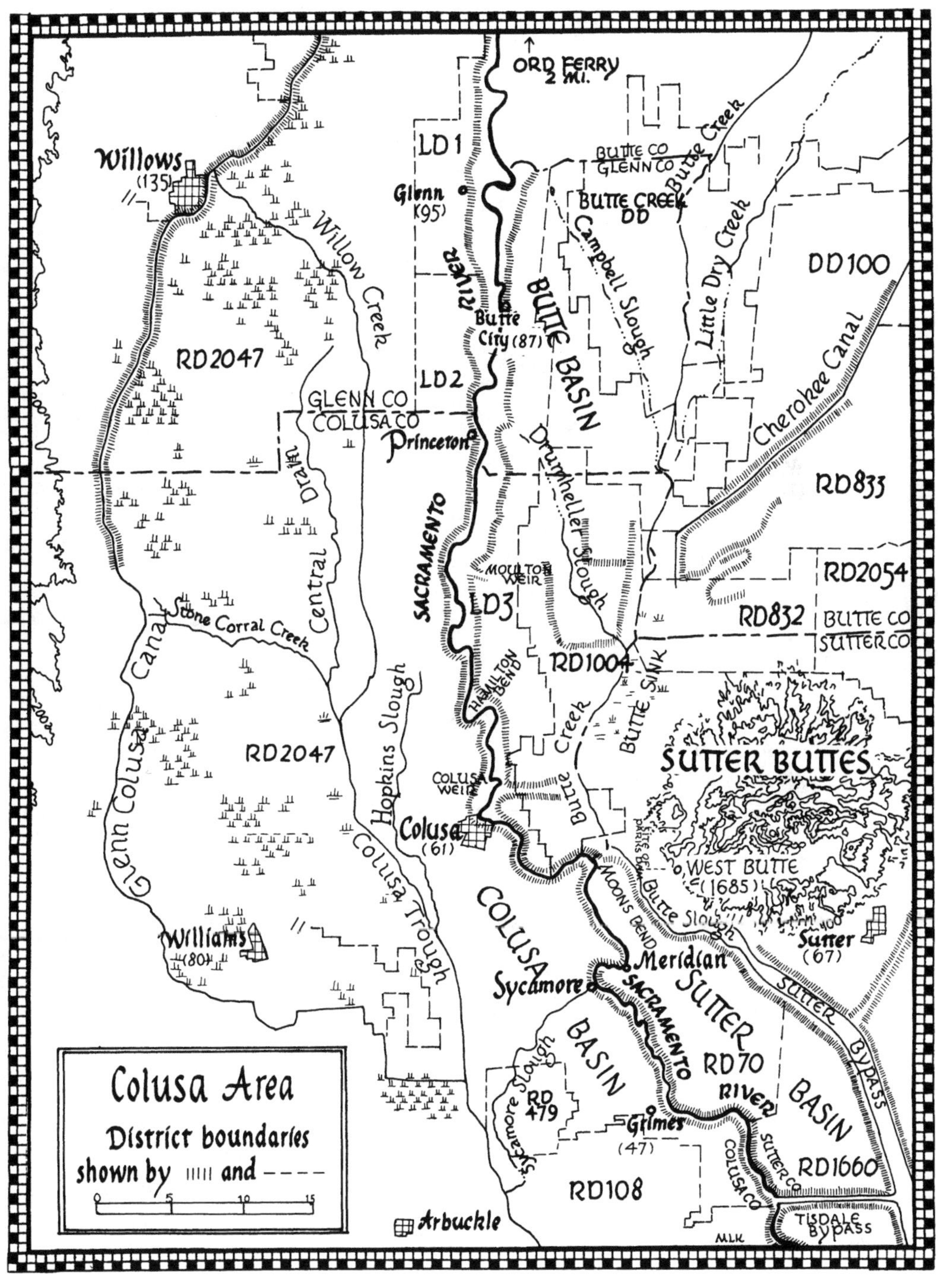

Colusa Area
District boundaries shown by ||||| and - - - -
0 5 10 15
ORD FERRY 2 MI.
Willows (135)
LD1
Glenn (95)
BUTTE CO
GLENN CO
Butte Creek
BUTTE CREEK DD
Campbell Slough
Little Dry Creek
DD100
Willow Creek
RIVER
Butte City (87)
BUTTE BASIN
RD2047
LD2
GLENN CO
COLUSA CO
Princeton
Cherokee Canal
Drumheller Slough
Central Drain
RD833
SACRAMENTO
MOULTON WEIR
LD3
RD2054
RD832
BUTTE CO
SUTTER CO
Stone Corral Creek
HAMILTON BEND
RD1004
BUTTE SINK
Glenn Colusa Canal
Hopkins Slough
Butte Creek
SUTTER BUTTES
RD2047
COLUSA WEIR
Colusa (61)
Colusa Trough
MOONS BEND
Butte Slough
WEST BUTTE (1685)
COLUSA
Williams (80)
Meridian
Sycamore
SACRAMENTO
SUTTER
Sutter (67)
SUTTER BYPASS
BASIN
Sycamore Slough
RD 479
RD70
RIVER
BASIN
Grimes (47)
COLUSA CO
SUTTER CO
RD1660
RD108
Arbuckle
TISDALE BYPASS
MLK

Sacramento was in heavy flow. The large inland sea up to a hundred miles long which appeared almost annually in the center-line of the Valley began right here, in the overbank flows in the Colusa vicinity. Local people would try again and again to push the water back into the river's channel and protect themselves from overflow, but it would burst out, first in one location, then in another, to resume its immemorial flooding out over the countryside.

From the point about twenty miles upstream from Colusa where the Sacramento in its natural condition began flowing overbank in both directions, the river runs on an elevated bed, for, having lost some of its volume, it begins dropping silt onto its bed, building it up as a platform. Thus from here to its mouth, the Sacramento runs on a ridge just like the Mississippi River. From the elevated river bed and the stream's natural levees the land on either side falls slowly away for a distance of three or four miles, after which it tilts gradually upward to rise to the foothills. Thus, the water that poured out of the river in high water times through slough openings flowed out into these "troughs." Further down the Valley, the troughs eventually widened into great tule basins.[3]

When Will S. Green, a Kentuckian then eighteen years of age, came up the Sacramento River in July of 1850 to help found the town of Colusa, he was steering a small steamer, the *Colusa.* And he was in a rapture, filled with visions of an imagined future. "How often did the boy," Green wrote many years later,

> allow his imagination to run on [to the time when] . . . the trackless plain . . . would be covered over with garden and orchard and vineyard and lowing herds, possessed by a happy and prosperous people, while upon the bosom of the river, so new, so beautiful, would float a commerce richer than that of the fabled Indies. . . . [This vision] has been the life-dream of the man.
>
> On and on steamed the little craft, scaring myriads of ducks and other water fowl by the newness of its form and voice, scaring deer that hid in the tangled woods, and even the grizzly bear, so abundant in the river bends. . . . [At the site of Colusa] . . . the wild oats that surrounded me were much higher [than six feet] . . . [and] beyond was as beautiful a scene as ever met the vision of man. There was one endless sea of white and blue, purple and gold. It seemed a sea, as the gentle

> breeze made those myriads of wild flowers wave and glisten. . . . I seemed to be reveling in a very Garden of Eden.[4]

When the Sacramento River approached the choke in the Colusa area and sent floodwaters out of its channel, those flowing westward ran out into the lowlands that form the long, wide Colusa Basin, while those going eastward moved into Butte Basin, north of the Sutter Buttes, and thence down into Butte Sink. The sink, whose thousands of waterlogged acres are still one of the great bird gathering places on North America's north-south coastal flyway, is an exceptionally low and flat depression about a dozen miles long lying between the Sutter Buttes and the Sacramento River, its southerly terminus roughly opposite the town of Colusa. The sink's surface is more than fifteen feet below that of the river, which passes by on its silt-created platform.

Floodwater rushed down into the sink not only from the Sacramento River, through openings in its east bank above and below Colusa, but large flows also entered the sink from another major participant in this complex scene: Butte Creek. It originates near Chico and angles southwestward down-valley, flowing through the trough that parallels the Sacramento at a few miles distance to the east. Butte Creek, in other words, passes through Butte Basin, and then curves around the west side of those Buttes to empty into the sink.

Here the commingled waters from all these inflowing sources form a deep lake in floodtimes which empties slowly southward through a channelway only a couple of miles across at this point which lies between the Sacramento River (flowing on its elevated bed) and Sutter Buttes. When this region was in its natural condition, the southward-flowing Butte Sink waters were shortly joined by another large waterway: Butte Slough (now closed off). It poured eastward out of the Sacramento River about five river-miles downstream from the town of Colusa. A stream more than a hundred feet wide and thirty feet deep, Butte Slough was the largest out-flowing slough on the Sacramento's east bank. It was the eastern counterpart to Gilsizer Slough at Yuba City, both sloughs pouring floodwaters into the tules of Sutter Basin.

These complicated overflows above and around Colusa were

what made the town an island in a surrounding expanse of water during the flooding months. Along both sides of the Sacramento River north and south of Colusa the somewhat higher land beside the river escaped prolonged flooding, but it was a regular occurrence for the Butte Sink pool to expand practically to the edge of the river itself, in the Colusa vicinity, and to remain in that condition for long periods.[5]

The high thick-stemmed tule rushes, which stood massed and forbidding far out into the sink and into the basins, created tule swamps that ran continuously on both sides of the Sacramento River (though back some distance from its banks, the strip of river lands intervening) from at least twenty-five miles north of Colusa southward to the Sacramento-San Joaquin delta islands, seventy miles down-valley from that town. In their original condition the Sacramento Valley tule rushes formed a high wall blocking cross-Valley travel until slowly and progressively hacked down or in dry periods burned out. In the 1850s they were "fifteen feet high [in the Colusa vicinity]. They had not been burned for a long time, and the old and new stalks stood so thick and matted that it was almost impossible to penetrate them, except on the wagon trail."[6] As late as 1886, as shown on an early map of the Geological Survey based in a survey of that year, the tules spread in a band up to five miles across on either side of the Sacramento, their eastern fringes reaching within about ten miles of Yuba City.[7]

These fertile, waterlogged lowlands were those officially classified as "swamp and overflowed lands." Will Green himself even became for a brief period the owner of large holdings, though apparently these were not in the swamps but out on the plain lands.[8] From the late 1860s on, such swampland owners in the Colusa region as William H. Parks and L. F. Moulton, with their princely but, for the present, unproductive swampland territories, would take a giant role in the long local struggle to get control of the Sacramento River and turn its tule-choked lowlands into a fruitful farming empire.

≈≈≈

Will Green was fascinated by the dream of transforming the flood-ravaged wilderness (as the nineteenth century conceived of it) that surrounded his town into a farming paradise. When he attempted the farming life himself, however, he soon failed at it. Why? Because of the Valley's long dry periods between rains, each year, and their erratic nature. When the rains were good, anything at all, it seemed, could be grown in the Valley's fertile soils, under that cloudless sky and warm sun. But the Valley's periodic droughts could blast everyone's hopes and send bankruptcy through the countryside. The answer? Seize control of the Sacramento River, Green would say, by taking off its abundant waters and carrying them out into the flatlands, lacing the Valley with irrigation canals.[9]

At the age of thirty-one, in September 1863, Green bought the town's newspaper, the *Colusa Sun.* Thereafter, we have in its columns that close-running account of water matters that for forty years into the future this river-obsessed man would produce. The *Sun* had begun publication in January 1862 in the midst of the historic double flood of 1861–1862, and it could record that Colusa itself was safe, as it would be in all future floods, and that the mail was cut off from Marysville for two weeks, due to water "which now covers nearly the whole country between Colusa and that city."[10]

Almost four years later Colusa entered on that historically crucial cycle of floods in the late 1860s which as we have seen stimulated mid-Valley people to begin taking steps to protect themselves. The Sacramento rose fast about the 21st of December 1866, reaching its high water mark on the 24th. Green remarked that "without doubt, more water passed down the valley than ever before since its settlement by whites in the same length of time." The river tore out several large cuts in its east bank, and torrents of water flowed out into the tule lands. "All this immense volume of water [pouring southward out of Butte Sink]," wrote Green, "could not pass between the high land of Butte slough and the Buttes, so it ran [back] into the river again at the head of Butte Slough." "In fact," he went on, "the current of the river running into the river was so strong that it ran square across the river, carrying drift, etc., over on this bank, and overflowed it for several miles two feet deep," the water running westward into Colusa

Basin.[11] Now, farmers on the west side of the river, north of town, first began talking about plans to build a levee several miles long to protect themselves.[12]

A year later, in February 1867, another flood arrived. The river swelled, rose higher and higher within its banks, and then broke over them to flow out on the valley floor to either side, creating "one continuous body of water" along the whole course of the Sacramento River, from three to eight miles wide on the west side of the river, perhaps half that area being covered on the east.[13] By midmonth, sheep herds were fleeing from the bottom lands near the Buttes, for the Butte Sink pool was getting larger and larger. Two months later, the Sacramento was once more out of its banks.[14] (It was this April surge of high water, valleywide, which set off Yuba City's first spontaneous effort to build a levee.) And in December 1867, the Sacramento River flooded once more, while across the valley, the Feather ripped through Yuba City's first levee across Gilsizer Slough. After two more weeks Will Green wrote that:

> Colusa and its environs is now an island; above, below, to the right and left is one vast sheet of water. Between town and the Coast Range the water presents the appearance of an inland sea. The . . . river has been within half an inch of high water mark.[15]

Within a few months, the river was once more on a rampage. By the first of March 1868, flooding was so general that all mail to Colusa from Marysville ceased and remained terminated for at least a week. The area downriver from Colusa was experiencing the highest water it had ever known. "The country . . . on either side," wrote Green, "is completely inundated."[16]

It was in the midst of this alarming cycle of floods that Will Green was elected by Colusa and Tehama counties to sit in the State Assembly, there to create the Green Act and drastically localize the state's swampland management system. Each group of landowners could now reclaim their particular swamplands holdings entirely as they wished. No public authority of any kind existed, any longer, to supervise the process so that valleywide drainage needs during floodtimes would be provided for, that is, appropriate channelways left open, and necessary levees constructed. The Green Act was passed within two weeks of the March 1868 flood; three days before, Sutter County had gotten its levee district bill enacted.

≈≈≈

For some time an argument of great seriousness and wide implications had been building up in the Valley, and it would go on for forty more years. The issue was a fundamentally simple one: what kind of *river control theory* should people rely on as they thought about flood control in the Valley? Within the argument a remarkably familiar order of battle shaped up, for the adversaries were the same kinds of people who had lined up against each other in the earlier and now-concluded debate over swampland policy. Once again, elitist Republicans were on one side, and populist Democrats were on the other.

We have seen that during the swampland debates the Republicans had thought in terms of large basinwide flood control projects based not on the knowledge of ordinary, self-taught people, but on the technical advice of engineers. For well-educated persons, who tended to be Republicans, engineers carried a special cachet, perhaps because they were the pioneering representatives of the new social order in America that Yankee-inspired Republicans, since the Civil War, had been trying to build. America was still an overwhelmingly crude and provincial society that lagged far behind the sophisticated nations of western Europe in its use, or nonuse, of educated expertise—or, for that matter, in its widely expressed contempt for that expertise. The masses who voted the Jacksonian Democratic ticket tended to be outspokenly antiintellectual, outspokenly distrustful, even contemptuous, of college-trained men. It was common for fathers to warn their boys not to pursue higher education, else they would be feminized. Get out of school, they would say, and learn in real life what you need to know; stay away from books! For his bookishness as a youth, his habit of getting to know the town gentry so he could get into their small libraries, Abraham Lincoln, classic Republican-to-be, was much derided.

Republican reformers in midnineteenth-century America were

in fact forever running into this national distrust of trained experts. The first public health crusaders in New York City, Republicans all, who in the 1860s tried to draw on the expertise of physicians, apply the concepts of the new germ theory of disease, and clean up the town, were buried in ridicule and contempt from the Democratic-leaning masses of that city. They bitterly distrusted modern science, the college-educated, and the reforming aristocrat, with the result that for many years public health efforts in New York City were quite frustrated.[17]

All of this was set within a broad cultural movement of national reform that came out of Republican America in the years after the Civil War. It was now, after decades of North-South rivalry and a bloody civil war, that the Yankee North, with its roots in New England, was finally in a position of national ascendancy and able to do the things that for decades, principally through Henry Clay's now-defunct Whig Party, it had been vainly calling for.[18] Essentially, gentlemen of Whig-Republican ideals hungered to create a more civilized, educated, sophisticated America, one that would turn away from amateurism and populist paeans to the limitless genius of the common man. The new America would apply learning and science and advanced technology to the creation of a thriving industrial society, city-based and cosmopolitan.

At the core of this dream for America were the new science-and-technology-centered private and public (land-grant) universities that Republican America in these post-1850 decades was self-consciously and proudly creating, from a vastly reorganized Harvard and Yale to such entirely new institutions as Johns Hopkins and Cornell and the state universities of Michigan, Wisconsin, and California—institutions that tended to be hotbeds of liberal Republicanism. Their role was to be the brooding places for the birthing of that trained middle class, that national community of well-educated young men and, eventually, women, who would build the more efficient, centralized, and productive national economy that Republicans envisioned. They were to bring in system and logic where, presently, amateur-created confusion and disorganization dominated the scene. They were to be the action-corps in that national search for order—in government (cleaning out corruption from top to bottom), in the running of industries and railroads, and in natural resource management—that historian Robert H. Wiebe has pointed to as the central impulse in middle-class American life from the late 1870s to the 1920s.[19]

There was something about the engineers' dedication to rational efficiency and disciplined technological adeptness which appealed strongly to the Republican mind, particularly since engineers were so crucially important in mining operations and in building the country's transportation network and industries. Within the engineering world, civil engineers (those who built public works, such as roads and bridges and railroads and canals) took the lead, for they had early emerged in the opening decades of the nineteenth century as an increasingly visible professional group whose skills were needed by the entrepreneurial corporate elite. In the thirty booming years from 1850 to 1880 the number of physicians and clergymen in the country increased six times, while the number of civil engineers multiplied sixteen times. In New York State there were 62 civil engineers in 1850, and 1082 by 1880; in California, the growth in these years was from 6 to 390. Nationally, the totals were 512 in 1850, and 8261 in 1880.[20]

By 1867 this elite corps among the engineers had reached a sufficient critical mass to create the profession's first permanent, national association to set standards and foster a countrywide sense of shared professional identity and community: the American Society of Civil Engineers. Meanwhile, in the late 1860s and into the 1870s formal civil engineering education expanded widely across the country. Its traditional lodging place had been at the Army's military academy at West Point, which from its founding in 1802 under the just-established U.S. Army Corps of Engineers had been for many years the country's only engineering school.[21] However, in the state colleges and universities which grew out of the Morrill Act of 1862, engineering instruction was from the outset installed as the centerpiece in their curricula. By 1870, over seventy institutions of higher learning offered students an engineering curriculum, so that the less than 900 engineers who graduated in the 1860s had become the almost 4000 who completed their training in the 1880s. As early as the mid-1870s, probably 80 percent of the nation's engineers were graduates of a college engineering program.[22]

They were, indeed, the most characteristic graduates of the new universities, which had seized on the ideal of public service to justify their existence in a country where most people still looked on colleges with distrust and, usually, disdain. In the engineer we may see a person, as Daniel Hovey Calhoun writes, "through whom the early possibilities of 'the new America' [most clearly] appeared."[23] It was engineers who "supplied the functional and professional leadership," Raymond H. Merritt notes, for the great transformation which, beginning in the 1850s, initiated America's technological revolution and the industrial revolution which flowed therefrom.

> By emphasizing mobility, efficiency, standardization, improved living conditions, and a less burdensome life, engineers ushered . . . [into American life] a cosmopolitan perspective, a new educational curriculum, and a new trend toward scientific management, and modified a whole maze of institutions.

They did all of this self-consciously, picturing themselves "as the vanguards of civilization who stimulated intellectual thought and promoted the expansion of cultural values, as well as developing natural resources and fulfilling material needs."[24]

The professional culture within which civil engineers were reared, their dominant ideal self-image, gave them a special energy and enterprise, and therefore a wide impact on national life. Civil engineers were trained not simply to be technicians who applied existing concepts in routine ways to the tasks they were given. Rather, they were to be men of inquiring minds, observers, analysts, creative problem-solvers who could innovate new methods, new techniques, and new materials. They were to advise their clients, either as independent consultants or as men high-placed in the particular corporations, usually as what were called "supervisors," by fashioning bold theoretical approaches to unprecedented situations. They were the key directing figures in such nationally prominent enterprises as the immense Hoosac railroad tunnel project in New England which, after many years of excavation in the mid-1800s transformed regional transportation patterns, or the decades-long struggle to get control of the mouth of the Mississippi River. It was civil engineers, their administrative skills honed by the tremendous challenges they had faced during the Civil War, who led the postwar managerial revolution in the American economy. It was a revolution that aimed at rationally and efficiently bringing together modern technology and new materials and carefully mobilized workmen, all of this coordinated by electrical communication.[25]

These daunting experiences and this much-respected national role induced a kind of imperial temperament in America's leading civil engineers. Confident of their skills and their analytical powers, they were extraordinarily ready to take on such huge challenges as the building of a railroad thousands of miles across the continent, or the reorganizing of entire natural environments to extract their minerals. And as they did so, their dramatic success stories induced Americans at large to develop an almost astonishing faith in their ability to do what they set out to achieve.

Perhaps engineers were so widely held in awe because they were well-educated men in an undereducated country; perhaps their status originated, too, in the fact that in America the profession of civil engineering had West Point roots. The very term "civil engineer" was adopted to distinguish midcentury civilian practitioners from the military engineers who had earlier done most of this work in the United States. Indeed, in the midcentury years it was a habit among the admiring public to attach military titles to leading engineers, such as "Captains" John Ericsson and James B. Eads, "Colonel" Octave Chanute, and "General" Herman Haupt, all of them men of great popularity and standing for their masterful engineering achievements.

As the century proceeded, engineering also attracted to its ranks many sons of the wealthy elite who could bear themselves with the assurance of established gentlemen. Their very professionalism, which set them off from the capitalists who employed them, their wide-ranging mobility as they took on project after project, seemed to make them an independent secular priesthood of scholarly experts, of the sort the contemporary Positivist philosopher August Comte in France envisioned as the elite who should govern modern societies. Whatever the sources of their extraordinary authority, by the mid-1870s we find such a man as A. P. Boller, a leading consulting engineer in New York, boasting "in his remarks to the 1874 graduating class of Rensselaer Polytechnic Institute [an early spin-off of West Point] that Americans placed such trust in the competence and integrity of his profession that they rarely questioned the stability and utility of their services and structures."[26]

There was always, however, a muttering conflict between the engineers, clothed in their capacious new garments of authority, and many in the lay public. As engineers were put in charge of great projects, the old guard that had formerly directed them, made up of entrepreneurs, political leaders, investors, and capitalists, often grumbled at being pushed aside. "There is no doubt who began the conflict," remarks historian Raymond Merritt. "Engineers had been openly opposing the management practices of 'lay' leadership [from the 1850s onward]. . . . In the succeeding quarter century almost every engineer participated in this conflict between laymen and professionals."[27]

These battles, which usually went on within the ranks of a particular corporation, also spread into the wider political arena. It was an obvious social fact, for one thing, that civil engineers and capitalists worked together in a natural, symbiotic partnership, creating an alliance that could be unpopular. During the 1860s, in California, San Francisco capitalists who were taking over and consolidating the hydraulic gold mining industry turned instinctively to the employing of engineers as they made their operations far larger and more efficient. Downstream, where the vastly increased flow of mining debris was received, men such as the North Bloomfield mine's chief engineer, Hamilton Smith—a person of aristocratic antecedents—were much distrusted.

Republicans and civil engineers: it was a fast and enduring alliance. Democrats certainly had, of course, their own learned elite, their own intellectuals, as a party with Thomas Jefferson for its founding saint could not help but have, but Democratic intellectuals tended to use their skills in social criticism, not in activities that met the needs of entrepreneurs.[28] Furthermore, while Republicans tended to believe that only the well-born, the educated, and the elite truly understood the nation's larger public issues, rank and file Democrats had a passionate belief in the wits of the common people and in common sense, not in book-learning. A consciously egalitarian movement that condemned every form of social distinction and privilege (except for slave-owning in the Democratic South, and after the Civil War, segregation), Democrats had insisted that ordinary men like Andrew Jackson, of little or no formal education, had simply in their natural intelligence and untutored instincts the ability to do anything that needed doing in America, even to taking on the presidency. They self-consciously contrasted this view with the Whig-Republicans' elitism and distrusted their colleges and universities, for none of which had they asked. The Morrill Land Grant Act of 1862, which created the network of state universities, was enacted by the Republican-led wartime Congress in response to no popular appeal.[29]

≈≈≈

It is within the larger setting of this continuing national confrontation that we can best understand the long debates that erupted in the early 1870s in California's Sacramento Valley over river control strategy. The issue was straightforward: who should be listened to in this matter, the experts of the new national engineering priesthood, or those who lived in the Valley and, self-taught and on the basis of actual observations, developed their own ideas about what needed to be done? Who needs experts, it would be asked, with their college-bred airs of superior knowledge and their lack of experience in everyday affairs? Like all book-educated people, engineers tended to bring abstract principles, based on bodies of learning acquired in faraway locations, to local questions, and this was instinctively distrusted by ordinary people who relied on the direct teaching of their own senses—in this case on walking beside and living with and observing daily the Sacramento River and its tributaries, and laboring through the long days and nights of actual floods. The new engineering elite seemed instinctively given to forming large theoretical conceptions and bold plans covering wide regions, and they had an unquestioning confidence in their own ability to do, in actuality, what in their minds they could conceive. It had been, in fact, this mentality that had led to the fiasco of centrally directed swampland reclamation in California, and to its repeal.

It was a significant moment in the Sacramento Valley, therefore, when in the early 1870s a new player, in the form of high-level engineering expertise, national in its networks and origins, entered the flood control dialogue. It made its appearance in the large and self-assured person of a general in the U.S. Army Corps of Engineers, Barton S. Alexander. A brusque, richly experienced, often overbearing man of massive proportions and absolute confidence in his own views, Alexander, born in 1819, was just past fifty years of age when swampland entrepreneurs in the Sacramento Valley first brought him into local debates.

West Point-trained, in the mid-1840s he had been put to work building fortifications during the war in Mexico within six years of becoming a second lieutenant of engineers. Thereafter Alexander had plunged into a wide-ranging career of planning and construction of military installations and hospitals, including the most difficult construction task to that point attempted in the United States, the rebuilding of the Minot's Ledge Lighthouse on the Massachusetts coast, which had been torn out by a great storm. An extremely complex, technically forbidding challenge for which Alexander devised brilliant solutions, Minot's Ledge took six years of his life and doubtless crystallized in him a personal character given to being decisive and authoritative.

Then Alexander was off to the Civil War as an engineer deep in battle after battle, from Bull Run through the bloody Peninsular Campaign to Fair Oaks and Philip Sheridan's lightning campaigns, in 1864, ranging the length of the Shenandoah Valley. At the same time, Alexander had heavy duties planning and constructing the defenses of numerous harbors and seacoasts and serving as chief engineer in charge of the defenses of Washington, D.C.[30]

Given ever higher rank for "gallant and meritorious services," at war's end Barton S. Alexander was a brevet brigadier general on his way to the Corps of Engineers' Pacific Territory, as senior engineer, charged with supervising all engineering operations on the Pacific coast. In 1873, after six years in that region, he was made head of a congressionally ordered irrigation survey in the Sacramento and San Joaquin valleys, the first such to be made. Typically bold, given Alexander's nature, the Alexander Commission took a large and confident view of the problem, preached the need for central planning, predicted that huge areas could be irrigated, and even suggested the location of major canals, including some dams in the Sierra Nevada. The commission "never questioned," as historian Donald J. Pisani writes, "the engineering feasibility of moving water over . . . great distances . . . [for] like most nineteenth-century westerners, they exhibited complete faith in technology and in California's master builders."[31] Though little came of the commission's report, as the first full-scale professional survey it was nonetheless historically significant in its stimulating effect on Californians' thinking about the potentialities of irrigation.

In 1874 and 1875 Alexander was on a board that examined the problem of maintaining sufficient depth at the mouth of the Mississippi River; during the course of that work he went off to Europe to inspect methods of improving deltas. Later in 1875, the State of California created the West Side Commission to examine a large proposed irrigation canal project in the San Joaquin Valley. Alexander, busy man, was appointed consultant, and his young protégé, the civil engineer William Hammond Hall, a man not yet thirty years old, was put in charge of the project. The two men were once again in an ebulliently confident frame of mind. They concluded that a multimillion-dollar canal almost 200 miles long was entirely feasible. In reality the concept was generations ahead of its time; nothing of this sort could in these years be built, nor was it. But as an admiring military associate wrote of Alexander, "Temporary expedients were his abomination. . . . There was nothing small or ungenerous in his nature. Little thoughts never entered his mind."[32]

≈≈≈

We have seen that half a dozen years before, in the period immediately following the passage of the Green Act in 1868, tens of thousands of acres of swamplands had been purchased in the Sacramento Valley by entrepreneurs. By the early 1870s, they were beginning to set about seeing how they could reclaim their vast waterlogged properties. In these circumstances, it was typical of men like Colusa-area swampland owner William H. Parks—a strong Republican who had sat in the Senate that, in 1861, had approved the ambitious if doomed swampland commissioners program—that he and others like him quickly turned to such a man as General Alexander for advice.

It was also fully in character for Alexander, when he gave the requested advice to Colusa-area swampland owners in 1870, to recommend a sweeping, almost arrogant assault on the Sacramento River. What he proposed was nothing less than a revolutionary rearrangement of the entire natural environment in the Valley, even though there were as yet no regularly gathered and coordinated bodies of observational data on stream flow on which to base his conclusions.

In the background was a brilliant, internationally famous study of flooding in the lower Mississippi River basin, commissioned by Congress in 1850, which was conducted by (then) Captain Andrew A. Humphreys of the Corps of Engineers, with the aid of a young assistant, Lieutenant Henry L. Abbot. An immensely detailed multivolume study presented to Congress in 1861, it was so powerful in its masses of data and its theoretical richness that it immediately made Humphreys a world-renowned figure among engineers (it also brought much-needed luster to the Corps itself); and, in 1866, it also made him commanding general of the Corps of Engineers, a post he would hold until 1879. His legendary Mississippi study burned deep into the collective consciousness of Corps of Engineers officers a rigid dogma on flood control. It called for "levees only": no bypasses, no upstream dams, no arrangements for allowing floodwaters to spread at controlled release points, but simply high levees and keeping rivers within single channels. This it was believed would, by increasing the velocity of flow, force streams to scour out and deepen their own beds, rendering them capable of carrying off all floods. (Twentieth-century research has not supported this thesis.) The Corps held unswervingly to its dogma in fair times and in foul, despite decades of criticism, until the 1920s (with an early breakaway by a brilliant young Corps officer in California in 1910, as we will see).[33]

Going entirely, then, on what had been learned of the Mississippi, General B. S. Alexander told Colusa-area swampland owners in 1870 that the Sacramento could and must be contained within a single channel, which according to the theory would increase its flood-bearing capacity so that it could carry all floodwaters down to the delta without overflow. The Humphrey thesis, hallowed in Corps memory, would be repeated over and over again for many years into the future by Corps engineers in the Sacramento Valley whenever they arrived to examine its great river and tributaries. It had, coincidentally, the crucially important spin-off of providing an engineering rationale from high prestige sources for the idea not only that the swamplands could indeed be quickly reclaimed, but for the assurance that no land need be set aside within them for bypass channels. Swampland owners took hold of Alexander's plans eagerly and gratefully.[34]

Will Green of the *Colusa Sun* flatly disagreed with Alexander. Himself a Southern Democrat almost entirely without formal education, Green was nonetheless a keenly intelligent man given to making careful observations of the natural scene around him, in the tradition of Thomas Jefferson, and he had good reason for believing Alexander's scheme disastrously wrong. He had, after all, been looking out on the Sacramento River from the town of Colusa for close to ten years. Learned men, he observed in a *Sun* editorial on March 4, 1871 in an obvious reference to Alexander, had been going by the example of the Mississippi River and saying that the Sacramento could be made by levees to carry off all of its waters in one channel, but the analogy was a bad one. Mississippi floods, gathered from a valley of continental proportions, rose very slowly, but in the Sacramento Valley they came from near at hand with surprising swiftness. The Valley was simply too close to the mountains that produced the floods, with the result that there were not thousands of miles of river channels as in the Mississippi valley, with their immense internal storage capacity, to absorb the high waters.

In fact, by the time Alexander had made his recommendations in 1870, Green had already arrived at a matured understanding of the Sacramento River that engineers of Alexander's national standing would not come around to until well after the turn of the twentieth century. In the crucial years of 1867–1868 when river planning ideas were in valleywide ferment, the legislature had created a commission to study the problem of how to control the Sacramento. Green, then an assemblyman and a member of that investigating body, developed at heavy financial cost to himself a plan, subsequently rejected by the legislature, that sketched out with eerie exactitude precisely the valleywide plan that the U.S. Corps of Engineers, forty years later, would eventually come to adopt, take to Congress, and over a long stretch of years construct as the flood control system that now protects the Valley.[35]

The Sacramento, Green said, could never be made to carry all of its flood waters within its own channel. There was just *too much water*. This was the crucial point at issue in the whole argument. How big was the river, when in high water? Green himself, in the late 1860s, had no idea exactly how much water the Sacramento in flood produced, for that matter no one did, since there was as yet no system of coordinated gauges on it and would not be for many years. The unassisted evidence of his own senses told him, however, that the river produced far too much water to be contained by the river's main channel, certainly below Colusa. As Green defined the problem, the Sacramento River was inevitably going to flow over its banks, no matter what anyone tried to do to it.

This, Green believed, meant accepting the Sacramento's outflows into the huge basins that paralleled it, but controlling those outflows. He would achieve this by limiting the river's discharging of water to a few carefully managed locations where concrete weirs (he called them "locks") would keep as much water in the channel as possible, so that it scoured out its bed to the deepest level manageable. When the channel could carry no more, the weirs would then allow the river to pass its excess waters out through structures that would be strong enough not to rip out and become deep crevasses. One of Green's more acute observations had been to note that when these crevasses formed and a heavy flow left the stream, the diminished volume remaining in the river itself, below that point, meant a considerably slackened current. This caused the Sacramento promptly to begin dropping onto its bed much more of its load of suspended silt. Thus, the channel below such breaks would fill, making it unable in the future to carry as much water as in the past. Maintaining deep main-channel integrity: this was central to Green's plan.

As to the water flowing out into the paralleling basins, it should not be allowed simply to spread freely and at will to form great lakes, but rather it should be contained within specific channels by means of canals (now called, in the existing Sacramento Flood Control Project, "bypasses") constructed through the basins' lowest troughs. This would allow the wide lowlands outside these canals to be lived on and put to the plow. Green envisioned, in short, a second, auxiliary river channel in the Valley, guided through the basins, which would carry the Sacramento's excess waters in floodtimes, but be dry the rest of the year—and presumably, as now, be farmed in those months. The inland sea would disappear, to be replaced by much narrower leveed overflow channels.

How could such an ambitious river management plan be put into effect? This was the tricky question, of course, for a Southern Democrat like Green. Clearly, a plan of this magnitude would never spring spontaneously into being by the action of many local, unsupervised authorities, as a Democrat would ordinarily prefer. Green solved the conflict posed by his Southern Democratic loyalties to laissez-faire localism, and his hard won sense of what the realities of the Sacramento River called for by going to a half-way position: he did not call for state construction of the system—as had been attempted by the ill-fated swampland commissioners program—but for having a state authority at least plan out what was needed and tell individual landowners where to put their levees.[36] Certainly there was no reason as yet, on the experience of the swampland commissioners fiasco, to believe that the state itself could successfully undertake the building of so large a project. Leave the actual construction and management, Green was saying, to local people, who would have a direct interest in seeing that the task was well completed. It was nonetheless a curious mixture, for a Southern Democrat, this blend of central planning and localism. In irrigation matters, too, Green displayed the same readiness to call for planned water management, if on a local foundation.

The available records do not tell us why the Green bypass plan was not acceptable to the legislature in the late 1860s or to the swampland owners in the year 1870 and beyond, but a number of explanations seem reasonable. Cost-benefit calculations play a large role in everyone's minds, even before they were given that name, and Green's proposal would at the least call on the swampland owners to set aside large areas of basin land to be used for the "canals," both for the construction of embankments and to provide channelways between them, and they would naturally resist this idea. Perhaps, too, Green's opponents turned away from his proposal for another economic reason: its very sweep and comprehensiveness would make it slow to achieve, since all would have to wait, who knew how long, until a valleywide drainage plan had been painstakingly surveyed and developed and the locations of privately constructed levees stipulated. Men with potentially fertile farmlands in front of them which they wanted to get into and drain as quickly as possible, and with funds ready to invest or already committed, would in this as in most such situations be worried about delays, especially indeterminate ones.

Possibly, too, people tested Green's idea logically and rationally, and simply on that ground drew back on the ground that what he called for was too visionary. Green was calling for a *system* to be put in place, based in the concept that the Valley was a single hydrographic unit that should be managed in a unitary way. He was urging a genuine innovation, a true policy leap as broad in scope as the swampland commissioners program itself. Most people, it would appear, were not ready for such bold policy changes. They preferred to do the job incrementally, step by step, each local landholding taking care of its own needs. People wanted, in short, to be left on their own to push ahead as they believed necessary, within their own angle of vision, within what they could see and their own wits prompted.

≈≈≈

There were, however, powerful forces at work in America's national political culture in the 1870s, more emotional than strictly logical, which make more understandable Green's failure to get his by-pass plan adopted. No one in public life is listened to simply on the basis of what he or she says, however logical it may be, but rather on the basis of who they are. In this case the contrast between the social standing and public image of the two kinds of people in 1870s America that Green and Alexander represented—their caste positions, so to speak—could hardly have been sharper. In the best of circumstances entrepreneurs like William H. Parks would be inclined to make up their minds in such crucial questions not by listening to an uneducated country editor but rather to a trained engineer, especially one of such an illustrious standing and background as Alexander. No one, living in that time, would have missed the social distinctions.

Furthermore, Green was not only a self-educated man with no college pedigree, he was a Southerner, indeed a self-described and outspoken "ultra states' rights man" who during the Civil War had argued the South's cause. He would be inescapably identified in the eyes of most Californians with rebels who had only just been bloodily defeated, at shattering national cost in lives and capital, in their effort to tear the Union apart. Partisan rancor nationally in the Gilded Age—the years from the 1870s to the 1890s—was deep and bitter. These were the years of what scholars now call "army-style" politics, with massed thousands turning out regularly to march in torchlight parades proclaiming hatred of their political enemies, not only in large cities but in small town America as well. These were the years of turnouts at the polls running regularly over eighty-five percent, so determined were the masses to "turn the rascals out." Independents, people who belonged to no party, were few, and they were hissed at as unmanly.[37]

In this context, the operative fact would be that Green was a Southern Democrat, and a publicly active one. He would be seen by Republican swampland owners as one of their sworn enemies, as a committed, true-believing member of a political party literally detested by all good Republicans as a mulish, perverse opponent to everything they regarded as civilized and forward-looking in national policy. Republicans firmly believed that their party, having saved the Union, was the practically divine instrument that now, in the post-Civil War years, was laboring to create what they proudly thought of as a progressive, rapidly developing, ever more civilized nation led by its true (Republican) elite.

The Democrats were the political home of the country's Roman Catholics, execrated by most Protestants, and of its drinkers of alcohol: the Irish and their whiskey, the Germans and their beer. Their name, too, was associated with steaming political corruption in the crowded ethnic wards of the big cities. In a classic utterance Governor Oliver P. Morton of Indiana in these very years publicly referred to the Democratic party as "a common sewer and loathsome receptacle, into which is emptied every element of treason North and South, and every element of inhumanity and barbarism which has dishonored the age."[38]

Republicans would believe that civil engineers, especially those honored men of the United States Army Corps of Engineers who carried glorious war records with them, were quite different people to listen to in difficult policy matters than men like Southern Democrat Will Green. Engineers had just helped to save the Union, they had been achieving prodigies of engineering brilliance in the storm of railroad construction that was sweeping the nation, and they had great prestige and moral authority in postwar America. They were also educated Northerners, usually college trained, and they had an honored national and international profession behind them.

Of course, no one knew anything, in any established, scientific sense, about the Sacramento River. Americans had been living in the Sacramento Valley only a few years, their flood experience was extremely limited, and there was no fund of river-flow data, created by a system of coordinated gauges. Few, therefore, who puzzled about what to do with the river, even Republican entrepreneurs, could say they in fact knew, out of their own knowledge and experience, the answer to the question: what to do? They had to rely on someone else to tell them. It came down to the fundamental matter of trust in this protracted debate over which definition of the problem in the Sacramento Valley to accept. Thus, in this as in so much of public policy making, it was a question not simply of economic interest or of logical analysis, though these influences were certainly at work, but of which people one was inclined to listen to, which views merited the most respect. When into the bargain the policy recommendations being received from that trusted person aligned well with one's own economic interest, as in the case of the swampland owners and General Alexander, the combination had to be irresistible.

≈≈≈

So matters stood in the 1870s. Who would make the decision? In the actual circumstance, in the Colusa region as elsewhere in the Sacramento Valley, it would be the swampland owners. Their authority, under the Green Act, was plenary. They had gathered their advice, they had decided on which policy to adopt and follow, and their plans were formed. We must now follow them into the always complex and surprising realm of implementation.

C H A P T E R

The Levee-Building Spiral Begins: *1867–1880*

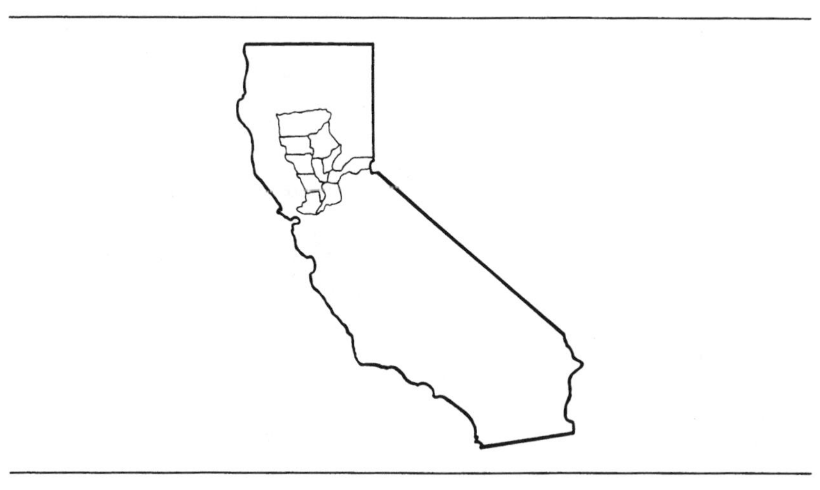

A torrent of water hit their single-story house, about 500 feet from [the] . . . Creek. The powerful, chest-high current carried [the] . . . Thunderbird, so new it didn't have license plates, two blocks. . . . [N]eighbor Greg Rianda dragged [a man with a leg in a cast] . . . to safety through waist-high water. . . . [Then they] sat watching cars floating by."

Stephen E. Wright & Dale Rodebaugh, San Jose Mercury-News, *February 19, 1986. Quoted in* Rivers of Fear, *p. 73.*

In the late months of 1867, the people living in Colusa County had read in their newspapers about Sutter County folk busying themselves with the building of their Gilsizer Slough levee, which for the first time in the mid-Valley region had closed off a major slough and had tried to deny a great river its usual outlet for overflow. Thus had Sutter County, as we have seen, taken the first decisive step toward trying to win freedom from the fear of floods by drastically reshaping the natural environment, whether or not their efforts harmed anyone else in the Valley. Self-protection, Judge Hurbert had said publicly and later proclaimed in his Yuba City newspaper, was the first law of nature.

Setting a process like this in motion had profound implications for the whole Valley. Once the river's natural overflow pattern was interfered with, a cycle was begun the end of which no one could see. The Board of Supervisors of Colusa County understandably derived from the Sutter County undertaking the conclusion that it was now open season on the Valley's rivers, if some local public purpose were being served, and in late 1867 it began to edge in this direction. Colusa County put a crew to work damming off Wilkins Slough, a

"The Climate of California on a Rampage." Sacramento Valley flood refugees depicted in The Pacific Rural Press *during the flood of February 1878, in a woodcut by Charles Nahl. The terror, the tragedy, the fate of livestock in such inundations, are graphically conveyed in this dramatic rendering.*
Courtesy: California State Library.

major Sacramento distributary on that river's west bank about eighteen miles downstream from Colusa. The purpose: to provide an embankment for a road.[1]

Editor Will Green of the *Colusa Sun* was worried. Here, he warned, was a test case for everything he had been saying about the river and its flooding behavior. The Sacramento River channel, he insisted, could not carry more water in floodtime. If it were denied an exit point where excess waters were normally released, then the river would necessarily be much higher downstream from that closed-off slough, producing higher and more threatening flood levels. When the river rose, as it did regularly, those below a cut-off slough outlet would be in considerably more danger than even at the present, bad as things already were. As a Colusa-area dispatch in a San Francisco newspaper had recently put their situation, "Every winter there is more or less of this submerging process."[2]

There was even talk in the Colusa region, Green warned, of leveeing, and thus closing off, the *entire west bank of the Sacramento from Colusa down to Knight's Landing,* a distance of some *forty river-miles*. The purpose: to close off the swamplands in the broad Colusa Basin, west of the Sacramento River, from overflow and reclaim them for agriculture. Such an undertaking, Green said, would simply push the river's floodwaters across the river and submerge all of the farms on the east side of the river from Butte Slough downstream. His words appear not to have gone unheeded. In the first outbreak of vigilante violence in the mid-Valley over river policy, within a week of Green's warnings local people in the Wilkins Slough area destroyed the county-built dam across the mouth of that watercourse.[3]

At the end of May 1868, the Green Act went into effect, and in the first day of filings, 15,000 acres of land in Colusa County were claimed under its provisions.[4] The county's economy soon began moving at a more bustling and abundant pace. After this date the region north of Colusa, which had long been quiet, began quickly to develop. The tiny communities of Butte City on the Sacramento's east bank, seventeen miles above Colusa, and Princeton, on the west bank three miles below Butte City, began to flourish.[5] Colusa County was entering on its amazing wheat boom of the 1870s, during which time a significant percentage of the entire world production of wheat would come from within its borders.

It was also in 1868, five months after the Green Act's effective date, that Levi Foss Moulton, a New England-born Yankee who was now approaching forty years of age, entered the local swampland story. An energetic and vigorously entrepreneurial man, he had come to California during the Gold Rush to mine for gold, then with his earnings had bought land in Colusa County in 1852, east of the Sacramento River and northward of the town of Colusa. Here he became the region's first large sheep rancher, battling in later years with the cattlemen to protect his herds. A staunch Republican, Moulton would eventually own as many as 35,000 acres of land, which amounted to most of Colusa County east of the Sacramento, and he lived in a grand five-story house far out on his property, about nine miles north of the county seat. Few men in the Sacramento Valley would be seized by grander dreams of bold reclamation projects than Moulton; few believed more confidently than he that out of his own genius and energies he could give peremptory orders to nature and push the overflowing Sacramento River off of his land.

Under the Green Act, Moulton bought immense holdings of swamplands in the low area between the Sacramento River and Sutter Buttes—that is, in the vicinity of, though apparently not in, Butte Sink. For more than thirty years Moulton would busy himself in ambitious projects aimed at turning his swamplands to irrigated agriculture, though not entirely with the success he hoped for. As local historian Charles McComish wrote of Moulton, he "spent several princely fortunes on levees, ditches, and other more or less experimental work." By 1891 his holdings had declined to the still comfortable expanse of 18,000 acres, about 5,000 of which were said to be reclaimed, the rest being given to stockraising and general farming. When he sold his ranch at the age of 75 in 1904, two years before he died in a buggy accident, it was for the sum of $300,000—though it was said that, at his death in 1906, he was largely bankrupt.[6] Nonetheless, in Moulton's untiring labors over many years, he succeeded eventually in laying out and building the first line of riverbank levees running for many miles northward from Colusa along the east bank of the Sacramento River.

His long adventure with the river began in November 1868, when he made his first appearance before the Colusa Board of Supervisors to petition for the formation of one of that county's initial swampland reclamation districts under the Green Act. On the 10th, the board issued its approval, creating District 87 (each county had its own numbering system). It consisted wholly of 4840 acres of Moulton's own land. In other words, there would be no one else with him in the project; he would be its entire board of directors. The district, situated largely in the unsectioned eastern half of Township 17 North, Range 1 West, lay about six miles north and east of Colusa. It was a very low-lying tract, its surface being some twenty feet below that of the Sacramento River, and thus it was in that part of the lowlands east of the river which were almost annually buried under deep floodwaters coming from the Sacramento itself and from Butte Creek. (In 1937, the Butte Lodge Outing Club, which was located in this area and at about the same elevation, reported floodwaters up to the floor of its lodge, even though it stood 16 feet above the ground.[7]) Running about six miles north to south and some three miles east to west, District 87 did not reach to the riverbank, though in its most westward extension, in Section 29, it approached within half a mile of it.[8]

Whatever Moulton planned to do with his new reclamation district, its existence did not lead as yet to the building of any levees along the river. The same was true concerning another and considerably older reclamation effort that also lay east of the Sacramento, though in this case downriver from the town of Colusa: that in the Meridian region of Sutter County. As early as 1862 farmers had seen that the swampland enclosed in this northwestern pocket of Sutter Basin—the section enclosed by Butte Slough to the north and east, and the Sacramento River to the west—was fertile soil. What they needed to do to clear out its thick stands of tules, put the land to the plow, and live on it was to dry it out by building a levee along the inside curve of Butte Slough. If successful, it would keep that stream from overflowing their land from the north and east. Meanwhile, they would rely on the natural levees of the Sacramento River to give them protection from the west. Accordingly, under the original swampland commissioners program of 1861, they had organized District 20, and had carried forward a small amount of leveeing along Butte Slough, doubtless at the upper, or northern, end of their pocket.[9] The hamlet of Meridian was laid out in their district in 1864, and by 1867 it had become a settled village.

When the Green Act was passed in early 1868, the settlers around Meridian moved quickly to reorganize under this more lenient legislation. Swamp Land District 20 became Meridian Swamp Land District 2, including some 10,000–12,000 acres of land, its eastern border beginning about two miles south of the "Long Bridge" over Butte Slough (on the road eastward to Yuba City and Marysville) and running northward along the Slouth.[10]

By its charter, none of the Meridian district's funds were to be used for building levees on the natural bank of the Sacramento. The higher and drier "river lands" that paralleled that stream were not classified as state-owned swamplands, they were federally owned and purchased directly from the national land office. The farmers along the river, therefore, would simply have to erect their own embankments against flood, if any were to be built.

In December 1868, District 2 was renamed as Reclamation District 70 (RD 70), which has remained its designation to the present day. In that year this emerging little principality—which now holds rich orchard lands—was bounded roughly on the south by the east-west road from Meridian to Long Bridge. (It would in later years expand considerably, eventually taking charge of the Sacramento riverbank levees, so that presently it fronts on about fifteen river-miles of the Sacramento, running downstream from Butte Slough and Moon's Bend.) Working entirely with tax moneys raised among themselves, RD 70 farmers by 1879 had constructed a total of thirteen miles of levee, eight feet high and four feet across on the top, along the westerly bank of Butte Slough and across the bottom of the district. Out on the main river, the farmers along the Sacramento's east bank had also built small private levees.[11]

≈≈≈

In 1870, two years after Moulton and the Meridian farmers had formed their districts, all eyes were turned downstream from Colusa by a dramatic public announcement that confirmed Will Green's earlier warnings about the planning and forming of a great levee project on the west side. A group of swampland entrepreneurs whose lands lay in Colusa Basin revealed that they had pooled their interests to form Reclamation District 108, a giant organization that is still, more than a century later, in active existence. RD 108's appearance was historically crucial. It did in fact initiate in a major way the building of levees on the Sacramento's banks, and its doing so set the whole process of enclosing that stream rushing swiftly along thereafter in a spiral of hectic construction, each project spurred into being as a riposte to prior ones. That is to say, now, along the Sacramento, as earlier along the Feather, the process of self-protection by pushing the river over on people living on the other side—the basic strategy in local flood control efforts in the Valley for forty years into the future—had begun.

Soon, these ambitious interventions into the natural floodtime flowage patterns of the Sacramento River would quite transform the mid-Valley environment. Before many years the cycle of riverbank levee-building up and down the river would fix irrevocably the future, long-term shape of flood control in this section of the Sacramento Valley and the character of this vast plain to the present day.

Reclamation District 108 began its public existence in September 1870, when a long article appeared in the *Colusa Sun* describing the plan of the Sacramento Valley Reclamation Company. Led by A. H. Rose, a prominent swampland owner, the trustees intended to reclaim 74,085 acres of Colusa Basin land, a bit more than half of which reached down into Yolo County. RD 108 would begin its levee at Sycamore Slough, a waterway opening out of the Sacramento's west bank about six miles downriver from Colusa. Specifically basing their project on advice from General B. S. Alexander, U.S. Army Corps of Engineers (USCE), the trustees of the new district took their stand firmly on the conviction that the Sacramento River could be made to carry all of its flow in its main channel by building high levees directly on its banks.

They did not, of course, intend themselves to build levees on both sides of the stream so as to complete Alexander's plan. Rather, they acted with apparent unquestioning confidence on the assumption that, given the existing context of ideas about property management in America, every property owner must look out for himself in a competitive war of each against all. The projectors of RD 108 had no sense of being trustees for the general welfare; indeed, nothing in the existing laws charged them with this obligation. Rather, they looked out only for their own interests, letting market forces thereafter tend automatically, as it was believed they would, to the needs of the community at large. This, after all, had been explicitly the public policy that the legislature had laid down in the Green Act of 1868. Thus, the projectors of RD 108 intended to do everything they could to prevent the Sacramento River from overflowing any longer on their side, whatever this might do to anyone else. If the farmers whose lands lay opposite to RD 108, easterly of the river, wished to protect themselves against the increased overflows now certain to come to their side, then it was up to them to set about erecting their own riverbank levees—and thereby complete Alexander's plan.

The trustees of RD 108 now proceeded to build a levee forty-five miles long, along the Sacramento's west bank from Sycamore Slough downstream to the town of Knight's Landing. It was set sixty feet back from the river bluff and constructed to a three foot height, judged to be one foot above the highest river level known. During the course of this construction, dams were put across the mouths of five sloughs: Upper Sycamore, Wilkins, Bear, Lower Sycamore, and Cache sloughs. What all of this meant for everyone else in the vicinity was well and fully understood and much talked of. A test case in the courts was for a time threatened, but nothing came of it.[12]

≈≈≈

Perhaps this was so because any such steps were for the moment quite overshadowed by an even bolder environment-transforming scheme soon set in motion on the river's easterly side, the Sutter Basin project. For the next five years it would set off an explosively angry and ultimately violent controversy. Its basic concept, which sprang, once more, from the fertile brain of General B. S. Alexander, was to emulate RD 108 by halting all Sacramento River overflows into the whole of the Sutter Basin, thus drying out its tens of thousands of acres of swamplands for agriculture. This ambitious goal called, first, for erecting a levee-dam that would shut off the huge floodtime outflow of the Sacramento River through Butte Slough and down into Sutter Basin, thus forcing those waters to stay in the Sacramento's channel. To keep them there, a levee would be built on the Sacramento's east bank beginning at Butte Slough and running about forty miles down river to about opposite Knight's Landing. Thus, as the eastside paralleling project to RD 108, the Sutter Basin project would realize Alexander's concept for the Sacramento River in this region by enclosing it on both sides within levees. The attempt was actually going to be made to force the Sacramento to carry all of its waters, even in floodtime, in one channel.

The projected levee-dam to close off Butte Slough would run west from the flanks of Sutter Buttes, from a point a quarter of a mile north of the hamlet of West Butte (on the east-west Pass Road, which runs through the Buttes). About a mile long, the levee-dam would run directly across and close off Butte Slough and tie into the levee of RD 70 a quarter of a mile north of Mawson Bridge, on Pass Road. A culvert in the levee-dam would allow water from Butte Sink itself to continue flowing on down into Sutter Basin, but direct Sacramento overflow through Butte Slough would be shut out.[13]

The moving spirit behind the ambitious Sutter Basin project was Ohio-born William H. Parks, the Colusa-area swampland owner earlier mentioned. Parks was a large man of powerful character, somber, heavily bearded, an entrepreneur of large vision and very great determination and persistence. He had arrived in California during the Gold Rush of 1849, had mined along the Yuba River for a time, and had then turned to raising stock for the price their meat fetched in the mines. Within four years of his arrival in California he had undertaken the extraordinary feat of twice returning to the midwestern states to bring livestock across the intervening plains and deserts and sell them in the mining towns, an incredible adventure, a highly dangerous one that required extraordinary courage and endurance.

In the spring of 1850, looking for a place to raise his cattle, he had taken up land in northwestern Sutter County, on the west side of Sutter Buttes, building his home near the hamlet of West Butte on Pass Road. For years he tended his herds, which grazed out in the grasslands and along the tule rushes in Butte Sink and Sutter Basin. In the mid-1860s, when the price of cattle plummeted, he added flocks of sheep. When in 1868 the Green Act opened the swamplands to purchase, he acquired, like Levi Foss Moulton, tens of thousands of acres lying in the tule swamps that paralleled the Sacramento.[14]

The 1870s, as we will see, would witness Parks at the center of a raging controversy set off by his Sutter Basin project. Later, in the 1880s this classic Gilded Age entrepreneur would emerge prominently in statewide politics as a dominating, strong-willed Republican Speaker of the State Assembly battling for a state-financed program of flood control in the Sacramento Valley. For his pains, he would be vilified as the archetypical representative of California's swampland owners, who together were regularly condemned in the Democratic press as thieving corruptionists.

Parks's progress toward this condition of statewide notoriety began in March 1871 when, with immense holdings of tule-choked lands to reclaim, he traveled fifteen miles eastward across the Valley to the courthouse in Yuba City, there to appear before the Sutter County Board of Supervisors. His purpose: to ask its formal approval for the Sutter Basin project. That county, it will be remembered, had in 1868 gotten special legislation from the state that authorized it to form levee districts to protect the county from overflow, leading to the creation of Levee District 1 and the erection of the Sutter County Levee. This unusual law had a unique provision in it, one not duplicated in the swampland legislation under which RD 108 and RD 70 were formed. It allowed the county to tax not only land values, as it gathered funds to pay for the building of levees, but the personal property, the private wealth and possessions, of all people living within the boundaries of any district formed for this purpose, whether or not they received any direct benefit. Thus, a levee project within Sutter County's boundaries could raise much more money than would normally be the case.[15]

Parks asked that under this legislation the Sutter supervisors create Levee District 5 to mount his great project, the supervisors themselves serving as its trustees. His proposal not only had the authority of General B. S. Alexander behind it, it was backed as well by the county's leading civil engineer, County Surveyor J. T. Pennington. A busy man whose name now adorns a county road and a hamlet on the north flanks of Sutter Buttes, Pennington formally presented the petition, which called for a district encompassing most of Sutter Basin, a princely domain of some 123,000 acres (excluding that included within RD 70), only a portion of which would include Parks' swamplands. Pennington himself was ordered to prepare the specific reclamation plan, and on April 3, 1871 he submitted his proposal. He would build levees around the entire Sutter Basin, with "Dams across Butte Creek, and Butte Creek Slough . . . the section of levee connecting them to be six feet above high water mark and eight feet wide on top." And so, on this day, it was ordered.[16]

Protests immediately erupted, since the project if built would close off an entire overflow basin. Leading the assault was Yuba City's *Weekly Sutter Banner*, a strongly Democratic paper that for years into the future would growl and snap at the swampland owners, and especially at the person of William H. Parks. The *Banner* condemned the scheme as impractical and ruinously expensive. Because it would back up huge volumes of floodwater denied their usual exit through Butte Slough, the project, warned the paper's editor, Judge Hurburt, would drown out everyone else nearby. It would create a choke in the Butte Slough area and force the water to pool far upstream. Meanwhile, by cutting off the normal flow, it would dry out those who lived below, where people depended on a steady inflow of Butte Slough waters for irrigation. For eight months of the year, he insisted, Butte Slough carried water from the Sacramento, while in floodtimes it carried fully one-third of the river's flow.[17]

On July 15, 1871 the supervisors then moved decisively ahead by letting a contract for Levee District 5 to erect a levee along the east bank of the Sacramento River from Butte Slough down to a point opposite Knight's Landing. On August 5th, they took the final step of adopting Pennington's detailed plan for a levee-dam across Butte Creek and Butte Slough, with appropriate flood gates "for drainage and Irrigation in said Levee District No. 5" to allow Butte Creek waters, coming down from Butte Sink, to flow on through.[18]

≈≈≈

By this time the entrepreneurs backing the huge Colusa Basin district, RD 108, were moving quickly to fend off the probable impact on their project of the Parks' plan. Since their west-bank levee running up from Knight's Landing terminated at Sycamore Slough, this left a wide unprotected gap upstream, some five river-miles long, which extended to a point opposite the mouth of Butte Slough, where levees would stand on the easterly but not westerly side of the river. Floodwaters pooled by Parks' levee-dam and riverbank levees would be deflected through this gap to flow around the upper end of RD 108's levees and down into their properties.

Two months after Sutter County authorized construction of Parks' levee-dam, RD 108's backers responded by leapfrogging beyond it on the west side of the river, that is, by building a new stretch of levee which would run up beyond the northern terminus of Parks' west side levee, thus pushing all the floodwater (when it arrived) back over on the east side. To do this, they formed a new reclamation district, RD 124, which brought an additional 20,000 acres into their project. Lying upstream of RD 108, its purpose was to build a levee beginning at the northerly terminus of the one they had recently completed (which extended up to and across Sycamore Slough) to run up the Sacramento's west bank to a point about seven miles, by the county road, above Colusa.

This would not only guard against Parks' project, it would shut off locations above the town of Colusa where very heavy westward outflows into upper Colusa Basin had always taken place during floodtimes: at Hamilton Bend, four miles in a direct line north of town; and three miles further on, at Seven-Mile (otherwise called Cheney) Slough. The water pouring out of the Sacramento River at these locations had traditionally run westward into the lowlands of Colusa Basin, and thence southward to assault RD 108 from the rear.

At the same time, in the first of many such decisions that in future years they would have to make, RD 108's trustees resolved to raise their levee. When these huge projects were first begun, the trustees appear clearly to have based their plans on the depth of the river's overflow in its natural condition, which by all accounts was in great shallow sheets perhaps one or two feet deep that could pass overbank for miles. Thus, in almost all cases the first levees thrown up were to a height of three feet, which would quickly prove to be not enough as the river, held back only briefly by such lilliputian fortifications, would simply rise on over them and resume its flooding. In the case of RD 108's levees, the decision to increase their height meant laying down an additional three feet of embankment to make the levee six feet high. The levee of the new district, 124, apparently the first such structure ever built from Colusa northward, was to be constructed "as near as practicable to the West Bank" of the Sacramento to a height of five feet, with a four-foot crown.

By early 1871 the Sacramento Valley Reclamation Company, the parent organization that created both RDs 108 and 124, was able to state that the last few miles were then being completed in what had become a levee sixty miles long, running along the Sacramento's west bank from Knight's Landing northward.[19]

Despite these efforts, in the coming years RD 108 (as in practice the combined 108–124 project was henceforth termed) would find that its levee system was a great disappointment. They had invested thousands of dollars, but received only a limited return. The river was simply much larger than their adviser, General Alexander, or apparently they themselves, believed it to be. Their new six-foot levee was not enough. Indeed, many years into the future RD 108 would still be struggling to find the answer to the question, how to halt overflows into their district? Almost twenty years after A. H. Rose and his colleagues had formed RD 108, we find the *Colusa Sun* remarking, during a flood, that the huge reclamation district was, as usual, badly inundated: "The landowners of 108 expect to be drowned out about two years in five. They fight the water like heroes."[20]

≈≈≈

East of the river and north of Parks' project, Levi Foss Moulton watched all of this leapfrogging of levees up the Sacramento River with alarm. As each project responded to each other's threat by building further upstream and thus outflanking the other side, he, Moulton, was going to wind up getting all the backed-up water dumped onto his own property. Worse, RD 108's new northward extension of its levee seven miles upstream from Colusa would push water directly over onto his land, which lay on the opposite side of the river from the new levees. He had been outflanked.

So he joined the game himself. In December 1870, just when RD 108 was first getting underway, he and neighbors had formed a district (RD 115) of some 16,000 acres that lay back from the riverbank two or three miles, paralleling the stream from a point opposite Hamilton Bend to another opposite Princeton, for a stretch of some fourteen miles.[21] They did not, however, get going in building a levee until spurred by the new large projects downstream. In 1871, to create a broader financial base, Moulton and neighbors brought RD 128 into being, enclosing 7,000 acres in the lowlands due east of Colusa.[22] Then in October of 1873 Moulton began surveying a riverbank levee from Butte Slough far upriver to the head of eastside overflow on the Sacramento, near Chico Creek, a distance of about forty miles.[23]

His final project, however, was not so ambitious. He envisioned, ultimately, a levee beginning right at Butte Slough and running up the eastside riverbank to the lower end of the Llano Seco Grant, eight miles north of Butte City, which as it happens is the very location where the Sacramento River's levees now end. "The map of the proposed levee," Will Green of the *Colusa Sun* remarked, "shows that if a similar levee should be built on the west side of the river [north of Colusa], the two would be nearly one mile apart." Thereafter, Green was regularly to agitate for "mile apart" levees in this reach of the river, a plan that actually made allowance for the river's heavier, more rapid, more meandering flow in this section. (The present levee system there essentially embodies this fundamental idea.)[24]

In 1874 and 1875, still looking for a stronger base for his project, Moulton established several more swampland reclamation districts: 206, 220, and 253. The first was a 3200-acre tract about two miles southeast of Butte City; the second was composed of land parcels located right along the riverbank, from a mile above Butte City down to the present vicinity of Moulton Weir (it would appear to have encompassed much of what is now Levee District 3); and the third a 6400-acre parcel in the vicinity of Butte Slough. The sum result was that by mid-1875 Moulton had in active existence five swampland reclamation districts—115, 128, 206, 220, and 253—to support the construction of a levee along the eastside riverbank some thirty miles long.[25]

Moulton had already launched construction in the fall of 1874, using $35,000 from the funds of RD 115 and RD 128 held by the Colusa supervisors, that is, from the price he paid to the Board of Supervisors, under the Green Act, for his county-surveyed swamplands. The supervisors, in turn, had in accordance with that act held his money in a special fund to be drawn on later for construction. Six years later, in 1880, Moulton was reported to say that "Excepting a few short reaches and some unimportant sloughs, our levees from just above Butte Slough to Llano Seco Grant have been completed," the total investment of the landowners, in addition to the funds returned from the County, being $75,000.[26]

≈≈≈

Like every other levee-builder in the Valley in this initial era of mutually destructive laissez-faire and general ignorance of the Sacramento's actual flows, in later years Moulton would see his painfully created embankment overtopped again and again and deeply crevassed by later floods. However, in the soaring confidence of his midlife years he had succeeded in fundamentally altering the physical nature of things in this midvalley region. Indeed, the present alignment of the Sacramento's eastside levees, north of Colusa, is essentially that which Moulton, at great cost and effort over an intense cycle of years, had conceived of and laid out in the busy, entrepreneurial 1870s. The history of flood management in the Sacramento Valley shows that few things are so resistant to later change as the alignments of a levee system once it is constructed. Landowners resist change in its route with implacable tenacity. So, in time, Moulton's creation would eventually become so fixed and accepted a part of the landscape that the levees became officially regarded as the "natural banks" of the Sacramento River.[27]

Moulton's great levee did not, however, do the entire job he had had in mind: completely excluding Sacramento River floodwaters from the eastside. In time it would finally be accepted that denying the Sacramento access to the eastside in high water times was literally impossible. It is determined to send its floodwaters out into Butte Sink, as it has for millennia; large breaks in the eastside levee stood open year after year. In the early 1930s, at two locations, large weirs on the easterly bank of the Sacramento were permanently opened out in Moulton's levee to allow for controlled outflows. One, called Moulton Weir, lies about a dozen miles above Colusa at a point where a large long-time break existed. The other, Colusa Weir, opens broadly in a location just across and slightly upstream from the town of Colusa.[28] A banquet was held at the scene of Moulton Weir when it was completed in March 1932, and speeches in the open air lauded the U.S. Army Corps of Engineers and the flood control plan that had produced the structure. "We are pleased with the work," said Ben F. Gould, a farmer whose holdings were nearby. "We are to live behind these ramparts and may now sleep peacefully and restfully for the first time in our lives."[29]

Not entirely. There would be more high waters and more bouts with floodwaters in the future, but the long line of farms and ranches which now runs up the eastside of the Sacramento in Colusa County does in fact lie reasonably well-protected behind high levees that no longer, because of the weirs, stand in such danger of sudden breaks and crevassing. And they have at their core the original embankment that Moulton had dreamed of and had built. His vision and his determined efforts to realize it, like those of his competing entrepreneurs downriver, left behind an enduring legacy: a profoundly reshaped river environment.

C H A P T E R

The Parks Dam War: The North and the South in Arms Again *1871–1876*

"I never thought I'd be so scared of water," said Greg Lawrence. . . . [A propane tank was on fire] and [he] swam to a neighbor's house and pounded on the second story window. . . . Now the flaming tank was floating loose. . . . He got away from it, but he was caught in the creek . . . and a . . . picnic table . . . bore down on him. . . . "I thought I was dead." He swam as hard as he could and was rescued by a boat.

> *Carl Nolte,* San Francisco Chronicle, *February 24, 1986. Quoted in* Rivers of Fear, *pp., 125–126.*

When Levi Foss Moulton was trying to exclude the Sacramento River from the eastside north of Butte Slough, William H. Parks was with enormous energy and determination pursuing his own dream: preventing the river from overflowing into Butte Basin. The key to the whole project was the levee-dam—"Parks Dam," as it was universally called—which he proposed to build from the highlands of the Sutter Buttes right across the wide channelway of Butte Slough to tie into the existing levees of Reclamation District 70. This, with a riverbank levee running many miles downstream from the Slough's mouth, aimed at keeping all of the Sacramento's floodwaters within its main channel.

Before Parks' dam was even completed across Butte Slough, Will Green of the *Colusa Sun* was publishing his fears that the project would drastically raise flood levels along the Sacramento River above, below, and to the west of the dam—and therefore put everyone else in the region outside of Levee District 5 in much increased danger.

An idealized, classically Victorian drawing of the farm and residence of George Ohleyer, Yuba City. For twenty years beginning in the mid-1870s Democrat Ohleyer, leader of the Anti-Debris Association and editor of the Sutter County Farmer, *carried on the struggle to shut down the hydraulic mines and to keep a close watch on them following their limited revival under federal controls in the 1890s.*
Courtesy: California State Library.

Parks' dam, he warned, together with the other riverbank levees being planned for construction along both sides of the Sacramento River upstream and downstream from Colusa would soon "make a very great difference at this place."[1]

Without question, Green and his neighbors faced a sobering prospect. Sacramento River floodwaters, once experienced, were the stuff of nightmares, and when they receded they left behind devastating financial loss. Who would protect those threatened? Who would indemnify those damaged? As it stood, there was no supervising public agency created by the legislature to which a Will Green or anyone else could turn to appeal for aid. A cruel irony lay in this fact. The very swampland reclamation policy built into the 1868 state legislation for which Green claimed authorship contained decisively and unarguably in its spirit and letter the principle that all those forming a levee-building district were henceforth free to consider only their own interest, not that of the general welfare, when they decided what to do to reclaim their land. The implementing of this policy, Green was now finding, had seriously disturbing and unanticipated results.

The unpalatable fact was that William Parks was proceeding in full accordance with public policy as it had been quite recently enacted. It was true that the actual putting into effect of these principles along both sides of the Sacramento in Colusa and Sutter counties immediately set up head-on conflicts of interest between entrepreneurs, conflicts that caught the community at large in between. Nothing, however, could apparently be done within the existing legal context to fend off what Parks had in mind.

Will Green was driven, now, to begin forming a new definition of the situation, a definition founded in the conviction that in some way not yet clear, the community at large had to begin regulating what people did with the Sacramento River, that is, that laissez-faire in a single hydrographic environment was unworkable. The Valley simply could not be fragmented into many small principalities, each of them doing whatever they pleased in their levee-building, if the people living in that Valley were to win freedom from the fear of flood. This realization, as we have earlier seen, was also in these years beginning to dawn in the minds of those who lived on the other side of the Valley, in and around Yuba City, but it would remain special knowledge. An intensive learning process was going on in the middle sections of the Sacramento Valley, but many years would pass before the rest of the state would acquire the new understanding.

Thus, the context within which mid-Valley people had to work was not encouraging. The time for political coalition building in the legislature to get new river policies enacted, as in the legislatively active 1860s, had passed, for those injured by existing arrangements were in a small minority. After all, in the Green Act of 1868 the entrepreneurs had gotten what they wanted—carte blanche to take up swamplands and reclaim them in any way they saw fit—and there were simply not any longer the votes to get the legislature to once again take up the complex task of rethinking what to do with the Sacramento River.

Will Green, however, was determined to *do* something. What he did, in fact, was to lose patience with the delays and frustrations in the democratic process and to push beyond it. This was not, in these years, a rare and unusual response. Americans in the nineteenth century, especially those living in frontier or near-frontier conditions, were often unable to accept the constraints of republican, constitutional government. The country was in some ways a bubbling pot of local conflicts and turmoils. People seemed determined to take the law into their own hands, whether in vigilante outbreaks or mob attacks on hated ethnic minorities or in the South's appalling lynch law.

Colusa's Will Green was, in short, ready to give way to a traditional frontiersman's impulse (an impulse, indeed, for which Southerners were legendary): negating the law by violence. In brief, he set out to create a new de facto public policy by extralegal means. Late in November 1871, we observe Southern Democrat Will Green, angry at Ohio Republican William Parks and genuinely anxious at what would happen to his town and its rural neighbors, issuing a long editorial appeal calling for someone to bust Parks' dam.[2]

Open conflict over the Sacramento River was drawing nearer, bringing with it overtones of the civil war between the North and the South, only six years in the past. Indeed, perhaps Green flung himself so bitterly into this campaign in part because through it he could lash back at a Yankee. Parks and his allies, meanwhile, continued to push ahead, playing their role in the opening confrontation. Two weeks after Green published his appeal, Sutter County Surveyor Pennington reported to the county supervisors on December 6, 1871 that Parks' earthen-embankment dam was in place: "That portion of the Levee," he stated, "for the protection of Levee District No. 5 from Overflow from the Base of Butte Mountains to the Sacramento River is completed." He had had the upstream side of the embankment thatched with willow cuttings to protect it against wave wash, and now, with an eye possibly to Will Green, he recommended that caretakers be placed on the dam. So it was ordered, and Pennington was appointed the project's superintendent.[3]

Soon the winter rains of late 1871 and early 1872 were falling and water was rising before the dam, for a flood was building up and the Sacramento River was trying, by means of its usual easterly outflows into Butte Sink and through Butte Slough, to send a huge proportion of its swelling current down into Sutter Basin. As the pool formed in front of the dam and flood levels upstream were pushed higher, tempers got hotter. During the night of December 27, 1871 Will Green's appeal was answered. Masked men arrived at the structure, overpowered the guards, and cut the structure at two places between Butte Slough and the highlands bordering Sutter Buttes.

Some five hundred feet of the dam quickly washed out. A rushing torrent of water poured down the formerly dammed-off southerly reach of Butte Slough into Sutter Basin with such force that it destroyed long sections of the still-building easterly levee of RD 70, which by this early date in its painfully proceeding evolution ran along some three and a half miles of Butte Slough's west bank.[4] In the following months the farms of RD 70 would slowly emerge from the inundation released on them by the district's shattered levees, and in the spring and summer of 1872 its people would toil at rebuilding many thousands of feet of embankment on the lands of farmers Tarke and Hoke. As they labored, dark things were doubtless said of neighbor William H. Parks, over in his high and dry ranch house at nearby West Butte.

The flood of January 1872 had not been a brief affair; it had kept mounting higher and higher. By January 6, the mail from Marysville had had to be carried for miles over open water in a small boat to reach Colusa (much of this journey being over the now flooded lands of Levee District 5), for "great oceans of water," Green observed, "are to be seen in every direction from town." The Sacramento River reached its highest mark at Colusa since American settlement.[5] How high the flood would have reached if Parks' dam had not been broken, could only be imagined. As it was, the town of Colusa once again passed through a flood season without itself going underwater, though later in 1872 it set about building a substantial levee.[6]

William Parks and the supervisors of Sutter County were as determined to have their way as Will Green. Would they give in to local vigilantes, Southern-inspired? Certainly not. The supervisors moved quickly to issue a contract for repairing the dam. Thereafter, it was built even stronger and higher, becoming a far more formidable structure than before. In early February 1872, angry farmers and townsfolk gathered in a large meeting at the county courthouse in Colusa to fire off a biting protest to the state legislature.

> You will please bear in mind [it said] that the bed of the tules is about eighteen feet lower than the natural banks of the Sacramento river, [and that in flood times Butte Slough carries a volume of water] equal to twice that carried by the rivers. . . . [Thus Parks' dam causes] the waters to rise and flow back over a large area of high land, doing great damage thereby to the owners . . . who have cultivated them for a number of years, they having always been considered as lands not subject to overflow.

A law, the Colusa petitioners insisted, must be passed to make it illegal to build dams across the natural outlets of rivers.[7]

This, of course, was an impossible appeal. The furthest thing from the mind of the California legislature in the 1870s or at any time in the future was enacting statutes that sweepingly decreed that in all circumstances the natural environment must be left alone, though in 1876 a bill declaring specifically that no dam could be put across the mouth of Butte Slough would at least make it through the assembly.[8]

Colusa's real answer came four months after this appeal had been sent to the legislature, when in June 1872 the landholders of Levee District 5 voted to proceed with completing their project. They authorized the issuance of bonds to pay for construction to the (then astonishing) total of $512,000. (By 1877, this would rise to $588,000.) When the strengthened Parks dam and levee was completed, a small barracks was put up on it to house its defenders.[9]

The year 1873 passed quietly, with little flooding, until the very last days of December. Then the rivers began rising once more. By early January 1874, a deep pool was again forming in front of Parks' dam and heavy damage was occurring to the lands upstream. On the property of an immigrant German farmer, Justus Laux, on the north bank of Butte Slough just half a mile in from its mouth, water was standing from four to seven feet deep, and had been from about Christmas time.[10] On Christmas day, Judge Hurburt, editor of the *Banner* in Yuba City, had made his way across the Valley to visit Parks' dam, which lay a mile downstream on Butte Slough from Laux's property. He noted that the "water in the basin above the dam was nearly eight feet above the lower side," and that there was "very bad seepage near the floodgate . . . from which enough water [was running] to be considered dangerous." When the river was rising, Hurburt noted, "the water from the [Sacramento] comes into the basin with great force from [Butte] . . . slough, running parallel with and close to the dam."[11]

The rains continued, sweeping in from the southwest day after day, and the great Sacramento River continued to swell and to push at Parks' strengthened barrier in its immemorial path. At four in the afternoon on the 19th of January 1874, while the storm raged, the water upstream from the embankment was still rising, and a full force of men was laboring frantically to save it, the structure suddenly gave way at the floodgate just east of Butte Creek. Fifty yards of the dam went out bodily. The immense backed-up pool drained rapidly away, boiling down through the crevasse—and the Sacramento River at Colusa, which had risen ominously to within a few inches of its highest recorded flood stage, and had been running over elevated banks above the town that formerly had been considered above the highest water, began to fall. By the time the first night had passed, it had dropped a foot. "We are glad," Green observed truculently five days after the dam broke, "[that] our citizens were saved the trouble of cutting it."[12]

A rash of protest meetings against the second rebuilding of Parks' dam now broke out. The January issues of the *Weekly Sutter Banner* in Yuba City were filled with attacks on Parks and his project. These were of course the corruption-filled 1870s, when in the noisome years of Ulysses Grant's presidency a series of national scandals alarmed the country and disgraced the Republican Party. Chief among them were the frauds connected with the building of the Union Pacific transcontinental railroad, in which the owners of the road engaged in special dealing, that is, they formed a separate construction company, the Credit Mobilier, through which they issued swollen construction contracts to themselves, thus diverting the railroad's funds into their own pockets. The contracts for building Parks' dam had in the same fashion been issued to Parks himself, by the Sutter supervisors, and now his project, with its $510,000 in debts, was condemned by the *Banner* as the "Credit Mobiler" [sic] of Sutter County.[13]

Soon another petition was making its way to the legislature warning that body that there would be bloodshed if Parks' dam were repaired again and angrily rejecting the idea that the Sacramento River could be made to carry all of its water within high artificial banks. Rather, as Will Green had long before maintained and the petitioners now insisted, the only answer was to accept the easterly overflows of the Sacramento in the Colusa vicinity as irresistible natural facts and build a large canal down through Sutter Basin to channel them, by this means opening up the rest of the Basin for agriculture without harming the general community. Three years of visionary bungling, the petitioners said, had gone for nothing save to fasten enormous debts on the taxed landholders. At a mass meeting gathered in Yuba City on the 23rd of February 1874, Levee District 5 was condemned as a "gigantic wrong," and a "farce and swindle."[14]

After some months, however, plans for a second rebuilding surfaced. In July the dogged Sutter supervisors again accepted a plan for "repairing the break in Butte Slough levee . . . and also for the construction of a bulkhead on the outside of the Levee East of Butte Slough." Two weeks later a bid to construct the works from entrepreneur William H. Parks was accepted.[15]

≈≈≈

At this point, Levi Foss Moulton decided to join the battle against fellow-Republican William H. Parks, though to reach his ends he had no interest in taking up the vigilante appeal to extralegal violence that Will Green had so readily issued. That might be suitable for a Democrat, he may have said to himself, but not for a law-abiding Yankee Republican. At least since the days of Andrew Jackson, in the 1830s, Whig-Republicans in the North had condemned the turbulent, violence-prone spirit that seemed to reside in the Democratic breast, producing ruckuses in the saloons and riots and mobbings in Northern city streets. Whigs in Jackson's time, and their descendants the Republicans in Lincoln's, thought of themselves as the exemplars of law and order in American life, the civilizing people who were trying to teach their disorderly countrymen the ways of peaceful, well-mannered, civil society. Lincoln himself was appalled at vigilante violence, it worried him deeply as a force sure to destroy America's still-new democracy, and he often publicly deplored it.[16]

Moulton's campaign against Parks, then, would not be in Will Green's style, but would be entirely within the law. Anything else would go against everything his kind of American believed in. Since the democratic process was not producing the desired result, since the legislature was not disposed to intervene, Moulton decided to bring a new player into the controversy. He would appeal to the court system, a distinctly nondemocratic institution where results would not flow from coalition-building, but, he hoped, from the application of reason and the law to the facts of the situation. Policy making by fiat, always possible in the American constitutional system in which the courts are so powerful, was now in the offing.

Characteristically, Moulton took an innovative tack. He would not appeal to the courts for relief under the centuries-old provisions of the common law. That is, he would not ask for civil damages, being financially compensated for the harm done to his property. Rather, he reached for a much more powerful weapon that the courts possessed. Under the law of equity, a system also many centuries old that was distinct from the common law, American courts had inherited from those in Britain the ancient, predemocratic power of medieval kings, still fully alive though little used, to issue injunctions quashing any activity found to be gravely destructive of the public welfare, whether or not it was in conformity with statute (legislature-enacted) law. To enforce such edicts, the courts could rely on the equally ancient sanction of "contempt of court," in other words, contempt of the king, with its almost unlimited options for fine and imprisonment. (Since about the 1860s the law of equity had in many states, as in California, been merged with the common law, so that the same judges and courts made use of and enforced both systems of law.[17])

This powerful, indeed almost ultimate, weapon in the armamentarium of policy making had not formerly been brought into flood management issues in California, for until now the universal impulse had been, in appropriate republican fashion, to look to the popularly elected legislature to enact, in statute form, all policies needed to resolve the country's problems. The courts were not well thought of, especially since the U.S. Supreme Court had intervened boldly and unprecedentedly in national policy making by ruling, in its ill-fated *Dred Scott* decision of 1857, that Congress had no power whatever over slavery.[18] For a number of years, during and after the Civil War, American courts had kept to a low profile, busying themselves primarily with ordinary property-dispute lawsuits, the particular subject of the common law. However, to legally sophisticated men like Levi Moulton the potential impact of the power of injunction was very great, if the courts could be persuaded to unlimber it in the direction he had in mind, and he resolved to spur them into action.

His specific request: he would ask for an injunction forbidding William Parks to rebuild his dam on the simple ground that the waters backed up by that structure flooded others' property more deeply and longer than would otherwise occur; in other words, the dam was harmful to the general welfare. Thus, by judicial decree if not by legislative statute, he would win establishment of a crucially important public policy: that Butte Slough was to be kept open, allowing the Sacramento River to overflow freely by that route into Sutter Basin.

In setting up an appeal for injunctive relief, Moulton was taking a historic step in the water management history of the Valley. His lawsuit would be the spark that in the ensuing years would deflect many others in the Valley away from the frustrating and usually deadlocked democratic process to the courts, in order to win new public policies by judicial fiat. This set off a rising storm of river management and flood control litigation in the Sacramento Valley. Something about the courts' almost biblical powers, if they chose to use them, to strike down the unrighteous in a bold, sweeping, magisterial decree, handed down as it were from on high, issued in the name of the much-abused general welfare, and won without the endless delays of the legislative process, had enormous appeal. As the people of the Valley asked the courts to intervene with growing frequency in the 1870s and 1880s, the cumulative result was to give that ancient, predemocratic institution the decisive and dominating role in making and presiding over flood control policy in the state of California, as it generally has also taken and exercises it in the much wider and even more complex and pervasive question of water rights in the western states.[19]

With the support of a group of backers whose land also lay upstream from Parks' dam, Moulton proceeded in October 1874 to get things in motion. He had, of course, a legitimate claim of action, for his own land, about 17,000 acres of it according to his later account, was harmed by Parks' scheme and had for that matter been deeply flooded before the dam's most recent rupture. However, he gave the undertaking a special twist. For whatever reasons, he decided not to put forward the action in his own name. Rather, he seems to have believed that the suit would have a better chance if it were filed by a much more ordinary person with small holdings whose land was close enough to Parks' dam to be demonstrably and unarguably damaged by the ponding that structure produced.

He found his catspaw in the modest personage of the German

immigrant farmer Justus Laux, a man of numerous progeny and siblings whose descendants still farm Colusa County land. The point was for Laux to agree to sue William H. Parks in his own name, Moulton and his backers paying Laux's costs and something in addition. The great landowner was himself, however, too grand a figure to speak to Laux personally. Rather, he sent his attorney to make arrangements. When to conclude the agreement Moulton and Laux later arrived in the same room, in Moulton's lordly fashion he continued to rely on intermediaries to go back and forth, conveying his wishes. After all, in the spring of 1873 the *Colusa Sun* had announced in its columns for all to see that Moulton's holdings had reached the princely total of 30,429 acres, while Laux was a small holder whose acreage reached to only 80 acres, who spoke only broken English, and was called "Gus."[20]

After his October agreement with Laux, for the next three months Moulton threw himself into a whirlwind of activity preparing his case. He hired a prominent Sacramento lawyer, Creed Haymond, who later in the legislature would take a major role in water policy matters; personally made all necessary land surveys (he had earlier been county surveyor); and traveled all over the mid-Valley region making arrangements. Meanwhile, on October 21, 1874, Judge F. L. Hatch, county judge of Colusa County, issued a preliminary restraining order against Levee District 5's reconstruction of its dam, pending settlement of the suit.[21]

Parks and the Sutter County supervisors were not, however, dissuaded. The intervention of the courts into all of this was, after all, a novel proceeding, so their moral authority was perhaps not as yet established, especially in a case such as this one where the project was otherwise entirely within the provisions of statute law. Parks ignored what was going on and continued to rebuild his dam.

On the 21st of November 1874, the *Banner* described the embankment of the dam to be "from four to nine feet above high water mark, with a slope on the outside of four to one, with two large and well-constructed gates for the purposes of irrigation and drainage. The one at Butte Slough . . . is built of brick and hydraulic cement, with cast iron doors and wrought iron frames, and has a capacity sufficient to irrigate the entire district in about thirty days." Levee District 5 had also constructed a similar drain far to the south which passed through the district's east-bank Sacramento River levee opposite the town of Knight's Landing, its purpose being to discharge back into the river any surplus irrigation waters that would have been let down into Sutter Basin through the gates in Parks' dam.

Meanwhile, all preparations for Moulton's case against Parks built toward their climax, the suit itself being scheduled to be heard in the last days of December 1874. However, when that occasion arrived it was immediately halted by a sensational development. Those who gathered expectantly in Colusa County courthouse on Monday, December 28, 1874 to listen to what promised to be a lively trial considering the two strong-minded men principally concerned were dumbfounded to learn that the canny Parks had quite outmaneuvered Moulton. Not long before the trial was to begin he had quietly prevailed on Gus Laux to sell him his farm, so that he, William Parks, was now both plaintiff and defendant in the suit! There was nothing for it: the case had to be dismissed.

For farmer Laux the event was an incredible and quite disorganizing windfall. For his modest eighty acres, said to be worth about $600, he had received from Parks the astonishing sum of $6000 in a box filled with gold coin, all of which he spent in one wild and bibulous day, to his wife's mountainous anger. For his part, Levi Moulton was infuriated—and he immediately filed two lawsuits: one against Laux to get the money back he had spent on the case, the other in his own name, finally, against Parks to plead for an injunction against the dam. He would lose the former, and the latter, filed on January 13, 1875 in Colusa's County court, a branch of the Tenth District Court, would not be decided for more than a year.[22]

Now, however, the enormous Valley-wide flood of January 1875, an event of historic proportions since it flooded Marysville, had arrived. Once again Parks' dam was under heavy pressure, as for many miles north and south of Colusa the Sacramento poured heavily through openings in its east bank and through the wide opening mouth of Butte Slough, all of this water piling up before Levee District 5's barrier. A force of thirty men labored on the dam through a howling north wind, on Monday, the 25th of January. Before the dam the turbulent, wind-whipped water pooled seventeen feet deep, creating a backed-up lake spreading fifteen miles northward—but the crest of Parks' dam was still three feet above the swells.

By Monday night and into the early hours of Tuesday, however, the waves striking the dam were so fierce that all its guards had been driven off duty. The wind sheered off to a new tack that drove the water even more sharply against the dam, and at 1:15 A.M. the embankment gave way at its west end, within a short distance of its juncture with RD 70's works. Some four hundred feet of the dam swept out immediately, the gap later increasing in size. As soon as the rupture occurred, floodwater began rushing down into Sutter Basin, engulfing several houses inside the levee in a sea of water reaching to their roofs, and overflows elsewhere halted. And so the "huge anaconda," exulted Will Green in the *Sun*, "that stretched its long and ugly body from the Buttes to the Sacramento [is gone]."[23]

Through the rest of the winter of 1875 Parks' shattered dam lay quiet, Butte Slough flowing unimpeded through the dam's great crevasse. Spring arrived, and once more William Parks, indomitable man, began stirring. Soon, the Sutter County surveyor was recommending reconstruction plans to the supervisors, and Parks was asking for the authority to rebuild for a third time. Petitions poured in on the supervisors protesting the project, and on June 3, 1875, in their capacity as trustees for Levee District 5, they finally denied Parks' request.

Once again, however, he had outmaneuvered his enemies. Probably anticipating this eventuality, on the 7th of May he had put in a formal request that he be allowed to form a Swamp Land District covering the area in which the dam was located. Such a step, by creating under the Green Act a district entirely under his own authority, would free Parks from having always to go to the Sutter supervisors for approval of his works. Such districts, as we have seen, had only to fulfill certain legal requirements as to the land included in the district, being thereafter perfectly free to build whatever they wished on their own authority. On the 16th of June, the supervisors had no choice but to approve formation of Swamp Land District 226, encompassing about 7300 acres of land in both Colusa and Sutter counties.[24]

The third rebuilding of Parks' dam now proceeded. By late October 1875, Will Green was noting that "the great Parks dam has again been completed. This time they say they have it strong enough to resist wind and water," building in also a new associated feature that would entirely close off Butte Slough, this time directly at its mouth.[25] The whole structure, as it happened, was quickly tested. The rivers were high early in January 1876, and the entire cycle was ready to start up again. A huge pool of water once more formed in front of Parks' dam. The unfortunate people of RD 70, whose fate had for years been pushed this way and that by Parks' various projects, saw that their own levee near the head of Butte Slough, which had been put under great pressure by the new barrier across that stream at its mouth, was washing badly. Then it gave way and water rushed down over their farmlands, washing homes away.

This new catastrophe, once more brought on the farmers of RD 70 by Parks' scheme, was too much to bear. On Sunday, the 8th of January, families living within RD 70 and along the banks of the Sacramento north and south of Butte Slough formed a naval war party to strike back at William H. Parks. At about 4 P.M. that afternoon a force of between thirty and forty armed and masked men arrived at Parks' dam in boats, overpowered the guards once more and put them under watch, sequestered their guns, and set about digging two small trenches a hundred feet apart to start water running over the dam. (The sheriff of Sutter County had earlier been on the scene, having been dispatched there by Parks beforehand because of rumors, but just before the masked party arrived he had left.) Soon a gap a hundred feet wide was opening; by Thursday, it had widened to seven hundred feet, and Parks' dam was again destroyed. "It was natural," wrote Green in the *Sun*, "that something should be done."[26]

≈≈≈

By this time, on January 3, 1876, the long-awaited trial of *Moulton* v. *Parks* had opened in the District Court in Colusa County courthouse before Judge Phil. W. Keyser, who had been brought over from the Yuba City branch of the Tenth District Court to hear the case. As it happened, the mid-1870s offered a welcoming judicial environment for Moulton's plea for an injunction, for America's courts, in these post-Civil War years, had their own reform agenda. It was an agenda with crucial implications for a pleading in a local state court, such as Moulton's, which asked severe new restrictions on business enterprise in the name of the general welfare. Before the Civil War, American courts, in what is termed their "instrumentalist" phase, had stood back on principle from much interference with entrepreneurs. The idea was to release them in every way possible to develop the economy. Even before the war began, however, a new mood was moving in, a fundamental shift in ideas about the law and its role in a democratic society.

American life in the postwar Gilded Age was not, in reality, a pleasing spectacle. Rampant corruption in Northern cities, a rising crime wave, mobbings and lynchings in the South, shameful behavior in jury-dominated criminal proceedings which threatened to make it impossible to prosecute the accused, ballot-box stuffing, rank scandals from city halls to the very porches of the White House, the rise of greedy robber barons in commerce, business, and banking who in the current laissez-faire conditions exploited the public at large to their own gross profit: all of it was alarming. Americans in general despaired of the future of their experiment in republican self-government, lawyers and judges grew deeply distrustful of the people at large and of the very concept of democracy, and they were skeptical of business enterprise.[27]

In place of "instrumentalism," a new judicial philosophy of "formalism" moved into the courts, that is, a concept that the law should not be regarded merely as an instrument, a servant, of business enterprise and of the people, it should be thought of as a powerful structure of justice inherited from the far-distant past, formally and independently existing, which should guide and restrain and instruct. In this view the courts and the law should not keep a low profile, allowing the community and business people to do largely what they wished, they should assume once more a majestic, supervisory, tutelary role.

They should, in brief, begin protecting the American people from their own democratic excesses. Judges felt free to be far more critical of legislatures than before and far more ready, under the principle and procedure of "judicial review," to treat the products of legislatures, their statute law, with skepticism. They were ready, sometimes with an almost cavalier readiness, to declare statute law on various grounds unconstitutional. A process was well underway in which the statutes enacted by legislatures would be "ordinarily regarded as isolated or sporadic encrustations upon the rational body of judge-made common law."

Judges turned often, instead, to apply ancient universal maxims of justice in human life, such as that of the general welfare, an admittedly broad and undefined concept that would nonetheless begin to be used in a wide variety of ways with much greater frequency than in the past as a basis for striking down statutes. "Judges of this [formalist] persuasion," observe constitutional historians Harold M. Hyman and William M. Wiecek, "tended to magnify their own role from will-less to oracular, to exclude questions of legislators' intent in deciding cases involving public law, and to wrest control from juries in criminal trials when questions of law wanted decision." "Formalism," they remark further, ". . . deified judge-made law as in [the law of] equity."[28]

So inspired, judges not only greatly expanded the practice of judicial review of statute law, they began, particularly in cases involving striking labor unions, to rediscover the law of equity's powerful weapon, the injunction, which they freely put to use to declare labor stoppages an illegal violation of the general welfare. "The injunction," writes Lawrence M. Friedman, the leading historian of American law,

> was an ancient, powerful, and honorable tool of courts of chancery [i.e., equity]. It had infinite possibilities and uses. Its suppleness and strength made it a deadly threat to labor. During a strike, a company might ask for . . . a temporary injunction. Courts . . . had the power to grant these orders quickly, without notice or hearing, if the court was persuaded that delay might irreparably injure the company. There

> was no need for trial by jury. If a union defied the . . . injunction . . . it stood in contempt of court. Hence, officers and members could be summarily punished, even thrown into jail.[29]

It was within this national judicial context that on January 3, 1876 Judge Phil. Keyser began to hear the case before him in Colusa courthouse. Moulton's plea maintained, essentially, that though the existing statute law governing levee-building, the Green Act of 1868, delegated total, plenary authority to landowners to put up whatever levees they wished and empowered them freely to push the Valley's watercourses this way and that, the law was defective and should be ignored. On the ground of the harm Parks' dam was doing to his neighbors in the Valley, his otherwise legal activities should be enjoined.

For years, the people of Colusa and Sutter counties had been wrangling, inconclusively, over this project. With all of that behind them, they must have been astonished at how quickly and decisively Judge Keyser now settled the matter, once and for all. After less than a week of hearing testimony as to the facts of the situation, Judge Keyser announced his preliminary ruling, coming down categorically on the side of Moulton and against Parks. In his formal findings Keyser stated that the dam had in fact put Moulton's land more deeply, and longer, under water than would otherwise have occurred. This was wrongful and must be stopped. On the 4th of March 1876 he followed these words with a perpetual injunction directed not simply against Parks' small principality, Swamp Land District 226, for this might have allowed Parks to form some other kind of legal entity to renew his project; rather, the injunction was directed against Parks personally and against his associates. They were ordered not to construct, maintain, or repair the dam, now or in the future. It was all over.

There was an immediate appeal, but Keyser's decision was confirmed by the Supreme Court of California in March 1878 and reaffirmed later in 1883.[30] Thus, by this action what would have been the law only within the jurisdiction of the Tenth District was made the law statewide. The courts throughout California now had a new and powerful precedent to which they could appeal in support of the concept of the general welfare.

When in later floodtimes great rushes of floodwaters tried to pass through the relatively narrow passage between the easterly levees of RD 70 and the westerly foothills of Sutter Buttes, a space little more than a mile wide, the remains of Parks' dam and levee across that gap, though deeply crevassed and abandoned, continued nonetheless to form a considerable barrier to the water's free flow. Particularly troublesome was the dense willow tree thicket that grew up along its length, descendant of the willow mattress that had been placed on the dam's upstream face to protect it from wave wash. In 1918, more than forty years after Keyser's injunction, state authorities moved in to clear out all but the dam's most resistant elements: its brick irrigation culverts and their steel doors.[31] The remains of these works may still be found a quarter of a mile out in the fields north of Mawson Bridge on Pass Road, buried deep in a quiet thicket of tenacious willow trees, all that now impedes the free flow of floodwaters from Butte Sink down into Sutter Basin.

C H A P T E R

California Mobilizes for a New Assault on the Inland Sea

1878–1880

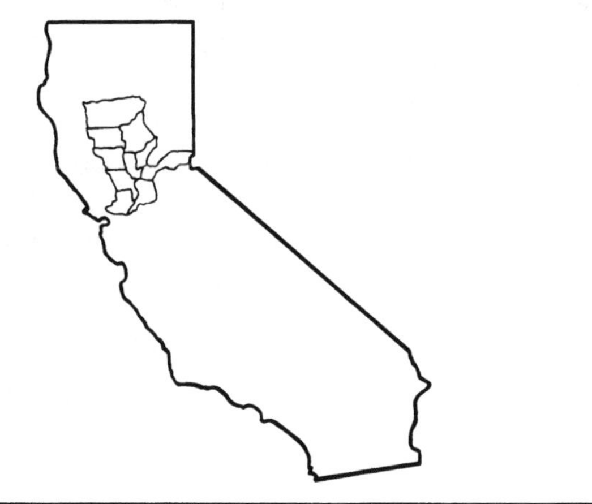

THE CHINESE

Bob Kinzan . . . noted that the people [who lived along the Feather river] . . . thought the danger of flood was over when the Oroville Dam was built upstream. "But I guess you can't say that you can move in between two rivers and not expect some kind of risk, because Mother Nature is going to do what she wants to do."

Carl Nolte, San Francisco Chronicle, *February 24, 1986. Quoted in* Rivers of Fear, *p. 126.*

Late in the 1870s California's politics spectacularly blew apart and then began reassembling in new ways. As the kaleidoscope turned and the various voting groups shifted about in their relations to each other, an unusually flexible and hospitable political context opened out. Windows of opportunity opened up for policy initiatives that had formerly been simply out of the question. In this fluid environment, new coalitions sprang into being which brought former enemies together, and for a time they were strong enough to do surprising things.

The first of these new coalitions won the convening of a constitutional convention; the second made the new constitution a boldly reforming document and drove it through to a narrow ratification victory. The third, quite differently constituted, then proceeded, in the first legislature to sit under the new constitution, not only to implement the new frame of government, but to enact the West's most sweeping effort to date at taking a great water management problem out of the realm of laissez-faire and putting a state government directly in charge of it.

The angry spirit of Denis Kearney, the anti-Chinese, anti-capitalist leader of the Workingman's party, is caught in this engraving. His movement endured long enough to help shape California's new Constitution of 1879, and by dividing the reform vote with the Democrats in the next state elections, turn the legislature and governor's office over to the Republicans. This led to the great Drainage Act experiment and the political crisis of 1880–1881.
Courtesy: California State Historical Society.

It was the nationwide Panic of 1873, instigator of one of the great depressions in American history, which by its successive hammer blows through the 1870s began the process of battering apart the existing structure of California's political culture. The 1870s were the "terrible seventies" in California, filled with widespread unemployment, farm distress, and social suffering. In July 1877, thousands of workers in San Francisco gathered in the "sand-lots" by the City Hall to hold meetings in support of a nationwide railroad strike then in motion. Quickly the mood escalated. The assembled multitude roared its approval of resolutions condemning wage cuts, graft, stock market cheating, subsidies for capitalists (read: the railroads, and monopoly public utilities), and above all, the continued immigration of the universally hated Chinese, whose presence was blamed for white men being unemployed.

Soon the sand-lotters were attacking Chinese dwellings, murdering inhabitants, and battling with the police. Setting a lumber yard ablaze next to the docks of the Pacific Mail Steamship Company, which was blamed for transporting Chinese to the state, the mobs were quickly in pitched battle with firemen. Shortly, men were being killed, and many others were injured. In a city built of wood and highly flammable, the authorities and the public at large were horrified. It seemed as if an insane civil war had broken out. Every armed resource available was mobilized to put down the rioters: the militia, federal gunboats, the police, and even a pickhandle brigade of 4000 vigilante volunteers who patrolled the city.[1]

By the autumn of 1877 a Workingmen's Party of California, mustering thousands of voters and practically dominating San Francisco, was in explosively oratorical existence. Denis Kearney, an Irish workingman immigrant, was the Workingmen's voice, and for four frantic years, "Kearneyism" transfixed the state. There must be, he cried, "a little judicious hanging" to bring an end to capitalist exploitation and to put down the "stock sharps" who were robbing the people. The owners of the Central Pacific Railroad, he said, who had brought thousands of Chinese workers to the state and were grinding down the whole community by their high transportation rates, were simply thieves. The workers, Kearney insisted, must control the state's politics and government; they must "meet fraud with force." Thousands marched behind him in great San Francisco parades. By "January of 1878," writes historian Alexander Saxton, "the Workingmen's party had become a major political force in California."[2]

Early 1878 was indeed a crucial, turning-point time in California's history, for in March the legislature finally passed an enabling act for the election in mid-June of delegates to write a new constitution for the state of California. Six months before, in September 1877, the people had voted overwhelmingly to have one, for there was massive anger at the railroads and other business monopolies, which were widely blamed for the long, cruel depression. As all parties swung into the campaign for electing delegates to the constitutional convention, an extraordinary political event occurred. The Democrats and Republicans, embittered antagonists, saw an even more dangerous common enemy in the Workingmen, and they joined forces to put a unified Non-Partisan ticket on the ballot.

The tactic worked: the Non-Partisan ticket won 78 delegates, to 51 for the Workingmen (23 more simply declared themselves Republicans or Democrats). However, what actually ensued in the convention was a working alliance between those Non-Partisans who were farmers, and the Workingmen, since they agreed that stringent regulations should be put on the railroads and business corporations.[3] The Non-Partisans who were actually Republicans railed angrily against "radicalism," but what went out to the people of the state for ratification in 1879 was a new constitution that called for innovative new public agencies that would regulate the railroads, public utilities, the stock market, and the corporations—as well as levy heavy penalties against the Chinese.[4] In the ratification campaign, the banks, railroads, manufacturing firms, mining companies, and water and gas companies crusaded vigorously against the new constitution, and the Republican party was outspokenly, fervently hostile.

The farm counties, however, were delighted with the new constitution, as indeed were Democrats generally. The vote in Colusa County, the "banner Democratic county" in the state, is revealing: it went for the new constitution almost two to one: 1419 for, and 753 against. It was on the basis of such majorities in the state's rural interior that in the May 1879 balloting, the Constitution of 1879 won its victory of 77,959 votes in favor, and 67,134 against.[5]

Now a last crucial election lay ahead. In four months time, an entirely new government, legislative and executive, would be elected to put the new constitution into effect. Would its friends, or its enemies, gain that coveted prize? The kaleidoscope turned again, creating a new political context. A clamor of voices broke out, for Republicans, Democrats, and Workingmen all ran separate candidates, and a new player, the New Constitution Party, which was composed of leading supporters of the new document from among Republicans and Democrats, ran its own ticket as well. Only one of these parties, the Republicans, was known to be essentially hostile to the new constitution. However, having lost in the ratification battle, the Republicans now announced that their party would accept it as the law of the land, though they were not in sympathy with its radical objectives.

The result was a dramatic turnabout: with the constitution's supporters so divided among themselves, and with thousands in the state recoiling in distaste against the Workingmen, the Republicans won not simply a victory, but a landslide. They gained control of the governor's chair, and they won almost every other elective office in the executive branch as well. In the state legislature, they swept up a strong working majority, and all of their candidates for the national House of Representatives were successful. The gubernatorial vote tells the story: the joint candidate of the Democrats and the New Constitution party received 47,647 votes, and the man run by the Workingmen got 44,482, for a combined total of 92,129. George Perkins, the Republican candidate, received 67,965 votes, a distinct minority of the total vote cast, but with a divided ballot it was to him that the victory went.[6]

Out of these turbulent, shifting, surprising two years, 1877 to 1879, the Republicans had emerged astonishingly triumphant. In a fashion denied to them since the heady years of the Civil War, and as the legacy of fortuitous events, they were once more in full control of the state government in Sacramento. The results, for water policy in the state of California, were to be dramatic.

≈≈≈

During the same months in early 1878 when California public life was being levered into fundamentally new paths by the rise of the Workingmen and the decision to write a new constitution, the struggle of mid-Sacramento Valley farmers and townsmen against their flooding problem shifted into a new course. Since the great Marysville flood of 1875, those who had called for a crusade to close down the mines had carried the battle into the courts and the legislature, but to this point without significant result. Now, however, the policymaking process was once again given a powerful nudge by another great natural crisis.

In early February of 1878 the Sacramento, which had been running higher than ever before because of debris in its bed, burst through a levee downstream from the city of Sacramento and inundated a vast area of farming countryside. Following this, torrential rainstorms swept over the valley one after another. Shortly, the Sacramento River at the state capital was higher than it had ever been known to be. More levee breaks spread disaster and alarm. Trains were halted, and a levee on the Bear River gave way, sending that stream's waters pouring over the flatlands.

By the twentieth of February 1878, the levee-encircled cities of Sacramento and Marysville were almost the only dry spots in the middle and lower Sacramento Valley. Outside of their great embankments only water could be seen in all directions; the ancient inland sea had once more declared itself with peremptory and apparently irresistible power. And now there were thousands more farmers and their families living on the Valley floor than in earlier years, drawn there in part by the illusion that the levee-building that had taken place since the last cycle of serious floods, in the latter 1860s, would protect them. For this reason the disaster was greater than ever it had been in the past. Great excitement rocked the middle and lower Sacramento Valley: cursing, wild plans, frantic efforts at rescue, devastation, loss, desolation, and suffering absorbed everyone.[7]

A San Francisco reporter aboard a laboring steamer breasting the surging Sacramento somberly recorded the scene:

> The fundamental elements of the scenery, from first to last, were a wild waste of waters, fringes of willows, parks of oaks, broken levees, rows of earth bags, streaks of black mud sprinkled with green grass and yellow wheat, stock on the levees, fences peeping out of water, and houses in the water. . . . I counted over forty breaks in the west levee . . . through which the water was pouring from the river in torrents. On the east side there is but one break, and it extends to the mouth of Feather River, and through this break the water runs into the river. The only real solid ground on the east side were the Indian mounds, which had successfully battled with the floods . . . the great sea seemed to extend on the one side to the Coast Range foothills and the other to the Sierra. . . . Farms were cut up into gullies, with narrow strips between, and the stock was wandering and lowing over these patches, looking in vain for food. . . . The water was rushing around nearly all the houses, and the beautiful orchards were either in the water or covered with slime. . . . The Sacramento, from Knight's Landing up, is quite thick with sediment, though it decreases as you ascend. . . . During the recent flood the population along the river fought the floods as never men fought anything else since the world began, but all in vain.[8]

This was an earthquake event, of the sort that shifts the policymaking landscape into new alignments and opens doors formerly closed. The legislature of 1878 had already been in session for two months, and in desultory fashion it had been listening to proposals for major water management reforms—and turning away from them in indifference. Republican state senator Creed Haymond of Sacramento, a remarkable man who had already been deeply involved in water controversies in the state, had been sensing that a historic convergence of two immense water problems in the state, irrigation and flood control, was ready to be consummated. As historian Donald J. Pisani in his remarkable work *From the Family Farm to Agribusiness:*

The Irrigation Crusade in California and the West, 1850–1931 has recently explained, for years there had been agitated interest and much costly and usually ineffective activity in the building of irrigation systems in California, especially in the San Joaquin Valley, that great dry grassland that stretches hundreds of miles southward from the Sacramento-San Joaquin delta. From the early 1870s, engineers led by the redoubtable General B. S. Alexander, USCE, had been making sweeping surveys of irrigation possibilities in that valley and proposing bold projects, though as yet without success.[9]

During the two-year drought of 1876–1878, which saw annual rainfall in the San Joaquin Valley fall to less than four inches, farmers and ranchers there had endured terrible suffering, and there were, as Pisani writes, "countless battles over water."[10] Clearly, now, the time had come to try to solve the characteristic California problem of wild fluctuations in rainfall by constructing irrigation works that would tap the large snow-fed rivers that issue from the Sierra Nevada.

> Conflict between rival irrigators would not end [an] . . . editor warned, until a coordinated state irrigation system had been established. For years California's shipping, flood, arid and swampland reclamation problems had begged for a state water policy. Moreover, during the 1870s, the autonomous swampland districts had proven incapable of coordinating their efforts at flood control and reclamation, and hydraulic mining cast a shadow over the future of the Sacramento Valley's farms and towns.[11]

In January 1878, therefore, Creed Haymond had risen in the state senate to propose (at General Alexander's urging) that a broad engineering investigation of both the irrigation and the flooding and debris problems be set in motion, clearly hoping by putting these two issues together to be able to assemble a large enough coalition of supporters to get action finally underway. This had set off an explosive few days of debate during which suppressed animosities between the farms and San Francisco had startlingly erupted. The hydraulic miners angrily opposed it, for they had no desire to see their operations opened to official public inquiry. With the aid of senators from San Francisco, where the large corporate hydraulic mines were headquartered, Haymond's proposal was quashed on the ground that it was a waste of money.[12] Nobody, S. D. Pierson of San Francisco had scoffed, could solve such a problem by running around the state in a railroad car.

Then came the storms. Quickly, the whole complex of water problems assumed major stature. Just at this crucial moment, when in February 1878, an assembly committee was meeting in Marysville's City Hall to gather information and everyone's eyes were being directed to the issue, a familiar figure came forward: William H. Parks. He rose at the meeting to say that he had devised a plan that would, he believed, *solve the flood control problem to everyone's satisfaction* and *make it unnecessary to halt hydraulic mining.* There was, in short, a solution available, he was saying, which would bring the community together, not divide it into warring camps, and would meet the needs of all.[13]

This was an extraordinary proposal, advanced in the midst of a bitterly conflicted controversy, and its nature merits comment. Parks, after all, had in his LD 5 project been apparently looking out just for himself. And yet he might say that he was only following the best engineering advice, and that if his plan had been allowed to work everyone living in Sutter Basin, not just himself, would benefit, that if others living elsewhere did their part too, the "main channel" concept would protect the whole Valley from flood. Now he was simply expanding his concept Valley-wide, as will be seen. And in the complicated public debate now opening, he would remain devoted to the concept that the whole community had shared interests, not opposed ones, and that they could be resolved by joint action. This belief was in fact a classically Republican theme in national public life, one that Henry Clay's Whigs and now the Gilded Age's Republicans dwelt on endlessly, in contrast to the Democrats. Where the latter since Thomas Jefferson had always attacked the wealthy and the entrepreneurial as seeking advantages over the people at large, and had stressed that there is an inherent, inescapable, eternal struggle between the classes, who are natural enemies, Whigs and Republicans had insisted that this was a false and pernicious idea that did nothing more than create hatred between workers and their employers, and bitter, immobilizing social estrangement. Instead, they would say, we are an interdependent community, the interests of each class are mutually supportive. There is no inherent conflict in society between capital and the common people, there is actually a harmony of interests, an instinctive impulse toward cooperation and mutual assistance, each class playing its own part, if only "outside agitators" would let this natural harmony of the interests flourish.[14]

Parks, then, would continually urge the farmers and townsmen of the Valley floor to be sympathetic toward the miners, and not be rigidly locked into the gritty, unrelenting hostility called for by Democrats like Yuba City's George Ohleyer, or by the Democratic assemblyman from Sutter County, D. A. Ostrom, who in the legislature had been insistently calling for laws that would shut down the hydraulic mining industry. What was needed, Parks insisted, was to work out a solution that would benefit the whole community, not just the farmers. Earlier, in an 1876 protest meeting, he had asked, "are we ready to say that [the hydraulic miner must] . . . stop immediately? Are we ready for so radical a measure at once? For one, I dare not say it." He was, after all, an entrepreneur himself who had suffered bitter public attacks for his projects, he was a Republican, and he doubtless had an instinctive fellow-feeling for his entrepreneurial colleagues in the mountains and in San Francisco. In taking this position he struck a note, furthermore, which appealed to many in his audiences, especially to the Marysville businessmen who traded with the miners, selling them goods and supplies.[15]

What proposal was he now ready to put forward as the great problem's much awaited solution? He had observed, Parks said, that a river tends to deposit its sediment and thus raise its bed if it is allowed to spread. However, it will carry along in its waters a heavy body of silt and debris if it is constricted within levees and its current kept strongly moving. In this way, hydraulic mining debris could be moved right through the river system without spreading out to bury the paralleling farmlands. Parks then brought out a model of the Yuba River with movable sides to demonstrate his point.

He went on to propose a complete plan of reclamation and river control. Strong reservoirs should be built in the ravines and canyons of the mountains to hold back the heavier mining debris—rocks, cobblestones, and gravel—and keep it out of the flatland river channels. Downstream, a connected system of levees should be built along the Yuba, the Feather, the Bear, and the Sacramento, stretching as far as the broad islands in the delta of the Sacramento. The levees thus constructed would constrict the rivers, force them to scour out their own beds, and allow the lighter sediment that would flow over the mountain reservoirs into the streams to be carried through the rivers and deposited in Suisun Bay—concerning the fate of which, at this point, there appears to have been general indifference. To pay for this expensive and unprecedented scheme, he would tax the mines and the lands bordering the rivers, this fund to be in the hands of a commission created to build and oversee the entire project.[16]

Parks' own interest in this scheme was direct and obvious. Frustrated earlier in his efforts to put the Sacramento River within a single channel, and thereby protect his lands, he now had a new foundation upon which to build toward that objective. Indeed, as a side-feature of the plan, he proposed that it be constructed so as to use the swampland basins as settling ponds for mining debris, thus filling them and perhaps by that means making them accessible to agriculture. He was not a man, however, who was moved solely by self-interest. Parks would battle hard, year after year, for his plan because he believed in it and in its power to rescue the entire Sacramento Valley from periodic floods.

Seventeen years before, it will be remembered, Parks had sat in the state legislature, which in 1861, and with his support, had enacted the last effort at valleywide flood control, the doomed swampland commissioners plan. A central feature of that whole episode had been the impulse of Republicans to think in terms of the whole Valley, not just of its parts. Centralism, unity, team spirit, a holistic approach, an imaginative and active use of government to achieve common objectives: all of this had been at the core of the Yankee-Republican inheritance that California Republicans possessed. It was an inheritance in dramatic contrast to the ways in which Democrats thought about public issues and about the Valley, with their instinctive preference for localism, distrust of far-away government, and of entrepreneurs with large plans. We are not surprised to see, then, that leading mid-Valley Democrats like George Ohleyer, the major figure in the antihydraulic mining crusade—who would be delighted to shut down the hydraulic mines instantly, if he had the authority—and Colusa's Will Green, came forward outspokenly and persistently to condemn Parks and his plan.

Green doubtless opposed the proposal not only because he distrusted Republican development schemes, but on engineering grounds as well. Parks was presenting a new version of General B. S. Alexander's main-channel concept, which the people of the Colusa region had already been struggling against for years. Parks described his proposal as his own conception, but he doubtless derived so integrated and ambitious a main-channel plan, which reached out to include the idea of dams in the mountains, from direct conversations with his long-time friend and supporter, General Alexander (whose death would abruptly arrive nine months later, in December 1878). Green had always argued that it was impossible to keep the rivers within a leveed single-channel system; that one way or another, in floodtimes the rivers were going to spread their waters; and that the answer lay in accepting but controlling that spreading. He had argued for regulating floods by building overflow channels down through the basins to carry the Sacramento's excess flows, and from 1878 on he would take every opportunity to ridicule Parks' proposal.[17]

The crucial point now was that Parks had made a policy proposal so attractive to the interests of so many people, and so persuasive in its own terms, that a new coalition of former enemies began to form in its support. Though Ohleyer and Green might carp from the sidelines, their own answers to the problem—shutting down hydraulic mining, or building a bypass flood control system—were going nowhere. Parks, at least, had suggested something that might possibly meet everyone's needs. As the assembly hearings proceeded in Marysville, miners and farmers alike got up to say that they approved of Parks' plan; and in subsequent public gatherings in the mid-Valley region, similar things were said.[18]

Now Senator Haymond reintroduced his bill calling for an investigation by the state government of the twin problems of irrigation and debris, and in the subsequent debates strong criticism of the proposal was matched by mounting sentiment in its favor. Even though his bill would appropriate the then-extraordinary sum of $100,000 and create a new official called the state engineer with a salary matching that of the governor ($6000 a year), legislators from dry farm districts pleaded for it, farmers battling mining debris spoke eloquently in its support, and (crucially important) even some mining representatives recognized Haymond's bill as the first step, perhaps, toward providing a final protection for their industry. In these very months, as we have seen, the legislature was uncharacteristically in a shifting, flexible mood. Pushed about by powerful political forces arising outside its walls, most notably the Workingmen, it was ready to respond positively to innovation. Not only did it approve the convening of a constitutional convention, it now enacted the bold state engineer proposal. After passage by the senate, the assembly in late March, 1878, approved the bill by a vote of more than two to one.[19]

The state engineer was given huge tasks. Clearly, no one yet faintly understood how immense were the problems he was called upon to study and for which he was to recommend solutions. He was to locate and map all land capable of irrigation (in a state encompassing 156,000 square miles); "divide this land into natural drainage districts; designate the best water sources in each district; determine the average annual water supply; prepare plans for irrigation works; and give his opinion and advice to such parties as may be engaged in irrigating a district, or who may be about to undertake the irrigation of a district." Also the state engineer was to inquire into

> the relation which hydraulic mining bears to the navigation of the rivers, and to their carrying capacity; to inquire into the question of the flow of debris from the mines into the watercourses of the state; to ascertain the amount and value of agricultural land and improvements which have been covered up or injured by the overflow of deposit or debris, coming from the hydraulic and other mines in the Sacramento Valley, and to devise a plan whereby the injuries caused thereby can be averted *without interfering with the working of such mines* [emphasis added].[20]

All this was to be completed in time for the presenting of a full report and proposed plans for solving these problems to the 1880 meeting of the legislature.

≈ ≈ ≈

William Hammond Hall, a brilliant, irascible, idealistic, and impatient engineer, now enters the story. Some thirty-three years of age in 1878, close friend and protégé to General B. S. Alexander—whose death in late 1878 would be for Hall a grievous personal loss—he had been born in Maryland and reared in Stockton, California, where he attended an Episcopal academy. When twenty-one, he had gone to work for the U.S. Army Corps of Engineers as a draftsman and surveyor. He was to learn his profession, in short, not in a college program, but within that mother-institution of civil engineering in the United States, the Corps of Engineers. Before long he was a field engineer; by 1870, in his midtwenties, he was helping plan San Francisco's Golden Gate Park, after which he became its chief engineer. In the mid-1870s he was out in the San Joaquin Valley doing major irrigation surveys with General Alexander, soon assuming the post of chief consulting engineer for the huge project being planned by the West Side Irrigation District. In May 1878, Governor Will Irwin, a warm supporter of the West Side Irrigation District, at the recommendation of General Alexander chose Hall to be California's first state engineer.

William Ham. Hall, as he usually signed his name, plunged into his great 1878–1880 survey with enormous energy and high organizational skill. As eventually became apparent, however, he had a heavy burden to carry: his own personality. Hall utterly lacked, indeed scorned, the popular touch. Arrogant and vain, while at the same time remarkably gifted, if in ways that ordinary Californians little appreciated, his nine years as California's first state engineer would be filled with controversy, frustration, and disappointment. A passionate advocate of centralized control over water policy and management, and of careful preliminary planning before major irrigation projects were begun, legislators who distrusted strong central government regarded him with great impatience, and so too did entrepreneurs eager to open their properties.

Hall would leave behind, however, an astonishingly rich store of fundamental insights and descriptive statistical data about the Sacramento River and its tributaries that would be foundational to everything that followed. Though he never developed specific plans for irrigation, his meticulous survey of the irrigable regions in the San Joaquin Valley was of very great importance in the subsequent development of irrigated agriculture in the state. At the same time, he created a small corps of young civil engineers, of the college-trained generation, who in later years would develop his ideas further and become leading figures in California water management.[21]

To explore the flooding and mining debris problems in the Sacramento Valley, Hall sent out parties under such engineers as twenty-eight-year-old Marsden Manson, fresh out of Virginia Military Institute, where he had taken his degree in civil engineering just a year before joining Hall's project. Fledged in the intense public heat and swift pace of the state engineer's 1878–1880 survey, Manson was a man who, like his superior, blended a vigorous and contentious temper with the capability of completing a great volume of field work in remarkably short order and turning out swift-moving, graphic, skillfully written reports. Soon he was being picked up by the U.S. Army Corps of Engineers to conduct more Sacramento Valley flood control studies. In later years Manson would go on to a major engineering career in California, filled with honors—he would be chosen a Fellow of the Royal Geographic Society—which culminated in the great Hetch Hetchy reservoir controversy and project after 1900.[22]

An even younger man, at twenty-three in 1878, was California-born C. E. Grunsky, who had gone off to Germany for university studies and would eventually take a doctorate in engineering from Rensselaer Polytechnic Institute in New York. Working as a topographer for William Ham. Hall in the 1878–1880 survey was his very first job, and he would remain with Hall until 1888, when the state engineering office temporarily collapsed upon Hall's resignation. Flood control, irrigation: these were to be Grunsky's early specialties.

In the 1880s his irrigation practice was particularly active, for he planned canal systems for the famous Henry Miller in his immense landholdings in the San Joaquin Valley and for Will Green's Central Irrigation District in Colusa County. His flourishing practice would eventually make him a man distinguished enough to gather many honors, among them being appointed in 1904 by President Theodore Roosevelt to the Isthmian Canal Commission.[23]

Hall's engineering parties examined in detail the damage done to the rivers by hydraulic mining debris and the existing condition of such levees as had to that point been built. When in 1879 another high water time struck the Valley, sending the rivers to flooding levels, the state engineer's office rushed out to study it closely and gain a systematic picture of how the great river system performed in such conditions. Meanwhile, carrying out for the first time the water-policy federalism that as we have seen *Gibbons* v. *Ogden* had in 1824 decreed, Hall had launched cooperative surveys of river-flow with the U.S. Army Corps of Engineers, making use of the first systematically emplaced network of river-flow gauges in the Valley.[24]

≈≈≈

Hall was able to arrange these cooperative activities because the Corps' California detachment had for some years been studying the Sacramento River and developing a basic store of fundamental engineering knowledge and skills concerning that stream. It had made its initial studies in 1873, submitting its first official description of the river in a report to Congress on that subject in autumn 1874. Then Congress, in belated response to an 1876 plea from the California legislature, had called on the Corps to examine the impact of hydraulic mining debris on the navigable rivers in the Sacramento Valley.[25]

The particular focus of the Corps' work—river navigation—bears remark. Since the landmark case of *Gibbons* v. *Ogden* had established the principle that Congress had control over the nation's navigable waters, that body had periodically appropriated funds for maintaining them in a useful condition. This had eventually led to the creation of that venerable, always controversial institution, the "pork barrel" rivers and harbors bills which at intervals issued from Congress. After considerable horse-trading among the members of Congress, the rivers and harbors bills handed out federal funds for local navigability projects constructed by the U.S. Army Corps of Engineers, such as removing snags and other impediments to navigation. After the Civil War, rivers and harbors appropriations skyrocketed.

Rivers have multiple impacts on the territory on either side of their banks, and it was inevitable that after *Gibbons* v. *Ogden* put the Corps to work on the nation's rivers, demands would eventually rise that it take on responsibility also for controlling floods. In 1850, floods on the Mississippi had got Congress sufficiently interested to put the Corps to work making extensive studies of that river, with a view to working up a full flood control plan. As we have seen, the Humphreys plan was in Congress's hands by 1861, just before the Civil War began. After that conflict, the issue was taken up again, but little came of these various proposals that the federal government begin flood control efforts, for they ran into determined opposition in Congress.

Other parts of the nation complained bitterly that they should not be taxed to benefit people who had bought land knowing that they were in danger of periodic flood, as was the case on the lower Mississippi River, and who in many cases had purchased their lands on the cheap under the Arkansas Act of 1850 (the swamplands giveaway, as it was called). Under that law, swampland owners were reminded, they were supposed to pay for their own levees and protect themselves. In 1882 the *New York Times* said that spending money on levees was "ridiculous," considering the undoubted unconstitutionality of such expenditures. In the same year the *Chicago Tribune* called it "confiscating the property" of the American people as a whole to benefit only those on the lower Mississippi. Senator Benjamin Harrison said that flood control was reclamation for the benefit of private property, and it was not constitutional.

The costs, if the principle of flood responsibility were admitted, would be potentially astronomical. Meeting such needs in a nation of 3 million square miles would be (as it is) practically an unlimited task. Therefore, critics grounded their resistance on the bedrock principle that federal appropriations for anything beyond navigability, certainly for flood control measures, would be unconstitutional. This position would be taken again and again in Congressional debates over the next fifty years, and repeated successfully, since in general terms the federal government did scrupulously stay free of flood control obligations.

The exception that proved the rule was the establishment in 1879 of the Mississippi River Commission, which was charged with developing flood control as well as navigation-maintenance plans on lower Mississippi. In practice, however, levee construction funds were subsequently provided by Congress for that river's needs only if they were part of a navigation project. Flood control efforts by the Corps of Engineers, such as they were—and the Corps itself pulled back from flood control obligations—had always to be masked under the rubric of navigation. As we shall see, not until the time of the First World War would Congress finally allow this barrier to be breached, and then only partially.[26]

≈≈≈

The cooperative state-federal survey activities in the Sacramento Valley to which State Engineer Hall in his 1880 report referred brought him into close working relations with the man who, upon General Alexander's death in late 1878, would become the Corps' chief officer in California and therefore for many years its leading voice in water matters: Lt. Col. George H. Mendell, USCE. Indeed, Mendell had been appointed to the post of consulting engineer to Hall's 1878–1880 survey of the rivers, so his links with the state engineer, as a much older man and as a seasoned, widely experienced engineer, were particularly crucial. Perhaps a decade younger and far less flamboyant than General B. S. Alexander, Mendell was also a West Point–trained engineer who had fought with great courage in the Civil War, winning a brevet-colonel's rank for gallantry in the long trench warfare before Richmond's fall. By 1878, he had been busily at work in his profession in California and the West for a dozen years. It was he who, as a major, had directed the Corps' first study of the Sacramento River in 1873–1874, and when Alexander had led his ambitious irrigation surveys in the San Joaquin Valley in the 1870s, both Mendell and Hall had been on his team. The two men had thus known each other for years.[27]

General Alexander and Lt. Col. Mendell shared one important characteristic: though federal military officers, they both got themselves deeply involved in California's internal water policy planning and politics. Alexander, indeed, had made the first recommendation to Senator Haymond that the state launch an engineering investigation of the combined irrigation and flood control problems, and we have seen that it was at his urging that Hall became the first state engineer. However, the bill authorizing all of this that had been passed in March 1878 was actually written by Mendell, a fact that greatly offended the general, who regarded his then-subordinate's action as impertinent interference.[28]

By the opening days of 1880 the state engineer's labors were completed, the surveys were made, and a plan for getting control of the hydraulic mining debris problem, and of the Valley's floods, was ready for submission to the legislature. That body, in its turn, was gathering for the very large task of putting the new constitution into effect. Its mood was highly mixed and disturbed, for as we have seen the Republicans, who had campaigned fervently against the "radical" new constitution, now had the controlling majority in the legislature, and their candidate, George C. Perkins, was governor.

He was, however, a special kind of Republican. A Yankee from Maine, he was of that prickly New England tradition in the party which was proudly independent-minded, looked on politics purely as public service, and was not comfortable with simple money-making even in the private economy. In the Gilded Age Yankee Republicans of this variety were offended by the corrupt power of great capitalists over governments large and small. And they had a special cause: fostering learning and public education as the ultimate solution to the nation's needs and problems. It was characteristic, therefore, that, true to this New England tradition, in 1869 it was Perkins, as a freshman state senator, who had pushed through the legislature the historic proposal that the state government provide support to the recently chartered (1868) but impoverished University of California.

At the age of forty-one when he became governor, Perkins was an energetic man who had come to California as a simple farm youth during the Gold Rush and had since become very wealthy. A remarkably imaginative entrepreneur, he now had large investments in merchant houses, sheep and cattle ranches, mining, lumbering, banks, and flour mills, and he owned a great fleet of merchant vessels. In San Francisco, he was one of its leading figures, being elected president of the San Francisco Merchants' Exchange in 1879. In the 1870s he had become widely noted as practically the only Republican state senator to kick over the traces of party discipline in the legislature and openly criticize land grants to the Central Pacific Railroad.

Perkins came to the governor's chair, therefore, with a reforming aura about him. As a firm Yankee activist and Republican of the Whig tradition, he believed government was there to be used for the good of the whole community, not simply to stand aside and let laissez-faire reign unchecked. In a style quite unlike his predecessors and most of his successors in the governor's office, in his messages to the legislature Perkins called for a simply astonishing array of reforms, many of them far ahead of their times and precious few of which would be enacted: regulation of railroad rates and fares; measures to break up land monopolies; an expanded board of agriculture; an income tax (not to be enacted for half a century); a labor bureau to resolve differences between employers and workmen; help for the unemployed; the conversion of the state prisons into reformatories, with a special school for boys to keep them away from hardened criminals; legislative examination of orphan asylums; the right for women to vote in school board elections; and an educational program that would do something about the 50,000 children who were not attending school, a fact he much lamented, perhaps by installing instruction in trade and mechanical skills in the public schools' curricula to make them more useful to the young.[29]

George Perkins, in short, was bringing an activist view of government to the executive office just as William Ham. Hall was preparing to recommend unprecedented measures in water policy and management. Perkins in fact chose the great questions of irrigation and the hydraulic mining controversy for extended, urgent words to the legislature. Concerning irrigation, the governor believed that, rather than leave that matter and its intimately related issue of water rights in the current anarchy of private enterprise, the state of California should move in to plan and direct a great system of irrigation, which was exactly what Hall himself and his engineering mentors had long been recommending. Though nothing would come of this initiative, in the other direction, the question of hydraulic mining debris, much more would eventuate. When on the 8th of January 1880, he took occasion in his inaugural address to remind the legislature of the conflict between the hydraulic mines and the farms, and to urge it to settle "this most important and delicate question . . . upon some broad and comprehensive basis," he had set the stage for the eventual enactment of an extraordinarily ambitious valleywide state-directed and -financed flood control project: the Drainage Act of 1880.[30]

CHAPTER

The Great Drainage Act Fight and the Reversion to Flood Control Anarchy: *1880–1886*

"We were at the Pay 'N Save standing back near the pharmacy. . . . There was a line of people filling their prescriptions when we heard someone running down the aisle . . . saying "everybody out of the mall! The levee has broken behind us!" I told my two kids to run as fast as they could to our car."

Harold Kruger, Marysville Appeal-Democrat, *February 25, 1986. Quoted in* Rivers of Fear, *p. 49.*

All the elements were now in place for a wholesale transforming of California's public policy toward the Sacramento River. The problem itself was growing more urgent, for as the river channels filled with debris the floods came more rapidly and were more destructive. By a fortuitous train of events the political context had also been put in the appropriate condition for something decisive to be done. The governor's office and the legislature were both in the hands of the Republicans, the political party that had always argued, nationwide, that government should be actively used to guide society, solve great public problems, and open the country's resources. Furthermore, the Republicans' favorite corps of experts, the engineers, had produced a plan that they said would solve the problem of the Sacramento River.

The new definition of the situation that the Republicans and such local entrepreneurs as William H. Parks were now putting forward—that the interests of the whole community, not just the farmers, must be protected, and that, by relying on an engineering solution, mining debris could be controlled and floods could be

Engineers were the pioneer professional "experts" in American life. In 1878 California created the office of state engineer, with a salary equivalent to the governor's, and charged this official with the task of developing solutions to the great flooding and irrigation problems. Brilliant, irritable, controversial William Hammond Hall held the post for ten years, building up a large body of fundamental information.
Courtesy: California State Library.

halted without shutting down the mines—was sufficiently persuasive to mobilize a strong coalition behind it consisting of representatives of the Valley, the hydraulic miners, and, crucially important, San Francisco.

As it happened, the existing moment was a particularly fortunate one for new initiatives. A kind of armistice had by default arisen in the farmer-miner battle, for the farmers' crusade to shut down hydraulic mining was in eclipse. Not only had the legislature adamantly refused all appeals from the farmers for laws limiting or prohibiting the discharge of mining debris into the streams,[1] the state Supreme Court had recently overruled a victory that the farmers had won in the case of *Keyes* v. *Little York*. The astonishing swiftness by which District Judge Phil. W. Keyser's 1876 injunction had settled the Parks' dam controversy had been a lesson not lost on others in the Sacramento Valley. In 1878, Valley people had gathered behind a Bear River farmer, James H. Keyes, whose property was being buried under mining debris, to ask this bold, activist judge for the same kind of decisive remedy against the hydraulic miners. That is, they asked that under the law of equity Judge Keyser issue an injunction that would close down all the mines discharging debris into the Bear River and its tributaries.

This was asking for a dramatic remedy indeed. Everywhere, the news of this request set off a start of surprise. There were nineteen hydraulic mines in Bear River watershed. Were they all to be shut down, simply by a court order, and on the plea of a single farmer downstream? How could such a thing be conceived? The farmers' attorney, a man of fertile mind and boundless energy named George Cadwalader, had a ready explanation. It was impossible, he pointed out, to establish which mine had sent down the sand and mud that was burying Keyes' property, so the only recourse was to put together as defendants all the mines in the entire watershed and ask relief against them jointly. Such an injunction, he argued, was justifiable on the ground that the miners were in fact, by their operations, destroying other people's property downstream. Despite the fact that there was no statute law declaring hydraulic mining, which had this inevitable effect, illegal, the process was disastrously harmful to the property of others. That is, in the Bear River watershed the state was facing exactly the kind of activity, destructive of the general welfare, that the law of equity had for centuries been in existence to strike down.

In March 1879, after delays induced by legal maneuvering, Judge Keyser, who was quite ready to bite the bullet, accepted Cadwalader's argument and granted the full injunction requested. He ordered that hydraulic mining cease in the watershed of the Bear River. Following this astonishing ruling, the subject of many angry editorials on both sides in California newspapers, in the succeeding months there was a good deal of scurrying about as the enraged miners tried to decide whether or not they would obey such an unprecedented decree. Eight months later, however, the state supreme court resolved the dilemma: in November 1879, it invalidated Keyser's order.

The court was simply not ready for so bold a leap into the use of the law of equity and the injunction. It insisted on seeing the case essentially as a property damage case and therefore as falling under common law tests. In that system a group of defendants could only be jointly charged if the plaintiff could prove that those being sued had actually engaged in a conspiracy to harm him. Lacking any evidence of such activity in the *Keyes* case, the court ruled that the miners had been improperly joined together in the suit, that is, that there had been a "misjoinder of parties."[2]

With the courts now closed to them, the people of the Valley had no choice, many among them now argued, but to give up on the campaign to destroy the hydraulic mining industry and swing behind the plan for valleywide protection and reclamation now being proposed.

≈≈≈

Soon after the legislature of 1880 began its sitting, on the 21st of January State Engineer William Ham. Hall sent his bulky report to that body on the twin problems of irrigation and flood control, with a letter of concurrence from Lt. Col. George H. Mendell, the consulting engineer. Hall's report was an extraordinary personal achievement. In the brief period of a single year, and working from ground zero, since his was the first such report ever to be made on the large issues he was given to study, Hall had managed to produce a document hundreds of pages long, jammed with facts and figures, clearly and gracefully narrated and analyzed. It did in fact offer to the legislature a carefully prepared examination of the two problems he was charged with studying, and a plan for reclaiming the Sacramento Valley's rivers that eminent authority—Mendell—declared was workable.

Few documents ever produced by the state of California have offered such rich reading. What lay spread out on the pages of Hall's report was a shocking picture, appalling in its detail and irrefutably damning in its implications, of the massive destruction of a natural environment and of a fertile farming countryside by an unrestrained industrial process. From this point on, pro-mining advocates could never again argue with any hope of being believed outside their own circles that the operations of the hydraulic mining industry were not damaging (as many had been insisting), that the harm it had worked had been hysterically exaggerated by the farmers. This element in the public argument which had been going on since the mid-1870s was now decisively concluded.

The deep river canyons in the mountains through which flowed the American, the Bear, and the Yuba, Hall reported, were choked, mile after mile, by immense deposits of mining debris which in some places were a hundred feet deep. For forty miles downstream from Oroville, with its cluster of large mining operations, the Feather's channel on the Valley floor was also filled in. And if some ten million cubic yards of debris lay in the bed of the Yuba before it issued from the mountains, in the fifteen-mile reach between the Yuba's canyon mouth and its juncture with the Feather at Marysville lay an immense deposit of sixty million yards which had totally obliterated the former channel of the river. It had overflowed so widely over the farms that had lined the river that its bed was now two miles wide.[3]

> The lands . . . [had been] dotted with prosperous homes, fruitful orchards, and luxuriant fields. . . . Levees that were thrown up to confine the waters to their accustomed courses only had the effect of

> causing the beds to rise still higher by the constant deposition of detritus between them, until they were finally overtopped by the floods, and the bottom lands were submerged from rim to rim of the adjacent plains with sand and clay sediment, to such depths that in places orchards, gardens, fields, and dwellings were buried from sight, landmarks were lost, and the course of the devastating flood was marked out by broad commons of slime and sand. Over these the streams now spread at will in many shifting channels, checked only by the dense clumps of willows and other semi-aquatic growth that thrive on the submerged territory, and confined between levees now set long distances apart, generally on the ridges of highland that formerly marked the boundary of the more fertile bottoms.[4]

Altogether, some 684 million yards of gravel had been mined along the Yuba, about 100 million on the Feather, 254 million on the Bear, and 257 million along the American. Later examinations by federal scientists and engineers revealed that a total of 39,000 acres of farmlands were buried under debris, at a total loss of almost $3 million. Another 14,000 acres were partially damaged, at a cost of over $400,000. Much of this damage was along the Feather River, since it carried debris from its tributaries the Yuba and Bear as well as that coming from the mines around Oroville, and its comparatively longer valley was thus subjected to greater destruction. However, along the Yuba 12,000 acres were buried, and along the Bear another 8,000 acres were destroyed.[5]

What was to be done? "The study of this subject," Hall wrote, ". . . [has] brought me to a sense of the absolute necessity for organized effort in these matters . . . I can only recommend that *the State take charge of the drainage ways and all drainage works [in the Valley]* [emphasis added], and exercise such control over them as will regulate their use, promote their improvement, and systematize the construction and management of all works designed to promote rapid drainage and prevent inundations."[6] The whole problem of controlling the Sacramento, Hall said, was for example greatly complicated and worsened because levees had simply been thrown up anywhere local people desired them, with uneven, conflicting results. From this cause, the Sacramento's carrying capacity had been "greatly injured."

What was needed was to treat the rivers "as water-carrying channels throughout their several courses, according to one broad design, executed in all and each of its parts."[7] A proper system of uniformly planned and coordinated levees would force the rivers to scour out their beds and carry their debris down to the bays.

None of this, Hall pointed out, would succeed if the massive deposits of mining debris currently lodged in the mountain canyons were not immobilized. He proposed that at a number of locations, especially at three sites in the canyons of the Yuba and at a location on that stream some miles outside the mountains called Daguerre Point, dams be built to hold back the coarse debris—the gravel, rocks, and sand—which would otherwise continue washing downstream to fill in the Valley's river channels. There should also, he insisted, be settling reservoirs in the rolling lands near the foothills, from which clarified water could be taken out for irrigation purposes, as well as measures taken to divert large portions of the sediment-charged river-flows into the swampland basins, which, thus filled in and raised, could be better put to productive agriculture.[8]

Dam-building technology was still at a primitive stage. As Hall pointed out, engineers had few examples to go on in the nation or the world at large. What he proposed, therefore, was a simple process of quarrying out heavy masses of stone from the canyon walls and having this material "dumped in rough massive structures across the gorges," raising them perhaps twenty-five feet a year as mining debris piled up behind them, eventually to reach heights of over two hundred feet. How long would this process be effective? For perhaps thirty years, by which time the dams would be filled up.

As to costs, Hall estimated that three dams on the Yuba would require an expenditure of perhaps $3 million, or $100,000 a year for thirty years—a staggering sum of money for Californians to read about while their minds were still full of the grinding economic suffering of the 1870s depression. And for this huge investment, dwarfing anything else the state had attempted, the people of the Valley would receive dams that by Hall's estimate would hold back only seventy percent of the debris. His plan would allow the clayey mud and slickens to continue percolating through his rubble dams and washing on downstream; anything further would call for shutting down the mines. The Valley floor, in other words, would continue to receive sediment-laden waters and the deposits they produced.

Hall appears to have sensed that those currently living downstream from his proposed rubble-stone dams would recoil at the thought of these loose structures standing in the mountain canyons, vulnerable, perhaps, to being swept away in high floodtimes and loosening sudden avalanches of water and debris on all below. He was in fact much concerned himself about them, for they would have to be built on the deep beds of sand which were already in the mountain canyons. In his report he worried a good deal about possible erosion under and around the dams, making them insecure. He was by nature, however, impatient toward lay criticisms, and in one of the more unfortunate passages in his report Hall lightly dismissed the matter: "but then nearly all engineering works are experiments to some degree, particularly those which are intended to cope with some active force in nature, as hydraulic constructions generally are, so that such works are often carried forward with a tentative policy and guided by experience constantly being acquired."[9] This cavalier remark was not enough to ward off the storm of protest against such dams that quickly arose in the Valley and roared on, year after year, with powerful political results.

In later decades, subsequent generations of engineers fell into the habit, as they wrote their own reports, of describing Hall's plan for controlling the floods of the Sacramento River as a "main channel" plan on the Humphreys thesis model, but it was not. He well knew that the Sacramento River was far larger, potentially, than most people then knew.

> [Let] it also be remembered [he wrote] that [this plan applies] . . . to the case where we deal with the ordinary floods of the valley, for no limit may be assigned to the amount of water which may at some time in the future come down this valley; and, as in the past there have been phenomenal inundations, now spoken of as "the flood of '62," "the flood of '52," etc., so may there yet be others as great or greater

> than they, against the general spread of which no human foresight can provide, nor secure protection for the great body of the lands in the valley.[10]

Limited locations, Hall remarked, such as cities and towns, could be raised in elevation or so well-protected by high levees that they could probably be permanently protected. And yet, he observed wryly in one of his alarming asides, experience showed that there were two classes of levees: those that had been overtopped by floodwaters, and those that were *going* to be. He continued: "And so it should be fully understood that floods will occasionally come which must be allowed to spread." But they must be allowed to do so not in their ordinary way, by opening out crevasses in levees, but by putting strong weirs at several locations so that outflows could occur without causing damage. There should be one, for example, near Colusa. Once given release from the main channel, the overflowing water should be conducted "in embanked channels to the low basins from whence it could be drawn out again so soon as the river would fall."[11]

Hall was especially worried about the vast lake of waters that in floodtimes formed in Sutter Basin, created by the many overflow channels on either side such as Butte Slough near Colusa and Gilsizer Slough running down from Yuba City. In a brilliantly graphic passage revealing how deeply he had pierced that former mystery, the actual course of a flood, and how successful he was being in visualizing it (this was all a reconstruction, derived from a close analysis of scattered flood height figures in various locations; there were of course no aerial photographs to read), Hall remarked that a strong north wind, sweeping down over

> the twenty-seven miles of this lake [i.e., Sutter Basin] [would] pile up there such a volume of water to be carried away as would bring disaster to works and lands far below. . . . [In the flood of 1878 a] large portion of the great flood-wave which over-threw the levees of Grand Island [in the delta] was blown out of the Sutter Basin 59 miles above. Entering the head of the lower Sacramento [i.e., the reach below its juncture with the Feather] from this basin, the flood line was raised at the point of junction about five feet in a few hours. This wave went

> down the river, caused breaches in the levees, and swept into the head of the Yolo basin, diagonally across which it coursed, running well up on the west rim [of the Valley], and making higher water there than on the east side at opposite points; thence, turning, it again crossed the basin and was projected out into the Steamboat Slough and [the delta region], where it overthrew portions of all levees.[12]

However, save for brief lists of needed projects dropped in here and there, the flood control plan that Hall had in mind for the Valley was only verbally painted in his report. Nowhere was there a map that set out where existing levees were located and which of them should be raised, where new ones should be constructed, or what an integrated system of levees would look like. Even the location of the dams in the mountain canyons, he said, could at this point only be roughly guessed at; if his overall plan were approved, later engineering studies would firmly establish the best locations. What Hall had given the legislature, in short, was a mass of graphic material describing the state of the rivers and the Valley, and a sketch of a plan for restoring them. Much would have to be taken on faith.

≈≈≈

Many in the legislature were now in a mood to take the engineers on faith. On the fourth of February 1880, a newly elected Republican assemblyman and hydraulic miner from the mountainous region of Yuba County, J. P. Brown, rose on the assembly floor to begin the process of putting Hall's plan into effect. He introduced a bill prepared by no less a personage than William H. Parks, entitled "An Act to Promote Drainage." In its finally amended form, it would create a much more powerful central authority in Sacramento by putting the state government in charge of flood control statewide. It would carry out this immensely complicated (and enormously expensive) new duty through the instrumentality of an independent public commission, a Board of State Drainage Commissioners. This body would have authority to establish various drainage districts around the state. They would not, however, design their own works. In a classically Whig-Republican arrangement, local drainage districts would have their works planned by the governor's own appointed expert, the state engineer, subject to their final approval. By this means, coordination of all works would be assured. The districts were then empowered to raise and expend tax moneys to build their particular projects and subsequently oversee all construction and operations.

Two months of heated public debate over the drainage bill, inside and outside the walls of the legislature, now ensued. Clearly, under color of an ostensibly statewide arrangement the drainage bill was primarily aimed at constructing a flood control system in the Sacramento Valley. Most Valley people, it was soon clear, were ready to join the miners and San Francisco in supporting the Drainage Act plan, but it quickly had its determined opponents. There were many in the mid-Valley region who clung tenaciously to the belief that nothing would ever answer the problem until the mines were closed down; that so long as the flood of debris they poured into the streams continued, no engineering works could ever get control of it. They refused to have faith in the engineers, in the safety of their proposed dams, or in Hall's drainage plan.[13]

Yuba County's former assemblyman, Democrat D. A. Ostrom, came forward in legislative hearings to condemn the plan as a scheme of the miners and swampland thieves (read: William H. Parks) working together. In a public gathering in Marysville the mayor, C. E. Stone, one of Parks' inveterate enemies, warned of unlimited taxation, and George Ohleyer, repeating the assertion that it was all a swampland plot, insisted that the whole state would be bankrupted by the project, which could never achieve its goals. In reply, at legislative hearings and in other public forums Parks himself hammered repeatedly at the theme that the engineers had insisted that dams and levees would solve the problem, which for him closed the argument. Completely confident of their guidance, he said "I am not here to substantiate their conclusions, I accept their conclusions, and upon them I base this bill. . . . That there must be legislation if you accept their conclusions there can be no doubt."[14]

In the middle of March 1880, another voice chimed in: that of the federal engineer, Lt. Col. George H. Mendell. He had completed the preliminary examination of the debris problem which Congress had earlier requested, and in an arresting report he painted for that body essentially the same grim picture of the devastation worked by mining debris that State Engineer Hall had provided two months earlier to the legislature, describing its grave impact on the navigable rivers. Mendell recommended that, ultimately, *nine* dams be constructed in the mountains to hold back the rocks and gravel from the mines, which, he said, was just beginning to emerge onto the flatlands. This was, in other words, another "coarse debris" plan that assumed that the mines would continue operating, and that it would be essentially impossible in that event to prevent muddy, sediment-laden water from washing on over the dams and downstream. To ward off the most immediate dangers, Mendell recommended an appropriation of $250,000 to construct three of the most needed dams.[15]

By now, the legislature was locked in debate over Parks' bill. If it had its critics in the Sacramento Valley, the rest of the state, save San Francisco, was if anything even more furious. The proposed Drainage Act would call for everyone in the state to be taxed to help protect the Sacramento Valley farmers and allow the hydraulic miners to keep their operations going. This was a policy-leap that went far beyond the usual consensus as to what the government in Sacramento should be doing. There was simply not the necessary community of interest, throughout California, to build support in the outlying parts of the state for this unprecedented arrangement, nor was the idea that government should be actively used to solve such problems widely shared. A Santa Cruz assemblyman condemned the notion of the legislature delegating governmental powers to an independent commission, and a San Joaquin assemblyman insisted that "one man should [not] be taxed to improve another man's property. It is not right to tax the people of Santa Clara, or San Diego, or of any other county in the State, to help reclaim the lands in this proposed district."[16] The *Los Angeles Herald* said it "would be just as logical to tax the whole State to pay for a failure of the crops and fleece which have been ruined by drought in the southern counties as to levy a tax to repair the ravages of the debris of mines." There was even talk in the Los Angeles papers of secession by the southern counties, where bitterness was expressed at "the utter disregard the populous portion of the State has for a section which is weaker politically than the other."[17]

Nonetheless, with last-minute help from Workingmen assemblymen from San Francisco—who mysteriously found reason suddenly to switch their formerly negative votes to the affirmative side—the drainage bill was carried through the assembly on March 31 by a vote of forty-three to thirty-six, only one assemblyman not voting on this hotly contested question. Every representative from the core mid-Valley counties voted for it, as did the miners' representatives and three out of four of San Francisco's twenty assemblymen. In the senate the debate was again explosive, and accusations of corruption were once more heard.

At a crucial point the drainage bill was amended to remove that feature that looked toward aiding the reclamation of the swamplands by diverting mud-laden waters onto them. If their lands were incidentally aided by the project, the swampland owners were to be charged accordingly. Thus purified, the bill passed on April 9 by a vote of twenty-one to sixteen, with even more solid Sacramento Valley and Sierra Nevada support than it had mustered in the assembly, and a near-unanimous San Francisco bloc behind it: seven of that city's ten senators.[18]

Two months later, on the 14th of June 1880, the national government took up decisively its side of the now-emerging state-federal partnership in restoring the rivers of the Sacramento Valley. Through the rivers and harbors act of that year Congress asked Secretary of War Robert T. Lincoln (the assassinated president's son) to have the Corps of Engineers "devise a system of works to prevent the further injury to the navigable waters of California from the debris of mines arising from hydraulic mining." Lt. Col. Mendell was given that most-cherished of tasks for a professional person: preparing a detailed plan to embody his earlier general suggestions.[19]

Meanwhile, the statewide argument over the Drainage Act raged on. While Sacramento Valley papers expressed their pleasure that a drainage system was finally to be built, the *San Francisco Chronicle* claimed that up to $1000 a vote had been paid over to legislators to pass the bill. A San Joaquin Valley newspaper, the *Stanislaus County News,* said the $5000 annual tax that property owners in its county would have to pay was a "heavy luxury," for Hall's plan was "a scientific experiment for the benefit of another part of the State. . . . The law is wrong in principle, doubtful in expediency, and liable to many abuses." Looking on the one hand at the fact that the legislature had refused to fund prisons or hospitals or a normal school in the southern counties, and on the other at this apparently lavish outlay for the Sacramento Valley, the *Los Angeles Herald* railed that "no more iniquitous measure ever passed a California legislature."[20]

≈≈≈

What remained now was to implement the complicated drainage plan that the engineers had brooded. The statewide Board of Drainage Commissioners, consisting of the governor, the surveyor-general, and the state engineer, took the first step, authorizing the forming of and establishing the boundaries for Drainage District 1, which included the Sacramento Valley and the adjacent hydraulic mining regions in the Sierra Nevada. Its three-person board of directors included a member from Sacramento and another from the mountains, and, of course, as its elected president, William H. Parks, who represented the Valley floor. They quickly plunged ahead, authorizing State Engineer Hall to throw up two brush dams, one across the wide sandy bed of the Yuba River, outside the foothills, and another in a similar location across the Bear. The purpose of these structures was immediately to halt the further downstream flow of the avalanche of rocks and gravel which, as Mendell in his U.S. Army Corps of Engineers report to Congress had noted, was just beginning to come out of the mountains.[21]

By early November the dam on the Yuba, which was about nine miles upstream from Marysville, was finished. The river here, a *Record-Union* reporter wrote after visiting the site, was "a shallow and muddy sheet of water [which] wanders aimlessly over the shining bed of sand and yellow mud cement from one to two miles in width, and in flood times pours its waters here and there over the land . . . destroying towns and villages, and covering farms and orchards and agricultural lands with the gritty sands and cement-like slickens." The dam itself, which varied in height from five to twelve feet, stretched "in a direct line southward two miles across the sandy bottom, its farther end being scarcely distinguishable from this point. Its top is as level as engineering science and skilled workmen can make it, and it reaches across the desert waste like a great prism." Composed of wired brush and logs cut out of the forest of willow trees that occupied much of the Yuba's bed, it was about seventy feet wide at its base. Two levees, on either side of the Yuba, completed the project by enclosing the stream from the mouth of the Yuba's canyon to its junction with the Feather at Marysville. The Bear River was similarly dammed and guarded by levees.[22]

Hall pushed ahead energetically on other levee projects in the Valley, too. By January of 1881, the secretary of the drainage board could report to the assembly that under the Drainage Act eighteen levee projects, in addition to the two brush dams, had been constructed in the Valley, at a total cost, thus far, of $463,153.21.[23] All of this was encouraging to mid-Valley people, who looked forward to the progressive construction of the integrated valleywide system that Hall, in his 1880 report to the legislature, had stated as his ultimate goal.

≈≈≈

It was all, however, built on sand, both literally and politically. As soon as the legislature of 1881 gathered, a powerful campaign rising from all over California to repeal the Drainage Act immediately got underway in the state capitol, and the act's supporters found their former strong political coalition melting away. At the same time, a rhetorically violent uproar burst out in the assembly over the Bear River brush dam, whose sandy foundations, it was loudly and repeatedly alleged, had been washed away by recent high waters in the river, so that the structure was failing—and with it, the engineering rationale for the entire Drainage Act system.[24]

All the passions of the repealers focused on the Bear River dam, whose uncertain condition quickly flared up into a major point of contention in legislative hearings. On January 27, over a hundred assemblymen, senators, and reporters entrained from Sacramento to travel to the Bear River and examine the dam. As they straggled out on the structure itself they broke into angry arguments, some insisting that the dam was failing, others that it was only suffering from a few easily repaired settles here and there. State Engineer Hall placed himself where he could explain to all and sundry how such a structure had to go through an initial period of settlage until it found a firm foundation. Many legislators were outspokenly skeptical, however, and finally, out of patience, Hall threw up his hands: "You expect miracles! send for a magician. I appeal to any practical man, with these evidences before him, if this dam, in the few days of its first test, has not accomplished wonders."[25]

The repealers, however, were in truth not interested in engineering explanations. Their constituents were up in arms at the Drainage Act tax, the whole undertaking had been built on a politically vulnerable and unstable base, and the Drainage Act was going to be assaulted unmercifully until in some way it was destroyed. William Parks was a member of the 1881 assembly, and in a short, sharp political struggle at the beginning of its sitting had won the Speaker's chair. Through several hard-fought months of confused, embittered, and often noisy parliamentary battles in the legislature, with a hard core group of assemblymen supporters behind him from the Valley and the mountains, Speaker Parks was able by skillful maneuvers to hold off the repealers.

At a climactic moment, someone, perhaps the corporate hydraulic mine owners from San Francisco, appears to have used graft to get the votes of key San Francisco legislators to defeat the repeal bill. Meanwhile, the fight caused a log jam in the legislature so unbreakable that not even the appropriation bill, providing funds to run the state government, could be enacted. The entire 1881 sitting of the legislature was a disaster, especially for the Republicans, who held a majority in it and had authored and pushed through the hated Drainage Act.

Governor George Perkins was deeply alarmed. In mid-January 1881, he had sent a long and urgent special message to the legislature calling for repealers to accept the concept of community of interest, statewide, and cease their attacks on the Drainage Act. Returning to the old system of local initiative and laissez-faire, with each city and reclamation district trying to control the river piecemeal, and producing mutually conflicting levee systems in a war of each against all, would be catastrophic. "I think it must be admitted," he went on, "that the relations between the various parts of the State are too intimate to permit of the decline of one without reactionary effect upon the fortunes of the others. Neither can in fact afford to seek a policy of isolation."[26] His appeal was fruitless; the repeal crusade mounted in intensity. When the governor had to call a special session to get the appropriation bill passed, once again the battle was underway, this time to strike out the Drainage Act tax.

Failing at this, the repealers began a suit at law, and now, finally, the Drainage Act was quashed. In March 1881, one of the leading repealers in the assembly, W. W. Camron, in the case of *The People* v. *Parks* asked to have the Drainage Act declared unconstitutional, and six months later, on the 26th of September, the state supreme court so declared. In the high court the Drainage Act had run full into a solid reef of adamant, ideologically undiluted, Jeffersonian public policy. The whole idea, dear to Republicans, of creating an independent public body called a commission and giving it broad, vaguely stated powers to carry out a major public task at its discretion, guided by experts, was anathema to the court. "The very first sentence of the act," as the presiding judge, C. J. Morrison, observed categorically in his opinion for the court,

> is fatal to whole of it. "The Governor, Surveyor, and State Engineer shall be the *ex officio* members of, and constitute a Board of Drainage Commissioners to divide the State into several drainage districts, and organize the same as hereinafter provided." Here is a wholesale delegation of general legislative powers to executive officers—the power of organizing districts in which taxes are to be levied, fixing boundaries, etc. . . . Any act which attempts to substitute the judgment and discretion of any person for the judgment and discretion of the Legislature

> in a matter committed to the Legislature, and not expressly authorized by the Constitution to be delegated, is void.[27]

The *Legislature*: this was the duly elected body that represented the people directly and was charged with plenary legislative powers. It was this body that should be making the state's policies. Executive officers must do things only as specifically guided in detail by the legislature, Morrison observed, even in so mundane a matter as the repair of streets. If legislators are wise enough to frame codes of civil procedure or laws governing contracts, lands, and corporations, "all the complicated affairs of life, even for the government of cities and counties," why are they not wise enough to manage the particular subject of drainage? "The proposition is too absurd to be considered," observed the judge.[28] The legislature "can not delegate its powers, except as expressly authorized in the Constitution . . . for, if [it] . . . could transfer its authority in one instance, it might in all others, and it could thus change the nature of the government entirely."[29]

In the Drainage Act the judgment of an executive officer called the state engineer as to what territory should be drained, was substituted for that of the legislature, and he was not even called on to make reports to that body, but rather to the commission. Commented Judge Morrison: "If the argument is good for anything, it will enable the Legislature to substitute the 'wisdom' of experts for their own in other matters as well as this. . . . why not with reference to all other matters requiring special knowledge?"[30] The Drainage Act even gave to executive officers the judgment of "when and where taxes shall be levied—that is the sole prerogative of the Legislature. . . . This is not only shocking to the natural sense of liberty, but it is contrary to the settled policy of this State, and of all the other States."[31] If this were not enough, the storage of mining debris was not, in fact, a matter of public concern, but rather a private enterprise "in which only the few are interested. . . . the Legislature has no power to impose taxes for the benefit of individuals connected with a private enterprise, even though the private enterprise might benefit the local public in a remote or collateral way."[32]

It was all over. The Republican concept of strong government through independent public authorities sited in a new and as yet unoccupied terrain between the legislature and the executive was not going to be allowed to become an enduring fixture in California government. The Drainage Act had finally fallen foul of the surrounding context of basic ideas and values which in the Gilded Age set out the boundaries as to what government could do, how far it could call on trust in executive officers—which, since the nation's founding, were regarded with brooding skepticism—and how deeply that government and those executive officers could draw on a statewide sense of community of interest, which as yet, in California, had not taken form. The drainage program had been created in unusual and fleeting political circumstances when visionary Republicans, aided by a succession of increasingly severe natural disasters, could for a brief period put in place in Sacramento their vision of what government in America should be and do—but the program could not survive. The whole effort at creating strong centralized control of natural resource management in the Sacramento Valley, for that matter anywhere in the state, by an agency of the state of California—save by its legislature acting directly, hardly a practical prospect—was in ruins, not to be revived for more than a quarter of a century, that is, not until Americans were thinking differently about society and government.

As we learn in Donald Pisani's *From the Family Farm to Agribusiness,* arduous efforts made in these same Gilded Age years by William Ham. Hall and others to get public policy toward irrigation reformed, so that central state authorities would take over direct management of water rights and the planning, construction, and administering of irrigation systems, would also fail. The immensely complicated matter of irrigation was left to local irrigation districts, which emerged triumphant, in their relative autonomy, from the intense public argument over this issue in the 1880s. In flood control as in irrigation, the result for many years into the future was a tale of confusion, anarchy, and a near-catastrophic record of bankruptcies and the wholesale wastage of invested funds.

≈≈≈

In January 1881, while the legislature was debating whether or not to repeal the Drainage Act, a monster flood, one of the greatest in the history of the Sacramento Valley, suddenly surged out of the mountains to spread devastation, suffering, and loss on the flatlands. Once more, nature had produced an appalling event that wrenched the course of public events into new paths. Frightened by the experience of fighting this massive inundation and appalled at the destruction, at this point the Anti-Debris Association, which the farmers had formed in 1878 to focus and give enduring strength to their efforts, gave up on the Drainage Act program. It could never protect them, they decided, so long as hydraulic mining continued to pour debris into and further destroy the river channels. The flood of 1881 had revealed that in the existing situation the region's levees, both locally built and those constructed by the state, were pitifully inadequate barriers, and the performance of the Yuba and Bear river brush dams was not encouraging. The Anti-Debris Association decided, therefore, once again to take up its crusade to close down the industry; the two-year armistice was over. It was hopeless to believe that the legislature would ever enact a statute declaring hydraulic mining illegal—one more vain attempt in this direction was made in February 1881—and so the people of the Valley turned again to the courts to ask injunction relief under the law of equity.[33]

A long series of lawsuits ensued over the next several years, culminating in a climactic January 1884 decision by Judge Lorenzo Sawyer of the federal Ninth Circuit Court in San Francisco, in the case of *Edwards Woodruff* v. *North Bloomfield Gravel Mining Co., et al.*[34] After listening over many months to testimony that filled thousands of pages of transcript, and twice visiting the affected areas, Sawyer issued a categorical ruling that remains the governing decree concerning hydraulic mining to this day. He had concluded, he said, that since hydraulic mining was doing such widespread damage, unless dumping mine tailings into the rivers was authorized by law (that is, it was not enough that existing laws did not declare it illegal) it constituted a general, far-reaching and most destructive public and private nuisance that must be halted. The suit covered all mines discharging into the Yuba and its tributaries, and at the end of his 225-page decision, Sawyer declared that the defendant companies in that watershed were "perpetually enjoined and restrained from discharging or dumping into the Yuba River . . . [or its tributaries] any of the tailings, bowlders [sic], cobble stones, gravel, sand, clay, debris, or refuse matter." This was not, in short, an injunction aimed only at "coarse debris," but at everything the mines produced. The mines were absolutely forbidden to allow any of their tailings to get into the rivers; the hydraulic mining industry, the whole of it, simply had to cease operations.[35]

In the year 1884, therefore, what appears to have been the first major federal court decree ever to be issued aimed at protecting a natural environment from further destruction had been handed down. It was declared, furthermore, in the midst of the Gilded Age, a time legendary for its indifference to the depredations of free enterprise, at the cost of closing down an entire industry that was owned and directed by otherwise-powerful capitalists despite the loss, to those gentlemen, of millions of dollars. It was of course not a decision made within the framework of the environmentalist values that would flourish a century later, but within the terms that Americans of the Gilded Age could understand and accept: that hydraulic mining inevitably destroyed the property of others.

It would take the rest of the 1880s fully to enforce Sawyer's decree, since ordinary miners living in the mountains continued to use the mining facilities that the corporations had abandoned.[36] Meanwhile, the great question of the rivers themselves—the focus of this history—remained. The mining debris that thirty years of operations had piled up in the mountain canyons was not halted by Sawyer's injunction. It continued to wash downstream, filling in the Valley's river channels more deeply with each high water season. By 1886 the rivers would begin running clear, hydraulic mining itself having been largely shut down so that mud was not floating downstream, but not until 1905 would the bed of the Yuba River at Marysville cease rising, and thereafter begin trenching out.[37] What was happening, in short, was that the peak of the debris-wave was passing that community to move thereafter into and on down the Feather and the Sacramento rivers.

In the 1880s, therefore, the problem of how to restore and reclaim the rivers still faced the Valley, unsettled. In February 1882, Lt. Col. Mendell had already proposed his own detailed plan for halting the downstream flow of stored-up debris in the mountains by building restraining dams on the Yuba, Bear, and Feather rivers, recommending that Congress appropriate $500,000 to fund the project.[38] His proposal, however, set off a great clamor in the Valley, for at that moment hydraulic mining was still not yet enjoined, the monitors were at work day and night, and many feared that the prospect of a forthcoming system of such dams would only encourage the courts to allow hydraulic mining to continue. Furthermore, Valley folk deeply distrusted dams, fearing for their safety. The Anti-Debris Association condemned Mendell's plan and even called for his dismissal, one Colusa County supervisor terming him a tool of the hydraulic miners.[39]

When in September 1882 a Republican-dominated U.S. Congress appropriated $250,000 to fund the building of three debris dams, appeals went off to Secretary of War Lincoln that he impound the funds as "an utter waste of the People's money [which would] . . . increase the already imminent danger." After some deliberation Lincoln agreed to do so, since the continued operation of the mines, he had decided, made it unwise to build the dams. In 1884 Congress stipulated that even the usual $40,000 Corps of Engineers annual appropriation for pulling snags in the Sacramento River could not be used until the Secretary of War was satisfied that hydraulic mining was halted. And so, the federal-state partnership that had been aborning was quashed, at both ends. This general impasse remained in effect until the latter 1880s. All efforts at the federal as well as the state level for restoring the Sacramento River and its tributaries were either terminated entirely, or suspended.[40]

CHAPTER

Reentry:
1886–1902

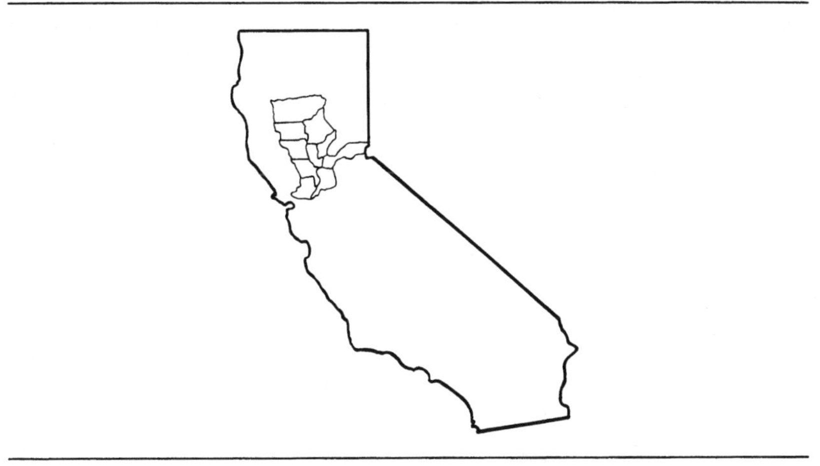

The boat struck [the light pole] with a loud clang, spilling all seven passengers . . . the boat started to turn upside down, and the world seemed to do likewise. . . . the next 10 minutes [were] . . . the most terrifying minutes of my life. . . . I felt the pull of the numbingly cold water and heard the roar of a river that ran 15 feet deep through what the day before had been [the] downtown. . . . then I hit something. My neck was caught on a wire strung between two poles. My jacket snagged around my head, and I was swallowing a lot of water. I thought then that I might die.

Brad Kava, San Jose Mercury-News, *February 22, 1986. Quoted in* Rivers of Fear, *pp. 53–54.*

For the second time in California, the Republicans had sought to shift public policy in natural resource management over to a centralized, Hamiltonian base, and the effort had again been beaten back. The courts, deep in a Jeffersonian distrust of independent public authority, had stripped California of the means to take arms against its great problem in the Sacramento Valley. In flood control, for many years into the future the result in that Valley was a story of confusion and failure. The Green Act was once more the only policy in effect; localism and individualism were dominant, which meant that joint efforts against floodwaters, the common enemy, were exceedingly difficult to mount; and mining debris washing down from the enormous piled-up deposits in the mountains filled the rivers deeper and deeper, so that the flood level kept rising.

In 1889, the people of Colusa County flung themselves into an

In 1893 the federal Caminetti Act allowed hydraulic mining to resume if miners impounded their debris behind dams. To angry complaints from downstream residents, log-crib dams were allowed. Before long, they were giving way. Requiring more permanent structures put costs of operations too high; by 1900 the briefly revived industry was once more moribund.
Picture source: Grove K. Gilbert, Hydraulic Mining Debris in the Sierra Nevada, *Professional Paper 105, U.S. Geological Survey (Washington, D.C., 1917).*

almost desperate outburst of levee building, putting up many miles of costly new levee, but it was all lost labor. In 1892, after a huge storm, the Sacramento reached its highest mark ever at Colusa, there were many levee breaks above and below town on both sides of the river, and thereafter Colusa County people seem to have fallen back exhausted, unable to do more.[1]

The only hope lay in action by state and federal authorities. Until they could be induced to move back into the Valley with a renewed program of centralized plans and funding, it would remain as it had been for many years: a flood-ravaged backwater, declining in population while the rest of the state boomed, shunned by investors and settlers, heavily burdened with debts people could not pay, and equipped with a patchwork levee system that had absorbed immense funds but provided little or no protection.

≈≈≈

The process of reentry was in fact already underway. People in the city of Sacramento had long before taken worried note of the steadily worsening condition of the rivers. Within two years of the decision in the North Bloomfield case, merchants there began calling for the launching of a renewed campaign to get the federal government back into the business of thinking about restoring the Sacramento and its tributaries.[2]

New economic and political currents nationwide were creating a welcoming context for such initiatives, provided they were linked, as it was often said they should be, to the revival of hydraulic mining. The entire national economy in the latter 1880s was entering on grave times. The massive migration of grain farmers out into the Great Plains which had marked the 1870s was by this time producing mountainous overproduction of wheat, while at the same time new grain-producing regions were being opened in other parts of the world. The result was a catastrophic slump in grain prices, which put debt-burdened grain farmers under cruel pressures. Southern cotton farmers, too, were being crushed by similar problems, the price of cotton having plunged to starvation levels. Out of these grave circum-

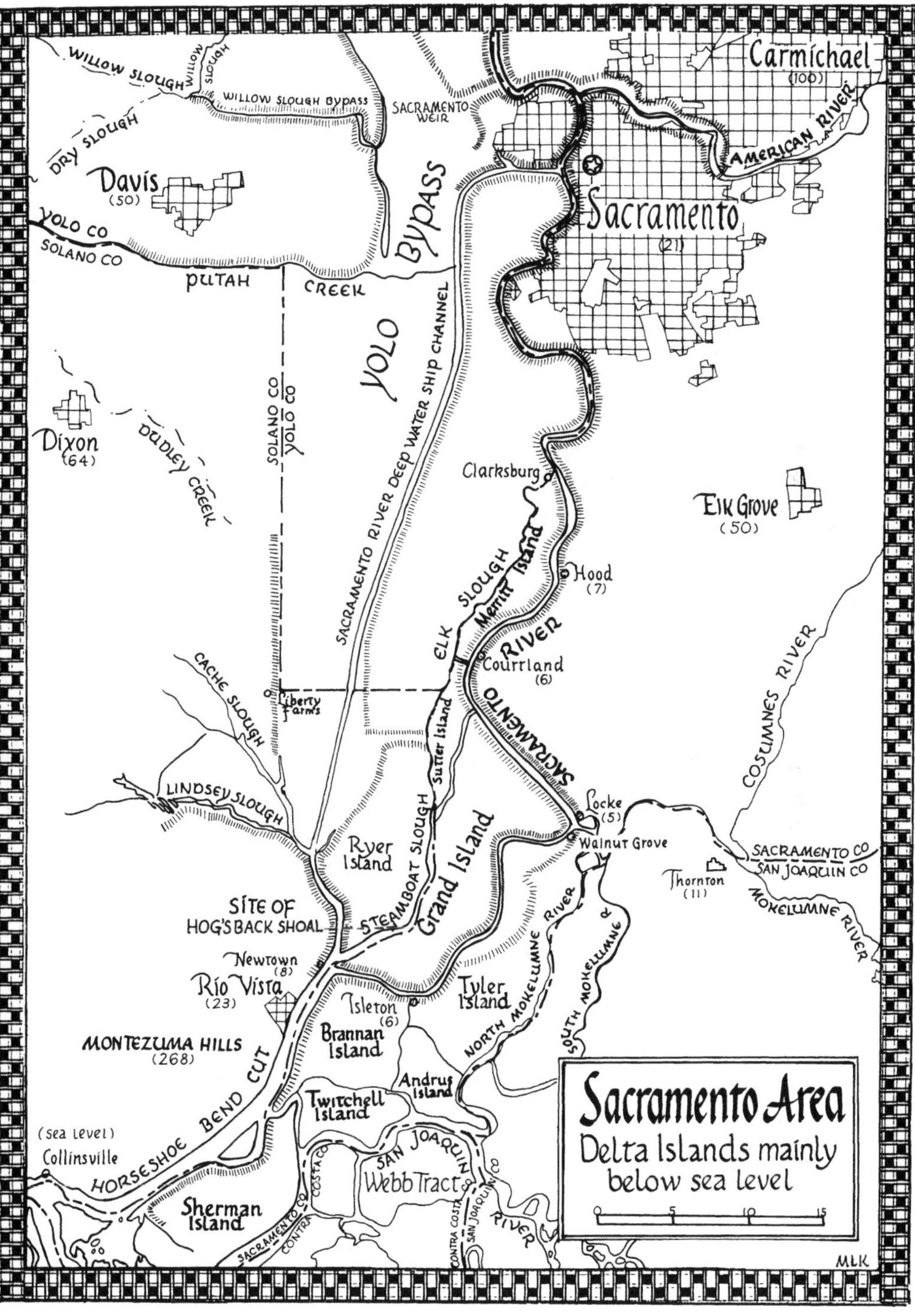
Sacramento Area
Delta Islands mainly below sea level
0 5 10 15
MLK
Carmichael
(100)
American River
Sacramento
(21)
Sacramento Weir
Willow Slough
Willow Slough Bypass
Dry Slough
Davis
(50)
Yolo Co
Solano Co
Putah Creek
Yolo Bypass
Sacramento River Deep Water Ship Channel
Solano Co
Yolo Co
Dixon
(64)
Dudley Creek
Clarksburg
Elk Grove
(50)
Hood
(7)
Elk Slough
Merritt Island
River
Courtland
(6)
Sacramento
Cosumnes River
Cache Slough
Liberty Farms
Sutter Island
Lindsey Slough
Steamboat Slough
Locke
(5)
Walnut Grove
Sacramento Co
San Joaquin Co
Thornton
(11)
Ryer Island
Grand Island
Site of Hog's Back Shoal
Mokelumne River
North Mokelumne River
South Mokelumne
Newtown
(8)
Rio Vista
(23)
Tyler Island
Isleton
(6)
Brannan Island
Montezuma Hills
(268)
Horseshoe Bend Cut
Andrus Island
Twitchell Island
(sea level)
Collinsville
San Joaquin River
Webb Tract
Sherman Island
Sacramento Co
Contra Costa Co
Contra Costa
San Joaquin Co

stances erupted a powerful national crusade for currency inflation, in the hope that large increases in the money supply would produce corresponding rises in commodity prices.[3]

From this new perspective, the closed-down hydraulic gold mines in California assumed a new importance. The grain farmers were agitating for a return to silver coinage, but certainly an increase in gold production would have the same effect of increasing the nation's total stock of currency. As the *San Francisco Call* would later put the question in the mid-1890s when the free-silver campaign was reaching its climax, "If we had it to do over again, we should not throw away $10,000,000 a year in gold as light-heartedly as we did when we allowed hydraulic mining to be suppressed without a serious effort to harmonize the conflicting interests." This picture of how productive the mines had actually been and of what had been attempted in the Drainage Act years was grossly miscast, but it accurately reflected the mood in which many people looked back on hydraulic mining. Farming had gone down with grain, the *Call* remarked, and therefore "our minds turn again to the industry that made California a state, and the product for which the whole world is scrambling."[4]

A concerted pro-mining campaign had got underway in the year 1887. The legislature was asked by the miners to authorize the building of high dams in the mountains which could impound the debris of entire watersheds (such a structure, for example, could be put in the Narrows of the Yuba River, a deep, steep-walled crevasse through which that stream flowed, some miles before it issued from the mountains), thus allowing hydraulic mining to revive. The proposal was only barely fought off by Valley people, once more with the odor of purchased votes floating through the legislature's chambers.[5]

In the minds of the legislature as a whole, however, this was not enough. The flooding situation in the Sacramento Valley was too desperate, and the belief that hydraulic mining should be resuscitated was too strong, to let the matter thus die. Feelings were thoroughly aroused, a new definition of the situation was forming up, and a coalition in favor of doing *something* important about these twin problems was taking shape. The result was unanimous passage of an urgent memorial to the national Congress pleading for aid to California. In what way? By authorizing a fresh examination of the entire problem by a specially appointed commission of Army engineers who, keeping in mind the protection of the people of the Valley floor, were to decide

> whether some plan can be devised whereby the present conflict between the mining and farming sections may be adjusted and the mining industry rehabilitated; second, to the carrying out of such plans, in the event any suitable ones be determined on; third, for a complete examination and survey of the injured river channels, with a view to their improvement and rectification; fourth, providing sufficient means to accomplish said purposes.[6]

Many in the Sacramento Valley still deeply distrusted the federal engineers to the point of paranoia, and they reacted in alarm to this new initiative. Boards of supervisors passed hostile petitions, but in September 1888, Congress reentered the Sacramento Valley problem by creating the appealed-for commission, composed of U.S. Army Corps of Engineers officers. The Biggs Commission—named for Marion Biggs, the California congressman who had authored the bill—was soon at work. Its report, rendered in February 1891, was perhaps predictable. Hydraulic mining could certainly be revived, the engineers confidently asserted, without damaging the rivers further. This could be achieved if the miners themselves put up dams near their operations to restrain their own debris. Meanwhile, the federal government could proceed to restore the rivers' navigability by such simple means as installing brush wing-dams in their channels to constrict their flow and force them to scour out their own beds.[7]

Of all the proposals cast up by the U.S. Army Corps of Engineers in its long affair with the Sacramento River, that of the Biggs Commission was the most overconfident, cavalier, and misguided, as later experience would abundantly demonstrate. It had, however, a powerful impact upon Congress, for the context was just right. The Biggs Commission report came off the presses in a Washington, D.C., which was warmly approving toward anything that might increase the volume of the national currency, and was therefore friendly toward the hydraulic gold mines. Thus the Biggs Commission report, for all its errors, was the germ out of which, eventually, an effective flood control system in the Valley would finally evolve—though there were many twists and turns in the road ahead toward that goal, which would not be realized until well beyond the turn of the twentieth century.

The mining industry was of course tremendously excited by the Biggs Commission report, and it had powerful pro-mining friends in the national capital to help bring its proposals to reality. Key California public figures also swung vigorously behind the new cause, urging it eagerly on the Congress. We see at a crucial nodal point a key person, Governor H. H. Markham, who had been almost peculiarly shaped by his experiences to play a strategic role in hurrying these events onward. Markham was a Yankee Republican who was twice wounded in Civil War battles and had become a distinguished attorney and entrepreneur in southern California. A seasoned and rather dashing public figure, Colonel Markham, as he was called, had served in Congress in the 1880s, where membership on the Rivers and Harbors Committee (which worked directly with the secretary of war and the Corps of Engineers) and success in winning large appropriations for improving Wilmington harbor had apparently converted him to the belief that Army engineers could work miracles. In his gubernatorial campaign he had urged that the Sacramento and San Joaquin rivers be improved at federal expense, and he had been swept to victory.[8] In his inaugural and subsequent addresses in 1891 Markham called repeatedly for reviving the hydraulic mining industry.

In 1892 a long-time pro-mining legislator, Congressman Anthony Caminetti of mountainous Amador County in the San Joaquin Valley, where hydraulic mining had once flourished, submitted a bill in Congress which would put the findings and recommendations of the Biggs Commission into effect. Caminetti proposed that a federal agency to be called the California Debris Commission be created and given authority to license individual operators to begin hydraulic mining, provided they built dams to restrain their tailings, and these dams were built according to Debris Commission regulations. Fueled by a flood of petitions in its support from California—one from the legislature was particularly important—the Caminetti bill swept through the

House in July 1892, though Congress thereafter adjourned before the Senate could consider the bill.[9]

Now a thoroughly aroused Sacramento Valley produced a storm of protest. Not only was the principle of debris dams still distrusted, it was widely feared that once miners had been thus encouraged to begin operations, they would pay slight attention to Debris Commission regulations and pour debris into the rivers with only token restraint.

> Rules and Regulation be blanked [cried the *Marysville Appeal*]! Will they impound debris? Will they prevent the filling up of navigable streams? Not much, and if we mistake not the valley people will see that more than "rules and regulations" are stretched across the rivers to restrain the debris from the hydraulic mines.[10]

There was a hurried calling of meetings by a revived Anti-Debris Association which led to strenuous and eventually successful efforts to give the Caminetti bill real teeth. By amendment, a penalty clause was inserted which stipulated that a $5000 fine or one year of imprisonment would be the lot of anyone violating the act.

In March 1893, the Caminetti bill came before President Benjamin Harrison, then in the last few days of his term of office, since Grover Cleveland had defeated him in the previous November's balloting. Here was a man who more than anything else, as president, had preached with a missionary's fervor the theme of development! development! In classic Republican fashion Harrison had eagerly supported the idea that government should do everything possible to assist private enterprise in opening the nation's resources and creating jobs. Clearly following his deepest instincts, he signed the legislation, and the Caminetti Act was law.[11]

As the fruit of just the right combination of converging influences—key players in strategic places, an expert report arriving at the right time, a political party still holding the reigns of power whose ideas were welcoming to it, and a hospitable context in state and nation—a new fundamental policy toward river management in the Sacramento Valley had finally been established at the federal level. It effectively recreated for this purpose the kind of independent expert commission, with broad powers, which on two occasions California had been unable to keep in place and operating. If even a few more weeks had passed, bringing the stern Grover Cleveland to the White House and into Congress the strong Democratic majority that had been elected with him, both of them nourishing their traditional distrust of entrepreneurs who asked for government help, the window of opportunity for the creation of the California Debris Commission would have closed decisively.

River management in the Sacramento Valley, with its complex of dams, canals, and governmental agencies, begins with the Caminetti Act, the end product of the mining debris struggle. What was publicly noted in California at the time of its enactment was that hydraulic mining could again revive, under Debris Commission oversight, and that now a federal body existed specifically charged with improving and maintaining navigability in the Valley's rivers. Less noted was a crucial provision in the Caminetti Act which would have decisive importance in future years. Doubtless without realizing its implications, Congress in that act surprisingly expanded the range of federal responsibilities toward the Sacramento and its tributaries. As we have earlier seen, Congress had traditionally and scrupulously held to the principle that in river management matters, it was responsible under *Gibbons* v. *Ogden* only for maintaining navigability. However, the Caminetti Act gave the new California Debris Commission not simply the combined tasks of regulating hydraulic mining and making plans for the purpose of "improving the navigability, deepening the channels, and protecting the banks of the rivers," it was also to make plans for "*affording relief from flood damages* [italics added]."[12]

Thus, a new and historic policy had been established, apparently by inadvertence, since the Corps of Engineers would not actually follow up on it for many years. When it did, Californians would finally discover that in the California Debris Commission the Sacramento Valley had won what it most needed: a strong federal agency which, if it so decided, had legal authority to do something about flood control. As Congressman Caminetti remarked, "The people of California do not yet realize what a tremendous advantage this bill is going to be to them. It is usually spoken of as a measure for the benefit of the miners, but its provisions for the improvement of the rivers will be found to be still more important. It gives us a River Commission—the third in the United States [after the Missouri and the lower Mississippi]."[13]

≈≈≈

Now a complex and as it turned out lengthy learning process had begun: discovering how to implement so novel a public policy as the Caminetti Act had established. The California Debris Commission, which was composed of three officers of the Corps of Engineers, was not, in truth, in an easy position. In an important sense it was exposed and vulnerable, for it embodied what was yet a new idea in the federal government. It was a *commission*—and not simply an investigatory one such as the Biggs Commission which would go out of existence at the end of its work—but a permanent governing body. It was given the kind of large, vaguely stated powers—leaving the details of implementation to its choice—that in 1881 the California Supreme Court in *The People* v. *Parks* had sternly quashed, declaring that in a democracy such authority should never be handed over by legislatures to "expert" commissions.

In Congress itself an agitated debate fueled by these Jeffersonian sentiments had raged for years over the idea of establishing independent commissions with broad discretionary governing powers (in this case, to regulate railroads). Widely reiterated were the criticisms that they were undemocratic and improper delegations of legislative authority. Because they would concentrate large powers in a few hands, critics said they were potentially vulnerable to takeover by the very interests (the railroads) they were created to regulate. In this same spirit, the Sacramento Valley's farmers had argued against having a commission, particularly one composed entirely of engineers, regulate the hydraulic mining industry precisely for the reason that they believed any such body would be in the miners' pocket—and engineers, in truth, were regularly the partners of men of large capital, not of the simple folk.

The American polity, as political scientists term a governing system taken in its totality, was in the Gilded Age (the years from the 1870s to the 1890s) essentially a bare Jeffersonian system of legislatures and courts, guided by the political parties, and this was the way most people wanted it to be. Men like Democratic Congressman John Reagan of Texas, who took a leading role in late-1870s congressional debates over creating a federal railroad-regulating commission, led the fight with eloquent and urgent power. He was deeply suspicious of this new kind of governing entity which would carry on its duties from a position somewhere between Congress and the courts, forming what is now termed the "fourth branch" of government. If the railroads were exploiting the community, Reagan said, let Congress stipulate in detail, in statute form, what practices were illegal, and then let the courts enforce that law.[14]

However, the nation's emerging problems in the new industrial and urban society being born in the Gilded Age were too complex and changing for this ancient vision of the American republic to survive. As political scientist Stephen Skowronek has described, in the 1880s the movement toward building a stronger, more centralized national administrative authority with wide powers to regulate key aspects of the new economy was beginning to build a constituency in Congress. The goal, as in the case of the California Debris Commission and the hydraulic mining dilemma in California, was "to remove all politically divisive and potentially dangerous policy decisions from the legislative arena," and to do so by "avoiding all hard-and-fast rules."[15]

Advocates of commissions said it was impossible to pass a law sufficiently detailed and superhumanly wise in foresight that would anticipate and list every stratagem skillful railroad entrepreneurs would use to gain advantages over their customers and their competitors, and simply rely on the courts to enforce the legislation. Rather, a federal railroad commission composed of (presumably) educated gentlemen of seasoned public wisdom must be created and given broad powers and wide latitude to enforce them, in light of expert knowledge and ongoing, existing circumstances. After a long debate, which raged through the mid-1880s, in 1887 Congress swung over to this elitist, essentially Whiggish concept (critics even warned that it was Hamiltonian Federalism revived) and created the Interstate Commerce Commission (ICC). In this measure the first step had been taken toward fashioning a new kind of administrative state in America, one which in many ways would resemble the stronger centralized governments in Europe. The ICC would have a difficult time establishing its role; through the 1890s the courts would stringently hobble its authority, but after 1900, with Theodore Roosevelt in the presidency and the dawning of the Progressive Era, it would grow into the powerful agency its creators had had in mind.[16]

The California Debris Commission, which was established just six years after the ICC (and would endure until its termination in the latter 1980s) was part of this tentatively emerging new regime in American government. It, too, would have a difficult time establishing its role, for the CDC was also a new thing in an overall institutional setting that was not particularly friendly or supportive. The Jeffersonian polity would endure in America for many years. The CDC would go through a long and wearing time of learning how to do what it was charged with achieving and getting Congress to take it seriously, that is, to fund its proposals.

Its tasks were certainly large enough. They were complicated, too, by the fact that the Caminetti Act required the Commission finally to put into effect the working federal-state partnership, concerning the navigable rivers, that *Gibbons* v. *Ogden* had mandated. Breaking new ground in this direction, the act required the state of California to share equally in the costs of such physical works as would be built, which meant state appropriations matching federal funds dollar-for-dollar. California was also to establish parallel state officials to work with the Commission.[17]

Sacramento took up eagerly its part of the bargain. Under the activist Governor Markham, in the very month of the Caminetti Act's passage in Congress the legislature created two new officials: a debris commissioner, who was to sit (in a nonvoting capacity) with the California Debris Commission (CDC) as it proceeded to issue licenses for hydraulic mining, and a state commissioner of public works. The latter would cooperate with the CDC in its efforts to reestablish navigability. That is, the public works commissioner's jurisdiction reached from the mouth of the Sacramento River to its juncture with the Feather, while that of the debris commissioner extended above that point. The Caminetti Act had adopted the specific proposals of the Biggs Commission, which had recommended a massive $500,000 dam project on the Yuba River. Therefore, in the legislation creating the debris commissioner's office California seized the nettle and appropriated $250,000 to be its half of the cost of such works. In these years of small and tightly controlled state budgets, this was a huge sum. Accordingly, the legislature cautiously stipulated that no money would change hands between the state and federal governments until Congress had also appropriated a like amount.[18] This was a prescient step; it would take years to get the funds from Washington.

≈≈≈

The California Debris Commission was soon at work, opening its meetings in June 1893, in its San Francisco headquarters. It had, however, but a slim purse to support its operations: $15,000. To get anything more—certainly the soon-to-be famous $250,000—it had to convince Congress that it actually had a viable and necessary plan for a major project. The commission had an abundance of experience and knowledge in its membership for the development of such a proposal. A familiar figure who had been at work in the Sacramento Valley for decades, Colonel George H. Mendell, was its president. The other two commissioners, Lt. Col. W. H. H. Benyaurd and Major W. H. Heuer, had been on the Biggs Commission. Indeed, Heuer's knowledge of the Sacramento River went back to the early 1870s, when as a young lieutenant he had nosed around the Hog's Back Shoal, making surveys.[19]

Since the early 1880s Mendell had been urging that a debris dam be constructed at Daguerre Point on the Yuba River. Accordingly, the commission was promptly launched on preparing a proposal to Congress that such a project be funded. Nothing whatever could be effectively done, the commission insisted, about restoring navigability on the Feather and the Sacramento rivers, which were downstream from the avalanche of mining debris that was coming down from the mountains, unless that immense mass of sand, gravel, and rocks was immobilized and, in effect, held in place. Otherwise, the river channels below would eventually be obliterated.

The watershed of the Yuba had held far the largest concentration of hydraulic mines, and the debris it was washing down into the Valley posed the greatest single threat to its rivers. Daguerre Point, a natural feature about six miles out from the point where the Yuba emerged from the mountains, had long been noted as an excellent location for some sort of restraining work since here a southward-thrusting spur of the foothills narrowed the river's channel. In the Commission's preliminary proposal to Congress, made in its first annual report, it informed that body that a "suitable appropriation for this work will be $300,000."[20]

Things were very different now in Washington, however, than they had been before the last election. As we have seen, Democrats, not Republicans, controlled Congress and the White House, where a somber Grover Cleveland, scourge of special interests since his days as mayor of Buffalo and governor of New York, sat on brood. He and his party had been condemning subsidies to private enterprise at the top of their lungs for generations, reaching back to Thomas Jefferson himself. Special legislation in aid of entrepreneurs was the fundamental source, Democrats insisted, of the corruption that stained the republic's government from top to bottom.[21] Sacramento Valley farmers, who were still fearful of the safety of debris dams such as the proposed Daguerre Point structure, attacked the CDC's proposal as one that would only aid the hydraulic mining companies, and their criticisms much harmed the CDC's proposal in Congress.

Furthermore, the nation was caught up in the agonies of a great national depression. Within months of the commission's creation in 1893, a massive nationwide slump, one of the worst in the nation's history—only the depression of the 1930s would be more severe—had drastically reduced all sources of revenue. For several years, until prosperity returned, Congress would be reluctant to fund public works projects, for it was forty years away from its New Deal discovery that such measures created jobs and would aid in recovery from depressions. As late as 1896, therefore, the California Debris Commission and the state of California were still looking in vain for river-improvement public works funds from Washington, whether the funds were the federal government's half of the $500,000 called for in the Biggs Commission report, or its share of the $300,000 that the CDC had requested.[22]

With its Daguerre Point project stalled in Washington, for several years the Debris Commission simply turned away from thinking about reclaiming the rivers and focused on its primary responsibility: reviving the hydraulic mining industry. From the state of California, however, in the mid-1890s there came a surprisingly energetic burst of planning activity directed at restoring the rivers and at flood control. Now it had a new instrumentality, in the public works commissioners' office, charged with thinking about these matters, and things swiftly began to happen. Governor Markham had made a shrewd choice when he selected a veteran swampland entrepreneur, A. H. Rose, to be state commissioner of public works. In an earlier chapter we have seen that he first came to public attention in 1870 as president of the huge Reclamation District 108 (RD 108) then being formed in Colusa and Yolo counties, which had proceeded to build sixty miles of river levee along the banks of the Sacramento and set off the levee-building spiral in the mid-Valley region.

Thereafter, at huge expense RD 108 had battled the river and its floods year after year, raising levees again and again only to have them overtopped or broken through, in part because levee-builders on the opposite side of the stream were crowding their embankments to the river's edge and leaving too narrow a channelway for floods to pass through. Few men, in short, had a more intimate knowledge than A. H. Rose of the results of flood control efforts in a setting of laissez-faire anarchy, under Will Green's 1868 legislation.

With Rose and Mendell rising to strategic positions of authority in the 1890s, it was finally the case that those in authority actually knew a great deal, in a concrete, factual sense, about the problem of the river. Gone were the heady years when a group of visionary young men were in charge who knew nothing, essentially, of the Sacramento River, but who were marvelously fertile in conceiving great visions about what they could do to it to get their way—as for example in reclaiming the swamplands—especially when prompted to spend money on bold schemes by distinguished engineers. Now a leadership cadre of seasoned men who could make realistic definitions of the situation had finally come into being.

Looking out on the Sacramento Valley in 1895, a quarter of a century after he and his fellow investors had launched RD 108, Commissioner Rose saw a discouraging scene. Vast sums of money, he remarked in his first annual report to the governor, had been spent on levees, and much of it had been wasted. The subject of flood control in the Sacramento Valley needed to be treated as a whole, he said, but instead the Valley "is divided into several hundred [independent] Reclamation Swamp Land or Protection Districts." Some of them had natural boundaries, but most were "arbitrarily bounded by property or other lines." Each district was supreme so far as the location and height of its levees were concerned, which in many cases they had built with no attention whatever to their effects on anyone else or on the river, "the prime object being the protection of the lands of their district according to the local objects to be obtained, which generally means the construction of levees powerful enough to overtop or force a break on the other side." Quite out of their concern had been making certain that channelways were of appropriate size, or that there was suitable outfall for floodwaters to flow down valley. How had this happened? Reported Rose: "This unfortunate condition has been the direct outgrowth of the policy of the State to sell these lands prior to their reclamation by the State; or even to prescribe the limits and location of levees and drainage channels."[23]

> As a general thing, these attempts were the result of the efforts of adjacent owners, with no conception of the fact that the works they were endeavoring to construct and maintain were parts of the great arterial drainage systems of valleys receiving the flood waters of 57,000 square miles of mountain and rolling lands. When we compare their disconnected and systemless efforts with the volumes and forces of the floods which they attempted to control, the cause of failure stands out in bold lines, and the useless character of a systemless struggle becomes very apparent. . . . the prime cause of failure has been the same throughout

> namely: the endeavor to construct through individuals or small districts, and without unity of action, the integral parts of a vast drainage and protection system, itself without design or conception.[24]

The language was revealing. *Design, cooperation, system, treating the subject as a whole, prescribing the limits and location of levees and drainage channels*: in these key words and phrases in Rose's powerful report the organizing impulse, Whiggish in spirit, was again at work. Clearly, in his mind the time had come for the state of California to move in once more on this wilderness of confusion and failure, which had produced a Valley still ravaged by massive flood and desperately insecure, and take central control of the planning and building of flood control works valleywide.

For this, a comprehensive proposal was needed, and with this in mind Rose had made well-thought appointments to his staff. He brought to it as consulting engineers two men who, as we have seen, were richly experienced in the Valley: Marsden Manson and C. E. Grunsky. As young men just entering their life work they had served under former State Engineer William Ham. Hall in the intense learning experience of his Drainage Act river surveys, conducted from 1878 to the early 1880s. Manson had gone on to make more studies of the rivers for the Corps of Engineers, and Grunsky had remained on Hall's staff until the state engineer's office essentially closed down in 1888.

In consequence, the body of knowledge that Manson and Grunsky brought to their task was deep and well tilled. So ready were they, in fact, to produce almost instantly a detailed, carefully wrought, essentially complete plan for valleywide flood control that with Commissioner Rose's very first annual report, sent to the governor in December 1894, sixteen months after beginning operations, he was able also to present the historic Manson and Grunsky report.

It was a brilliant achievement, a master stroke of planning which laid down the basic structure of flood control in the Sacramento Valley as it exists today, though the Corps of Engineers would not accept its principles for another decade. More than seventy pages long, the Manson and Grunsky report was a lucid, closely argued document written with energy and confidence, dense with fact, and skillfully reasoned. After a lengthy description of the nature of the Valley's rivers and basins, and an analysis of river-flow which relied heavily on the data they had gathered a decade and a half before under William Ham. Hall—little more was yet available—they proceeded to their plan, presenting it, they wrote, in a form of "extreme simplicity" so that their intentions would be entirely clear and understandable.

One point was fundamental: it was clear that they disagreed categorically with everything the Corps of Engineers had been and would go on saying about the river: that, following the Humphreys thesis, its waters could be put into a single, main channel. The river in floodtime, Manson and Grunsky warned, was just too large ever to be contained in this way. In fact, just four years before Manson and Grunsky made their report, General Cyrus Comstock of the Corps of Engineers, while serving as president of the Mississippi River Commission, had told Congress that the Humphreys thesis would not work. On the lower Mississippi, he called for release points to let excess waters escape down side channels—but the Corps itself disagreed, holding hard to its "levees only" policy.

Manson and Grunsky were sophisticated engineers; they doubtless had paid close attention to Comstock's publicly expressed views on the lower Mississippi. Besides, their mentor, William Ham. Hall, had demurred in his 1880 report from the strict "main channel" concept that General Alexander had earlier preached. It is understandable, therefore, that by implication in their 1894 plan they came down strongly against the Humphreys thesis. First, they said, it was certainly true that existing channels should be enlarged so that they would carry floodwater to "their maximum capacity as drainways." However, they went on, the fact must be accepted that the Sacramento River was going inevitably to flow overbank in floodtimes, not simply during rare monster floods, as in 1880 Hall had warned, but rather as a common event in even ordinary high water times. The outflow of "surplus waters" should be allowed at selected points, where strong weirs could be constructed, thus preventing the opening out of deep crevasses. From the weirs, the overflowing waters would pass out into the basins, as in the Valley's natural condition they had done. Indeed, Manson and Grunsky were at pains to say that their plan simply reproduced nature, which was why it would work.

However, they would introduce a large modification to nature's way of performing, and here, they were once more picking up themes briefly stated by their mentor, State Engineer Hall. In his 1880 report to the legislature he had said that escapeways, with embanked channels leading out from them into the basins, should be constructed to carry off overflowing floodwaters. However, his observations were made almost as an aside, they were not developed further. What would happen, for example, to the water after it was sent out into the basins? Presumably, it would occupy the basins until lower river-levels in the spring and summer allowed it to drain away. However, it was not necessary, Manson and Grunsky remarked, "to abandon the large and fertile areas represented by the basins to the surplus waters." Rather, the embanked "by-pass channels" (the term being here used for the first time) would be so planned and constructed that they would extend right on through the basins, thus keeping the floodwaters from spreading. Furthermore, in their plan each bypass would lead to the next one. This arrangement, which would in effect create a second river channel down through the Valley paralleling the main one, would allow the surplus waters to be quickly taken down-valley for discharge into Suisun Bay.[25]

Manson and Grunsky remarked that, in fact, Grunsky himself had presented the first recommendation of bypasses fifteen years before, in the fall of 1880, at a levee meeting in Princetón, Colusa County. We are aware, however, that Will Green, who in 1895 was still editing the *Colusa Sun,* had recommended this very bypass plan for the Valley in the pages of his newspaper and to the legislature as long ago as the mid-1860s. He must have found the Manson and Grunsky report a mixed experience to read. It offered him both long-overdue confirmation of his prescience and another snub given to a self-taught man of Southern sympathies who had not gone to an engineering college, and who was now thought to be, perhaps, simply an elderly country editor.

On the other hand, we are aware that Grunsky and Green knew

each other, for they worked together in the latter 1880s in the planning of Green's irrigation projects. Possibly this relationship actually began when Grunsky as a young engineer was in the Colusa vicinity in 1880 to attend his levee meeting, at which time voluble Will Green may have filled his ears with his long-ignored plan. It may have been that many years later, in 1895, it was not thought that publicly giving such an origin to the bypass concept would aid its chances of acceptance.

Having presented their broad plan, Manson and Grunsky needed to provide details of implementation, and they were ready with them. They described proposed bypasses through the several basins; urged that the mouth of the Sacramento be opened out, especially near Newtown Shoal, where a "choke" hampered egress and forced floodwaters to pile up, producing immense inundations; and proposed that all river levees "be brought to a uniform standard." What would be the result? The protection, they said, of 1,090,500 acres of Valley land that, with its improvements, was valued at more than $100 million. All of it in high water years was in danger of being flooded, while even in years of average rainfall a third of this vast area was in current conditions underwater. The cost of such a system? Some $9 million, to be raised by taxes on the property benefited and in proportion to the benefits realized by each landowner.[26] This "would seem to be large," Commissioner Rose wrote to the governor, but if built the plan would "bring into existence a wealth several times the cost of the works, at a figure less than one half that which has already been expended upon the existing lines of levees and protection works."[27]

Governor Markham urged the Manson and Grunsky plan on the 1895 legislature, but he went out of office as it began its sittings; a passionate antitax and budget-cutting Democrat, James H. Budd, succeeded him as governor;[28] the great depression of the mid-1890s had shriveled everyone's readiness to take on a huge new expenditure; and the plan languished.[29] Its role thereafter was to serve as a powerful guide and model for all future thinking about how to solve the Sacramento Valley's flood control problem. For the present, however, it appeared that nothing whatever would be done by either the federal government, through the California Debris Commission, or by the state, through the commissioner of public works, to make even a start on reclaiming the rivers.

The opening of the year 1896 saw the log-jam breaking rapidly. The whole movement toward ever more ambitious responses to the challenge of flooding in the Sacramento Valley was crisis-driven, and in familiar fashion, natural events now burst in to shake everyone out of their immobile positions and begin a new cycle of policy making. A major storm ravaged the state in January, many of the debris dams, constructed of logs, which the miners had built in the mountains under authority of the CDC broke, loosing large volumes of fresh mining debris to start moving down the rivers. The Valley protested vigorously, pointing to these events as proof that its people had been right to distrust the commission and its engineers. The gross errors embodied in the proposals of the Biggs Commission, which had confidently asserted that, under the supervision of U.S. Army engineers, hydraulic mining could be revived, were now surfacing for all to see. It had given advice to the federal Congress which had proved disastrously wrong.

The California Debris Commission, in an effort to save the situation, now began demanding the construction of more permanent and expensive restraining works by the miners, but even so, hydraulicking could only proceed intermittently. Sustained operations and a heavy flow of water inevitably had the effect of sweeping debris on over the lips of the dams, whether constructed of wood or masonry. In turn, the people downstream would clamor for injunctions and get them, for the creation of the CDC did not lift or affect in any way the continued jurisdiction of the courts over the industry. The categorical prohibitions of the *North Bloomfield* decision against discharging debris into the streams were still the law of the land. The boom in the mountains which had followed the Caminetti Act had busted. By 1900 not one mine in the Sierra Nevada was even capable of large-scale resumption of operations. Their water systems had been extensively damaged during storms, and their water rights were sold or lapsed. Though small operations would intermittently be possible in future years, the hydraulic mining industry was essentially dead.[30]

In January 1896, the State Anti-Debris Association sent representatives off to Washington to plead for help. The specific point at issue: the continued failure of Congress to appropriate its matching $250,000 for the project on the Yuba, its reluctance to do so springing from continuing allegations that only the hydraulic miners would be aided.[31] At the same time, after the disastrous flood of January 1896, the state commissioner of public works' chief engineer, J. R. Price, issued a colorfully written, dramatically appealing report that made it inescapably clear that the Sacramento Valley's rivers had reached such an advanced state of uncontrolled flooding that major new steps, on both the federal and state levels, had to be taken.

If the Sacramento River, he wrote, were allowed to continue filling up with debris, and crevasses in its levees such as existed on the river's right bank for miles below its juncture with the Feather were allowed to remain open—the heavy sands of the Feather, flowing into the Sacramento, were now beginning to wash far out into the Yolo Basin, reaching deposits as deep as six feet—then every basin would eventually be in grave, potentially terminal, danger. They would fill with floodwater and stay that way, all reclamation of any sort being impossible. Deep river channels, he insisted, had to be created to carry off the floods, and this work had to begin, as Manson and Grunsky had recommended, at the bottom of the river, at its mouth, where a "cork," as Price termed it, existed in the form of the Newtown Shoals. Extending for miles above Rio Vista (and including, apparently, the ancient Hog's Back Shoal), their removal would give the river more fall, accelerate its flow, and allow its power to reassert itself. The result, by scouring action, would be a progressive deepening of the stream, and a much increased capability for passing floodwaters out into the bay. "Without this," Price warned, "all other work is, in our estimation, useless."[32]

> The National Government must give us aid, or the destruction of the navigability of the Sacramento River is only a question of a few years. The damage now existing will take years to repair, but if permitted to continue, not only will it destroy navigation, but it will depopulate the wealthiest portion of the Sacramento River Valley—a kingdom in itself, a principality given to the energy of the nineteenth century, but

> without assistance destined to disappear in tule swamps and frog ponds before the dawn of the twentieth century.[33]

Congressman Grove L. Johnson, a Republican of Sacramento who since the days of the Drainage Act controversy in the early 1880s had long been active in Sacramento Valley flood control issues, now moved vigorously to secure federal funds. He was successful, for in April 1896, the long-awaited $250,000 for the Daguerre Point project was finally appropriated by the House in the Rivers and Harbors Act of June 3, 1896. All references to assistance for hydraulic miners were eliminated, however. The appropriation was specifically directed to be used for rehabilitating the navigable rivers.[34] Then in 1897, the state legislature formally charged the commissioner of public works with responsibility for flood control planning and operations for the entire Sacramento Valley. It was no longer simply to work with the CDC in its efforts to restore navigability. The legislature went on to adopt the commissioner's proposal as to specific projects and appropriated $300,000 to be spent on improving the Sacramento River's channel from its mouth to the Feather River. This set in motion the first engineering operations on the rivers for many years.[35]

From 1896 to 1898, the state got to work on Newtown Shoals by building jetties that narrowed the river, produced a stronger flow, and induced the scouring out of debris in the stream's bed. Then the state's engineers began step by step to build other projects up-valley, such as weirs to control overflow, though everything done in these early years was piecemeal and fragmentary, considering the immensity of the problem. In any event, navigability was quickly improved. By 1902, river depths at the Newtown Shoal, which formerly had been from zero to seven feet, were approaching twenty feet. By 1906, tidal action in the Sacramento, which formerly had not gotten closer to the city of Sacramento than ten miles, was reaching above that community, and river steamers could begin to keep their schedules.[36]

The California Debris Commission was fully aware by the latter 1890s that hydraulic mining was dead. Leaving essentially behind the impossible task of reviving it and funded now to move ahead on its navigability responsibility by building the Daguerre Point project, the CDC turned decisively in that direction. Without realizing it, by taking this step the commission was entering on a long, painful, error-filled effort; the imperatives of this effort, by its own internal logic, would finally lead the commission to take up the last in its Caminetti Act–listed duties, which to this point it had assiduously avoided: affording relief from flood.

After several years of painstaking engineering studies, a complex plan was evolved by the CDC for immobilizing the debris moving massively down the Yuba River. Several low, but progressively higher, concrete barriers would be built upstream from Daguerre Point, behind which the downstream-moving debris would be caught in a series of wide stair-steps, together with a settlage basin. The river's flow would also be diverted through a sill cut in the solid rock that composed the Point. All of this would cost, however, some $800,000, and this meant that California and the Congress would have to appropriate an additional $150,000 apiece.[37]

California soon provided its share of the money, but there were widespread suspicions in Congress that the Daguerre Point project was actually a covert plan for aiding in the revival of hydraulic mining. Accordingly, during a tour of West Coast public works sites the entire Committee on Rivers and Harbors of the House of Representatives descended upon the small town of Marysville on June 27 and 28, 1901. The committee appeared with wives, staff, and apparently every state and federal official resident in California who was in any way connected with the Yuba project. A crowd of horse-drawn rigs, carrying a total of 140 people, streamed out eastward of town on the Brown's Valley Grade to visit the hydraulic mining pits at Smartville, and then the sites for the restraining works at and near Daguerre Point.

It became clear to all that the project was not a hydraulic miners' scheme, but an undertaking vitally necessary to protect the state's navigable rivers. The party's steamboat had itself gotten stuck in the debris-fouled river on its way to Marysville. The redoubtable chairman of the committee, T. E. Burton of Illinois, was a particular center of interest and attention. He had decisive power of life and death over all rivers and harbors projects in the nation, and he was famously close-fisted with the public's money.

Victory was at hand, however, for subsequently, in the Rivers and Harbors Act of June 13, 1902, the project as described in House Document 431 was approved, and the necessary $150,000 was appropriated (and later matched by California). On October 16, 1902, the construction bids on the first works to be built by the California Debris Commission since its establishment nine years before were opened. The first major river-rehabilitation project undertaken jointly by the state and the federal government, urged for more than twenty years, was at long last underway.[38]

CHAPTER

A Policy Context Transformed: The Progressive Era and the Revival of Planning *1902–1906*

They found Robert Ainsworth's body lying in a grassy ditch next to a rice field along Kimball Lane, just off the Jack Slough Road north of Marysville. . . . Officers found prints matching Robert's boots on the pickup's hood and cab. Perhaps he had escaped from the back of the truck and crawled up on the hood, where he had decided to throw off his boots and socks for what he hoped would be a swim to safety.

Bob Teets, "The End of the Storm," in Rivers of Fear, *p. 127.*

While from 1897 on the state of California, through the Office of the Commissioner of Public Works, and the U.S. Army Corps of Engineers, through the California Debris Commission, were beginning jointly to try to restore limited portions of the damaged river channels of the Sacramento Valley, the political situation nationwide was shifting and changing with almost bewildering speed, ushering in an ebullient era for new policy making. Put simply, from about the middle of the 1890s, when the country was stunned by the great depression of those years, American political culture responded by moving into one of its most profound remakings in the nation's history.

The key feature in this transformation was the essential collapse of the Democratic party in the North and West, so that in its weakened condition what now came to be called the solid South remained its sole and solitary bastion. The great depression of the 1890s and Grover Cleveland's response to it as president had dealt a body blow to the party. Inheriting the traditional Democratic belief that the

In 1903 crusading San Francisco Chronicle *editor E. D. Adams—a classic Progressive Republican—led in creating the Commonwealth Club as an elite public forum for evolving solutions to California's problems. In 1904 he convened a State River Convention and proposed a plan for flood control which called on the legislature to scuttle localism and build a strong state-directed flood control system, later embodied in the state's Reclamation Board and the U.S. Army Corps of Engineers' Sacramento Flood Control Project.*
Courtesy: California State Library.

government should stand back from the economy, that it should take a passive, laissez-faire stance and let natural forces work their way out, Cleveland's administration was based in pure Jeffersonian doctrine, but it was murderous politics. Ethnic working class voters had traditionally voted strongly for their friends, the Democrats, who not only shared their distrust of capitalists and special privilege, but had tried to ward off nativist-inspired Republican attacks (primarily at the state level) against ethnic culture—Catholic, foreign language speaking, alcohol-using, parochial-school centered—as un-American.

Now, however, working class voters suffered from the shock of massive unemployment, and during the elections of the mid-1890s, which saw Republican leaders sternly quashing antiimmigrant agitation in the party's ranks, tens of thousands of laboring men swept in a great tide to the Republican party. After all, as the Republicans reminded the nation endlessly in the depression-era elections, they had always insisted that government, at all levels, should intervene actively in the economy to create good conditions for investment, aid entrepreneurs, stimulate industrial development, and thereby create jobs and economic well-being. Republicans such as the 1896 presidential nominee William McKinley insisted that they, not the Democrats, were the true party of working people. Furthermore, in the 1896 election the Democratic nominee, William Jennings Bryan, demanded free and unlimited coinage of silver to inflate the currency and raise grain prices, helping farmers out of their long depression. This pushed even more city workers over to the Republicans, since low food prices were a boon to them, not a curse.

These seismic underlying shifts in ethnocultural voting loyalties produced a *new politics* and a *new policy-universe* in America. The knife-edge balance between the two major political parties which had characterized the Gilded Age, first one and then the other in power, quite disappeared. Save for Woodrow Wilson's two terms in the White House (1913–1921), for the next thirty years, from the mid-1890s until the Great Depression in the 1930s, the Republicans ran the country. A solid Republican North and West faced a solid Democratic South, which meant that in most national elections the Democrats could hardly mount a believable challenge. In this long

Republican golden era, what in a later period would be called WASP (white, Anglo-Saxon, Protestant) America was ascendant in government, literature, scholarship, the arts, and the economy. What political historians refer to as the era of the Fourth Party System (1894–1930) was firmly in place.[1]

For a crucial run of years after 1900, the positive-government mentality of the Republicans—in effect, a reborn Whiggery—flowered in the rise of Progressive Republicanism. With activist governors in key state houses like Robert LaFollette in Wisconsin, the classic insurgent, and Theodore Roosevelt in the White House, a massive remaking of the American way of life took place. Among other transformations of the Progressive Era, these were the years when the "New American State," as political scientist Stephen Skowronek has recently termed it, was fledged. The "modernization of national administrative controls," he writes, "did not entail making the established state [of courts, legislatures, and parties] more efficient; it entailed building a qualitatively different kind of state."[2] The new American state the Progressives constructed relied on a greatly expanded and strengthened bureaucracy and on a comparatively lavish use of expert-guided independent commissions insulated from detailed supervision by legislative bodies. The ancient Whig dream of elite authority in charge of the country's key nodal points, and buffered against populist interference, was finally taken far toward its realization.

Paradoxically, all of this swept forward within an extraordinary renaissance, at the same time, of the country's essential democratic faith. At the Progressive Era's heart lay a bursting new faith in "The People," a term trumpeted forth probably millions of times in these years, in oratory and in print. It was this faith that led to the establishment in many (by no means all) states of the referendum, the initiative, and the recall, which together comprised the goals of the passionate crusade for "direct legislation" to battle corruption and give the people a direct voice in policy making. Progressivism actually began at the grassroots in the 1890s, rising up through American public life from the towns and cities to the state capitals, and after 1900 arriving in Washington, D.C. Americans to a degree far beyond anything in their past began forming hundreds of citizen organizations aimed at developing and advocating reform legislation. Working together, they created new centers or organized citizen power which succeeded eventually in getting legislatures drastically to reform the old order of political corruption, purchased privilege, unchallenged elite power, and unrestrained freedom of enterprise.[3]

≈≈≈

As these deep changes worked themselves out within each state and nationally, they created a fluid public scene, replacing the impasse of earlier years. A blizzard of reforms swept in, and in no realm more dramatically than in natural resource management. At the center of the Progressive Era as a fertile source for headlines and front-page stories was that many-sided and bitterly conflicted movement, in these years reaching its first climax, which took the name *conservation.* In this cause, the dearest to President Theodore Roosevelt's heart, reforms were launched which among other things saw Chief Forester Gifford Pinchot struggling vigorously with lumbering interests, to much newspaper attention; at issue was whether or not the national government through an active new regulatory bureaucracy could halt the denuding of the national forests by logging companies and begin the restoration of these lands. In another direction, the conservation movement saw Congressman (and later Senator) Francis Newlands carry on his long and dogged labor to create a federally financed and managed irrigation program in the arid West, under the Reclamation Service, which would attack land monopoly by revitalizing the family farm.[4]

Conservation was many things, among them a campaign to eliminate waste and inefficiency in the country's use of its natural resources. A passion for "efficiency" at every level of government and in every social and economic pursuit, whether it be in city government or industrial production or social welfare, was in the Progressive years one of the master impulses of reform throughout the country and even abroad, in Great Britain, from which Americans appear to have derived the term.

Several historians have described the movement. It was an "efficiency craze," writes Samuel Haber, "a secular Great Awakening, an outpouring of ideas and emotions in which a gospel of efficiency was preached without embarrassment to businessmen, workers, doctors, housewives, and teachers, and yes, preached even to preachers."[5] For this reason the Progressive Era, observes Stephen Skowronek, "is celebrated as the age of economy and efficiency, the period in which business principles and scientific management techniques turned the battle against profligacy and waste in government." In Washington the early twentieth century saw a cascade of new agencies aimed at bringing about efficiency in the federal government's operations, among them the Commission of Economy and Efficiency, the Bureau of Efficiency, the Central Bureau of Planning and Statistics, the Bureau of the Budget, and the General Accounting Office.[6]

In sum,

> the broader significance of the conservation movement, [Samuel P. Hayes has written], stemmed from the role it played in the transformation of a decentralized, nontechnical, loosely organized society, where waste and inefficiency ran rampant, into a highly organized, technical, and centrally planned and directed social organization which could meet a complex world with efficiency and purpose.[7]

Destructive waste in the natural realm was widely symbolized by the chaos of cut-over forests and heedless, destructive mining operations. Getting efficiency into such areas would be best achieved, Progressives were convinced, by taking the country's abused natural resources out of the realm of entirely unrestrained private enterprise and putting them under the (presumably) rational, consciously scientific management that trained experts could provide and that corrupt legislative bodies, with their infinity of self-serving mutual bargains, seemed never able to produce. "This was the gospel of efficiency," Hays remarks, "efficiency which could be realized only through planning, foresight, and conscious purpose."[8]

At the heart of the Progressive Era, giving it ideas and momentum and leadership, was an essentially new middle class in America. Schooled in the drastically reformed public and private universities that the Gilded Age had created, and after 1900 moving into the business and professional classes, the new middle class rapidly gathered strength and influence in government and in society at large. Its members wanted to bring order to a disorderly society and build a new America no longer guided by the venerable Democratic belief that in a democracy anyone at all, without the need of formal education, could run the country, teach its schools, heal its sick, argue cases in its courts, and build its public works. Rather, America should become a far more elitist country in which learning, rather than being scorned as effeminate and disabling, would be looked on as a source of power and leadership and needed expertise; in which access to membership in the professions would require formal entry requirements, college degrees, state-administered licensing examinations.[9] Richard Hofstadter long ago pointed out that the Progressive Era was preeminently the time in American life when that special kind of social personality, the expert, rose to major national leadership.[10]

Among businessmen and even among farmers, a new type of entrepreneur emerged, usually college-educated, who also made use of new knowledge, new methods, and put great faith in experts. Chief among the latter, nationwide, and symbol for an entire age in industrial history, was the famous mechanical engineer, Frederick W. Taylor. From 1895 until the 1920s, as a self-conscious practitioner of what he took to be science in the production process, he was the inspiring spirit in that post-1900 drive toward industrial efficiency which was linked to time and motion studies.[11]

Americans of the new middle class had soaring visions of what science, as they understood it, could do in every realm of national life. The new way, they believed, would replace unrestricted economic competition, with all that it appeared to bring in the way of waste and exploitation and destructive rivalry. Proceeding by means of economic planning, it would bring the American people to heights of prosperity and material abundance that they had never formerly known.[12]

What gave these attitudes a transforming power in American life was that in the Progressive Era this reemergent faith in government by a learned elite was rising within an educated class that was far larger, in relative as well as absolute numbers, than ever it had been before in American life. Thus, this revived Whiggery had much greater leverage on public affairs than that political faith had had in the past.[13]

≈≈≈

It was early May of 1902 in California, and swampland owners from all over the Sacramento and lower San Joaquin valleys and the delta were gathering in Pioneer Hall in the city of Sacramento. The rainy season that year had been relatively modest, and yet the rivers had reacted violently. Levees were broken through and floodwaters rushed out widely over the Valley floor, demonstrating with unmistakable urgency that whatever the commissioner of public works had been doing in his jetty-building at the Sacramento River's mouth and in scattered levee and weir projects—whatever, indeed, the landowners themselves through their many reclamation districts had for decades tried to do—the inland sea could still reclaim its ancient territory whenever the rivers rose. Suppose, it was asked, a flood season like that monster of the Valley's river legends, that of 1861–1862, were to arrive again, as some day it must, what devastation would then come to the Valley?

To many, the situation seemed hopeless, unless landowners were ready to "join hands," as they put it, "and set to work."[14] Their team spirit impulse, now rising, was revealing. The dogged reliance on individualism and localism which Valley landowners had clung to for many years, reaching far back into the nineteenth century, was fading. A flood season such as many in the past that the Valley had borne stoically was now enough to set people stirring, in an effort to begin mobilizing their joint energies.

There was much in California's political context to encourage those who hoped to get the state government actively involved, once more, in regulating resource management. The nationwide victory of the Republicans in the climactic election of 1896 was duplicated in California. The political balance between the two major parties which had existed in the state for many years "came rapidly to an end," historian R. Hal Williams writes, "as California became a solidly Republican state. . . . With rare exceptions California's one-party status continued until 1932 as the Republicans almost completely monopolized the governorship, the legislature, and the congressional delegation."[15]

Much of this Republican surge arose from a deep ethnocultural change in the state: a massive migration into southern California, beginning in the late 1880s, had brought a flood of Protestant Middle Westerners to that region that would continue right on into the twentieth century. Firmly Republican in their voting loyalties and often New England in their remote ancestry, the new southern Californians soon shared that region's historic antipathy to the dominant north in state politics. They set themselves in firm opposition to traditionally Democratic, Roman Catholic, ethnically mixed, labor union-dominated, politically corrupt, and (as they believed) immoral San Francisco. The Progressive movement in California, as a reform crusade directed against much that San Francisco represented, would be born in southern California and given much of its leadership by that section.[16]

Shifting economic as well as political tides were also aiding California's rural entrepreneurs in these years. The long depression for American agriculture which had begun in the 1880s had come to an end as the entire world economy felt an upward lift beginning in the late 1890s, following large gold discoveries in Colorado, South Africa, and Alaska which poured new capital into world trade and investment. For the first time in many years, the agricultural community began to experience prosperity, and the boom times for farmers would run right through the First World War. For twenty years, all plans for large investments in agricultural enterprises would operate in a buoyant atmosphere. Once more, as when the wheat mania gave a strong push to the swampland rush of the late 1860s, economic forces were converging with strong currents already underway in the national political culture to produce dramatic policy changes.

There was another new element in the equation. While in the depression years of the 1890s ambitious schemes for flood control and reclamation had had little hope of being funded, now in the prosperous Progressive Era large ongoing engineering projects like President

Theodore Roosevelt's huge Panama Canal adventure created a climate of opinion friendly to major public works at the state and city level, as seen in the long Owens Valley aqueduct project that Los Angeles launched and completed in these years with Roosevelt's explicit blessing.[17] The Panama Canal was in everyone's minds in California, for it offered an exciting prospect: the opening of huge new markets in the Eastern states, reachable by low-cost water transport that would avoid railroad monopolies.[18]

The men who came together in Sacramento in May 1902 to talk about flood control were hardly simple farmers. Their holdings were often so large it is inappropriate to speak of them under that rubric; they were rural entrepreneurs. Some, like F. F. Ryer, of Ryer Island in the delta, listed San Francisco addresses, for they were absentee landowners. The leading men in the meeting were overwhelmingly Republican and uniformly figures of substance. The president of the meeting was Frank Miller, head of the powerful National Bank of D. O. Mills & Co. He was shortly to publish an article on "reform" in *Out West,* the word meaning to him the development of means to quicken the development of land, cheapen grain transport, and establish clearinghouses for land advertisement.

The convention's vice president was George F. McNoble of Stockton, the California born past president of the State Bar Association. Others included Jesse Poundstone, long a major swampland owner south of Colusa and president of Reclamation District 108. A member of the wealthy Boggs family, whose extensive holdings north of Colusa went back at least to the 1860s, was there. J. H. Glide, a leading Sacramento County stockman, was another participant. In 1917 he was to be the chief figure in a reclamation company owning 12,000 acres in Yolo County, capitalized at $2.5 million, whose main function was subdividing for resale. His father had built the first system of big levees in the Old Lisbon district of Yolo County.[19]

What did the gathering hear? From Miller the exhortation that they must stand together if they would live on land subject to overflow. The struggle they were in, he warned, would last twenty years and cost millions, but Holland had done it and they could. "You are here," he said, "to make California the greatest country in the world."

Theirs was no solitary task, he warned; thousands waited to see what would happen at this meeting.[20] John Ferris of San Francisco, a large swampland owner who was eventually to become son-in-law to sugar millionaire Claus Spreckels, and in January 1906 the first California delegate ever to attend a national river and harbor congress (held in Washington), warned of the cost and that they could not count on tax funds if the people at large did not benefit.[21]

As the meeting proceeded, it was clear that, as the *Sacramento Bee* had earlier warned, upriver and downriver people had, as always, sharply differing ideas as to what should be done. P. J. Van Loben Sels stood up to declare in a major address that the choke at the river's mouth, below Rio Vista, had to be the first item of business. Then, however, Will Green of the *Colusa Sun* rose to warn in similarly urgent tones that the upper river had to be got to in a hurry, for its bed was filling in, the water was spreading, and soon there would be no river channel left at all.[22] State Senator R. T. Devlin, an attorney who was soon to be chairman of the Republican state committee, and for many years was a member of the board of the Crocker Bank, then urged the meeting to take the necessary next step: they must form a permanent and active organization if they wished to achieve any of their goals.[23]

The gathering thereupon created a standing organization that they named the River Improvement and Drainage Association of California. It turned over its actual deliberations to a "Committee of 24," most of whom were large landowners and bankers.[24] Its executive committee of seven included, besides Miller, McNoble, and Glide, the downriver advocate P. J. Van Loben Sels, who was a major figure in reclamation south of Sacramento; B. G. Peart, superintendent of the 10,000-acre Fair Ranch near Knight's Landing, some fifty miles downriver from Colusa; and Louis Tarke, whose holdings in RD 70, in the upper part of Sutter Basin, amounted to 4,500 acres. Like most of the others, Tarke was an ardent Republican and held stock in banks.[25]

In June, the Committee of 24 embarked on a three-day tugboat tour of the Sacramento River, with (now) Col. W. H. Heuer of the Corps of Engineers and State Engineers M. A. Nurse and George N.

Randle in attendance, to examine the great problem they proposed to take on.[26] They found a deplorable situation. For many miles below Colusa, in the region where the giant RD 108, now decades old, and Meridian's more modest RD 70, equally venerable, had for many years battled the river, there were broken levees and deep cuts on both sides through which water had long been washing. This allowed three-fourths of the river's floodwaters to pass out into Sutter and Yolo basins, inundating them deeply. The water continued to flow through these deep crevasses until the low water stages of the summer season arrived. The Sacramento itself suffered severely from these conditions, for, robbed of a strong flow between its banks, its channel velocity was low and the deposition of silt in its bed was heavy.[27]

At the mouth of the river the committee found the severe choke that Van Loben Sels complained of, a choke that had survived all the state's labors at clearing out Newtown Shoals. In the flood of 1902, because of breaks near the state's Elkhorn weir (upstream from the city of Sacramento and on the river's west bank), so much water had rushed down Yolo Basin and piled up near Rio Vista, where all the discharge of the Sacramento River came together, that it "seemed to accumulate . . . all at once in enormous volume." The entire basin in front of Rio Vista "seemed one roaring sea, spreading waste and devastation, threatening dikes which had been supposed to be safe beyond peradventure, and overtopping others." So high was the water at Rio Vista that it acted like a dam. The Sacramento River actually stood still far upstream to Walnut Grove.[28]

What was the cause? The committee's analysis was familiar: valleywide flood control had been left in many private hands and executed through a wilderness of reclamation districts, each of which believed "that the only way to keep their heads above water is so to protect their own land as to drown out their neighbors, opposite, above, or below." In words that echoed William Ham. Hall's warnings from far in the past, and the later laments of the first commissioner of public works, A. H. Rose, the committee went on to deplore the fact that one broad, comprehensive scheme on scientific lines had never been undertaken. The universal cutting off of drainage channelways, as in the mass closing of sloughs, had by forcing more water to stay in the main channel produced "a rise in the flood line to elevations never before dreamed of; hundreds of thousands of dollars," the committee observed, "were in years gone by spent . . . in the vain and foolish attempt to have the size and height of . . . levees keep pace with the constantly rising flood marks." The results of a half-century's efforts in the Valley were clear: mass failure, and an incredible wastage of capital and potentially valuable resources.[29]

What must be done? The river's mouth was far too narrow and tortuous as it wound through the delta's meandering channels, a condition worsened by recent levee-building in the delta islands, and it must be opened out drastically with a wide straight cut right across Sherman Island in the delta, creating a single capacious outlet for the river. This recommendation, formerly unthinkable, was the child of new technology, for the necessary immense dredges had been recently invented. (In his 1902 *Annual Report,* the commissioner of public works also recommended such a cut, which he referred to as being across Horseshoe Bend.) A large deep-channeled new mouth for the Sacramento would lower its fall and induce scouring.

As to the river as a whole, the committee urged that it be put into one channel (landowners always liked the Humphreys thesis) by repairing and raising existing levees to prevent all lateral escapes of floodwater during ordinary high water periods, thus keeping as much water between the levees as possible, with overflow weirs for use during times of extreme flooding. The result? These measures would open prospects, they insisted, which would be sparkling enough to excite all landowning entrepreneurs: the five overflow basins with their million acres of fertile soils—Butte, Sutter, Yolo, American, and Sacramento—could all be thoroughly reclaimed, "creating conditions of wealth and prosperity for the waste lands . . . as far [north, up-valley] as Jacinto and Chico." To achieve this the next legislature should be asked for $750,000, for the entire state would benefit, and the entire state should share the cost.[30]

Nothing came of this obviously self-serving appeal. Californians as a whole were no more ready to pay out tax funds to help the swampland owners of the Sacramento Valley than they had been twenty years before, in the time of the Drainage Act. And there the matter may have lain, save that this was the Progressive Era and the community at large, in California as in other states, was coming busily alive, networks of discussion and debate were proliferating, the impulse to pull people together to address the great public issues of the day was strong, and no great unsolved evil was allowed simply to persist for lack of attention.

A year after the Sacramento meeting, in May 1903 a group of civic-minded reformers in San Francisco, led by the editor of the *San Francisco Chronicle,* Edward F. Adams, formed the Commonwealth Club to provide a forum for the organized investigation and discussion of the day's pressing public policy questions. Born out of the breakup of an earlier effort devoted to irrigation and water law reform, which seemed to have come to grief because of sectional rivalries between the northern and southern parts of the state, the club aimed at representing all of California. Inspired by the planning ideal, and committed to the belief that localism must give way to managed regional development, its membership, which ran upwards of a hundred by 1904, included such water activists as prominent San Francisco attorney William Thomas, President Benjamin Ide Wheeler of the University of California, San Francisco's mayor James D. Phelan, and Governor George Pardee, an ardent conservationist.[31]

The reform-minded journalist Edward Adams was in his attitudes classically emblematic of the efficiency-oriented and resource-management dimension in the Progressive mind. His specialty in his editorials was economic topics, particularly those having to do with finance and agriculture. In 1899 he had published a book called *The Modern Farmer* which urged making use of the teachings of science and recent technology to turn traditional farming into efficient agriculture.[32] As organizer of the Commonwealth Club he conceived of it in bedrock Progressive terms as a kind of impartial research institute and debating society. The Progressive mentality had immense faith in "The People" and in the sovereign wisdom of their common sense. In this spirit Adams, as Donald Pisani writes of him, "had deep faith in the rationality of man and assumed that people usually disagreed over issues out of ignorance rather than economic self-interest, personal rivalries, or other 'sordid' motives." As he saw it, the Commonwealth Club should embody in its work the scientific method for finding truth that the universities taught, and to which the new middle class was deeply devoted. The club's

> basic job was to gather "the facts." Individual sections collected information, compiled reports, and drafted bills for consideration by the entire club. Adams believed that the club's "impartial" data allowed it to propose much sounder legislation than members or committees of the railroad-dominated legislature could produce. During the first few years of its life, the Commonwealth Club tackled such hot Progressive issues as civil service reform, the California penal system, the referendum, tax reform, and government regulation of railroads. It first considered water law reform at a meeting held on November 9, 1904.[33]

Even earlier, Adams had taken a strong interest in the flooding problems of the Sacramento Valley. To a resource-conservationist, here was a dramatic tale of wholesale wastage of resources and capital, and he was convinced that a systematic, fact-centered analysis would yield a solution. As first president of the Club, in the fall of 1903 he had gotten the permission of its governors to make such a study of the Valley's flood and reclamation crisis. Thus was set in motion a most extraordinary feat of historical scholarship. Adams was the first person to think of going back into the records to put together a legal and economic history of the whole problem, from its origins, and to pull together the relevant public documents. It took him months to conduct the research, since the information had never before been assembled. In the midst of his labors, in March and April of 1904, a disastrous outflow of floodwaters into Sacramento Basin occurred, immense areas of the Valley long thought well-protected were buried deep in torrential flows pouring out of levee breaks, and millions of dollars in damages were suffered.

People now began actively to help Adams, men of large landowning interests and long experience. On May 11, 1904, he was ready to come before the club to read his paper on the history of the flooding issue, the first formal public presentation of the subject in San Francisco. Its contents apparently came as a great enlightenment even to men like Colonel Heuer, USCE, who had had thirty years on the river, but had never had the full story presented to him, inclusive of all the relevant laws and court decisions. The purpose of the enterprise was to arrive at new public policies, and what were Adams's recommendations? In mainstream Progressive fashion, he called for the state of California henceforth to take full control of all reclamation activities, all planning and building of levees, in cooperation with the federal government.

Recognizing that the Valley was a hotbed of endless argument over what should be done to the rivers to get them under control, and that each plan had its committed enthusiasts, he recommended the appointment of a supervising chief engineer who should come from out of state, to clear him of all charges of prejudice or political involvement. Then the local reclamation districts, those dogged bastions of selfish and destructive localism, should eventually be dissolved and replaced with one large district that would take in the entire Valley. Lastly, there should be a moratorium on all further expenditures on flood control measures until "a complete plan has been worked out."[34]

After the flood of 1904, the impulse to organize expanded tremendously through the state's business community. The River Improvement and Drainage Association issued a call for a State River Convention to be held in San Francisco, and more than a dozen other bodies joined in as sponsors of the gathering.[35] It was preceded by weeks of newspaper attention, with Adams's *San Francisco Chronicle* devoting column after column of analysis and exhortation almost daily to the subject of the rivers and reclamation. Adams was especially adamant that those attending should *leave all matters of flood control design to the experts, the river engineers* (emphasis added); that those who lived in the Valley should not get caught up in their ancient wrangles as to how best to control the river; and he warned that "So long as they fight among themselves it will be useless to try to arouse interest in the general public." On their way to the river convention, two hundred and fifty participants boarded the river boat *Valletta,* which navigated down the Sacramento from Colusa to offer a direct examination of the waterways and the delta.[36]

On the 23rd of May some 400 delegates gathered in the American room of the Palace Hotel in San Francisco to spend two days listening to speeches and formally prepared papers and debating resolutions. The roll of those attending read like a roster not only of the major landowners who had led the 1902 meeting in Sacramento—such as Loben Sels, Snowball, Devlin, McNoble, and Ferris—but also of the leading figures in California's water policy establishment and public life, including Governor George Pardee ("welcomed with much applause"), Commissioner of Public Works Frank Ryan, and U.S. Senator George C. Perkins, who more than twenty years before, as governor, had pleaded in vain with the legislature to adopt the concept of statewide community interest and save the Drainage Act of 1880.

Governor Pardee, a Republican—as were all California governors for fifty years, from 1887 to 1939, with one exception in the late 1890s—urged the delegates to consider the futility of the great and largely ineffective investments that had been made in reclamation. The recent floods, he warned, had proved "that individual effort is insufficient." Senator Perkins advised them to see to the swift perfection of an integrated, engineer-developed plan for valleywide flood control, after which they should make strong appeals to Washington for help.[37]

The old conflict between amateurism and expertise, however, flared up dramatically. Will Green, patriarch editor of the *Colusa Sun*—at age 72, he was in the last year of his life—who as we have seen had been a self-trained leader in reclamation and irrigation campaigns for forty years, rose to criticize at length the idea of turning over the task of preparing a comprehensive flood control plan to, as it was said, the best engineers who could be found, nationwide. All past plans developed by such men, he said scornfully, had been failures—as indeed they had been, whenever put to the test. The landowners themselves, Green insisted, could solve their own problems, using common sense. J. W. Snowball of Knight's Landing, downriver from Green's Colusa, agreed, saying he did not want any "fool engineer" telling him how to reclaim his 1000 acres of swamplands.[38]

However, Will Green, aged Democrat, promptly found his views held up to ridicule before the convention by Ferris, Loben Sels,

McNoble, and Devlin. Republicans all, they had the great faith of their breed in credentialed experts. The Colusa editor's speech, they said, was sheer populist demagoguery.[39] The most violent and derisive critic who rose to condemn Green's words was a wealthy southern Californian, an entrepreneur named Lee Allen Phillips. An archetypical symbol of historian Robert Wiebe's new middle class who had risen out of that status to wealth and power, Phillips was a lawyer, financier, and executive of the Pacific Mutual Life Insurance Company. He was perhaps the most sophisticated of the new entrepreneurial generation. A Republican and a Congregationalist, his father was dean of the University of Southern California, and he had been college-trained at DePauw University. Phillips then became a "masterful and skillful financier," as his biographer admiringly comments, in time branching out into reclamation projects in the islands of the Sacramento-San Joaquin delta. He took a great interest in this work, living in Stockton from 1902 to 1907 to supervise it. Afterwards, he organized a number of corporations, both holding and construction operations, to reclaim delta lands, leading to the farming of more than 100,000 acres, which were then subdivided and sold to small operators. It was said that two-thirds of the potatoes grown in California in the following twenty years were grown on this land. Emboldened by this success, he reclaimed the Cienega Swamp in Los Angeles and several thousand acres in New Mexico. His proudest achievement was the building of the $10 million Biltmore Hotel in Los Angeles.[40]

Now, before the assembled delegates in San Francisco, Phillips joined with others of similar mind to warn the convention openly that they would withdraw entirely if engineers of national standing were not consulted. Though a Marysville delegate protested against this threat, the men of the new order in California had the convention with them: Green was voted down two-to-one.[41]

A continuing organization was now formed which assumed the name of the earlier group formed in Sacramento, the River Improvement and Drainage Association of California (RIDA). Under that rubric it issued a long public declaration that lamented the vast losses to floods in the Central Valley; warned that scattered individuals could no longer hope to solve the problem, that collective effort was mandatory; and lauded the huge potential for development which beckoned in the Sacramento and San Joaquin valleys, with their rich lands, bordering the rivers, which could maintain a large and prosperous population. The federal government to this point had done nothing but maintain navigability, the RIDA statement pointed out, but the time had come for both Sacramento and Washington to help in ways "that will benefit a large number of people where the work could not have been done by private enterprise." Avoiding any attempt to settle on a specific flood control plan, which would have set off interminable arguments, the convention appealed to the legislature to appoint a commission of five eminent engineers, at least three of them from outside the state, to report a plan "in time for action to be taken upon it by the next State Legislature." For their part, the members of the convention pledged themselves to damp down their differences as to river control strategies and "give full moral support to the plan when adopted."[42]

Editor Adams of the *Chronicle* was delighted. "For half a century," he remarked, "the people of the State have been watching this river vendetta, hoping against hope that the combatants would tire themselves out and be ready to turn to and pull together for the good of all." It was clear, he said, that the delegates "had not left their belligerent spirits at home . . . as any very positive assertion as to definite plans of controlling the floods would at once cause a rising of the bristles from the opponents of the plan." He went on:

> As a rule, combination is the result of unendurable competition, continued until all concerned are exhausted and can fight no more. . . . If the present flood season has proved to be the final knock-out blow, it will be a blessing to the State. . . . So far as one can judge . . . the war is over, and from now on the river men will be a band of brothers, ardently laboring for the common good.

What was needed now, remarked Adams, was "to arrange for a scientific commission in which confidence could be placed, and instruct it to go ahead and protect everybody and all interests under some comprehensive plan."[43]

The succeeding years in California saw swift steps being taken.

By January 1905, the RIDA's committee on river gauges had got the state to put in a complete system of water gauges on the Sacramento and San Joaquin rivers, and in cooperation with the federal government a uniform datum line was being established. In this arrangement, the state would take readings, and the U.S. Geological Survey would make the necessary compilations. The long-elusive foundation of reliable and comprehensive data on river-flows, about which engineers were still uncertain, was finally being created.[44]

Then at the RIDA's urging, Governor Pardee appointed a commission chosen from among the leading river engineers in the nation—the RIDA's executive committee actually picked them—to devise a plan. Major T. G. Dabney, U.S. Army Corps of Engineers, for twenty years chief engineer of the Upper Yazoo District on the lower Mississippi (Californians were eager to learn what had been done there) was its chief officer, its other members being Major Henry B. Richardson, USCE, of the U.S. Mississippi River Commission; Major H. M. Chittenden, USCE, experienced on the Ohio and in charge of all federal works on the Missouri; and M. A. Nurse, chief engineer to the state's commissioner of public works.

Almost as soon as Dabney was appointed he was in San Francisco, where the RIDA's executive committee listened in great excitement while he painted a dramatic picture of the transforming of the Yazoo district on the lower Mississippi, a once moribund and abandoned region many thousands of square miles in extent, by an integrated levee system. "Today," he said, "I can show you flourishing crops growing on land where the water-mark is twenty feet up on the trees. There is now no land in the Upper Yazoo Levee District that is too low to cultivate if local drainage can be had for it."

Prosperous towns, railroads, banks, businesses, and villages were everywhere, Dabney said. Land bought for a few cents an acre was now going for excellent prices—delicious news, doubtless, to his California audience of swampland owners. Where fifteen years before there had been but one bank in the basin, now there were more than fifty. What had been the key? Putting real power, Dabney said, in the hands of an independent levee commission that moved decisively to establish a flood control plan, take private land when necessary to build levees, issue bonds to get funds, and worm a lot of money out of the federal government.[45]

In August 1904, the Dabney Commission organized and got quickly to work. Settling into offices in the Flood Building in San Francisco, which for many years had been the headquarters of the California detachment of the U.S. Army Corps of Engineers and therefore of the California Debris Commission, it held daily sessions and periodically headed out on inspection trips. The commission was much on the road, traveling over the affected Central Valley regions not once but several times. The existing information system was fully mobilized. All the accumulated knowledge that Californians to this point possessed about their rivers, not simply in their writings but in their heads, was tapped. The head of the state's commissioner of public works engineering staff, M. A. Nurse, was of course on the Dabney team; Colonel Heuer, president of the California Debris Commission, was talked with extensively; and so too were people like the aged William Ham. Hall; his brilliant former associates Marsden Manson and C. E. Grunsky, now full of honors; as well as Governor Pardee, members of Congress, and longtime swampland owners from the River Improvement and Drainage Association.[46]

It was a whirlwind performance that produced a long and confident report, in the imperial tradition of the Corps, before the year 1904 was even out. First, the commission summarily dismissed the flowage figures relied on by Manson and Grunsky in their 1894 plan, terming them impossible. They would indicate, the Report said, a total discharge by the Sacramento River of over 300,000 cubic feet of water per second in extreme floods, and this was out of the question. The entire Manson and Grunsky concept of bypasses—in effect, a second, auxiliary river channel to be used in floodtimes—was then rejected. Such a system would be much too costly to build, the Dabney Commission said, and it would spread the water instead of concentrating it.

Then came the Dabney Commission's prescription, which applied the Humphreys thesis full and undiluted. All existing outlets for overflow which the state since 1897 had building, *including all weirs,* should be closed. The entire river must be kept between wide-apart levees (considerably wider than the existing ones). That would force it (the Dabney Commission believed) to scour itself out to a depth that would allow it to carry all of the anticipated 250,000 second-feet that the commission estimated was the most the Sacramento would ever produce. They proposed, in short, that familiar object: a main-channel plan.[47]

Even William Ham. Hall, a quarter of a century before, had said in his largely main-channel plan that there would be floods coming downriver that no conceivable levee system could contain and that provisions for controlled overflow had to be made. The Dabney Commission, however, was cavalier with the views of the locals. The Sacramento was going to be *made* to stay within its levees. The people of California would simply have to close down everything their state government had been doing, shut off the weirs, and commit themselves finally and conclusively to the main-channel concept. Large areas of the Valley floor would henceforth find themselves within the wide-apart levees the Dabney Commission called for, rather than outside of them, as at present.

The landowners of the RIDA had always liked main-channel plans, and they had also made their internal bargain to accept whatever the men whom the RIDA termed "distinguished engineers" would say. Accordingly, the RIDA did so, mounting a major campaign to have both state and federal governments act upon it. Congress refused to take action, largely because the House's Committee on Rivers and Harbors, under its strong-minded chairman, T. E. Burton, was adamant in opposition to expanding the federal government's role in river management beyond maintaining navigation.[48]

Burton took this stand in dogged resistance to a recent proposal, the multiple-use concept, enthusiastically favored by Theodore Roosevelt and conservationists, which in these Progressive years was being widely advocated. Multiple-use advocates insisted that the federal government should use the nation's rivers not only for navigation, but also for irrigation, power production, recreation, and flood control. To achieve this, and thereby realize the most rational basinwide developments throughout the country, the federal government should construct *plans* for each watershed so that one function did not harm but enhance all others.

This was a concept Burton would never accept. To begin with, navigation was for him the rivers' primary function, one far above all the others in priority, for like so many in his time he was obsessed with river transportation as competition to the railroads, which in the Progressive Era seemed to have the nation's economy by the throat. Secondly, he believed transportation was the only function that Congress, under the traditional reading of *Gibbons* v. *Ogden* and the Commerce Clause, could constitutionally support. For its part, the U.S. Army Corps of Engineers, which was essentially under the control of the Rivers and Harbors Committee, would be dragged to the multiple-use concept only after the passage of many years of intense intragovernmental negotiation and political maneuver. Congress itself, to whose moods the Corps was always sensitive, did not warm to the planning concept either. Legislators much preferred the traditional arrangement by which, through individual bills, they got particular rivers and harbors projects funded for their districts whatever harmful impact they might have on basinwide needs.[49]

Though Congress proved resistant to the RIDA's appeals, the state of California was successfully prevailed on to push ahead vigorously in putting the Dabney Report into operation. In February 1905, the RIDA took the extraordinary step of publishing a pamphlet that set down in complete and exacting detail its precise wishes as to how each of the bills it wished passed in Sacramento should read, including the distribution of powers to various agencies. The result should be, it urged, the establishment of a strong independent commission that "WILL IN FACT BE A GOVERNMENT FORMED OF OWNERS OF SWAMP LANDS FOR THE ADMINISTRATION OF SWAMP-LAND AFFAIRS" [*sic*]. The RIDA bill would split three ways the cost of the whole project between the federal government, the state government, and the landowners.[50]

So instructed, in the following month the legislature created a Sacramento Drainage District to encompass both the Sacramento and lower San Joaquin valleys (the only region in the Central Valley with similar problems to those along the Sacramento). Its task was to regulate private levee building in an area that included over 60,000 parcels of land, owned by about 42,000 owners. Aside from initial organizing activities, however, its powers were suspended until either the state or the United States government joined in to provide funds to handle the "entire estimated cost of river improvement."[51]

Since these moneys were never appropriated, this first commission eventually expired, but not before performing an important and lasting function. Its initial assessment on property owners had led to a court challenge. On July 22, 1907, the constitutionality of such a commission was affirmed by a decision in Sacramento superior court, and later confirmed by a state supreme court decision on March 24, 1909. More than twenty years before, in *The People* v. *Parks*, this same court had ruled that the legislature could not constitutionally delegate such powers to an independent commission. By the Progressive Era, however, the traditional Jeffersonian notion that only legislatures could make discretionary decisions in government, that everything the executive branch did had to be spelled out in detail in a specific law, even when repairing streets, was quite dead.

The decision in *The People ex rel W. G. Chapman* was sweeping and categorical, one issued in the full Rooseveltian mood of the Progressive Era. The court had no difficulty whatever with the legislature having created a commission and given it broad, general powers to carry out a task that would benefit the public welfare, even if, the court said, a similar law were nowhere else to be found in the statute books. The existing arrangements of anarchistic localism in reclamation, it observed, had resulted in gross wastage of capital and resources, and doing something decisive about this problem was without question a legitimate governmental activity.

As to the new commission's supervisory powers over long-existing local reclamation districts, which, appellants alleged, had vested rights that it could not override, the court in a tone verging on arrogance remarked dismissively that had it wished, the legislature had full powers to dissolve each and every local district at one stroke and put all of their powers into the hands of a single large unit. It could even tax local landowners without giving them any voice at all in the matter, had it wished, as when the state's roads were built and maintained. The fact that the lawmakers had not gone so far as that "is but an exercise by the Legislature of less than its plenary power."[52]

The door to bold policy innovations in natural resource management was now wide open. The new American state, expressed in independent commissions equipped with strong, discretionary governing authority, could be brought into being.

C H A P T E R

The New American State Drains the Inland Sea: The Sacramento Flood Control Project Becomes Reality *1907–1920*

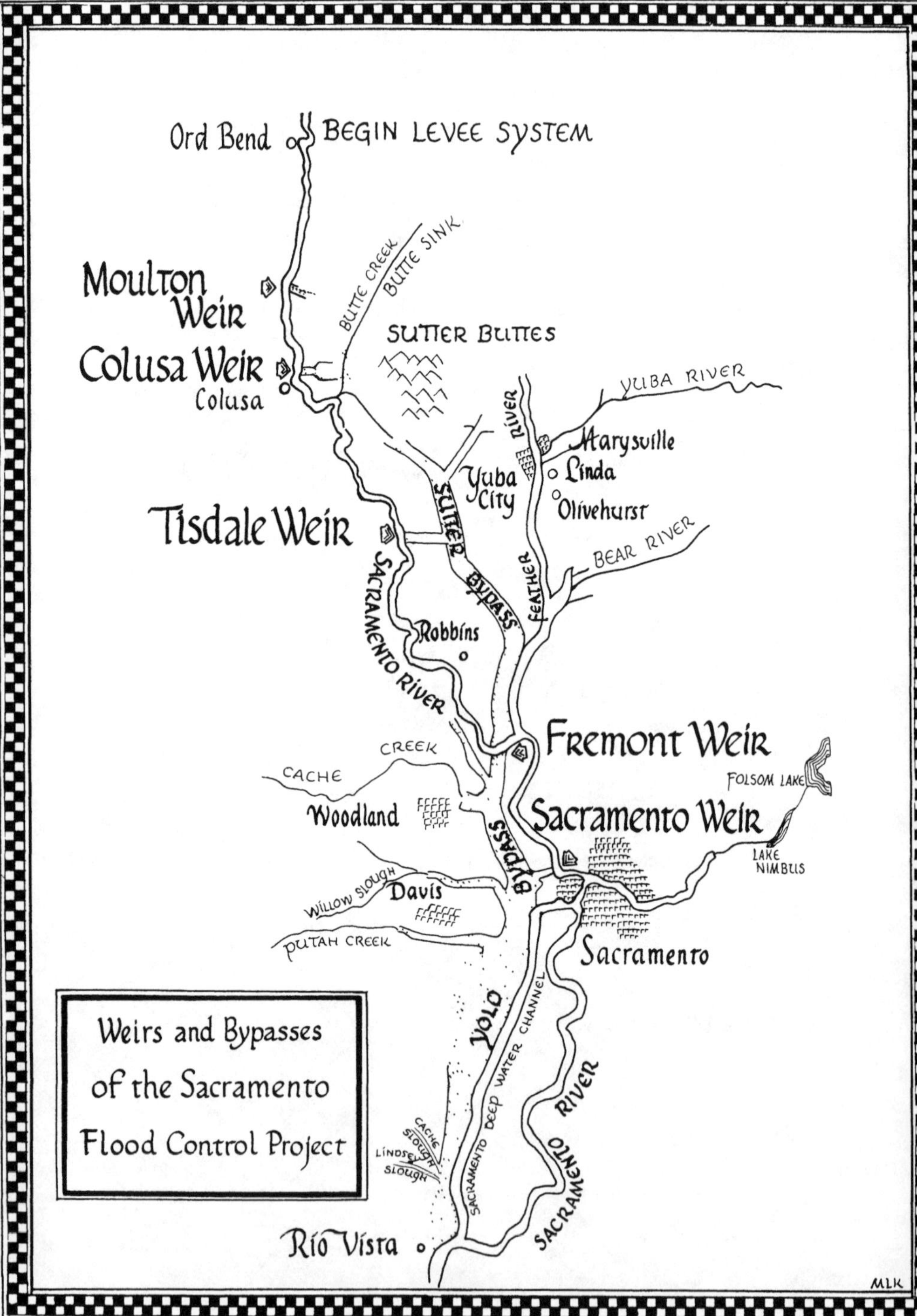

Weirs and Bypasses of the Sacramento Flood Control Project

In Strawberry Manor, mechanical trash collectors came by after the flood to pick up soggy sofas, chairs, carpets, dressers and mattresses that had been stacked in front of virtually every ranch house in the subdivision. The trash collectors crushed the junked furniture, then dumped the loads into waiting garbage trucks.

> *Thom Akeman,* Sacramento Bee, *March 3, 1986. Quoted in* Rivers of Fear, *p. 23.*

It was the 19th of March 1907, and newspapers all over the Sacramento Valley were dark with screaming headlines: flood, torrential flood, flood to heights never known before! Out of the mountains huge outflows were pouring onto the Valley floor such as no one had experienced, save the few who could remember the storied inundation of 1861–1862 almost half a century in the past. The mid-valley region from Marysville to Colusa, like the Valley as a whole, was devastated. The Feather River, which was raging out of the mountains at Oroville and flowing down-valley in a gigantic torrent, rose over its embankments at Hamilton Bend, several miles downstream from Oroville, to send a great arm of surplus floodwaters bursting entirely out of the Feather's watershed and running southwesterly across Butte Basin, north of Sutter Buttes, to rush into the Sacramento River above and below Colusa, overwhelming local levees. Even so, below Hamilton Bend the Feather still had too much water in its channel for the levees to contain, and six miles above Yuba City it overtopped them again, flowing a foot and a half deep over the District 9 embankment. Four miles further and it made

In 1911 the U.S. Corps of Engineers' California Debris Commission reported the Sacramento Flood Control Project plan to Congress. Based on the bypass concept, it would create a second river channel into which the Sacramento would overflow in high water times. Immediately adopted by California, whose Reclamation Board began bringing California's part of the plan into being, it was adopted by Congress in the historic Flood Control Act of 1917, which first made flood control a federal responsibility.

another escape from its channel, at the Starr place, while on the following day the river broke through the levees below Yuba City, at Shanghai Bend, the countryside for many miles around being swiftly flooded.

On the Marysville side of the Feather worried townspeople watched the swollen Feather hurrying by, and men labored frantically, hour after hour, to shore up weak places. Upstream, at the U.S. Army Corps of Engineers project on the Yuba, where the California Debris Commission had built a concrete barrier 1200 feet long across the river's bed to hold back mining debris, the entire south half of the barrier was gone, unable to bear the "awful force of the rushing waters."[1]

> Thomas Gianella [the *Appeal* stated on the 22nd] . . . reports that he climbed upon a high mole south of Oroville and with a powerful pair of field glasses could see the entire plain surrounding Gridley and Biggs covered with water. [Oroville was terribly flooded, the] Feather river [having] surpassed all previous records so enormously that the ordinary precautions against . . . high water were as nothing. . . . On the east the flood ran for a distance up the slopes of the low foothills. . . . The Nelson ranch, on the Honcut, where high water had never been known to be, was inundated.[2]

Some miles below Oroville on the Feather a mining community called Dredgerville had sat on the flatlands bordering the river, but "today where the town once stood is a raging river two miles in width."[3]

The "entire town of Biggs was flooded [by Feather River water], that portion north of B street being fully five feet deep," reported the *Sun* on the 19th; nearly as much water was pouring down east of the river as there was in the river itself. Across the Valley, at Colusa, the Sacramento was utterly out of control and running wild over the countryside, having burst its banks north as well as south of the community. On the following day the paper carried familiar words: the "entire east side is a vast sea of water as far as the eye can see." On the west side, below town, the whole of Reclamation District 108 was flooded out, there being at least ten breaks in the Sacramento's west bank between Colusa and Sycamore. By the 21st the levees around District 70 had gone out, and it filled like a bowl, the water within the district being at about the level of the river. A new heavy storm then struck, producing immense flooding west of the town of Colusa.[4]

By this time the U.S. Geological Survey had been long enough at work in the Valley to establish a datum reference line, its gauges were in place on the rivers to measure the great flood of 1907, and out of them came astonishing news. The Dabney Commission had scoffed at Manson and Grunsky's estimate of 300,000 cubic feet per second as the most the Sacramento, in extreme peak flow, would produce, but in March 1907, the government's observers found that a monster flow of 600,000 cubic feet per second had poured out of the Sacramento's mouth into Suisun Bay.[5] (Two years later, in 1909, the Sacramento would produce another gigantic flood of almost exactly the same magnitude as in 1907.)

If anyone still clung to the Dabney Report's principles, they would have to accept levees (below the juncture of the Feather and the Sacramento) expanded not simply to 1200 feet apart, from the existing 600, but to as much as 3000.[6] A single channel more than a half-mile wide down through the center of the Valley? The prospect was absurd. Once again the engineers had been seriously wrong. Had the monster floods of 1907 and 1909 not come along so soon after the Dabney report had been presented, millions of dollars would probably have been wasted in the construction of its recommended works, and the Valley would have been in a far worsened situation with a massive and nonfunctional project in place. Fortunately, the report could simply become a historical curiosity in the archives.

As we have seen, things had not, in fact, been going well for another band of engineers on the Yuba River. Here, where the California Debris Commission had for years been focusing literally all of its attentions and, since 1902, had been engaged in building its massive concrete barrier across that stream, in the flood of 1907 the barrier had utterly failed (as it had already done in previous flood years). The remorseless erosive power of the torrent of gravel and rocks that, making a cacophonous roar, swept over its lip simply wore down through the concrete and repeatedly destroyed the structure.

The commission doggedly kept repairing it and pushing ahead to complete its planned erection of several barriers, but the mining debris could not be contained and by 1910 the barriers were abandoned.[7] Yet again, the engineers had been wrong.

The U.S. Army Corps of Engineers had to reinitiate its learning process once more, only this time it undertook its catechism in a different frame of mind and through different eyes. There was, for one thing, a new person on board. A gifted young engineer, Thomas H. Jackson, who was only eight years out of West Point and already a captain, had arrived in California just a month before the flood of 1907 to become a member of, and apparently the leading spirit in, the California Debris Commission. Canadian-born but Michigan-raised, Jackson was a strong-minded, able, and forceful man who was ready to innovate. He had an unusually deft touch at organizing large enterprises and leading them with energy and foresight. He would serve brilliantly in France during the First World War, earning a cascade of honors—and the purple heart for wounds—and would rise to become chief engineer officer.[8]

Though in 1907 he was only a junior officer, Jackson seemed to bring a fresh wind into the deliberations of the California Debris Commission, giving it a readiness to scuttle long-held Corps dogma about the river which, it had now to be admitted, was simply wrong. He brought to the commission, too, another rare commodity: the power of mind to produce, over the next several years, the brilliant proposal in 1910 which, known ever thereafter as "The Jackson Report" in recognition of its moving spirit and authorship, won its eventual way to congressional approval and endures as the foundational plan for the Sacramento Flood Control Project.

As it happened, at his arrival Jackson found a commission that had already, in 1905, begun tentatively to work itself over to a new role by initiating wider studies of the Valley's river problems. Until that point the CDC had been a dutiful team player, in deference to deeply rooted Corps and congressional policy, limiting itself to the view that the flood control was not its concern, only the task of insuring that there were navigable depths in the river's main channel. It is interesting to speculate why this key player in the Valley, the CDC, switched course, always a rare and risky tactic for a subordinate bureaucratic agency to undertake, to begin working out a new and much bolder definition of its task and of the situation. The commission broadened its view to take in the entire Sacramento Valley and its recurrent inland sea as its subject and thrust itself forward to become the lead agency in finally solving the Valley's great problem.

Certainly the policy context, as we have seen, had changed dramatically by the middle of the decade. Perhaps, therefore, it was simply that the 1904 river convention in San Francisco and the powerful advocacy and lobbying activities of the River Improvement and Drainage Association had made flood control such a high voltage issue that the CDC felt impelled to join the new policy surge that was building up in California. Perhaps, too, it envied the great public splash made by the Dabney Commission in its whirlwind foray into the state, and wanted to demonstrate that the California Debris Commission, too, had engineering expertise that could minister to the Valley's needs. The commission, furthermore, was certainly in the midst of a compelling learning process that pointed irresistibly in the direction of innovation. Its increasingly frustrating experiences on the Yuba were teaching it by the most telling method that something new had to be thought about, that the approach the commission was taking was not working.

There is another consideration: these men were river engineers, and in the White House the era's most exciting Republican in the land, Theodore Roosevelt, was trumpeting the cause of conservation, efficiency, and the need to end the wholesale wastage of natural resources. Furthermore, he urged a potentially central role for experts in this new order. How could working-level professionals in the Progressive Era not be aroused by all of this? How could they not want to take a larger part in what was going on?

Whatever the reasons, beginning in 1905 and then with accelerating energy after the flood of 1907—and the advent of Captain Jackson—the CDC rediscovered that its original charge in the Caminetti Act of 1893 had given it a much wider responsibility than that simply of regulating hydraulic mining and aiding navigation. Its long-ignored third task was "to afford relief in flood times." Taking up this duty, the commission in its wider studies of the Sacramento River learned, as Captain Jackson later said in an address to the Commonwealth Club, "that the problem of the debris and navigation and flood control were so closely associated that it was almost impossible to deal with one without considering the other. . . . Following that, we came upon other difficulties, and it has resulted in our taking up more of the flood problem as a whole."[9] As Edward Adams wryly remarked to the club, the good news was

> the somewhat belated discovery that in the California Debris Commission we have a body composed of the same officials who, as members of the board in charge of rivers and harbors [a recently-created Corps agency], will not even think of the reclamation of swamp lands, but, as members of the Debris Commission are ready and willing to give that subject their most careful attention and who find themselves instructed thereto by hitherto neglected expressions in the Act of March 1, 1893."[10]

As Jackson and the commission got to work on developing a flood control plan for the entire Valley, one thing was clear: whatever they devised, they would have to mold all their thinking to the fact that they had a far larger river to deal with than any of their engineering predecessors had imagined. The information base had changed utterly, everything would have to be reconsidered, and this would take time. There were to be, in any event, no more swiftly constructed plans that nature in the due course would destroy; that would confirm once more Will Green's dictum that engineers did nothing but make mistakes.

However, if they were going to begin thinking in valleywide terms, a first item of business was inescapably at hand. As for years everyone had been saying, something simply had to be done about the mouth of the Sacramento River. Will Green had long rightly insisted that the river in the mid-Valley region, above and below Colusa, was in deplorable condition, but the commission had to agree with P. J. Van Loben Sels and others like him in the lower Valley that everything depended on the choke in the river's lower sections being removed, and the opening of a wide-enough mouth to allow the Sacramento's immense outflows to pass through unimpeded. The technical means, too, were finally at hand in the newly developed dredges of which there had for some years been much talk.

In June 1907, therefore, the first step taken by the CDC (within four months of Captain Jackson's arrival) in its new activist role was to send a request to Congress for $400,000, to be matched by the state of California, to buy two mammoth dredges. They would undertake a major widening of the mouth of the Sacramento, by means of a large cut across Horseshoe Bend, to accommodate an outflow of 600,000 cubic feet per second. This project, the commission recommended, should be set in motion right away, though it could not be looked on as anything more than a first step, to be taken while the commission itself settled down to a careful, step-by-step development of a comprehensive valleywide flood control plan. The national capital was rocked throughout the years of the Roosevelt and Taft presidencies by high-intensity political debate and maneuvering over conservation policy, and it was not until the 1910 Rivers and Harbors Act that funds for the two dredgers, matched by California, were appropriated. The dredgers themselves were constructed by 1913, beginning their work in that year. They had an enormous task before them, digging out a wide curving channel from above Rio Vista to Collinsville. It is traditionally said that this cut removed more soil than that excavated to create the Panama Canal. This is shown in the fact that eleven years later, in 1924, the dredges had only succeeded in opening the Sacramento's mouth sufficiently to allow an outflow of 400,000 second-feet.[11]

For more than three years after the flood of 1907, the engineers of the California Debris Commission traveled up and down the Sacramento River and its tributaries, making surveys and compiling data. The CDC's motivating concept was a conviction that the "great amount of reclaimable land in the Sacramento Valley, its high value after being reclaimed, and the great damage to the land already reclaimed, wrought every few years by floods, render the problem of flood control a vital one which must be solved in the immediate future." Also, by the long investigation it had undertaken, the commission was convinced that navigation, debris control, and flood control "are inseparably connected, [and accordingly they properly comprised] . . . one general project."[12]

By August 1910, the lengthy labor was completed, and the commission was ready to submit its plan. At its core was a recommendation that the federal government provide $11 million (a very large sum in these pre–First World War, pre–New Deal years) to pay for one-third of a proposed Sacramento Flood Control Project, which Jackson estimated would in total cost $33 million, the state of California and local landowners being responsible for the other two-thirds. As to the physical works proposed, Jackson broke decisively with Corps dogma and came down squarely for a bypass plan. His generation presumably knew nothing of Will Green's bypass proposals of almost fifty years before; the country editor was by now half a dozen years in his grave and was denied the gratification of this ultimate vindication. Jackson, however, made gracious acknowledgment of Manson and Grunsky's 1894 plan as the first public statement of such a concept and openly adopted it. He remarked admiringly that, even though in the mid-1890s they had had little reliable data upon which to make their proposal, and the peak river-flows they had assumed were too small, its "principles . . . are believed to be sound." His own project, Jackson remarked, "differs from [theirs] . . . principally in providing for the complete control of a much larger flood discharge."[13]

The Jackson Report was still a strongly navigation-centered plan. These were the years when a nationwide enthusiasm for river navigation, as competition to the railroads, had seized the country, producing repeated appeals to Congress on this score, and no proposal going to that body without navigability at its center could possibly be funded. Accordingly, Jackson called for keeping a heavy flow within the Sacramento's main channel by means of high, strong levees not too far apart. This would induce scour and maintain an excellent navigable channel. At the same time the river's excess waters, which to this point had generally broken through levees to spread widely in the basins, would be made to overflow in a controlled way through weirs. Thereafter they would be put under the strict discipline of being held within leveed bypass channels within those basins, the beds of which could be farmed between inundations.

The main stem of the Sacramento Flood Control Project as Jackson conceived of it (and as, with some modifications, it was been constructed) had its northern terminus in the vicinity of Ord Ferry, thirty miles north of Colusa, where the Sacramento in its natural condition began its first overbank flows into the paralleling basins. From that point Jackson planned the project's levees to run downstream for more than 200 river-miles, the southernmost point of the project being at Collinsville at the river's mouth. Sutter Bypass, opening out on the east side near Colusa to receive the huge overbank flows north of that point which pour into Butte Sink, takes the excess water down through Sutter Basin. It terminates at an extraordinary crossing point at the juncture of the Sacramento and the Feather where the flow coming down the Bypass mingles with and crosses through the waters in the Sacramento's main channel to Fremont Weir, on the other side, thence to flow down-valley westerly of the main channel through the ever-widening Yolo Basin bypass. It, in turn, discharges through Cache Slough back into the main river near its (expanded) mouth, and the recombined waters of the Sacramento River thereafter pass on out into Suisun Bay. The expectation was that this combination of works would carry floodwaters down through the Valley and out into the bay much more rapidly than in the past, so that the inland sea, which in the past had been created by backed-up and wide-spreading waters, would no longer appear. And so, indeed, has it worked out.

To complete his plan, which also included the building or upgrading of levees along the other major watercourses on the Valley floor such as the Feather and the Yuba, Jackson reported that almost 500 miles of riverbank and bypass levees would be needed, valley-wide. Some 391 miles of such structures were already in existence, but only 74 miles of them were high enough and strong enough to be considered up to necessary standards and grade. The Jackson Report anticipated that the state of California would do its part by spending, or causing landowners to spend, millions of dollars to build levees or bring them to proper heights.[14]

An historic moment in policy making for the Sacramento Valley had arrived. All the lines of thinking had finally converged. The point had at length been reached when people knew enough, and conceived of what they knew within a sufficiently sound conceptual framework, to put together a viable proposal. It had taken forty years, but the experts and the laymen, the upriver and downriver people, the engineers of the Corps and those of the state, as well as those, like Manson and Grunsky, now in private practice, were in agreement. The argument over river control strategy was over.

Jackson's report, with its essential lineage running back to Will Green's proposals in the 1860s, and its data foundation many-layered and venerable, beginning with William Ham. Hall's surveys in the late 1870s and culminating in close multigauged and accurately calibrated studies of the latest inundations, was henceforth to be the apparently universal consensus on what to do with the Sacramento River. In 1914 congressional hearings a major figure in California flood control matters, V. S. McClatchy of the *Sacramento Bee* publishing dynasty, stated categorically that "There is now absolutely no difference of opinion on the part of the landowners on that subject," and thirteen years later, during congressional hearings in 1927, Clarence F. Lea, a local congressman, spoke in similar terms: "Everybody, practically, is agreed that the plan is an appropriate one, that it is going to accomplish the purpose for which it is designed."[15]

In the late summer of 1910, the CDC dispatched the Jackson Report to the U.S. Army Chief of Engineers in Washington and an uncertain fate. It was given a lengthy, wary examination. The Corps, after all, continued to be firmly committed to the Humphreys thesis, as it would be until the late 1920s. Furthermore, it was beset on all sides. The Corps was the target of ceaseless cannonading from Theodore Roosevelt's Inland Waterways Commission, pressuring it to swing over to the multiple-use concept and provide for the many potentialities of water management in its plans. The Corps should take account "of the purification of the waters, the development of power, the control of floods, the reclamation of lands by irrigation and drainage, and all other uses." Marshall O. Leighton, chief hydrographer of the Geological Survey, had conceived another large new concept of historic dimensions: building dams in watersheds to impound flood waters, make electrical power with them, and out of those revenues pay for the whole project.[16]

The Corps' engineers disagreed violently with this new turn of affairs, insisting that reservoirs could have no effect on floods, that the answer was still "levees only," indeed that another key conservationist concept, maintaining well-forested watersheds to reduce flooding, would not work in that way. They also had survival anxieties, fearing that if the multiple-use concept won out the Corps would eventually lose its domestic public works mission to a new civilian federal department created for this purpose, as urged by the Waterways Commission (this idea had been in the air, in Washington, since the 1880s). The Corps was of course caught between a single-project-conscious Congress, which loved the pork-barrel system, and its planning-conscious critics. The latter worked ceaselessly for the idea that the needs of whole watersheds should be merged and considered together, a process that would often reveal that a congressman's favorite special project in his district might actually be harmful in its overall impact.

At the same time, the embattled Corps had to endure the criticisms of the national engineering profession, whose four major societies enthusiastically trumpeted the virtues of watershed planning, the conservation cause, and the drive for efficiency. They warmly supported Theodore Roosevelt in his crusade, as well as everything that "sought to bring order, efficiency, and business methods into government." Most civil engineers strongly favored the idea of building reservoirs on the nation's rivers and had hard words for the Corps on this ground.[17]

By December of 1910, the examination of the Jackson Report had reached the point where the U.S. Army Board of Engineers for Rivers and Harbors was ready to make a cautious judgment. *If* Congress decided to cooperate with California in "a comprehensive project of this magnitude for the purpose of flood control," then the CDC's plan should be adopted, for it was well designed. However, despite what Jackson had said in his report about flood control and navigation being inextricably mixed together, the plan's execution, the Board insisted, was "not necessary in the interests of navigation." The chief of engineers, in similar gingerly fashion, merely concurred in these views, and six months later the secretary of war in June 1911 presented Jackson's plan to Congress without recommendation. He referred to it simply as "a project . . . for the relief from floods in the Sacramento Valley and the adjacent San Joaquin Valley," going on to remind Congress that the fault for its appearance before that body lay with itself, since the proposal had been "made in accordance with the requirements of the act of Congress approved Mar. 1, 1893, creating the California Debris Commission."[18]

It was clear, then, that in the hands of Congress the Jackson Report would have to stand or fall on its own merits. The bureaucracy was standing back from Congress on this one, hat in hand. T. E. Burton was no longer chairman of the House's Rivers and Harbors Committee, where he had long sat bulldog-like turning back everything but navigability proposals and approving precious few of those, but the committee's attitudes were not much changed. In November 1910, the Democrats had won an immense victory nationwide in the congressional elections, and they now controlled the House. With their traditional Jeffersonian, laissez-faire attitudes and their distrust of anything that could be thought a subsidy for wealthy entrepreneurs—and it would be hard, as we have seen, to speak of California's River Improvement and Drainage Association as a society of simple farmers—the Jackson Report was certainly in for a long hard look.

≈≈≈

While a reluctant Committee on Rivers and Harbors was undertaking its lengthy, deliberate consideration of the Jackson Report, California moved swiftly. And it did so in a pubic context that had entered one of those rare periods when great bursts of reform legislation would be possible. A ground-swell of Progressive sentiment had built up behind a long-delayed revolt against the corrupt rule of the Southern Pacific Railroad over the state's legislature, courts, executive branch, local governments, and even its newspapers.[19] Led by progressives in the Republican party, in the election of 1910 the crusade carried the incomparably exciting Hiram Johnson, the quintessential Progressive, to the governor's chair.

No one save Earl Warren would ever have a stronger hold on the loyalties of the state of California. For six years, from 1911 to 1917, Johnson would be a crusading governor, enacting an incredible volume of reform legislation, and then for twenty-eight more years, until his death, he would be California's United States Senator. Johnson was Sacramento-born, an attorney who had been educated at the University of California, and son to Sacramento's perennial public figure and political agent of the Southern Pacific, Grove L. Johnson, with whom in time he had a bitter falling-out. From 1906 onward Hiram built a spectacular reputation as a prosecutor in a lurid cycle of graft trials in San Francisco. Seizing the Republican party's gubernatorial nomination in 1910 by means of the direct primary, in use for the first time (thus, nominations were no longer by Southern Pacific-dominated political conventions), he was carried to office over the broken power of the railroad. With him he brought into the legislature a broad tide of progressive Republicans.[20]

As Johnson plunged with tremendous energy into his duties as governor, he had a crowded agenda. A blunt, pugnacious (and inordinately sensitive) man widely regarded as a kind of western Theodore Roosevelt—whom he deeply admired—Johnson clearly shared all of Roosevelt's ideas about the pressing need for strong administrative authority, dispensing efficiency and social justice from the center. Government should intervene boldly in society and the economy by offering regulation and expert guidance.

When his first legislative session convened, Johnson asked for a much more powerful rate-setting railroad commission; state control of public utilities; enactment of the initiative, referendum, and recall; the installation of "efficiency" in government by establishing a regular administrative budgeting procedure (one of the premier efficiency-oriented reforms being urged nationally) and a strong civil service built around the merit system; direct election of U.S. senators; the vote for women, as well as an eight-hour day; county home rule, thus ending corrupt Sacramento meddling in local affairs; workmen's compensation in the form of an employers' liability law; free state textbooks in the public schools; and a broad push on the conservation front, primarily in forest management (following the ideas of T.R.'s Gifford Pinchot), the protection of water-power sites from speculators, and water-law and irrigation reform.[21]

In a virtuoso display of public policy leadership, in the 1911 and 1913 legislative sessions Johnson got practically the whole of this reform agenda. It was no wonder that in 1912 the California governor was chosen T.R.'s vice-presidential running mate when Roosevelt vainly sought the presidency on a hastily assembled Progressive Party ticket. It was no wonder, too, that when Sacramento Valley people went to him in 1911 to urge that he ask the legislature to create a state Reclamation Board with regulatory authority over the Valley's reclamation districts, a commission that would have approval power over all of their levee-building plans and keep them in conformity with the hoped-for Jackson Report project, he readily agreed. In effect, he made flood control one of his administration's conservation measures.[22]

In light of all past history in the Valley, with its generations of gritty local loyalties and hostility to central authority, this was a revolutionary proposal. Even more remarkable, when it came before the senate and assembly, it was passed not merely by simple majorities, but unanimously, in both houses.[23] So powerful was its supporting consensus, and so ascendant for this moment were the policy-outlook and political context of the Progressive Era, that there was no significant debate on this bill, which in any other time would have set off torrents of argument. Lacking this visibility, the birth of the Reclamation Board, in subsequent years one of California's most controversial public agencies, does not even surface in Spencer Olin's or George Mowry's otherwise excellent histories of Hiram Johnson and the Progressives.

Thus the new American state, in one of its provincial embodiments as an independent commission in California, on this occasion arrived quietly and almost anonymously, as if it were in the midst of a hurrying crowd too busy at many different reforms, each of them drastic innovations, to make a public stir at its advent. The Reclamation Board arrived in this muted style even though henceforth it would vastly expand the power and outreach of the state government in one of society's most sensitive domains: property management. It would take thousands of properties under its supervision and require landowners to spend millions of dollars on levee-building to meet not their desires, but a centrally developed plan.

By this means, however, California had finally made it possible to transform a marvelously fertile but flood-cursed valley. Lifting from it, in time, the incubus of a periodically reappearing inland sea, the new authoritative state resuscitated a region large enough to have been thought an entire principality in other countries and other times: the Sacramento Valley, as well as the adjacent Sacramento–San Joaquin delta and the lower San Joaquin Valley. All of this vast area was placed within the Sacramento and San Joaquin District, created in 1913 by state enactment. It included "practically all of the swamp and overflowed lands . . . from Chico Creek on the north to Fresno Slough on the south," or some 60,000 pieces of property in fourteen counties.[24]

The state's Flood Control Act of 1911 explicitly adopted the Jackson Report "with such modifications and amendments as may hereafter be adopted by the [state's] reclamation board mentioned in section two of this act . . . as a plan for controlling the flood waters of the Sacramento River and its tributaries." The Reclamation Board was empowered "to pass upon and approve plans that contemplate the construction of levees . . . along or near the banks of the Sacramento River or its tributaries . . . or within any of the overflow basins thereof. Any original plan of reclamation hereafter adopted . . . must be approved by the reclamation board," or else it would be adjudged void. If any levees were built without that approval they would constitute a public nuisance, and the board was "hereby empowered to prosecute any suit or suits . . . for the prevention or abatement" of them.[25]

≈≈≈

All eyes now turned to Washington, where it was hoped Congress would soon agree to play its part in controlling the floods in the

Sacramento Valley. However, the Democratic chairman of the Rivers and Harbors Committee, Stephen Sparkman of Florida, announced at a February 7, 1912 hearing before that body that Congress "could only deal with navigable streams . . . he did not regard the government of the United States as committing itself beyond a question of navigation." Ten months later, in its leisurely fashion the committee sent the Jackson Report back to the chief of engineers with instructions to pare down the federal share in the costs of the project to those aspects having only to do with navigation, that is, just the river levees. Forget the bypasses. California would have to build them.[26] Before action could be taken on the pared-down appropriation, World War I intervened, halting all such spending.

This delay meant that for many critically difficult years, almost the entire burden was placed on California. The pressures built up in the Valley for launching new reclamation districts and opening major agricultural developments were now too intense to deny, and much had to be done despite the lack of federal help. Furthermore, the outbreak of war in 1914, followed by United States entry in 1917, placed huge demands on the national farming community. Fervent appeals were sent out from Washington asking for rapidly increased production, and at the same time prices for farm goods rose rapidly. In the background was widespread confidence, in the Sacramento Valley, that the federal government would soon step in to carry out its part of the Jackson Report. As the years passed without this actually taking place, overcommitments on both the private and state level grew heavy indeed.

Despite these difficulties, the state forged ahead. In 1913, the Reclamation Board was given much stronger powers. At the request of many swampland owners, who gathered in Sacramento to urge their needs on the legislature, it was given power not only to approve private levee projects, but to force private interests to make their levees conformable to the Jackson Report plan. It thereafter required landowners throughout the Valley to spend millions of dollars of their own money in such undertakings.[27] The board was also empowered to collect funds by itself, by special assessment, so as to construct major features of the project which the federal government and private enterprise could not or would not encompass (for example, the bypasses), and it proceeded to purchase spoilage lands for the deposit of dredge tailings near the Horseshoe Bend cut and contract to buy weir sites.[28]

Meanwhile, the Reclamation Board was assaulted on all sides by litigation. As the board's attorney Stephen W. Downey would say of it in the mid-1920s, "The Reclamation Board has been called by almost every profane word in the English language and by some not in the English language."[29] Those in favor of collective action to solve a common problem had won the legislative victories, but those opposed fought bitterly in the courts. One suit, by the huge landowning Miller & Lux company in Merced County, attacked the constitutionality of the basic legislation, but the state supreme court upheld the law. Over a hundred suits in many counties were launched against the first general assessment on property owners in the district. Furthermore, suits were soon underway to force the board to pay higher prices for land claimed for bypass areas. In Sutter Basin, there was a clamorous fight over the location of Sutter Bypass, which local people insisted was placed so as to specially benefit the huge holdings of the Chicago-based Armour interests. These cases were all fought through to a successful conclusion, from the standpoint of the board, but they occupied much of its time in the early years.[30]

Meanwhile, the stubborn roadblock in Washington, D.C., was finally removed. Great floods in the Ohio and Mississippi watersheds in 1912 and 1913 had created intense public interest in having a federal flood control program, all of which put tremendous pressure on Congress to change national policy and take up that task. When it began to appear that the Corps might lose out entirely, it fell in line and from 1913 on willingly undertook flood control tasks, though still resisting the multiple-use concept and the building of reservoirs. National magazines explored the flood control subject, symposia were held, and the entire country was aroused. In the presidential election campaign of 1916, both major political parties included flood control in their platforms.

After years of intense congressional political maneuvering, congressmen Benjamin Humphreys of Mississippi and Charles Curry of

California, who spoke from the only states in the union that as yet had fully developed flood control plans, finally persuaded Champ Clark of Missouri, Speaker of the House, to create a new standing body, a Flood Control Committee, with Humphreys as chairman. It was charged with "regulating and controlling the flood waters of the country by all practical means, through levees to prevent overflow, through arid land reclamation, through swamp land reclamation, through storage for water power and other purposes."[31]

In 1917 the new Flood Control Committee put together in a single bill the plans for Mississippi flood control and the amended Jackson Report for California (in which the federal share had been reduced to $5.8 million). On March 1, 1917 it was enacted as the nation's first Flood Control Act, thus finally giving official sanction to the Jackson Report and Corps participation in the full Sacramento Flood Control Project.[32]

In California, the litigation against the location of the Sutter Bypass, whose easterly levee was not yet constructed (RD 1500, the large Armour-interests reclamation district, had already constructed the western side), was in 1917 terminated by a state supreme court decision favorable to the state. At that point the legislature, with the recently enacted federal Flood Control Act as encouragement, in the closing hours of its 1917 session urged the Reclamation Board to move promptly on building the eastern levee of the Sutter Bypass, thereby putting it into operation. Lacking adequate funds (not until 1919 would the legislature appropriate $3 million for the project), the board had to scramble in all directions for money, even borrowing it from private interests and locating a contractor who would do the work on credit. Nonetheless, it was able to push ahead. Employing at times over 500 men and 200 livestock in six camps, the contractor tore out about half a dozen old cross levees and removed exceedingly dense brush from about 3500 acres. Then, using many dredges, some twenty-two miles of earthen levee were built, 20 feet high, 20 feet across at the crown, and on a base 120 feet wide.[33]

Much had been done, too, by this time under the direction of the Reclamation Board in building river and bypass levees, either by bringing existing structures up to grade or by starting new projects. As board chairman W. S. McClatchy said in an address before the National Drainage Congress in Cairo, Illinois at the opening of 1916, "The Sacramento flood control project . . . is the greatest project now in progress or under consideration in the West, and is exceeded in importance by few in the Nation."[34] In that year, too, the California Debris Commission could report that it had completed the most important single feature of the project, the huge dredger cut across Horseshoe Bend, though it was not as yet as wide as it ultimately would be.[35] Before the eyes of California, the Sacramento Flood Control Project was becoming reality.

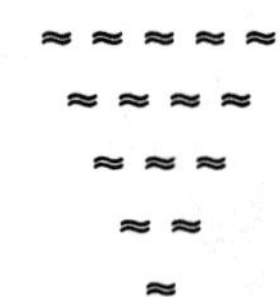

CHAPTER

A Valley Transformed: *1905–1986*

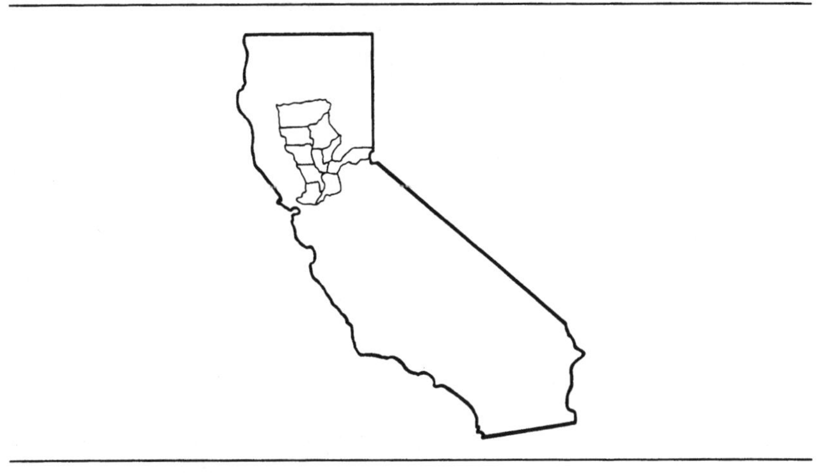

A
B

The major storm that devastated portions of northern and central California in February 1986 was in some ways the greatest storm of record. Flooding and heavy rains raged through the state for more than a week . . . causing damage over more than half the state. The Governor proclaimed a state of emergency in 39 counties and damages totaled more than $500 million. More than 50,000 people were forced from their homes, and at least 12 people died. An estimated 1,380 homes and 185 businesses were destroyed and more than 12,000 homes and 950 businesses were damaged.

Department of Water Resources, The Floods of February, 1986, *p. 1.*

In its own way it was an eerie event, though the men involved were unaware that they were engaged in anything more than the day's business. They were on the steamboat *Colusa,* and their vessel was pushing upstream on the Sacramento River while they looked at the land on either side and entertained dreams of rich farms, happy toiling farm families, and a finer California. However, the time of their voyage was not July of 1850 with young Will Green heading upriver on another vessel *Colusa* and daydreaming about the agricultural glories to come, and what they saw around them were not virgin fields choked with head-high wild oats and splashed with wild flowers. The time, rather, was sixty-five years later almost to the day—July of 1915—and what they were looking out on were long miles of orchards and farmhouses, country roads and church steeples. It was in fact the Sacramento Valley that Green had envisioned as

The flood of February–March 1940 from above in the Sutter Buttes–Colusa vicinity (the town is at the lower right, on the banks of the Sacramento's main channel), showing how the massively overflowing water passed down over the Butte Sink area and inundated the farms of the "east side." The successfully holding levee in the foreground illustrates graphically how vitally important to huge Valley areas is an effective system.
Courtesy: Murray, Burns, and Kienlen, Consulting Civil Engineers, Sacramento.

long ago he had stood at the wheel of his boat, though as yet still in its beginnings and hardly a patch on the even more populous and prosperous scene that the men of 1915 hoped to see rising up in their own lifetimes.

Their day's business was trying to convince a skeptical group of congressmen from the Rivers and Harbors Committee that in the interest of expanding farming Congress should take on the flood control burden and approve the Sacramento Flood Control Project.[1] In truth, it was astonishing what even the hopes inspired by the Jackson Report, and the early work of California's Reclamation Board, had already created in the way of a much expanded farming world in the Valley. Since the first beginnings of the Progressive Era stirrings about the Sacramento River, from the creation of the River Improvement and Drainage Association in 1902, the State River Convention in 1904, and the subsequent agitations of the Commonwealth Club, the Sacramento Valley had begun a long transforming economic boom. Encouraged by evidence that something decisive about the river was in the offing, investors were so active that as early as 1909 Edward Adams of the Commonwealth Club had been able to report a remarkable upsurge in entrepreneurial developments in the Valley. The Farm Lands Investment Company, below Marysville, had by that year a 14,000-acre project underway, as did the Lovdal district opposite Sacramento (6,000 acres), the Fair Ranch near Knight's Landing (10,000 acres), and the Egbert District near Rio Vista (10,000 acres). Just getting going was a huge project set in motion by Natomas Consolidated of California, a former gold dredge operating company, which planned a development just above the city of Sacramento which would enclose the largest part of the American Basin.[2]

By 1915 the spectacle in the Valley was even more remarkable.[3] The launching of large private reclamation schemes, the building of new railroad lines, the introduction of new crops that became huge producers, swift rises in the acreage under irrigation, and sharply increased land values: all of these testified to a revolutionary new era in the Valley's history. In 1913 about 400,000 acres in the Valley were reported to be in a "comparative state of reclamation"—that is, private landowners, operating through reclamation districts, had constructed levees, drained the swamps, and put the land to farming—as against some 300,000 in 1910. In the following five years, more than 300,000 more acres were reclaimed, involving a total of over 350 miles of levee construction. In 1918 alone, private interests spent $2 million on reclamation works.

By 1918 the Reclamation Board could report all of the following as having come into existence since 1912: Sacramento River West Side Levee District (below Colusa), 107,000 acres; Reclamation District (RD) 1500, 63,735 acres (the huge Armour property in Sutter Basin); RD 1000, 53,040 acres, and RD 1001, 31,420 acres (the Natomas project); RD 1600, 6,150 acres; RD 999, 23,855 acres; RD 900, 10,400 acres; RD 1002, 5,830 acres; and reclamation in the delta islands amounting to 26,915 acres.[4]

Typical, if larger than most, was the ambitious Natomas Consolidated operation in the American Basin, which was fully completed in 1915. It enclosed the basin entirely, for a total area of over 80,000 acres. The company constructed model levees, with crowns of twenty-four feet, placed a hundred feet or more back from the riverbank, the intervening berm grown up with trees and brush to protect against wave wash. Their average height was fifteen feet. Thus for the first time in fifty years, the Reclamation Board observed, "the sea of flood waters [in the American Basin] was replaced by a sea of waving grain."[5]

Meanwhile, a railroad net was being rapidly built throughout the Valley, the lines generally converging on the city of Sacramento. In 1913 alone the following railway roads were under construction or recently placed in operation: the Sacramento South, to Walnut Grove; the Oakland, Antioch, & Eastern, an electric from Oakland to Sacramento; the Vallejo Northern Railroad, another electric, connecting Vallejo and Sacramento; the Sacramento & Woodland, an electric; the Northern Electric Railroad, which in 1906 connected Chico and Oroville, in 1907 built to Sacramento via Marysville from Oroville, and in 1912 constructed a branch from Marysville across the Valley to Colusa; the Southern Pacific Railroad, which was building branches all over; the Central California Traction Company, an electric that had been operating between Sacramento and Stockton since 1911.[6]

River navigation was also surging. It was revived not long after the initial federal river navigation project began in 1899; but before the flood control program got into operation there were years (1908, 1911, 1912) when navigation was actually halted because of low water and too much mining debris in the stream. Other critical low water years came in 1920, 1922, and 1924, when the Sacramento practically ceased having any outflow at its mouth—a condition in part created by extremely heavy irrigation withdrawals in these drought times—but in these latter seasons, because of the effects of the project, navigation never ceased.

The opening of the mouth of the Sacramento River by the cut across Horseshoe Bend, which began in 1913, far exceeded expectations as to its effect upon the navigability of the river, even though by 1927 this particular part of the project was only 80 percent complete. Because the river by this step was given greater slope, mining debris (of which several hundred million yards still remained to be washed through the river system) was so eroded out of the Sacramento's bed as to lower the height of extreme low water at the city of Sacramento to about ten feet below what it had been in 1905, or practically to its original elevation before the impact of debris. The clearing of the river channels even extended far up the Feather, amounting to about a seven-foot lowering in the Yuba, at its mouth, by 1925.[7]

Part of the reason why there were so many more vessels navigating the Sacramento lay in the fact that, with greater freedom from flood, Valley farmers could turn to intensive agriculture—that is, to orchard crops, rather than simply planting wheat and other field crops. They were therefore producing far more tonnage. What they all had in mind, of course, was the long-awaited opening of the Panama Canal, which would allow them to tap Eastern markets, and this event took place in 1914. One great holding of 54,000 acres which had produced approximately 35,000 tons of freight per year when it was in ordinary field crops was by 1916 divided up into smaller holdings (as was typical of orchard farms) and producing 150,000 tons.[8] Thus the July 1915 voyage of the Rivers and Harbors Committee on the steamer *Colusa* presented the congressmen with a practically continuous orchard on both sides of the stream. Pears, plums, peaches, cherries, prunes, apricots, and pears were being grown, with grape vineyards beginning also to spread.

The rivers, therefore, carried hundreds of boats. Some would go far up the river, pulling empty barges, and begin loading as they came down river, adjusting to the depth of the stream. Such operations as the Sacramento Transportation Company maintained fleets of the new gasoline-powered trucks going ten miles on each side of the river to pick up crops and deliver goods. If the farmer had freight, he would put up a little flag, each line having its own ensign. Boats would stop for even one bag of potatoes. Carrying the equivalent of twenty-two carloads of freight, boats from the Valley could tie up directly beside ocean-going vessels in San Francisco harbor, short-circuiting all the switching and handling of railroads. So low were water freight rates that in 1916 some 90 percent of the freight between San Francisco and Sacramento was carried by boat. The value per ton of this freight was almost the highest of any river in the United States, in addition to which thousands of passengers annually took the overnight steamboat ride from Sacramento to San Francisco to conduct their affairs.[9]

In the year 1916, four navigation companies operated on the Sacramento, owning 26 steamboats and a large number of barges. On the 200 boats of all kinds in this traffic, the following tonnages and passengers were carried:

1910:	496,147 tons;	180,405 passengers
1913:	733,594 tons;	212,114 passengers
1918:	1,053,510 tons;	91,540 passengers
1922:	1,291,135 tons;	93,903 passengers.

Sacramento River commercial transportation reached its peak in 1925, when 1,366,780 tons of freight were moved on the river. (It declined steadily thereafter through competition from gasoline-powered transportation, to 623,422 tons in 1938, rising to 832,656 tons in the war boom years of 1943.)[10]

Of all the transformations in the Valley, most astonishing was the explosion of rice culture. In 1911, 160 acres produced rice in the Sacramento Valley. In 1915, 720,000 sacks of rice came out of the Valley, valued at $1.5 million, and in 1916 the incredible total of 2.5 million sacks, valued at $5 million. The crop matures late and therefore must be moved quickly before the rain falls. This made water navigation in many parts of the valley more critically needed then than ever. Much of the rice culture in these years was in the delta islands, where the peat soil would not bear rails, making boats mandatory.[11]

This whole spectacle of swift development in the Sacramento Valley gave men in high positions visions of truly grand scope. V. S. McClatchy, chairman of the Reclamation Board, exulted before the California State Bankers' Association in 1914 that water transport, with its cheap rates as against railroads, meant that California crops could go to all the markets of the world through the Panama Canal. Waterways could touch "the important towns of the valley. Lateral canals could tap every important point on the floor of both valleys."

McClatchy, agrarian visionary, believed the ultimate result would be a grand and healthful social transformation. The one million acres in process of reclamation then lay largely empty of population, he said, growing only field crops. There had been no markets for anything more than small grains, and it was unsafe, because of flood dangers, for families to live there. But all that was now to change. With flood protection, excellent navigability, and the Panama Canal, the great holdings would break up into family farms of twenty acres each, and where there were then few residents, there would soon be as many as 400,000 people, ultimately a million. And consider, McClatchy said, "how much more desirable is increment to the population of this character than the operatives of factories and sweat shops, living in congested tenement districts, deficient physically and necessarily narrow in their lives and their ideals."[12]

This was not a solitary dream in these years. Rather, it had been much in the American mind for decades. The swift rise of populous industrial cities, beginning in the 1880s, had produced great lamentation, nationwide, as Americans bitterly deplored the draining away to those cities of millions of young people from the farms and country towns who sought a different kind of life there but only found, it was said, temptation and demoralization. The decline of the small family farm was widely grieved. In Theodore Roosevelt's years in the White House one of the causes to which he gave some of his most urgent thoughts and support was the "Country Life" movement, which sought to stem the cityward-rush by revitalizing conditions of life in the farms and bringing them up to city standards in such public services as schools and roads.[13]

California, as Kevin Starr has recently written, had a special problem, created by land monopoly. The rural life produced by the bonanza wheat farming that exploded in the 1860s and boomed on into the 1880s presented an unedifying social scene, one that in reality was much like mining. The bonanza farms were usually owned by absentees, and they used up the soil with no thought of renurturing it thereafter, just as the miners had used up the mountains. The gangs of migratory wheat workers

> were single men, as were most of the miners, and when they returned from the fields they lived, as did the miners, in shacks or bunkhouses devoid of domesticity. Coming into [small nearby towns] . . . they drank, fought, gambled, and whored as had the miners in Marysville and Sacramento a generation earlier.[14]

In the late 1870s the *Sacramento Daily Union* sketched the typical wheat farming scene graphically:

> We are all but too familiar with the picture: A level plain, stretching out to the horizon all around; for a few months a wavering sea of grain, then unsightly stubble; in the center a wretched shieling [hut] of clapboards, weather-stained, parched, and gaping; no trees, no orchard, no garden, no signs of home . . . on everything alike the tokens of shiftlessness and barbarism. . . . we see nothing in prospect but a shiftless drifting backward further and further into barbarism, until, the fertility of the soil being exhausted, the reckless and half-civilized tillers of it shall be compelled to migrate.[15]

Wheat culture peaked in the middle 1880s, when California, then ranking as the state with the second largest wheat crop in the nation, put something like two-thirds of its cultivated property to this purpose, making a total of 3.75 million acres of land. From increasingly exhausted soils came an ever lower quality of wheat, while at the same time rising competition from other parts of the world sent wheat prices plummeting. By 1900 only 2.6 million acres were in wheat, and by 1910 this had dropped sharply to about 478,000 acres. The plains, said an 1899 traveler in the Kings River region of the San Joaquin Valley,

> are given up to desolation. Eight or ten years ago large crops of wheat were raised on this land . . . and farmhouses built on nearly every quarter section. . . . But not a spear of anything green grows on the place this year. . . . The houses of former inhabitants are empty, the doors swing open or shut with the wind. Drifting sand is piled to the top of many fences. The windmills, with their broken arms, swing idly in the breeze. Like a veritable city of the dead, vacant residences on every side greet the traveller by horse team as he pursues his weary way across these seemingly endless plains.[16]

In direct contrast, however, in fruit culture, in the planting and harvesting of orchards, there lay, Californians believed, the hope of a family-farming future. Kevin Starr writes:

> No agricultural endeavor stood in greater contrast to the get-rich-quick, land-hungry exploitations of wheat. Fruit culture was a work of time and patience. Capable of generating livable incomes from smaller land plots, fruit culture encouraged families to live on the land. Fruit culture nurtured values of responsible land use, prudent capitalization, cooperation among growers in the matter of packing, shipping, and marketing. Above all else, fruit culture encouraged a level of rural civility in the care of homes, the founding of schools, churches and libraries, the nurturing of social and recreational amenities which stood in complete contrast to the Wild West attitudes of wheat.[17]

The whole burden of Donald Pisani's absorbing recent book on the history of irrigation in the Western states is to show us how much this generations-long crusade was fueled by the dream of creating and spreading, preserving and enhancing, the family farm, with its broad hoped-for social consequences.[18]

One of the conservation causes into which the Hiram Johnson administration poured intense energies and labored through heavy political battles to produce was the reform of California's water laws to prevent water monopoly, eliminate litigation over water rights, and ease the spread of small-farmer dominated irrigation districts. Former Governor George Pardee, who served on Johnson's Conservation Commission, exulted that when millions of acres currently lying bare, with little population, were irrigated, "and only when they are irrigated, there will live, in cities, towns, villages, and on ten and twenty acre farms, in California comfort, ten millions of happy and prosperous American people."[19] It was certainly true that the peculiar history of land policy in the state, which had produced immense landholdings and land monopoly, had meant that wheat farming as it developed in California was a bleak industrial process. It was no wonder that men like McClatchy watched enthusiastically as that world began slowly giving way to intensive agriculture and small farms.

It is always difficult to measure outcome against dream, but there are facts at hand to sustain the view that for at least a time in California, much of this dream came true. "By 1920," Starr remarks, "a vast fruitbelt—eight-hundred miles in length, two hundred miles in width—extended down the state."[20] The Sacramento Valley, as is evident yet in the 1980s, remained a land of immense open spaces given over to field crops, especially rice, the Valley's giant crop, but orchards expanded tremendously, and so did both the number of people on the land and the number of individual farms. Though the Sacramento Valley did not grow in population after 1900 as explosively as did the San Joaquin Valley and southern California, where there was much more land and irrigation expanded tremendously,[21] it did dramatically end its long stagnation.

To look again at a single mid-Valley farming county, Sutter, which has taken our attention before (concerning the 1850s and 1860s), major changes may be seen in the structure of its life. In the thirty years from 1870 to 1900, Sutter County's population essentially did not grow at all; that of other mid-Valley counties actually declined. From 1900 to 1910, when California as a whole was growing 60 percent in population, Sutter County grew only 7 percent.[22]

The next decade, from 1910 to 1920, witnessed a completely new pattern. It was in these years that the great boom took off in the Valley, following upon the Jackson Report and the building of major features of the flood control system. Sutter County mirrored this development by growing from 6,328 people to 10,115, or an increase of close to 60 percent, while California as a whole, though it swelled mightily, grew at a slower rate: about 40 percent.[23] The next ten years, from 1920–1930, did not see this Sutter County surge continue quite so spectacularly, but even so it grew by 44 percent, California as a whole increasing by 66 percent in the same period.[24]

Other aspects of the picture are equally revealing. There were 728 farms in Sutter County in 1900, growing to 873 in 1910, a modest increase, then leaping to 1,437 in 1920, roughly 70 percent more in ten years. By 1920, there were 1,758 farms in the county. Meanwhile, total acreage in farms did not increase at all in this proportion (from about 290,000 in 1900 to 340,000 in 1930). Farms, in other words, got much smaller, there were far more of them, and as statistics on valuation show, they were also far more expensive, rising from a total value of $7 million in 1900 to $41 million in 1920. In the decade 1910–1920, the key years of this study, land values almost tripled.[25] In short, in these years more costly and smaller orchard farms, tilled by resident families, flourished.

≈≈≈

Beyond the year 1920 the Sacramento Valley, and the flood control project upon which it now desperately relied, entered on a long span of troubled and complicated years running through the Depression era, the World War II, and beyond—a period that warrants another book-length work of scholarship. These difficult years began in the working-through of a frustrating time of growing economic crisis during the 1920s. Spurred on by the high food prices that erupted when the First World War began, and then pressed by the government in Washington to redoubled efforts after the American entry into that conflict, the Reclamation Board had made heroic efforts to complete the project's levees and bypasses through heavy assessments on landowners.

Then came a catastrophic drop in farm prices after the war ended, after which American farming nationwide began its cruel depression of the 1920s. Large assessments that had been levied to build the state's share of the Flood Control Project could never be collected; the costs of construction (which under the Flood Control Act of 1917 the landowners of the Sacramento Valley had agreed to shoulder themselves, since Congress had sharply reduced its financial share) soared far beyond the ability of many people to pay. Eventually, after years of studies, hearings, and complex state-federal negotiations that were spurred onward by disastrous national floods in 1927, in the Flood Control Act of 1928 the federal government assumed most of the costs of flood control in the two regions thus far covered by federal policy, the lower Mississippi and the Sacramento Valley.[26]

Thereafter, the Sacramento Flood Control Project passed from the first phase of its history, that in which it appeared, was largely constructed, and had its primary impact on the life of the Valley, into the second, "in-being" period. Now it was a question of dealing with the next generation of difficulties, arising out of the existence and nature of the Flood Control Project itself and its functioning. If the water was not to be allowed to spread over the Valley floor but kept strictly within leveed channels, this meant long periods of heavy flows within those embankments, which were now many hundreds of miles in length, and a continual problem of maintenance. Being constructed only of piled-up dirt and sand, the levees could suddenly slump or collapse during floodtimes. They needed to be carefully watched for seepage problems, during extended periods of high water, and for such simple but fatal illnesses as gopher holes. These and other causes could produce that alarming sign of imminent levee-failure, great boils of water erupting on the landside of a levee which needed quickly to be rendered harmless by the hasty building around them of sandbag coffer-dams.

Then, during the New Deal years the national government began taking on flooding problems nationwide, especially after enactment of the historic Flood Control Act of 1936, and its legislative sequelae. In the 1930s the projects that the Progressive Era had thought ambitious became tentative by comparison. A government that had accepted costs reaching about $20 million only after almost two decades of pleading suddenly became a source of vast funds. At the same time, the multiple-use controversy that had gone on for years in the federal government was finally won, in the New Deal years, by those who argued in favor of that principle. The result was a major policy transition nationwide to what had been dreamed of for many years: the building of very large headwater dams. They were constructed to serve a wide range of functions, including irrigation, power production, and recreation, and during floodtimes they could also offer crucial aid by slicing off the peaks of the flows. That is, they would release less water downstream during high water periods than was flowing into the reservoirs behind them.

In California, the launching in the 1930s of the state-planned but federally built and managed Central Valley Project, involving many dams, canals, and complex water interchange systems between basins, altered the whole frame of reference within which flood control arrangements and planning operated. The U.S. Bureau of Reclamation's Shasta Dam at the head of the Sacramento Valley, completed by the early 1940s to serve as the foundation of the Central Valley Project, was so immense (it would impound 4.5 million acre-feet of water) that it could simultaneously manage flood control, irrigation needs, navigation, salinity problems in the delta, and power production. Also, in the mid-1940s, the U.S. Army Corps of Engineers was authorized to build a number of large headwater dams in the Sacramento and San Joaquin valleys, including Folsom Dam on the American River. In the 1960s, the voter-approved California State Water Project produced in 1967 the damming of the last major uncontrolled tributary of the Sacramento, the Feather River, by means of Oroville Dam.[27]

However, the basic geographic and hydrographic natural facts of the Sacramento Valley remained. It was still a province given to frequent periods of high water and threatened flood, so that the fundamental challenge the Sacramento Flood Control Project was created to master remained as pressing as ever. There were many years, furthermore, when it had to do its job without the aid of large headwater dams. Therefore, the building-out of the valleywide flood control system dreamed of by Thomas H. Jackson and his successors among the federal and state engineers continued steadily. By 1944, the Sacramento Flood Control Project was regarded as about 90 percent complete, having cost a total of $89 million, some $66 million having come (before the Flood Control Act of 1928) from state and local sources. Its authorized works included 980 miles of levees; 7 weirs or control structures; 3 drainage pumping plants; 438 miles of channels and canals; 7 bypasses, 95 miles in length, encompassing an area of 101,000 acres; 5 low water check dams; 31 bridges; 50 miles of collecting canals and seepage ditches; 91 gauging stations; and 8 automatic shortwave radio water-stage transmitters.[28]

Though it was not until the 1940s that the Project was strongly enough built to go through a flood season without major levee breaks, its protection did allow for continued population growth. Taking the four rural counties in the heart of the Valley—Colusa, Sutter, Yuba, and Yolo—we see that while they had grown only 58 percent during the fifty years from 1860 to 1910 (and were essentially stagnant from about 1880), in the next forty years, to 1950, their population increased 170 percent, from 38,018 to 102,950; by 1980 they would be up 500 percent over 1910. The large rural and urban county of Sacramento, with the state's capital city, grew 181 percent in the half century between 1860 and 1910, but from then to 1950—a time before the impact of the high-technology revolution, and California's overall skyrocketing in population from that cause—it spurted up 309 percent, or from 67,806 people to 277,140. (By 1980, Sacramento County would be up the astonishing total of 1055 percent in population over 1910, reflecting a rate of growth somewhat higher than the state as a whole in this span of years.)[29] If the Valley were still subject to frequent ravaging floods, very little of this swelling of population could have taken place.

In reality, the Valley's flooding dangers have much increased, due to variations in climate that are not understood. Beginning in the 1950s, the Sacramento River and its tributaries have in floodtimes been producing more and more water. In 1955, when a tragic levee break at Yuba City caused heavy loss of life, the Feather River had produced in that flood its highest outflow ever measured, some 203,000 cubic feet per second, and since then, this flow has been exceeded three times. In the 1950s, to strengthen the levees for heavier flows, the U.S. Army Corps of Engineers began a long and extremely costly program of levee "hardening" in various locations by covering them with rocks and cobbles.

At the same time, the Flood Control Project has entered an ironic phase. Aided now by the presence of five large headwater dams—in addition to enormous Shasta, there are Black Butte on Stony Creek, New Bullard's Bar on the Yuba, Folsom on the American, and huge Oroville Dam on the Feather—it has been so successful over the long term in providing protection to the Valley that, because of the resulting immense population growth, each overflow or levee break, when they do occur, is fantastically more costly and dangerous than in the older times. The Sacramento Flood Control Project was conceived and designed to protect farmers, and now it is having to protect large urbanized metropolitan areas holding populations running to the hundreds of thousands. In round figures, while it protects some 900,000 acres of farmland, it also is responsible for shielding 100,000 acres of urban structures from flood.[30]

Not only do these urban structures include heavily capitalized commercial and public buildings that by their complicated technological interiors are more vulnerable to flood damage than their nineteenth-century predecessors, the homes Valley people live in are no longer prudently "flood-proofed" by being built on high foundations—they sit flat on the ground. In addition, as American affluence rises and lifestyles soar even among the broad masses of the people, these dwellings are now filled with expensive furniture, appliances, rugs, and art objects. It is no longer a matter of widely scattered farm homes with their simple wooden floors and austere furnishings being assaulted by floodwaters, but densely packed neighborhoods containing valuable residences and fleets of expensive automobiles, travel trailers, and, in backyards, stored recreational vessels.[31]

The surprising fact, in light of these conditions, is how well the project works. After the high water season of 1981–1982 the state's Department of Water Resources could remark that the system

> has proved to be highly efficient over the years and today, except for additional flood-control reservoirs, it remains essentially as originally constructed. The Sacramento Valley portion of the project has been severely tested on several occasions and in general has performed effectively.[32]

The flood season of 1982–1983 was a particular challenge for the project, since "more than four times the average volume of runoff passed through the system." Even so, during that period "the project performed as designed without major problems."[33]

≈≈≈

Then on the evening of February 11, 1986, the first in a series of massive rain storms sweeping northeastward from the region of the Hawaiian Islands, taking up more and more vaporized moisture as they passed over those thousands of miles of warm open ocean, and building huge energies, began to move in on central and northern California. By now, the state's Department of Water Resources Flood Operations Center in Sacramento was in "flood fighting" trim, and so too was the U.S. Army Corps of Engineers; the federal-state partnership so long ago decreed in *Gibbons* v. *Ogden* was in full operation. The National Weather Service's California-Nevada River Forecast Center staff was also at work, alerting everyone to the looming crisis. And so it began. In a ten-day downpour, the storms arriving on shore one after the other disgorged incredible volumes of rain on the land below. In a broad band of territory reaching 200 miles north and 100 miles south of a line from San Francisco to Sacramento and Lake Tahoe, one river system after another, from the Russian River in Sonoma County to the Truckee flowing through Reno, swelled gigantically, in many locations producing uncontrollable flooding. The cities of the Napa Valley, from St. Helena at its head to Napa near its mouth, were brutally assaulted by overflowing waters.[34]

In the Sacramento Valley, the Sacramento River's main channel was soon chockfull, and north of the Sutter Buttes the immemorial pattern was once again displaying itself: below Chico Creek heavy overbank flows to the east and out into forty-mile-long Butte Basin began taking place at points above the beginning of the project's levees. Then, downstream, excess waters started pouring out Moulton Weir and Colusa Weir, joining the southward flowing Butte Basin waters in Butte Sink, passing thence down into the wide mouth of Sutter Bypass. Meanwhile, over in the Feather River's watershed, in the vicinity of Yuba City and Marysville, the Feather and the Yuba were at the 65-foot warning stage by the 17th of February. Releases from Lake Oroville down the dramatic falling plunge of its long concrete overflow spillway poured a torrent into the Feather River—producing great clouds of vapor boiling up from the contact point—which reached the figure of 150,000 cubic feet per second.

Further down the Valley in the vicinity of the state capital, hundreds of volunteer workers were by then laboring day and night in drenching rains and violent winds to strengthen the levees enclosing the American River. That stream was roaring along in a torrent of 130,000 second-feet, rushing down to its juncture with the Sacramento River and gravely endangering hundreds of thousands of people on either side. Water from the Sacramento's main channel crowded through the Sacramento Weir, running westward to join the southward-moving flows in the Yolo Bypass. That ever-broadening channel was carrying its wide sheet of excess floodwaters downvalley into Cache Slough, whence they flowed on past embattled Rio Vista—its people turning out to tend hastily constructed flood-barriers—through the long, wide Horseshoe Cut out into Suisun Bay. During these outflows, the *low* tides at the river's mouth would reach higher on the measuring staffs than any prior *high* tide. On the 19th, levee breaks on the Mokelumne River, south of the city of Sacramento, flooded Thornton and delta islands.

In the evening of the next day, at a time when people were briefly comforted by falling river levels, a flow of water suddenly erupted outside of the Yuba's southerly levee by the community of Linda, followed abruptly by a sudden yawning levee break that sent 24,000 people fleeing from their homes, to which they could not return for two weeks, some for many weeks. It took two days simply to close the break (after which 37 pumps flown in from all over the nation labored at nine pumping stations for six weeks to drain the flooded region). Something like 3,000 homes were damaged or destroyed from the Linda break, 150 businesses were wiped out, many of them in a low-lying mall, approximately thirty square miles were flooded, and overall costs ranged from 50 to 100 million dollars.

Meanwhile, the American River levees just barely held as Folsom Dam, like Oroville, released unprecedented volumes of water. Over on the east side of the Sacramento River, near the Sacramento Metropolitan Airport, at many locations crews worked desperately to repair large boils, seeps, slumps, and sloughing off of levee material from its landside bank. If either the American or the Sacramento Rivers had broken through—and it was a close-run thing—they would have buried deep under water a large recently built-up region of homes, condominiums, businesses, and even an under-construction sports palace, all of it spreading energetically in recent years out into the southern end of the American Basin (which, we will remember, was regularly described in the nineteenth century as "a sea of floodwaters").

The headwater dams played an absolutely crucial role in shaving off the flood peaks, and thus protecting the Valley from an even worse fate. At its peak inflow, Shasta was receiving over 150,000 second-feet, but it kept its downstream releases to 70,000 second-feet; Lake Oroville's inflow reached more than 260,000 second-feet, but it held its releases, during a climactic two-day period, to 150,000. Folsom's largest inflow reached in excess of 200,000 second-feet (much increased for a brief period when an upstream cofferdam gave way), and it released 130,000.[35]

At the latitude of Sacramento city, at the flood's high point, something like 650,000 cubic feet per second of water passed down-valley. This was at least 50,000 second-feet beyond the volume of water that Thomas Jackson and his successors had designed the project to contain; it will be remembered that the largest flood of record they had to refer to, and around which they planned the system, was that of 1907, which produced about 600,000 second-feet. However, the amazing fact is that, had it not been for the dams holding back peak flows, that total Valley peak outflow in February 1986 would have exceeded *a million second-feet*![36]

As State Engineer William Hall had prophetically warned the legislature in his remarkably prescient 1880 report, there would be floods coming down the Valley, some day, far larger than any they had yet seen. And so it had eventuated in 1907, and once more, far more astonishingly, in February 1986. Perhaps an even greater outpouring, on some future occasion, is yet to come. The Sacramento Valley, after all, is millions of years old, storms have been coming up from far out in the Pacific for many millennia, and Americans are only into their second century—but a tiny slice of time—of observing floods in that venue. Their experience to this point, given the great age of the natural environment, can only be described as shallow in the extreme.

Even so, in its official report on the awesome flood season of 1986, the Corps of Engineers was able to state that the Sacramento Flood Control Project had "prevented widespread flooding and damages."[37] Of course, along the Sacramento River below Shasta dam there were $17.4 million in estimated damages in 1986; $21 million along the Feather; $95 million by the Yuba River; and in the American Basin, north of Sacramento city, various overflows produced over $17 million in costs.[38] Along the American River alone, however, if Folsom Dam and the river levees had not existed, flood damages in this heavily urbanized area would have approached $5 billion. Considering the whole broad band of California and Nevada struck by the storms of February 1986, the Corps estimated that existing flood control structures prevented approximately $13.4 billion in losses.[39] As the state's Department of Water Resources could report, despite the heavy damages, the more than 50,000 people forced from their homes and the dozen deaths,

> the local, state and federal flood protection facilities worked. The levees, with thousands of workers patrolling and repairing them around the clock, for the most part withstood the greatest volumes of water ever recorded on the lower Sacramento River system, flows that exceeded the system's theoretical capacity.[40]

After all, though Yuba County suffered grievously from the Linda levee break, across the Feather River in Sutter County, where now-populous Yuba City and its surrounding countryside neighbors in their dense fruit orchards and wide alfalfa fields live cupped between the Feather and the Sacramento, there were *no* damages in the flood of 1986. Colusa County had only 24 houses and 4 businesses damaged, none destroyed; in Yolo County, the comparable figures were 34 and 5, with none destroyed; and in vast Sacramento County, with its many thousands of structures, the figures were only 1730 and 73, with none destroyed.[41]

In conditions none of the Sacramento Flood Control Project's founders could have visualized, at a time when any significant failure would have had vastly multiplied effects over those of a comparable event in 1910, and in the face of an outflow far beyond anything anyone in those years could have guessed might occur, the system had worked surprisingly well. Quite aside from the water held back by the dams, 1986 had put 650,000 second-feet into the leveed channels, and they had essentially held. Had Captain Jackson and E. D. Adams of the Commonwealth Club witnessed these days, they would have marveled at the immense soaring dams, and at the same time could have felt themselves happily confirmed by that ultimate tribunal, the verdict of history. So few had died! Floods worldwide commonly produce, and even in the United States have in past years produced, thousands of deaths. In the Johnston, Pennsylvania flood of 1889, 2200 people were drowned. Now, in the Sacramento Valley, more than a million people could live on a floodplain and though on occasion sorely harrassed, could not simply survive, but flourish.

Meanwhile, the continuing joust goes on, yearly, between the Project, fortified by the great dams, and the Sacramento River. This is very much a live, ongoing encounter. The inland sea has disappeared, but it is now clear as it never was before how powerful a river system has been put under control, and how vulnerable that structure of control will always be. Thus that ancient activity in the Sacramento Valley, that local cottage industry, the study of the Sacramento and its tributaries, also goes on, as it has since the days of Will Green and William H. Parks. After its long 1986 siege of flood fighting had passed into history, the U.S. Army Corps of Engineers first undertook some $11 million of levee repair projects, and then initiated an as yet unfinished five-year study to see, in light of the 1986 events, how well matched are the Project and its great antagonist.[42]

≈≈≈

When the weather forecasters were first warning that a big storm was coming, a columnist in the San Francisco Bay Area, new to California, scoffed. "My question—and I ask this without ever having seen Pacific Storm Bob or whatever it's called—[is] why do we have three days of front page stories and TV news stories about a rainstorm? Is it because Californians are sissies?" It was because, as his Bay Area colleague Carl Nolte later replied in print, "Nature in California is a smiling killer than can turn on you at any time."[43]

CHAPTER

Reflections:
The Sacramento Valley as a Case Study in American Political Culture and the Policy Process

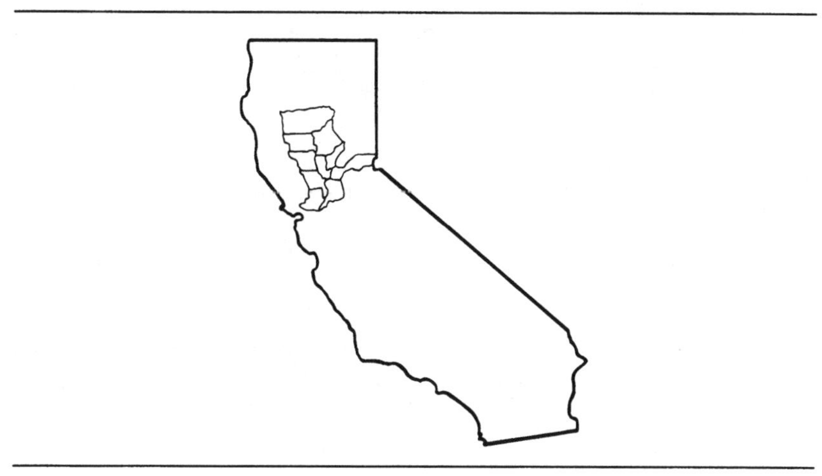

ALICIA AVE

The first factor is the context of the problem. . . . *The political culture of the system should be considered. . . . A sensitive appreciation of specific, realistic contexts in which decisions are made and results sought is a necessary prerequisite to understanding.*

> *Garry Brewer and Peter deLeon,* The Foundations of Policy Analysis, *pp. 191–192, 260.*

This is the story of an encounter between a natural environment and a people. In it, we follow that people as, within the context of their particular political culture, over more than half a century of trial and error they worked out and applied a series of decisions which in time empowered them to master that environment's complex challenges. In the 1850s the Sacramento Valley offered to the newly arriving Americans, then predominantly a farming people, the promise of an agriculture bountiful beyond anything they had formerly known. At the same time it denied them more than a partial and embattled access to that promise by periodically sending destructive floods pouring down over Valley floor which endangered life, destroyed property, obliterated crops, drowned livestock, and left behind a great inland sea of ponded waters which consumed several months in draining away. In time that wild and threatening environment was tamed and disciplined, as the people of the Sacramento Valley, putting painfully learned skills to use which called on resources continental in scope, created their Holland in California, their protected and fruitful garden.

My purposes in this book have been to narrate the course of

A day after a sudden break in the Yuba River levee at Linda, during the February, 1986, flood season, homes on Alicia Avenue sit up to their eaves in water. It will take weeks of pumping before tens of thousands of Linda residents can return to their residences to begin cleaning everything out, and starting over again.
Photo: David Parker, in the Appeal-Democrat, *Marysville-Yuba City, Feb. 28, 1986.*

these events for their intrinsic human interest—it has seemed to me, most of all, simply a rattling good story—and also for what they tell us of the policy process. My aim has been to gain a specifically historical insight into policy making in the American setting, and by this means to find a reasonable explanation for the particular outcome of this encounter in the Sacramento Valley.

Many models for policy analysis present themselves in the work of scholars in disciplines outside history. The more traditional simply trace how decisions are shaped by the structure of the country's formal governing system; similarly venerable are emphases on policy as the product of political party activity, or as what the elite leadership wants. More fashionable since the 1950s has been the view that it is the balance of power between interest groups in the community at large that is the most crucial influence—or that an essentially logical cost-benefit calculation by participants forms the driving force in all public affairs. This one-factor "rational actor" thesis, which holds that all participants ask solely how they, personally, will benefit materially from the various decision-options available, is actually very old in explanations of the course of history and public affairs, going back to Karl Marx and beyond. Then there are such recent theses as what is termed the incrementalist approach, which holds that because of deep commitments to existing arrangements ("sunk costs"), policy decisions are rarely more than step-by-step limited modifications of what already is in place. Another is a version of the rational actor model which relies on game theory, while systems theory looks holistically at the entire governing arrangement as a kind of impersonal computer that receives inputs and generates outputs.[1]

All these approaches, as they are dealt with among social scientists, tend forbiddingly to be architectonic and mechanical, using a kind of dehumanized engineering language about public affairs which deals in leverages, numbers, stress-points, structures, and fulcra. They are based, too, on theories of human nature which are much too simple. Thus, while each model has its quantum of insight, what strikes the policy historian, whose daily task it is to examine real people doing actual things in real circumstances, is how much they leave out.

Public life as it has in fact taken place is formidably untidy, unpredictable, filled with chance and surprise. Analytical models are useful, but life is not logical, it is historical. We cannot force it to fit preconceived categories and theories. As Garry Brewer and Peter deLeon have written, "There is nothing quite so irrational—and misguided—as [analytical] approaches that claim to be rational and then operate as if the world ought to be the same—neat, simple, and orderly."[2]

My preference has been, therefore, for the much more pluralistic, human-centered "policy sciences" (that is, multidisciplinary) approach that such scholars as Brewer and deLeon have developed, with its more complex notions of human motive and character. Their emphasis is essentially clinical, not discipline-based; that is, they begin with the problem that the people involved faced, not with a theoretical principle, and then ask a series of questions. At what stage is the process of decision making (that is, is it at the stage of initiation; estimation of the problem and selection of policies; or implementation)? Who are the players? What ideas (ideologies, worldviews) inspire them? What values, what dreams for America, do they entertain? What are their interests? How do they define the issue before them? Who do they conceive to be the enemy? How do the parties involved image each other—what preconceptions do they bring to the controversy about their rivals? How do affective factors, such as fears and anxieties, historical memories, conspiratorial delusions, and prejudice, shape their actions? And what part is played by the personal factor, by the unique character and actions of key individuals?

Then, moving outward from the players, the policy sciences approach asks, what is there in the *context* that influences the policy making, that sets frameworks and limitations and possibilities? Specifically, what is going on in the country at large, and what is the state of the national or local mood; how does the governing system work; and what is the encompassing political culture, the whole pattern of behavior and believing in public life, like? How is the information system working, how well do the parties involved actually understand, in a factual sense, the problem? In what ways does the time dimension, and even chance events, both of which continually shift and change the context, affect the proceeding? Then, lastly, how do the decisions made work out, in practice, and what does this lead to?[3]

Guided by this systematic approach, in the story of the Sacramento Valley and its great flooding rivers we have learned that such nonquantifiable influences as values and ideologies, contrasting visions of America, and related beliefs about government, in addition to economic interest, did in fact powerfully influence what happened. That Americans were profoundly an individualistic and localistic people, one of the most enduring and internationally identifying attributes in their national political culture to this day, immediately put a stamp on everything that was done from the 1850s to the Progressive Era. So, too, Democrats and Republicans were sharply set off from each other in their ideas and in what kinds of people were in their ranks, so that it mattered decisively which of them was in power. Working from their own political worldviews, their own distinct notions of what government should do and America should be all about, they adopted policies that even in natural resource management were profoundly different from each other, producing drastic oscillations in what was done as first one and then the other would predominate in Sacramento. Their definitions of the situation were crucial for they stimulated conflict and flowed directly into the decisions, the tactics and the strategy, that were adopted.

The roster of players was at first a short one, but as important new ones entered the picture—as, for example, the courts—we observed that they changed the entire policy-making universe, making it considerably more complicated. Paying close attention to the players alerted us to the need to examine the nature of the engineering profession, its imperial mind-set and boldly intervening national and local role, and its symbiotic relations with the Republicans, when it entered the scene and began playing a major part in the action. The flow of the time dimension and the intervention of that sovereign and unpredictable power, chance, regularly shifted the terms of action and opened windows of opportunity, hitherto closed fast. In 1880 the peculiar politics leading up to the writing and adoption of the new State Constitution of 1879 put the legislature and governor's office fortuitously but firmly in Republican hands, so that there took place the brief and dramatic episode of their ambitious, centrally managed, and ultimately failing Drainage Act program of 1880.

In Democrat Will Green, a man of Southern loyalties who with a number of others we followed closely through the decades, we witnessed that absorbing phenomenon: an encounter between a gifted person and his or her principal life challenge at a certain stage in the history of the problem they seek to solve. Green, a kind of untutored Jeffersonian genius, encountered the Sacramento Valley context when it held a low level of reliable information about the rivers and high residual Yankee-Southern hostilities, so that his brilliant insights into river management would be rejected as unsubstantiated or as coming from a suspect source. By contrast, many years later a gifted young captain in the U.S. Army Corps of Engineers, Thomas H. Jackson, encountered the Sacramento Valley context when it was chockfull of tested information and, at the touch of such a person, ready to spring loose a universally accepted theory that half a century before was spurned when it came from Will Green.

Focusing on the learning process as the continuing thread that tied together this whole experience, we saw how strong a part it plays in policy making, having within it the ultimate key to success or failure. We followed a people slow to learn, reluctant to take up activism because of their deep investments, psychological and sociological as well as material, in the existing situation. They constantly underestimated the problem and overestimated their knowledge and capacity—trained engineers as well as ordinary citizens and politicians alike. They continually deluded themselves as to costs, as to the seriousness of the situation they faced; they regularly let themselves be misled by visionary, self-deluding experts with the highest professional credentials. Even the most well-trained and experienced U.S. Army Corps of Engineers officers clung to fundamental flood management misconceptions of great importance, decade after decade, culminating in the imperial (and, as it turned out, absurd) pronouncements in 1906 of the distinguished Dabney Commission. Here again, chance, in the form of the almost unprecedented monster floods of 1907 and 1909 which followed hard upon, and the recent installation of flow-measuring gauges in the Valley entered to dictate events. It finally and conclusively toppled the Corps' obsession with unsound theoretical principles by dramatically altering and perfecting the fundamental information base upon which every hope of a viable public policy rested.

However, these remarks on the policy process need coherence, continuity, and cumulative point. This will be best achieved by taking one major theme that runs through all of these events and following it: the nature and shaping influence upon policy of the political culture, particularly as it expressed itself in the tradition embodied in the Whigs of the Age of Jackson, and their legatees, the Republicans. The point that will here be made is a simple but historically central one: the Sacramento Flood Control Project, the culmination of this long struggle, was the product of a nationally reborn and triumphant Whiggery which in the Progressive years reached an extraordinary apogee, what might be called the "Whig Moment" in twentieth-century American life.

≈≈≈

The Whigs, who as we have seen in the second chapter were alive only for the brief twenty years from the early 1830s to the mid-1850s, should be thought of not just as a political party with a legislative agenda but as a cultural world within American life, a whole stratum of kinds of people, often but by no means always New England in origin—they were the archetypical Yankees—who lived in distinctive ways and possessed a coherent, identifying worldview. (There were multitudes even in the South, usually amongst its urban peoples, great plantation owners and independent upland farmers who disliked slavery, who admired and emulated the Whigs and voted their ticket.)[4]

As a political party the Whigs were not so successful at winning presidential elections as their rivals, the Jacksonian Democrats, those skillful adepts at party politics who loved the game of it, for as men devoted to the ideal of the independent gentleman Whigs recoiled in distaste from that arena. However, it was they who in what they built into American culture shaped the society and nation that was to come. They may have finally stumbled and collapsed as a party, but recongregating themselves within the Republican party as it took form in the 1850s they survived flourishingly as what would before long become the vital and shaping core culture in American life. Whig-Republicans were practitioners and symbols, and therefore, by example, teachers of distinctive values, habits, and preferences and ideas about government and society which in time would take form as the dominant American way. In short, America has evolved into a Whiggish country.

As the original Yankees (this name has come to be generally applied to all Americans abroad, though Southerners reject the appellation), Whigs thought of themselves as the very heart of the country, as its most virtuous and enlightened element. In their own words they were America's "sober, industrious, thriving people." It was they who preached the values of hard work, punctuality, thrift, and education which after the Civil War penetrated ever more deeply into all parts of the country. Whigs admired entrepreneurs and risk-takers, though they were not comfortable with the person who merely made money at whatever cost to the community. Public spiritedness: that was their ethic. Whigs particularly looked to the college-trained, the professional person, to provide leadership, and they cultivated the life of learning.

Where the Democrats saw a threatened as well as a real force for social exploitation in the rise of manufacturing, new technology, and an employing class, Whigs saw progress in all of this and applauded it. As investors, bankers, employers, and industrialists, they set America moving toward what it has since become: an urban and industrial country tied compactly together by complex transcontinental transportation networks and an intricate financial web. Whigs were many things, but for our purposes in this history we note especially that in economic terms they were the modernizers. (The Democrats, by contrast, were the modernizers in cultural terms, stressing individual choice, social equality, secularism, and tolerance for divergent ways of life.) That is, it was the Whig-Republicans who pushed America toward a national style of living that became predominantly entrepreneurial in mood and fascinated by, almost entirely absorbed in, thriving economic development.

This was not a process, however, that Whigs believed could get going simply on its own steam. Letting everyone do only what they wanted to do, that is, following a policy of laissez-faire, would in their minds mean drift and inefficiency. Though Whigs joined the Democrats in regarding powerful, nobility-directed European governments with distaste, they believed that their countrymen had gone too far in the other direction. They needed to get over their love affair with pure and unregulated individualism and begin thinking of the whole nation as a family that required paternal leadership. If there was to be real progress, a *plan* needed to be imposed from above, in the same way that God, as Whigs would say—they were a devout, churchgoing people—has imposed his plan of salvation upon humanity. Then the United States of America would achieve an "organic unity of society," a phrase Whigs like to use. Whigs especially approved of joint government-private business enterprises, such as the public provision of water-power sources to drive privately owned factories.

Since the 1820s Henry Clay, the Whigs' leader and inspiration, had offered the national plan that Whigs supported. He called for an "American System" that would include protective tariffs to keep out foreign goods and allow factories to spring up within the country to produce the things people wanted; a national bank to pool the country's capital; and federally constructed roads and ports to open up and link together natural resources. This, Whigs believed, would have many admirable results. It would open a wide array of opportunities and occupations to gifted young Americans—and they were passionately interested in releasing this spirit of enterprise.

In short, Whig-Republicans wanted government at all levels to intervene actively in cultural and economic life. After all, they would say, government is God's earthly magistrate whose task is to promote the general welfare in many ways. They found their social ideal in an idealized memory of the New England town, in which the community gathered together to work out ways for jointly meeting common goals; in which unfettered individualism was frowned upon. Where Democratic intellectuals of the nineteenth century tended to distrust such institutions as churches, courts, executive governments, and corporations as constricting and oppressive, Whigs thought of them as almost divine instruments for creating law and order, for organizing and therefore liberating society's productive energies.

Whigs, in short, had an appetite for managing, for *governing.* As the historian Daniel Walker Howe points out, "most of the . . . important organizations of the day—voluntary associations, school systems, and business corporations in particular—were run by Whigs."[5] When Jefferson Davis found he had to lead the Confederacy in a great war, he turned to the Southern Whigs to take over its management, create and direct its quickly founded war industries, and order its finances.[6] We see in the Whigs, then, a people who were never uncomfortable with rule from above by qualified and public-spirited elites, for they were instinctive paternalists.

In California's early years Whig-Republicans had a hard time winning enough elections in the state to gain majorities in the legislature and win the governor's chair. It took unusual national circumstances, such as the Republican-led Civil War, to put them into authority. When that happened, they immediately put into place the kind of swampland reclamation policy that their political tradition urged upon them as suitable and appropriate. That is, in 1861, as we have seen, they scuttled the formerly localized arrangement that the Democrats had enacted and created a strong central authority in Sacramento, guided by experts (engineers), which devised a plan for the whole valley. Its ambitious goal was to build a uniform system of levees which would solve the flooding problem in toto, not simply farm by farm and on the basis of ordinary wits, as the Democrats had intended. This program collapsed of its own weight, but in 1880 the Republicans attempted once more a similar undertaking. They did so under the direction this time of an official whose office the Republicans created, denominated the State Engineer, who was much disliked and condemned by the Democratic masses. They disliked on principle this elite leadership and expert management arrangement.

In a keen insight, historian Howe remarks that we can once again recognize the Whig-type in our own century. They reemerged most visibly, he maintains, after 1900, in the form of Theodore Roosevelt's Progressive Republicans. The conservation movement, the use of strong commissions to regulate railroad rates, the creation of new government agencies to police the making of food and drug products, joined to T.R.'s respect and admiration for learning, for experts, and also for powerful, imaginative businessmen (though he was ready sternly to regulate any who flagrantly exploited the community): all of it was indeed in the temper of the Whigs.

No more Whiggish figure exists in all of twentieth-century American history than the aristocratic, European-trained Gifford Pinchot, sign and symbol of Roosevelt's conservation crusade. As T.R.'s chief forester, for the first time he put centralized regulatory policies and an expert Forest Service in charge of lumbering in the national forests to halt their wholesale destruction and yet make them also continuously productive. Pinchot was no populist; small lumbermen all over the West hated him perhaps more passionately than did the great corporations.[7]

≈≈≈

It is clear that this model of the Progressive Republicans as Whigs applies with special aptness to California's public life after 1900. We note that it was the Progressive Republicans in the state, behind Hiram Johnson, who in the climactic legislative sessions of 1910–1913 built the basic structure of an energetic, intervening government system in California public life which shapes it to this day. Their agenda was a sweeping one: social welfare services that set the state on the trajectory that would put it in the forefront, nationally, among the states in this field; establishing strong commissions to regulate transportation and public utility rates; reforming the laws governing water rights to elevate the public's sovereignty over this vital public resource; vastly transforming the public schools; establishing stringent rules on child labor, hours of work, and wages for women; creating a pioneering workmen's compensation, insurance, and safety act; and beginning the first assault on disgraceful conditions in migrant labor camps.[8]

It is revealing that the Whig-Republican remaking of post-1900

California even extended deeply into its cultural life. As Kevin Starr has written, no more central and characteristic creation of the California Progressives exists than the University of California, which they intended would become an essentially Whiggish institution built in the mold of the Yankees' cherished Harvard, Yale, and Cornell. In the very years when the Sacramento Flood Control Project was being proposed and established, the Progressives were beginning their reconstitution of the university into precisely the kind of intellectually elitist institution—research-oriented, devoted to high culture and the training of professionals and community leaders—that California's Whig-Republicans dreamed of possessing in their state.

As the Progressive Era was being born in the late 1890s, a great scholar from Cornell, Benjamin Ide Wheeler, was brought out to undertake his twenty-years' revolution in the University of California. A warm personal friend of Theodore Roosevelt's and a classic Progressive, it was characteristic for Wheeler to be involved in the Commonwealth Club deliberations that set the Sacramento Flood Control Project in motion as a public crusade. In this way, Wheeler gave personal expression to the fundamental Progressive principle that those of learning should help lead in the solving of the nation's problems.

Thus for the Progressives, as Starr observes, the "university was their Progressive dream come true, their vision of elite high-mindedness in the public interest translated into buildings and libraries, faculty and students, research and teaching programs. Appointed regents as young men at the height of the Progressive Era, [Chester] Rowell, [John Francis] Neylan, and [Edward A.] Dickson served well into the 1940s and 1950s . . . providing a Progressive continuity that became, in effect, the formative philosophy of the university. Finding a haven at the University of California, the Progressives kept their dreams alive for another half century."[9]

≈≈≈

Within this general context in American political culture, the final outcome of the decades-old policy struggle over how to manage flooding in the Sacramento Valley, and the particular form of the arrangement adopted to achieve this goal, falls into place as reasonable and appropriate. It is the culmination of a half-century joust in California between what might be termed Democratic America and Whig-Republican America, one that concluded in the years after 1900 in a solid and enduring Whig-Republican victory.

For the fact was that in the area of resource management, the great experiment, the Jeffersonian system in America, had failed. In the world it was radically new, based as it was on the belief that the common people are wise enough and virtuous enough to govern themselves, strictly through their own local institutions; that there was no need for European-style centralized rule by remote and educated aristocracies, by self-styled experts in the art of governing and statecraft. The simple Jeffersonian state of legislatures, parties, and courts took a long step toward its demise in the Progressive Era, with the emergence of the country's first cluster of strong bureaucracies and independent commissions with generalized authority to preside over major segments of the national economy. The Madisonian constitution of sharply limited government, its elements at war with one another, had bogged down in impasse and needed, in the twentieth century, to begin its radical reforming, though the process would move ahead erratically in the succeeding decades.

It is appropriate, therefore, that with Republicans overwhelmingly in charge in California after 1900, the flood control controversy came to an end in the building of the kind of rationally planned and integrated flood control system for the whole Valley, managed from the center under strong public authority, that Henry Clay himself would regard as a splendid model of Whig public policy. The fact that its eventual creation was the fruit of a long learning process conducted by a corps of experts and brought by them to such disciplined and polished form that it served as the essential basis of policy, would make Whigs nod in approval.

That the movement for flood control reform was made up in its rank and file as well as in its leadership of large landowners and urban-based entrepreneurs of almost exclusively Republican loyalties confirms the picture. That they were college-trained men who, impatient with Democratic populists like Will Green who distrusted engineers, by contrast trusted them and envisioned large corporate agricultural enterprises made possible by cooperative partnership with government, makes the creation of the Sacramento Flood Control Project match even more closely the Whig model of paternalist public policy. The very protestations in the Commonwealth Club's deliberations that landowners must submerge individualism and join together in a common enterprise came from mentalities that were classically Whig in spirit.

≈≈≈

What has happened to the Whig impulse since these Progressive Era years? Why does the picture given in the narrative to this point of the Whig-Republicans stand so at variance with the modern anti-government Republican party and its ideas? Is there an essential discontinuity here which reveals that, whatever we may observe in this long affair in the Sacramento Valley, there is no line of connection, as to political culture, between the Whig Moment in the Progressive Era and the present public scene?

It would require, of course, another book to trace in detail the massive political transformations in twentieth century American politics which have led to the reversals in party policy that have occurred, but the larger outlines (which I have discussed elsewhere) may be traced in.[10] To begin with, from about 1910 onward the Democrats learned, first within such urban and industrial states as New York and Illinois, and then nationally, under Woodrow Wilson and Franklin Roosevelt, how useful government could be in regulating powerful business interests, and also in bringing European concepts of social welfare into American life to moderate its free enterprise austerities and minister to the needs of the unfortunate and the helpless. As this learning process and this major reversal took place, culminating in the New Deal years, the Republican party recoiled from its ancient love affair with strong government to take up the former Democratic cry of laissez-faire and individualism.

Indeed, a minority of those who were of the essentially Whig tradition had not been, in fact, ever entirely comfortable with membership in the Republican party. They were repelled by its increasing identification with capitalists during the Gilded Age, and with money making pure and simple. The searching doubts on this score of the Adams family, and other so-called "Mugwump" Republicans like them in the Gilded Age, are well known. Later, after Theodore Roosevelt's failure to build progressivism lastingly into the Republican party, many Progressive Republicans (by no means all) would on this ground eventually cross the Rubicon to become part of Franklin Roosevelt's following and administration. Here under one of Woodrow Wilson's Progressive Democrats was where the venerable Whig concern for the whole community and its needs, the Whigs' team-spirit mood and impatience with unfettered individualism, as well as their taste for central planning, had found its lodgment. (On these themes, see Otis L. Graham, Jr.'s *An Encore for Reform: The Old Progressives and the New Deal* [New York, 1967], and *Toward a Planned Society: From Roosevelt to Nixon* [New York, 1976].)

As the Republican appetite for *governing,* in the public interest, was slowly stripped out of the Republican party, the university professoriate also shifted from its traditional Republican base to the Democratic side, in the process taking with them much of the idea of using the government to plan the nation's growth and development. With them, too, went a good deal of the Republicans' former identification with learning and science. Many New Deal era Republicans filled the air with a ranting anti-intellectualism, and the McCarthyite anti-communist crusade of the Republicans in the 1950s reeked of a sour hatred of academics redolent of the Jacksonian Democrats.

However, these historic changes of front toward active government must be accurately understood: they did not reach to the essence of the political culture; they were essentially shifts in tactics only. The two parties' larger goals remained largely the same. The basic continuity in the overall strategy of the two parties, and in their enduring cultural nature, itself the origin of that strategy, has persisted.

The Republicans remain the party that looks with admiration and trust on the business community, and works so to bend public policy as to encourage and stimulate it. Vigorous development of the nation's resources, usually by means of large projects relying heavily on expert guidance, continues to be that party's central obsession as it was in the days of Benjamin Harrison. For this reason the nation's engineers still constitute an overwhelmingly Republican profession which finds its most congenial home working with pro-development entrepreneurs. It is simply that the Republicans, as a great national community in the population at large, put this impulse to use now almost entirely in the private domain, where their center of gravity has come to lie almost exclusively. In the private economy, the ancient Republican appetite for large-scale planned development flourishes mightily.

And when they find themselves in economic environments, as in oil management policy, which call pressingly for cooperation among producers, Republicans are as ready as ever they were in the Sacramento Valley to set aside laissez-faire and make use of government to intervene (with the willing assistance of oil-state Democrats), in this case by means of production and import quotas. That venerable Whig preference for a government-business partnership in high-risk situations, where the former makes entrepreneurship possible by providing facilitating aids, public works, and services, is still active in public affairs. The most immense public works project in not only American but possibly world history, the building of the interstate highway system, was one of the Eisenhower administration's most cherished achievements, reminding us of the chartering of the transcontinental railroad under Abraham Lincoln.

Republicans continue to have their heartland essentially within the boundaries of the core culture; that is, in what is now termed the "WASP" (white, Anglo-Saxon, Protestant) community. They are stiff and uncomfortable with minority outgroups (their one minority client, black America, was thrust over to the Democrats during the New Deal years); in presidential elections, since 1968 the majority of white Americans have begun to vote Republican. It is Republicans, furthermore, who in the traditional Puritan-Whig style (which we observed at work in the Age of Jackson) remain friendly toward moralistic crusades which seek to use the power of government actively to intervene against life styles regarded as both immoral and destructive to mainstream American life. The "Moral Majority" movement of the

Ronald Reagan years accurately perceived the Democrats as its proven enemies.

The Democrats, for their part, still look on the wealthy and the powerful through Jeffersonian lenses; that is, with distrust and skepticism. As they have been since the nation's beginnings, they are wary of large-capital-driven economic development, that wariness now finding its expression through the strongly Democratic-leaning environmentalist movement. In Jefferson's mode they talk endlessly of equality (a word never heard in Reaganesque rhetoric) and through affirmative action and entitlement programs labor in its cause; and they remain the political home of the outgroups and the culturally divergent. Democrats instinctively nourish a reluctance to sanction government campaigns against private moral behavior. The abortion issue now provides the revealing touchstone between the two parties that prohibition did in earlier generations, the Democrats in both situations continuing to favor cultural laissez-faire.

≈≈≈

We note, then, that the fundamental political culture, springing from the nation's beginnings, which helps so much to explain the course of the long battle against the Sacramento Valley's inland sea is still alive and well, though its particular forms and modes of action have changed. It was not, of course, the "cause" of all that happened in the Valley. A major thesis in this book is that one-factor explanations are fatally too simple, and it is not my intention to commit that time-worn error in analysis. Without question there is much more than simply political culture that helps to explain the outcome of this story. The physical facts of life in the Sacramento Valley pushed powerfully toward overturning the solitary rule of individualism and localism. Simple economic interest, entirely without the aid of party ideology, also gave a great impulse to the willingness after 1900 among landowners to accept central regulation. If cost-benefit studies had been then in vogue, it would have been a small task to demonstrate the costs of the existing anarchy and the benefits of cooperation, especially with Eastern markets ready to open via cheap water-level transport through the Panama Canal.

That behind these events there had been a decades-long learning process meant that by the Progressive years, certainly after the enormous floods of 1907 and 1909, there was a firm foundation of bipartisan consensus that something of the sort Captain Thomas Jackson of the U.S. Army Corps of Engineers was proposing would have to be adopted. There were no Democratic alternatives to his plan recommended, when it went to Congress, and the Reclamation Board legislation of 1911 did win passage in the legislature by unanimous vote during the whirlwind of that session.

It remains, in fact, to entertain the thought that, given these converging influences, perhaps political culture was in reality largely irrelevant to what finally happened in the Sacramento Valley; that the existential facts of the situation, joined to pressing economic interest, dictated the outcome, whatever party was in power. This "rational actor" position, which thinks of politics as largely a side-show, is seriously unhistorical. The two parties were not, as we have seen, essentially identical in interests, ideas, and behavior. The most powerful and enduring single force in shaping political mentalities is the sense of who the enemy is, and Republicans and Democrats differ profoundly in this regard. Thus they differ widely, too, in their definitions of the situation, whatever it might be, and in the things they are determined to ward off or to achieve.

Thus, if the Democrats had been strong and in full voice in the legislature, instead of weak and demoralized, when proposals came to it from a cabal (as they would term it) of capitalists in San Francisco calling for a centralized flood control plan, ranks of circling skeptics would have been mobilized to pick and probe at its every joint and rivet. As we have earlier seen, at one point the advocates of centralized flood control had even publicly stated, with astonishing political insensitivity, that the independent commission they were proposing to regulate levee-building in the Sacramento Valley "WILL IN FACT BE A GOVERNMENT FORMED OF OWNERS OF SWAMP LANDS FOR THE ADMINISTRATION OF SWAMP-LAND AFFAIRS" [*sic*]. Ever since the wholesale steals of the swamplands after the Green Act's passage in 1868, the appellation "swamplander" had been a term of opprobrium in California politics, and especially within the more militant Democratic and Workingman circles.

It would require a setting aside of everything known of the two parties, therefore, to believe that a Democratic plan for the Valley would not be significantly different from the one actually adopted. These differences would probably not be in the plan's overall physical nature, that was agreed on, but in its financing, in its specific governing arrangements, possibly in the local alignment of levees (there were bitter complaints on this score from wheelhorse Democrats alleging special treatment of great corporations), probably in its degree of centralization, certainly in its readiness to accommodate large corporate interests or in the voice given them in the system's management by the appointments made to the Reclamation Board.

It may be useful, to gain some perspective on this question of the relevance of party in policy making to consider for a moment a contemporary course of events which was taking place on the national stage, in a setting where the Democrats were strong and vigorous. In 1907, while the climactic California flood control crusade was building momentum, a serious "banker's panic" occurred nationally which caused great alarm. It was the catalyzing event which, with a man like Theodore Roosevelt in the White House, set finally in motion a long-brooding movement to reform the country's banking and currency system. By 1912 a Republican commission after years of study was ready with a solution. It was based fundamentally in deep respect for the banking and financial community, and a readiness to hand directly over to it, in effect, the task of regulation. It called for a powerful nationally chartered central bank in Wall Street, privately owned, which through branches around the country would discount commercial paper, issue currency, and hold the tax receipts of the national government. It would be essentially a recreation of the Bank of the United States long ago destroyed by President Andrew Jackson, and accordingly the proposal was almost universally approved by the banking community.

Then chance intervened. In the presidential election of 1912 the Republicans angrily divided, so that Theodore Roosevelt and William Howard Taft split that vote. Only this event allowed the sending of Woodrow Wilson to the White House, with but a plurality of the nation's ballots, not a majority, behind him. This, in turn, led in time to a Democratic solution to the problem everyone said needed to be solved and upon which the "experts" had formed a consensus agreement. Breaking with that consensus, the essential point of the Democratic plan, which was driven in its crucial formative moments by militant populists from the poorer sections of the country, was to take the control of banking and currency out of the hands of the private bankers. The legislation finally enacted created a public body, the Federal Reserve Board, which would not only regulate the currency supply but print and issue it, thus making that crucial economic task a public, not a private function. This principle was immediately condemned as socialistic, vicious, and "the preposterous offspring of ignorance and unreason."

Furthermore, in place of one central bank, there were now no less than twelve regional central banks, for the Democrats had always been localists, and they bitterly distrusted not only bankers as a class, but Wall Street in particular. Each regional bank was given its own board, with bankers limited on such boards to a minority membership. To a torrent of bankers' criticism, the regional banks were even authorized to issue loans, that is, print and hand out currency, on short-term farm mortgages, an arrangement scoffed at as "cotton currency" and "corn tassel currency." As Woodrow Wilson's biographer Arthur S. Link has written, "in the face of this torrent of abuse and criticism, Wilson stood immovable." And so, the reforming of the nation's banking and currency system, "the greatest single piece of constructive legislation of the Wilson era"[11] and a task the need for which both parties accepted—indeed upon some of its major aspects there was consensus—came out very differently in Democratic hands than it would have if entrusted to the Republicans.

Thinking by analogy in history is a risky undertaking, as Richard E. Neustadt and Ernest R. May have recently informed us,[12] but in this case the controversy over banking and currency policy was so close in time to the flood control debate in California, and its working out took place within so similar a universe of ideas and motives, that it appears reasonably useful as analogy. It confirms the position that in all large policy matters affecting economics—to speak of no other policy realm—Democrats and Republicans would reach significantly different decisions. As this book has in good part been written to demonstrate, context in policy making is powerful, probably dominant, and it does in truth make real differences which party makes the decisions.

The fact is that, historically, the two parties have carried distinctive policy potentials deep within them through the generations, policy potentials that are released when history, as it moves, periodically opens windows of opportunity. When the nation's economy collapsed in 1893, taking down with it the once-powerful Democratic party and inaugurating what historians call the Fourth Party System, a thirty-year period of overwhelmingly Republican dominance in Washington and in the Northeastern, Middle Western, and Far Western states—especially in California—a climactic sequence of events was set in motion. An historic window of opportunity, hitherto only partially ajar and often closed, swung wide open to the Whig-Republican mentality in California. In one of the more revealing episodes of public policy making in the Progressive Era, a valleywide flood control system was created that strikingly duplicated the basic picture Whig-Republicans had always carried in their minds about how America's affairs should be managed, and the remaking of the Sacramento Valley was at long last carried through to completion.

≈ Notes ≈

~ PREFACE ~

1. Elna Bakker, *An Island Called California: An Ecological Introduction to Its Natural Communities* (Berkeley, Los Angeles, London, 1972), pp. 149–153.
2. This is in fact the impulse behind the nationally emerging field called "policy history" and of its new *Journal of Policy History*; it is also the purpose of an undergraduate major in the history of public policy which in recent years I have set in motion in my own institution.
3. Garry D. Brewer, and Peter deLeon, *The Foundations of Policy Analysis* (Homewood, Ill., 1983), p. 13. Other comments on this score: The analyst must "identify the relevant contextual or environmental parameters . . . determine how the problem fits into the general organizational environment" (p. 45). "The first factor is the *context of the problem*. . . . What are the environmental, normative, technological, and political constraints? . . . A primary consideration for the decision maker is the overall context. . . . The political culture of the system should be considered" (p. 191–192) "A sensitive appreciation of specific, realistic contexts in which decisions are made and results are sought is a necessary prerequisite to understanding and action" (p. 260).
4. Harry N. Scheiber, "State Law and 'Industrial Policy' in American Development, 1790–1987," *California Law Review* 75 (Jan. 1987), 425–444; Donald J. Pisani, "Promotion and Regulation: Constitutionalism and the American Economy," *The Journal of American History* 74 (Dec. 1987), 740–768.
5. Gertrude Himmelfarb, *Lord Acton: A Study in Conscience and Politics* (Chicago, 1962), pp. 146–155.
6. It may be of interest that since all of this demonstrated the power and usefulness of the historical method in public affairs, it eventually translated itself into major new programs of instruction. In the mid-1970s, at the University of California, Santa Barbara, I proposed the first

graduate program in what it seemed to me should be (and since has been) called "public history," a term whose purpose is to give a distinct identity to the professional service of historians out in the community at large, rather than on academic staffs. Approved in 1975, our Graduate Program in Public Historical Studies admitted its first class in fall 1976.

The students trained in our program, who now number more than ninety, have gone on to careers in a wide variety of public settings, either in positions connected with public policy (i.e., as historians in government agencies, or as consultants to public authorities in urban planning or natural resource management), or in the other precincts of public history: historic preservation, litigation support, archival management and corporate history, historical museums and parks, community history and oral history, and the like.

The public history movement has become national and international, creating programs in many colleges and universities, featuring its own widely circulated professional journal, *The Public Historian,* and marked by well-attended national meetings of public historians working in many professional settings, convened annually by the National Council on Public History.

1 ~ The Sacramento Valley: Eden Invaded

1. Theodora Kroeber, *Ishi in Two Worlds: A Biography of the Last Wild Indian in North America* (Berkeley, Los Angeles, London, 1971), pp. 21, 36; Erik H. Erikson, "Fishermen along a Salmon River," chap. 4 in his *Childhood and Society,* 2d ed., rev. and enl. (New York, 1963).
2. Donald C. Cutter, tran. and ed., *The Diary of Ensign Gabriel Moraga's Expedition of Discovery in the Sacramento Valley, 1808* (Los Angeles, 1957), p. 19. For a description of the Valley in its natural state, see Bakker, *An Island Called California*; and a remarkable early history, written by a man who settled in the Valley in 1850, Will S. Green: *Colusa County, California . . . With Historical Sketch of the County (San Francisco, 1880),* pp. 1–88, passim, particularly the *Supplement* contained in the 1950 photographic reproduction, which carries several published articles by Green describing the Valley's original appearance and state. See also John Thompson's dissertation, "The Settlement Geography of the Sacramento–San Joaquin Delta, California," Stanford University, 1957, which describes its original condition; and Kenneth Thompson, "Historic Flooding in the Sacramento Valley," *Pacific Historical Review,* 20 (Sept. 1960), 349–360, which is essential. On the tules in

the Valley's original condition, see, among other sources, Thompson and West, *History of Sutter County, California* (Oakland, Calif., 1879), p. 90. I have also drawn on extended reading in Sacramento Valley newspapers of the 1850s.

3. Sir Edward Belcher, *Narrative of a Voyage Round the World Performed in Her Majesty's Ship Sulphur during the years 1836–1842* (London, 1843), II, 123–124.
4. Charles Wilkes, USN, *Narrative of the United States Exploring Expedition: During the Years 1838, 1839, 1840, 1841, 1842* (Philadelphia, 1845), V, 178, 182; same author, *Western America, Including California and Oregon . . .* (Philadelphia, 1849), pp. 28, 44–45; Thompson, "Historic Flooding in the Sacramento Valley."
5. See Green, *Colusa County,* for a detailed description of the local Indians and their fate.
6. Ibid.
7. See County Assessor's report, printed in the *Weekly Sutter Banner,* Yuba City, Sept. 14, 1867. For information on the clearing and burning of the valley oaks, I have relied on extensive reading in local newspapers in the 1850s.
8. There is a considerable literature on Sacramento River navigation. For the specific points made here, see: *Placer Times* (Sacramento), May 5 and November 17, 1849; I. N. Irwin, collator, *Sacramento Directory and Gazetteer, for the years 1857 and 1858 . . .* (San Francisco, 1867), p. xii; State Engineer, *Report . . . to the Legislature of the State of California—Session of 1881,* part III (Sacramento, 1880), p. 13.
9. *Placer Times,* Jan. 26, 1850; H. William Hoffman, "History of Navigation of California's Feather River," Master's thesis, Sacramento State College, 1963; *Weekly Butte Record* (Oroville), March through May 1857; the *Weekly Sutter Banner* (Yuba City), which has many entries in these years on the regular comings and goings of steamboats along the Feather, as do the Marysville papers.
10. Thompson and West, *History of Sacramento County,* pp. 66–67.
11. *Placer Times,* Feb. 2 and 9, 1850; the *Star* is quoted in Thompson, "Historic Flooding in the Sacramento Valley," p. 357.
12. Testimony in 1927 by Major U. S. Grant, III, of the U.S. Army Corps of Engineers. See pp. 796, 800, 885–889, in: *Hearings before the Committee on Flood Control, House of Representatives, 70th Congress, 1st Session, on the control of destructive flood waters of the United States. December 12 and 13, 1927. Part 2: Sacramento–San Joaquin River System.* Washington, 1927.
13. Quoted in Thompson and West, *History of Sacramento County, California* (Oakland, Calif., 1880), pp. 66–67.

14. Ibid., p. 67.
15. Ibid., pp. 73–74.
16. *Daily California Express* (Marysville), Jan. 24, 1862, quoting earlier issues no longer available; De Pue & Company, *Illustrated Atlas and History of Yolo County, Cal.* . . . (San Francisco, 1879), p. 56; testimony, John H. Jewett, in *Edwards Woodruff* v. *North Bloomfield et al.* (cited as 9 Sawyer 441 or 18 F 753), pp. 1709–1710. The testimony in this 1883 case, which runs to more than twenty typewritten volumes, is in the Marysville City Library.
17. For the foregoing and following account of the evolution of the hydraulic gold-mining industry, its geological basis, and its water-gathering system, consult chap. 1, "The Rise of Hydraulic Mining 1850–1880," pp. 21–56, in Robert Kelley, *Gold vs. Grain: The Hydraulic Mining Controversy in California's Sacramento Valley* (Glendale, Calif., 1959).
18. I was able, in 1951, to watch one of the last California hydraulic mines in operation, that at Relief Hill near Nevada City, and the scene resembled in every particular the following description.
19. Quoted in Nevada City *Transcript,* July 30, 1879.
20. W. H. Hall, *Report of State Engineer to Legislature of California, 23rd Session,* part III (Sacramento, 1880), 49–50.

2 ~ The Interplay of American Political Culture and Reclamation Policy

1. *Marysville Herald,* Feb. 19, 1856.
2. Captain Wm. Corlett, "Testimony taken by Committee on Mining Debris . . . ," p. 9, appendix, *Journals of the Senate and Assembly,* 22d session, vol. IV (Sacramento, 1877).
3. Quoted in the *California Chronicle* (San Francisco), Feb. 7, 1856.
4. Quoted in ibid., April 9, 1856.
5. See the map with Lt. Wilkes' 1841 expedition report, cited above; and that in the earliest systematic survey: Cadwalader Ringgold, *A Series of Charts with Sailing Directions Embracing Surveys of the Farallones, Entrance to the Bay of San Francisco* . . . , 4th ed. (Washington, 1852), p. 39. Copies of these maps are maintained in the California State Library.
6. San Francisco *Bulletin,* Oct. 23, 1856, and Nov. 10, 1857; San Francisco *Herald,* Dec. 7, 1856.
7. Lawrence M. Friedman, *A History of American Law,* 2d ed. (New York, 1985), p. 261.
8. Archibald Cox, *The Court and the Constitution* (Boston, 1987), p. 86.
9. See Richard M. Frank's thorough exploration of this complicated legal matter in his essay, "Forever Free: Navigability, Inland Waterways, and

the Expanding Public Interest," in *University of California, Davis, Law Review* 16 (Spring 1983), 579–629.

10. For a more extended description and discussion of American political culture in these years, see Robert Kelley, *The Cultural Pattern in American Politics: The First Century* (New York, 1979); on the era's army-style politics, see also a book by Ronald P. Formisano, *The Birth of Mass Political Parties: Michigan, 1827–1861* (Princeton, N.J., 1971), pp. 22, 57–58, 70, 77–78.
11. To read of the enduring power of this basic national character, see: Robert N. Bellah, et al., *Habits of the Heart: Individualism and Commitment in American Life* (Berkeley, Los Angeles, London, 1985).
12. As explored in Bernard Bailyn, *Ideological Origins of the American Revolution* (Cambridge, Mass., 1967); and Gordon Wood, *The Creation of the American Republic, 1776–1787* (Chapel Hill, N.C., 1969).
13. For a solid discussion of state government efforts on behalf of entrepreneurs, granting them special privileges, see Pisani, "Promotion and Regulation," 740–768. For the persistent stands of the two parties, the Whigs and the Democrats, see Herbert Ershkowitz and William G. Shade, "Consensus or Conflict? Political Behavior in the State Legislatures during the Jacksonian Era," *The Journal of American History* 58 (Dec. 1971), 591–621. On the later decades of the century, again at the state level, see Ballard C. Campbell, Jr., *Representative Democracy: Public Policy and Midwestern Legislatures in the Late Nineteenth Century* (Cambridge, Mass., 1980).
14. See: Lee Benson, *The Concept of Jacksonian Democracy: New York as a Test Case* (Princeton, N.J., 1961), pp. 40–41, 52, 56; Charles Sellers, *James K. Polk: Continentalist 1843–1846* (Princeton, N.J., 1966), pp. 472–474.
15. This general sketch of the Democratic political mind has been drawn from many sources, including: Marvin Meyers, *The Jacksonian Persuasion: Politics and Belief* (New York, 1960); Arthur M. Schlesinger, Jr., *The Age of Jackson* (Boston, Mass., 1945); chaps. 7 and 8 in Robert Kelley, *The Transatlantic Persuasion: The Liberal-Democratic Mind in the Age of Gladstone* (New York, 1969); and chaps. 5 and 6 in same author, *The Cultural Pattern in American Politics.*
16. For the foregoing and following discussion of the Whig mentality, see Daniel Walker Howe's splendid work, *The Political Culture of the American Whigs* (Chicago, 1979); and chap. 7 in Kelley, *The Cultural Pattern in American Politics.*
17. *Marysville Herald,* Oct. 21, 1854.
18. William Henry Ellison, *A Self-Governing Dominion: California, 1849–1860* (Berkeley and Los Angeles, 1950); and Royce D. Delmatier, Clar-

ence F. McIntosh, Earl G. Waters, eds., *The Rumble of California Politics: 1848–1970* (New York, 1970).

19. United States, *Statutes at Large,* IX, chap. LXXXIV, 519–520.
20. See Richard H. Peterson, "The Failure to Reclaim: California State Swamp Land Policy and the Sacramento Valley, 1850–1866," *Southern California Quarterly* 56 (Spring 1974), 45–60. For the swamp land problem in general, see ibid.; and State of California, State Engineer (Hall) *Report . . . to the Legislature,* 1880; Joseph A. McGowan, *History of the Sacramento Valley* (New York and Palm Beach, 1961), I, 283–292; Thompson, "Settlement Geography of the Sacramento–San Joaquin Delta," doctoral dissertation, pp. 185–204, especially, as to total acreage, p. 186 (citing "Report of the Director of the Bureau of Land Management, Statistical Appendix" [Washington, 1950], table 106, "Acreage Granted to States and Territories," p. 126 [mimeographed]).
21. Thompson, "The Settlement Geography of the Sacramento–San Joaquin Delta," pp. 185–196; McGowan, *History of the Sacramento Valley,* pp. 283–284.
22. See chap. 7, "First Phase: Realignment and Disunion, 1856–1860," in Robert Kelley, *The Cultural Pattern in American Politics,* pp. 187–227.
23. Ellison, *A Self-Governing Dominion,* p. 269; Delmatier et al., eds., *The Rumble of California Politics,* pp. 42–43.
24. Ellison, *A Self-Governing Dominion,* pp. 268–314; and Delmatier et al., *The Rumble of California Politics,* pp. 15–30. See also, in ibid., John Bauer's essay, "The Beginnings of the Republican Party," esp. pp. 50–52.
25. See George M. Fredrickson, *The Inner Civil War: Northern Intellectuals and the Crisis of the Union* (New York, 1965).
26. Leonard P. Curry, *Blueprint for Modern America: Non-Military Legislation of the First Civil War Congress* (Nashville, 1968).
27. Thompson, "Settlement Geography of the Sacramento–San Joaquin Delta," p. 194.
28. See Peterson, "The Failure to Reclaim," p. 60.
29. California, *Statutes* (1861), chap. CCCLII, 355–361; California, *Journal of the Assembly,* April 8, 1861, p. 675; California, *Journal of the Senate,* May 1, 1861, p. 721; for 1860 county votes, see Bauer, "The Beginnings of the Republican Party," in *The Rumble of California Politics,* p. 51.

3 ~ The Failed Dream: The Swamp Land Commissioners Experiment

1. Donald J. Pisani, *From the Family Farm to Agribusiness: The Irrigation Crusade in California and the West, 1850–1931* (Berkeley, Los Angeles, London, 1984), pp. 130–135.

2. Peterson, "The Failure to Reclaim," pp. 50–51; Thompson, "Settlement Geography of the Sacramento–San Joaquin Delta," pp. 196–198; McGowan, *History of the Sacramento Valley*, pp. 284–285; Thompson and West, *History of Sacramento County*, p. 186.
3. Thompson, "Settlement Geography of the Sacramento–San Joaquin Delta," pp. 196–198; McGowan, *History of the Sacramento Valley*, pp. 284–285; Thompson and West, *History of Sacramento County*, p. 186; Peterson, "The Failure to Reclaim," pp. 50–52.
4. Peterson, "The Failure to Relcaim," pp. 51–52.
5. Ibid., p. 52.
6. Ibid.
7. Ibid., p. 54.
8. Delmatier et al., eds., *The Rumble of California Politics*, pp. 54–59.
9. Sacramento *Daily Union*, Mar. 1, 1866, quoting *The Colusa Sun* of Feb. 24.
10. There is an abundant historical literature on these national conflicts over race issues. The mainstream of the story may be followed in: Kelley, *Cultural Pattern in American Politics*, which contains extensive references to the relevant scholarship.
11. H. Brett Melendy and Benjamin F. Gilbert, *The Governors of California: Peter H. Burnette to Edmund G. Brown* (Georgetown, California, 1965), pp. 146–148.
12. Pisani, *From the Family Farm to Agribusiness*, pp. 5–11.
13. Sacramento *Daily Union*, Mar. 22, 1866.
14. Ibid., Mar. 1, 1866.
15. California, *Statutes* (1865–1866), chap. DLXX, 799–801.
16. Sacramento *Daily Union*, Mar. 22, 1866.
17. Ibid.
18. Ibid., Mar. 31 and April 2, 1866.
19. Green, *Colusa County*, p. 76.
20. *Colusa Sun*, Mar. 14, 1868.
21. Pisani, *From the Family Farm to Agribusiness*, pp. 93–97; "Report of the Engineer of the Sacramento Valley Irrigation and Navigation Canal," *Journals of the California Senate and Assembly*, 17th session (Sacramento, 1868), appendix 2; Frank S. Reager, "Will S. Green, 'Father of Irrigation,'" appendix VI, in Green, *Colusa County* (1950 edition).
22. State of California, *Statutes* (1867–1868), chap. CCCCXV, "An Act to provide for the management and sale of the lands belonging to the State, approved Mar. 28, 1868." (For its swampland provisions, see part II: "Swamp and Overflowed, Salt Marsh and Tide Lands," pp. 514–521.) See also *Colusa Sun*, Mar. 7, 1868, quoting the San Francisco *Bulletin*.
23. Green, *Colusa County, California* . . . . , p. 76; *Sun*, Mar. 28, 1868.

24. Quoted in *Colusa Sun,* June 6, 1868.
25. *Colusa Sun,* Mar. 28, 1868.
26. "An Act to provide for the management and sale of the lands belonging to the State, approved Mar. 28, 1868"; Green, *Colusa County,* p. 58; *Colusa Sun,* Mar. 18, 1868; McGowan, *History of the Sacramento Valley,* I, 283–292; California State Engineer, E. A. Bailey, "Historical Summary of State Legislative Action with Results Accomplished in Reclamation of Swamp and Overflowed Lands of Sacramento Valley, California," appendix D, *Sacramento Flood Control Project: Revised Plans* (Sacramento, 1927).
27. *Colusa Sun,* May 30, 1868; Charles D. McComish, *History of Colusa and Glenn Counties . . .* (Los Angeles, 1918), p. 95.
28. McGowan, *History of the Sacramento Valley,* I, 285.
29. Thompson and West, *History of Sacramento County,* p. 64; federal report listed in note 15, chap. 10, below.
30. Quoted in Sacramento *Daily Union,* Nov. 11, 1867.

4 ~ Crisis on the Yuba and the Feather

1. Kelley, *Gold vs. Grain,* pp. 32–33; *Marysville Appeal,* Mar. 31, 1860.
2. *Appeal,* Aug. 14, 1860.
3. *Appeal,* Mar. 28 and 30, April 2, Dec. 6, 1861.
4. *Appeal,* Jan. 27, 30, and Feb. 3, 1862.
5. Judge Lorenzo F. Sawyer, in January 1884 decision rendered in *Edwards Woodruff* v. *North Bloomfield et al.*, heard in the federal Ninth Circuit Court, San Francisco, in 1883–1884. (9 Sawyer 441)
6. Testimony in 1883 in note 5 above; remarks quoted on p. 1709 of the transcript (on file in Marysville public library).
7. *Marysville Herald*: Mar. 11 and May 6, 1851; Nov. 14, 1855; April 10, 1856.
8. *California Chronicle,* Jan. 13, 1856.
9. Mar. 11, 1856.
10. Richard Hoskins, inventor in about 1870 of the "Little Giant," as the monitor was called, had his factory in Marysville. See letter from Hoskins to H. G. Hanks, Jan. 26, 1882, quoted in California State Mineralogist, Hanks, "Placer, Hydraulic and Drift Mining," *Second Report* (Sacramento, 1882), pp. 68–69.
11. Duane Smith, *Mining America: The Industry and the Environment, 1800–1980* (Lawrence, Kans., 1987), pp. 29–41.
12. Ibid., p. 46.
13. Ibid., pp. 47–51.

14. *Marysville Appeal,* Jan. 25, 1862; *Daily California Express,* Feb. 3, 1862.
15. *Mining and Scientific Press,* Jan. 4 and Mar. 1, 1982.
16. Kelley, *Gold vs. Grain,* pp. 34–56.
17. *Weekly Butte Record* (Bidwell Bar), Feb. 11, May 6 and 20, Nov. 4, 1854; *The North Californian,* Nov. 17, Dec. 1 and 8, 1855, April 11, May 2, July 11, 1856, Mar. 6, 1857; *Weekly Butte Record* (Oroville), Feb. 10, April 7, Sept. 1 and 22, Oct. 5, Nov. 3, Dec. 29, 1855, July 19, Aug. 9, Sept. 13 and 20, Nov. 8, 1856, Jan. 3 and 17, Feb. 14, 1857.
18. *Weekly Butte Record,* Jan. 27 and Feb. 3, 1866.
19. Ibid., June 17, 1871; Rossiter W. Raymond, *Statistics of Mines and Mining in the States and Territories West of the Rocky Mountains: Annual Report,* V (Washington, D.C., 1874), 133–136.
20. *Weekly Butte Record,* Nov. 8, 1873.
21. For the foregoing, see: ibid., July 27 and Dec. 7, 1867; Feb. 29, Mar. 21, Nov. 21, 1868; Jan. 9, May 15, June 26, and Aug. 28, 1869; April 16 and Dec. 10, 1870; Nov. 8, 1873; Mar. 10, 1875; *The Weekly Mercury,* Feb. 11 and 18, 1876, and Mar. 22, 1878.
22. *Colusa Sun,* Dec. 29, 1866, and Jan. 19, 1867; *Weekly Butte Record* (Oroville), Dec. 22, 1866; *Marysville Appeal,* Dec. 29, 1866.
23. *Alta California* (San Francisco), Feb. 9, 1867; *Colusa Sun,* Feb. 14, Dec. 14 and 28, 1867; *Weekly Butte Record,* Dec. 28, 1867; *Weekly Sutter Banner,* May 4, 11, and 25, 1867.

5 ~ THE STRUGGLE BEGINS: SUTTER COUNTY IN SIEGE

1. *Colusa Sun,* Jan. 19, 1867; *Weekly Sutter Banner,* May 11, 1867.
2. U.S. Department of the Interior, Geological Survey, *Yuba City Quadrangle, California,* 7.5 Minute Series (Topographic), 1952; same, *Sutter Buttes Quadrangle, California,* 15 Minute Series (Topographic), 1954.
3. See J. H. Jewett testimony in *Woodruff* v. *North Bloomfield* transcript, p. 1774, for the slough mouth size.
4. Helen F. Belz, "History of Floods—Yuba City and Vicinity," local unpublished typewritten report, Yuba City, Calif., 1956.
5. *Weekly Sutter Banner,* May 25, 1867, June 27, 1868, and Mar. 17, 1874.
6. *Weekly Sutter Banner,* Aug. 3, 1867; Thompson and West, *History of Sutter County,* p. 99. The official map of Sutter County, issued by the board of supervisors in 1873, shows his plot of land, with the name "J. Gelshaouser," at the head of the slough. My spelling of it is the way he signed his own name.
7. April 15, 1867. The identity of the *Weekly Sutter Banner*'s editor, and

his status as judge, has been derived from the Feb. 27, 1875, issue, in a news item on the sale of the paper, which indicates that "H. W. Hulbert" (an apparent misspelling by the new owners) had been owner and editor, and from the April 25, 1867, issue in which the remarks of "Judge Hurburt" at a public meeting are quoted in relation to the levee project.

8. Ibid., April 20, May 11 and 18, 1867.
9. Ibid., May 25, 1867; and the 1873 Sutter County Map.
10. *Weekly Sutter Banner,* Aug. 17, Sept. 28, Oct. 12, Nov. 16, Dec. 21, 1867.
11. Ibid., Nov. 23, Dec. 28, 1867; and Jan. 4, 1868.
12. It is little realized in the United States how strange and unusual in the world is this country's localism, in constitutional, governmental terms. (Other countries in the world have far more specifically cultural localism.) The spectacle of 17,000 locally elected special districts, quite aside from the much-more-visible phenomenon of thousands of largely self-governing cities and counties, has no parallel elsewhere. Even Great Britain, historic home of political liberty and individualism, is far more centralized in its workings than is the United States; Canada is more centralized by comparison, and France and the northern European countries are well known for their intense centralization, even in the Federal Republic of West Germany. The USSR carries centralism to the ultimate extreme. While teaching American history at Moscow University for a semester in 1979, the extraordinary localism of our system was powerfully reemphasized for me; I saw how mystifying to Soviet scholars, whose country's governance has always been centralized (before as well as after 1917), was the decentralized American system, which to them appears to be rank anarchy. Learning from my lectures of the still highly decentralized and confusing arrangements for water management in California, they could not keep from asking, "but who's in charge?" A subsequent lecture tour in India, certainly a federal country, nonetheless brought me once more into contact with scholars and journalists who found the depth and extent of American localism surprising. The government of entire states, in that country, may be suspended and taken over by the central authorities.
13. AB 553, "To provide for the protection of certain lands in the county of Sutter from overflow," approved Mar. 25, 1868.
14. Sutter County, Board of Supervisors, *Minutes,* book C, pp. 67–68.
15. *Marysville Appeal,* Mar. 29, Apr. 1, 15, 17, 1868.
16. Sutter County, Board of Supervisors, *Minutes,* book C, pp. 90–94; *Marysville Appeal,* June 19, 20, 1868; *Weekly Sutter Banner,* Aug. 29, 1868.

17. *Weekly Sutter Banner*, Nov. 30, 1867; Mar. 21, Aug. 1, Oct. 17, 1868; and Jan. 9, 1869.
18. Testimony of William Ham. Hall (state engineer), D. J. Kertcham, and C. E. Stone, in *Woodruff* v. *North Bloomfield*, pp. 661, 1947–1949, 2156.
19. Thompson and West, *History of Sutter County*, pp. 65–66; *Weekly Sutter Banner*, Jan. 29, 1874, Jan. 30, Feb. 6, 1875; Kelley, *Gold vs. Grain*, pp. 41–53.
20. *Weekly Sutter Banner*, Feb. 24, 1874.
21. Ibid., Feb. 24, 1874.
22. Ibid., Feb. 21, 1874.
23. *Mining and Scientific Press*, quoting *Weekly Sutter Banner*, April 4, 1874.
24. See decision in *James H. Keyes* v. *Little York Mining Co.*, 53 Cal 724; also Yuba County statistics in *9th Census, Population* 15, 91–92, and *11th Census, Population*, 69–75.
25. *Appeal*, Aug. 26, 30, Sept. 12, 1874.
26. Peter J. Delay, *History of Yuba and Sutter Counties* (Los Angeles, 1924), pp. 101–103; Testimony, *Edwards Woodruff* v. *North Bloomfield et al*, pp. 1946, 2111, 3634, 5813, 5817, 7715.
27. C. E. Stone testimony, pp. 2030, 2032, and Eli Teegarden testimony, p. 2109, *Edwards Woodruff* v. *North Bloomfield et al.*
28. Nevada City *Transcript*, Jan. 22, 1875.
29. In Kelley, *Gold vs. Grain*.

6 ~ COLUSA, THE SACRAMENTO RIVER, AND THE ARGUMENT OVER WHAT TO DO

1. On the Sacramento River in this section of the Valley, see: The various descriptive passages in Green's *Colusa County*; and the report of Major G. H. Mendell, U.S. Army Corps of Engineers, to the Congress, carried in the *Colusa Sun*, Sept. 19, 1874. This first survey of the Sacramento River by the Corps of Engineers was authorized earlier in the year: See telegram from Washington, D.C., dated April 29, 1874, carried in the *Marysville Appeal*, May 2, 1874. This led to the original congressional appropriation for work on the Sacramento and Feather Rivers, March 3, 1875, for "extracting snags in the Sacramento River, and for the improvement of the Feather River, by removal of snags and by the construction of brush jetties." See document no. 123, *Sacramento and San Joaquin Rivers, Calif.*, House of Representatives, 69th Congress, 1st session, Dec. 12, 1925 (Washington, D.C., 1925).
2. See testimony of Etcheverry, and Gen. U. S. Grant, III, USCE, in

Hearings before the Committee on Flood Control, House of Representatives, 70th Congress, 1st Session, Dec. 12 and 13, 1927: Part 2, Sacramento–San Joaquin River System (Washington, D.C., 1927).

3. This and the following account of the region's physical character are drawn from Green, *Colusa County,* pp. 26–27, and passim.
4. From *Supplement,* p. vii, to Green's *Colusa County,* quoting his article in *Out West* magazine of April 1902, "The Sacramento Valley as Will S. Green Saw It in 1850."
5. This description draws upon the *Butte City* (1954) and *Sutter Buttes* (1954) quadrangle maps of the U.S. Geological survey (Fifteen Minute Series); and its specific information on flood performance is based on several decades of flood reports in the *Colusa Sun* from the latter 1800s, and on state and federal engineering reports cited hereafter through the course of the narrative.
6. Thompson and West, *History of Sutter County,* p. 90.
7. Department of the Interior, U.S. Geological Survey, *Reconnaisance Map: California–Marysville Sheet* (edition of 1895, reprinted 1920). In my own use of this map, as a historical consultant and expert witness in a series of lawsuits in the 1960s and 1970s, I found it to be exceedingly accurate, even in the depicting of quite small geographic features.
8. Donald J. Pisani informs us, in his *From the Family Farm to Agribusiness,* that in Henry George's account (*Our Land and Land Policy, National and State* [San Francisco, 1871], p. 63) Green was listed as one of thirteen individuals who had received 20,000 acres or more from the state. See Green's own account of how he got his land, and what he did with it, in Green, *Colusa County,* p. 76.
9. The power of this dream statewide, and the history of the long effort to build an irrigation empire in California, (including Will Green's own efforts in this direction [*Colusa County,* pp. 259–265]), is brilliantly described in Pisani, *From the Family Farm to Agribusiness.*
10. *Colusa Sun,* Jan. 11 and 25, Feb. 1, 15, and 18, 1862.
11. Ibid., Dec. 29, 1866.
12. Ibid., Jan. 19, 1867.
13. San Francisco *Alta,* Feb. 9, 1867.
14. *Colusa Sun,* Feb. 14 and April 20, 1867.
15. Ibid., Dec. 14 and 18, 1867.
16. Ibid., Mar. 7, 1868.
17. See Fredrickson, *The Inner Civil War,* on the rabid antiintellectualism and distrust of learned expertise in the prewar years; and James Mohr, *The Radical Republicans and Reform in New York during Reconstruction* (New York, 1973), on public health in New York City.

18. See Kelley, *The Cultural Pattern in American Politics*; and Howe, *The Political Culture of the American Whigs.*
19. For the foregoing, see: Fredrickson, *The Inner Civil War*; Laurence R. Veysey, *The Emergence of the American University* (Chicago, 1965), esp. chap. 2; Burton J. Bledstein, *The Culture of Professionalism: The Middle Class and the Development of Higher Education in America* (New York, 1976); Robert H. Wiebe, *The Search for Order, 1877–1920* (New York, 1967).
20. Raymond H. Merritt, *Engineering in American Society 1850–1875* (Lexington, Ky., 1969), pp. 9–11.
21. U.S. Army Corps of Engineers, *The History of the U.S. Army Corps of Engineers* (Washington, D.C., 1986), pp. 17–19.
22. Ibid., pp. 29–35.
23. Daniel Hovey Calhoun, *The American Civil Engineer: Origins and Conflict* (Cambridge, Mass., 1960), p. vii–viii.
24. Merritt, *Engineering in American Society*, p. 2.
25. Ibid., pp. 27–87.
26. Ibid., pp. 90, 118, 126–136.
27. Ibid., pp. 71–75.
28. I have followed the work of one such leading figure, Samuel Tilden, and traced the world of Democratic intellectuals within which he worked, in (Kelley) *The Transatlantic Persuasion.*
29. Valuable on the public distrust of colleges, universities, and higher learning is Veysey, *The Emergence of the American University*, pp. 13–18.
30. "Barton S. Alexander," U.S. Army Corps of Engineers, Office of History: Biographical Files.
31. Pisani, *From the Family Farm to Agribusiness*, pp. 113–120.
32. Ibid., pp. 143–144; "Barton S. Alexander," U.S. Army Corps of Engineers.
33. Martin Reuss, "Andrew A. Humphreys and the Development of Hydraulic Engineering: Politics and Technology in the Army Corps of Engineers, 1850–1950," *Technology and Culture* 26 (Jan. 1985), 1–33.
34. That Alexander was the principal engineering adviser to Colusa-area swampland owners may be seen in the original announcement of Reclamation District 108, an immense operation, and in an affidavit of one of the swampland owners, W. H. Parks: see *Colusa Sun*, Oct. 29, 1870, and "Affidavit" filed by W. H. Parks, Dec. 17, 1874, in *Laux* v. *Parks*, case no. 922, Tenth District Court, Colusa County. The substance of his advice may be seen in what these people, on the basis of his recommendations attempted to do, and in various utterances of Will S. Green, later cited.

35. The description of Green's plan, which follows, is based, as indicated in the following note 36 below, on his own account of it contained in articles in his newspaper. Official documents are unavailable. In the state legislature's printed records, there is a title page to the *Report of the Commissioners appointed to Examine into the Practicability of Making a New Outlet for the Flood Waters of the Sacramento Valley* (December 8, 1869), upon which body Will Green sat, but the report itself consists of a single plaintive page which asks for a sum of up to a thousand dollars to collate and print the large document they were ready to produce. The legislature was apparently not interested; it was never printed. See: *Journals of the California Senate and Assembly*, 18th session, appendix, vol. 3 (Sacramento, 1870).
36. For the foregoing, see Green's comments in the *Colusa Sun* on: Mar. 3, 1871; Dec. 6, 1873; and Jan. 26, 1878.
37. See: Richard Jensen, *The Winning of the Midwest: Social and Political Conflict, 1888–1896* (Chicago, 1971); Paul Kleppner, *The Third Electoral System: Parties, Voters, and Political Cultures* (Chapel Hill, N.C., 1979); Campbell, Jr., *Representative Democracy*.
38. Morton quoted by David Herbert Donald, "The Republican Party 1864–1876," in Arthur M. Schlesinger, Jr., ed., *History of U.S. Political Parties* (New York, 1973), II, 1281–1289.

7 ~ THE LEVEE-BUILDING SPIRAL BEGINS

1. *Colusa Sun*, Jan. 2 and 9, 1868.
2. San Francisco *Alta*, Feb. 9, 1867.
3. *Colusa Sun*, Jan. 2 and 9, 1868.
4. Ibid., May 30, 1868.
5. Ibid., Mar. 20, 1869, and Mar. 12, 1870; McComish, *History of Colusa and Glenn Counties*, p. 58.
6. *Colusa Sun*, April 12, 1873, and obituary, Dec. 8, 1906; *Marysville Appeal*, Dec. 9, 1906; McComish, *History of Colusa and Glenn Counties*, p. 95; Justus H. Rogers, *Colusa County . . .* (Orland, Calif., 1891), p. 364; James M. Guinn, *History of the State of California . . .* (Chicago, 1906), p. 1484.
7. *Marysville Appeal–Democrat*, Dec. 14, 1937.
8. *Swamp Land Record—Act of 1868*, book A, pp. 4–5; *Minutes*, Board of Supervisors, Colusa County, book B, p. 64.
9. Thompson and West, *History of Sutter County*, p. 66.
10. Swamp Land Survey Book A, Sutter County, pp. 150–151; Thompson and West, *History of Sutter County*, p. 80; *Colusa Sun*, Mar. 16, 1867.

11. Thompson and West, *History of Sutter County*, p. 66; *Weekly Sutter Banner*, Feb. 24, 1872.
12. *Colusa Sun*, Sept. 10, Oct. 8, 15, 19, 22, 1870; *Weekly Sutter Banner*, Feb. 24, 1872.
13. See "Affidavit," filed by W. H. Parks, Dec. 17, 1874, in *Laux* v. *Parks*; "Petition for Rehearing," *Moulton* v. *Parks*, 1883, 64 Cal 166 (State Archives file no. 6219); *Minutes*, Board of Supervisors, Sutter County, book C, Mar. 11, 1871, pp. 402–403, and April 3, 1871, pp. 410–412.
14. Obituary in *Marysville Appeal*, July 29, 1887.
15. *Colusa Sun*, Feb. 6, 1875.
16. *Minutes*, Board of Supervisors, Sutter County, book C, Mar. 11, 1871, pp. 402–403, and April 3, 1871, pp. 410–412.
17. *Weekly Sutter Banner*, April 15 and 22, 1871; Thompson and West, *History of Sutter County*, pp. 67–68.
18. *Weekly Sutter Banner*, July 15, 1871; *Minutes*, Sutter County Board of Supervisors, book C, p. 448.
19. *Colusa Sun*, Sept. 9 and Nov. 18, 1871, July 18 and Sept. 12, 1874. Jan. 3, Nov. 14, and Dec. 12, 1885; *Swamp Land Record—Act of 1868*, book A, Colusa County, pp. 21–25; "Report of Plans and Specifications of Trustees of Reclamation District 124," filed Nov. 9, 1871, Colusa County; McComish, *History of Colusa and Glenn Counties*, p. 94; Sacramento Valley Reclamation Company, *Tule Lands* . . . (1872).
20. *Colusa Sun*, Dec. 21, 1889.
21. *Swamp Land Record—Act of 1868*, book A, Colusa County, pp. 18–20; *Minutes*, Board of Supervisors, Colusa County, book B, pp. 196–200; *Colusa Sun*, Dec. 24, 1870.
22. *Colusa Sun*, Nov. 11, 1871; *Swamp Land Record—Act of 1868*, book A, Colusa County, pp. 27–30, approved Nov. 7, 1871.
23. *Colusa Sun*, Oct. 18 and 25, 1873.
24. Ibid., April 11, 1874.
25. *Swamp Land Record–Act of 1868*, book A, Colusa County, pp. 32–36, 39–40.
26. Green, *Colusa County*, pp. 59–60; *Colusa Sun*, Aug. 8 and 22, Sept 12 and 26, 1874, Mar. 27, Nov. 9, 1875, Jan. 15, Mar. 4, 1876, and Jan. 1, 1878.
27. This was the final ruling in a superior court proceeding to which I contributed expert historical testimony that essentially developed this point; *Sacramento and San Joaquin Drainage District* v. *Zumwalt et al.*, Butte Superior Court, Oroville, my narrative being presented on July 11, 1967.
28. These events may be followed in the *Colusa Sun*: Jan. 12, 16, 25, 27, 29, Mar. 4, 29, Sept. 30, 1932, Jan. 30, 1933. See also State of Califor-

nia, Reclamation Board, *Minutes,* pp. 6449 and 6483, Mar. 16, 1932, and p. 6496, Mar. 28, 1932.

29. *Colusa Sun,* Mar. 4, 1932.

8 ~ The Parks Dam War: The North and the South in Arms Again

1. *Colusa Sun,* Nov. 18, 1871.
2. Ibid., Nov. 25, 1871.
3. *Minutes,* Board of Supervisors, Sutter County, book C, pp. 503–504.
4. Ibid., July 13, 1872, p. 575; *Colusa Sun,* Dec. 30, 1871; *Weekly Sutter Banner,* Dec. 30, 1871, and Jan. 20, 1872; Thompson and West, *History of Sutter County,* pp. 67–68.
5. *Colusa Sun,* Jan. 6, 13, and 20, 1872.
6. Ibid., Dec. 14, 1872.
7. Ibid., Feb. 10, 1872.
8. See accounts of AB 15 in ibid., Jan. 29 and Mar. 4, 1876.
9. Thompson and West, *History of Sutter County,* pp. 67–68; *Colusa Sun,* Dec. 6, 1873.
10. Laux affidavit, Oct. 6, 1874, in *Laux* v. *Parks,* case no. 922, Tenth District Court, Colusa County.
11. *Weekly Sutter Banner,* Jan. 3, 1874.
12. *Colusa Sun,* Jan. 24, 1874.
13. *Weekly Sutter Banner,* Jan. 3, and 10, and February 24, 1874.
14. Ibid., Feb. 14 and 28, 1874; *Colusa Sun,* Feb. 7, 1874.
15. *Minutes,* Board of Supervisors, Sutter County, book D, July 12, 1874, pp. 154–155.
16. On this issue, see: Howe, *The Political Culture of the American Whigs;* David Grimstead, "Rioting in Its Jacksonian Setting," *The American Historical Review* 77 (Mar. 1971), 361–397; Kelley, *The Cultural Pattern in American Politics,* pp. 167–168, 214–215; Formisano, *The Birth of Mass Political Parties.*
17. Friedman, *A History of American Law,* pp. 391–398.
18. Don E. Fehrenbacher, *Slavery, Law, and Politics: The Dred Scott Case in Historical Perspective* (New York, 1981).
19. As to the latter, consult: Pisani, *From the Family Farm to Agribusiness,* in which this scholar, who is much interested in the impact of the law on the economy, discusses many court cases, as in his extensive exploration of one of California's landmark cases, *Lux* v. *Haggin,* pp. 191–249; and Robert G. Dunbar, *Forging New Rights in Western Waters* (Lincoln, Neb., 1983).

20. For the foregoing and what follows, consult: records in *Laux* v. *Parks*, case no. 922, Tenth District Court, Colusa County; in *Moulton* v. *Parks*, 64 Cal 166 (State Archives file no. 6219); and *Moulton* v. *Laux*, 52 Cal 81, "Transcript on Appeal" (State Archives file no. 3329). See also: *Colusa Sun*, April 12, 1873.
21. Ibid.
22. *Colusa Sun*, Jan. 2, 1875; and court cases cited in note 20, above.
23. *Weekly Sutter Banner*, quoting *Marysville Appeal* of Jan. 27, 1875; *Colusa Sun*, Jan. 30, 1875.
24. *Minutes*, Board of Supervisors, Sutter County, book D, May 7, 1875, p. 256; and pp. 260, 262, 266–268. A specific description of the district appears in Sutter County *Swamp Land Survey Book* "A," pp. 154–155, May 7, 1875.
25. *Colusa Sun*, Aug. 28 and Oct. 39, 1875.
26. Oral history interview on Mar. 28, 1972, by R. Kelley with (then 90+-years-old, and very alert) C. E. Reische, longtime secretary of RD 70, who had spent his entire life in the district. He reported family accounts of these events, in which a member of his family had participated. See also: the records, in *Moulton* v. *Parks*, above cited; *Weekly Sutter Banner*, Jan. 8 and 13, 1876; *Colusa Sun*, Jan. 15, 1876.
27. Of the many historical works exploring the ills of Gilded Age America and the grave alarm they induced in the national mood, I have found Paul C. Nagel's *This Sacred Trust: American Nationality 1798–1898* (New York, 1971) to be exceptionally useful.
28. Harold M. Hyman and William M. Wiecek, *Equal Justice Under Law: Constitutional Development 1835–1875* (New York, 1982), pp. 347–349. See also Friedman, *A History of American Law*, pp. 358–363.
29. Ibid., p. 556.
30. *Moulton* v. *Parks*, particularly "Findings of Fact" in "Transcript on Appeal"; *Colusa Sun*, Jan. 4 and 10, Feb. 14, and Mar. 4, 1876, Mar. 23, 1878.
31. State of California, Reclamation Board, *Fourth Biennial Report* (Sacramento, 1918), p. 30.

9 ~ CALIFORNIA MOBILIZES FOR A NEW ASSAULT ON THE INLAND SEA

1. Benjamin F. Gilbert, "The Period of the Workingmen's Party," in Delmatier et al., *The Rumble of California Politics*; Alexander Saxton, *The Indispensable Enemy: Labor and the Anti-Chinese Movement in California* (Berkeley, Los Angeles, London, 1971), pp. 104–114.

2. See sources in preceding note, pp. 75–78 (Gilbert) and 113–120 (Saxton).
3. Gilbert, "Workingmen's Party," pp. 85–88; Saxton, *The Indispensable Enemy,* p. 128.
4. On the Constitutional Convention, see: Carl B. Swisher, *Motivation and Political Technique in the California Constitutional Convention, 1878–1879* (Claremont, Calif., 1930); Gilbert, "Workingmen's Party," pp. 85–88; Saxon, *The Indispensable Enemy,* pp. 127–132; *Debates and Proceedings of the Constitutional Convention of the State of California, Convened at the City of Sacramento, Saturday, September 28, 1878,* 3 vols. (Sacramento, 1881).
5. Gilbert, "Workingmen's Party," p. 88; Green, *Colusa County,* pp. 36–38.
6. Mable B. Jones, *The Republican Party in California, 1877–1881,* unpublished master's thesis (Stanford University, 1957), pp. 66–67; Winfield J. Davis, *History of Political Conventions in California, 1849–1892* (Sacramento, 1893), p. 421.
7. *Sacramento Daily Record-Union,* Feb. 6, 1878; *Mining and Scientific Press* (San Francisco), Feb. 16, 1878; *Daily Evening Bulletin* (San Francisco), Feb. 18, 20, 23, 24, 1878.
8. *Bulletin,* Mar. 9, 1878.
9. See for example Pisani, *From the Family Farm to Agribusiness,* chap. 5, "Irrigation in the 1870s: The Origins of Corporate Reclamation in the Arid West," pp. 102–128.
10. Ibid., p. 162.
11. Ibid.
12. *Record-Union,* Jan. 5 and 14, 1878; *Senate Journal,* 22nd session, p. 93; *Bulletin,* Jan. 12, 1878.
13. *Marysville Appeal,* Feb. 17, 1878; *Record-Union,* Mar. 4, 7, 1878.
14. This core strand in the Whig–Republican mind and the opposing attitudes of the Democrats have been much illuminated in the historical literature on political culture previously noted. My own research into the minds of Gilded Age Republicans, as seen in the thought of James G. Blaine, Benjamin Harrison, and William McKinley, though as yet unreported, has confirmed for me the deep, persisting nature of this image of society and class relations which they inherited from their predecessors.
15. *Record-Union,* Jan. 5, 1876.
16. Ibid., Mar. 4, 7, 1878; *Marysville Appeal,* Feb. 17, 1878.
17. For a look into the Green–Parks argument over his plan, see the *Record-Union* for March 11, 1878, which printed a letter from W. H. Parks summarizing the controversy and condemning canals through the basins as harmful to real flood control, since they would spread the water.

18. *Marysville Appeal,* Feb. 19 and March 1–3, 1878.
19. *Senate Journal,* 22d session, pp. 310–379; *Assembly Journal,* 22d session, p. 710; *Record-Union,* Mar. 26, 28, 1878; *Bulletin,* Mar. 26, 1878.
20. "An Act to provide a system of irrigation, promote rapid drainage, and improve the navigation of the Sacramento and San Joaquin Rivers," Mar. 28, 1878, *Statutes,* 22d session, pp. 634–636.
21. Pisani, *From the Family Farm to Agribusiness,* chap. 7, "William Hammond Hall and State Administrative Control over Water in the Nineteenth Century," pp. 154–190.
22. Manson will continue to appear in this history. For biographical details, see *Who's Who in California, 1928–29,* p. 294; and a sketch of him at his death in *Western Construction News* 4 (Dec. 10, 1929), 655.
23. For biographical data, see *Who's Who in California, 1928–29,* p. 282; and Pisani, *From the Family Farm to Agribusiness,* p. 261.
24. For general information on Hall's survey project, see his first report to the legislature: *Report of the State Engineer to the Legislature of the State of California—Session of 1880.*
25. See *Colusa Sun,* Sept. 19, 1974, *Record-Union,* Mar. 13, 1880; and *Marysville Appeal* for background to Mendell's study. Kelley, *Gold vs. Grain,* pp. 77–83, describes the 1876 legislative debate and the appeal to Congress. The letter books of the chief Corps officer in California after Alexander's death, Lt. Col. George H. Mendell, are in the Bancroft Library, University of California–Berkeley; the 1878–1879 correspondence describes his river-survey activities.
26. U.S. Army Corps of Engineers, *The History of the U.S. Army Corps of Engineers,* pp. 47–50; Frank E. Smith, *The Politics of Conservation* (New York, 1966), pp. 80–86; Reuss, "Andrew A. Humphreys and the Development of Hydraulic Engineering," pp. 1–33.
27. U.S. Army Corps of Engineers, Office of History, Biographical Files; and *Colusa Sun,* Sept. 17, 1874.
28. Draft manuscript, U.S. Army Corps of Engineers, Office of History, "Engineers and Irrigation: The Alexander Commission's Report on Irrigation in the Central Valley of California, 1873," ca. June, 1987, p. 32, citing *Alta California,* Dec. 16, 1878.
29. Melendy and Gilbert, *The Governors of California,* pp. 137–140.
30. Quoted in *Record-Union,* Jan. 9, 1880.

10 ~ THE GREAT DRAINAGE ACT FIGHT AND THE REVERSION TO FLOOD CONTROL ANARCHY

1. See chap. 2, "The Farmers Begin to Protest 1856–1876," in Kelley, *Gold vs. Grain.*

2. 53 Cal 724; Kelley, *Gold vs. Grain,* chap. 3, "The First Battle: 1876–1879," pp. 85–130.
3. William Ham. Hall, *Report of State Engineer to Legislature of California,* 23d session (Sacramento, 1880), part III, pp. 48–59.
4. Ibid., pp. 14–15.
5. G. K. Gilbert, *Hydraulic Mining Debris in the Sierra Nevada,* U.S. Geological Survey, professional paper 105 (Washington, D.C., 1917), p. 43; Thomas L. Casey, *Mining Debris, California,* 51st Congress, House executive document 267 (Washington, D.C., 1891), p. 9.
6. Hall, *Report* (1880), part II, p. 75.
7. Ibid., part II, pp. 11 and 14.
8. Ibid., part II, pp. 13–14.
9. Ibid., part III, pp. 31–37.
10. Ibid., part II, p. 14.
11. Ibid., part II, pp. 15, 70–71.
12. Ibid., part II, p. 72.
13. For detailed description of this argument, see chap. 4, "Compromise—The Drainage Act, 1880," in Kelley, *Gold vs. Grain,* pp. 131–156.
14. *Marysville Appeal,* Feb. 19, 24, 25, 26, 1880; *Record-Union,* Feb. 27, 1880.
15. G. H. Mendell, "Mining Debris in Sacramento River," House of Representatives, 46th Congress, 2d session, executive document no. 69 (Washington, D.C., 1880); *Record-Union,* Mar. 13, 1880; *Marysville Appeal,* Mar. 12, 1880.
16. *Record-Union,* Mar. 19, 1880.
17. Pisani, *From the Family Farm to Agribusiness,* p. 170.
18. Kelley, *Gold vs. Grain,* pp. 144–150.
19. See House executive document no. 76, 46th Congress, 3d session: "Report of Chief of Engineers for 1881"; see letter of Secretary of War to Sacramento Board of Trade, quoted in *Marysville Appeal,* Jan. 3, 1886.
20. Pisani, *From the Family Farm to Agribusiness,* pp. 169–170.
21. "Report of the Board of Directors of Drainage District No. 1," *Journals of the California Senate and Assembly,* appendix, 24th session; *Record-Union,* Nov. 11, 1880.
22. *Record-Union,* Nov. 11, 12, 1880.
23. *Assembly Journal,* 24th session, p. 144; *Record-Union,* Jan. 27, 1881.
24. For a detailed account of the repeal controversy in the legislature, see chap. 5, "The Fight over Repeal: 1881," in Kelley, *Gold vs. Grain.*
25. *Record-Union,* Jan. 28, 1881.
26. "Special Message of Governor George C. Perkins," *Journals of the California Senate and Assembly,* appendix, 24th session.
27. *The People* v. *Parks,* 58 Cal 626.

28. Ibid., p. 628.
29. Ibid., pp. 625–626.
30. Ibid., pp. 627–628.
31. Ibid., pp. 630–631.
32. Ibid., p. 639.
33. See chap. 6, "The Second Offensive: 1881–1882," in Kelley, *Gold vs. Grain*, pp. 188–216.
34. Cited either as 18 F 753 or 9 Sawy. 441.
35. See chap. 7, "The Farmers Gain Total Victory 1882–1884," in Kelley, *Gold vs. Grain*, pp. 215–242.
36. See chap. 8, "The Occupation: 1884–1890," in ibid., pp. 243–270.
37. U.S. Geological Survey, Gilbert, *Hydraulic Mining Debris in the Sierra Nevada*, pp. 29–30.
38. U.S. Army Corps of Engineers, Lt. Col. G. H. Mendell, "Report on a project to protect the navigable waters of California from the Effects of Hydraulic Mining," House executive document no. 98, 47th Congress, 1st session (Washington, D.C., 1882).
39. Letter from Secretary of War to Sacramento Board of Trade, quoted in *Marysville Appeal*, Jan. 3, 1886.
40. See Kelley, *Gold vs. Grain*, pp. 236–237, 252–253, 263–267.

11 ~ REENTRY

1. *Colusa Sun*, Nov. 14, 1885; Aug. 31, Sept. 28, Dec. 14 and 21, 1889; Dec. 31, 1891; Dec. 31, 1904.
2. For the efforts of the Sacramento board of trade, see *Marysville Appeal*, Jan. 3, 1886.
3. Of the abundant literature on these national events, the following may be consulted: John A. Garraty, *The New Commonwealth: 1877–1890* (New York, 1968); Lawrence Goodwyn, *The Populist Moment: A Short History of Agrarian Revolt in America* (New York, 1978).
4. Quoted in *Grass Valley Daily Union*, Oct. 19, 1895.
5. Kelley, *Gold vs. Grain*, pp. 272–273.
6. *Marysville Appeal*, Mar. 10, 1887; *Assembly Journal*, 27th session, p. 739; *Senate Journal*, 27th session, p. 745.
7. U.S. War Department, *Report of Board of Engineers on Mining-Debris Question in State of California*, 51st Congress, 2d session, House of Representatives, executive document no. 267 (Washington, D.C., 1891).
8. Melendy and Gilbert, *The Governors of California*, pp. 237–245.
9. Kelley, *Gold vs. Grain*, pp. 279–280.
10. July 22, 1892.

11. For the foregoing, see Kelley, *Gold vs. Grain,* pp. 280–281. On Benjamin Harrison, see Harry J. Sievers, *Benjamin Harrison,* 3 vols. (1952–1968), and Benjamin Harrison, *Public Papers and Addresses* (1893). Concerning Grover Cleveland, see chap. 8 in Robert Kelley, *The Transatlantic Persuasion.*
12. For the later discussion of the significance of this phrase by the Corps of Engineers' officer-in-charge, when its implications were eventually discovered, see: California Debris Commission, *Flood Control—Sacramento and San Joaquin River Systems, California* (Washington, D.C., 1913).
13. *Grass Valley Daily Union,* Feb. 8, 1893.
14. Stephen Skowronek, *Building a New American State: The Expansion of National Administrative Capacities 1877–1920* (Cambridge, Eng., 1982), pp. 140–143.
15. Ibid., p. 145.
16. Ibid., pp. 145–162.
17. U.S. Government, *Statutes at Large,* Act of March 1, 1893, vol. 27, p. 507.
18. State of California, Commissioner of Public Works, *Report to the Governor of California* (Sacramento, 1895), printed as vol. IV in *Appendix to the Journals of the Senate and Assembly,* 31st session, [hereafter cited as Commissioner of Public Works, *Annual Report* (year)]; State of California, *Statutes, 1893,* p. 345.
19. U.S. War Department, Chief of Engineers, California Debris Commission, *Annual Report* (Washington, 1895). Published as executive document no. 16, House of Representatives, 53d Congress, 2d session; also as appendix YY, *Annual Report of the Chief of Engineers for 1895,* pp. 4049–4075 [hereafter cited as CDC, *Annual Report* (year)]. Concerning Heuer, see: U.S. Government, *Report of the Secretary of War,* vol. II, "Report of the Chief of Engineers" (Washington, D.C., 1871), pp. 914–917, appendix W5, published as executive document no. 1, part 2 (Series Set 1504), House of Representatives, 42nd Congress, 2d session.
20. California Debris Commission, *Annual Report* (1895), p. 8.
21. On the Democrats and their theory of corruption, see Kelley, *The Transatlantic Persuasion,* for extensive exploration of this theme.
22. Kelley, *Gold vs. Grain,* p. 290.
23. Commissioner of Public Works, *Annual Report* (1895), pp. 9–10.
24. Ibid., p. 17.
25. Ibid., pp. 58–59; and Reuss, "Andrew A. Humphreys and the Development of Hydraulic Engineering," p. 27.
26. Commissioner of Public Works, *Annual Report* (1895), pp. 61–70.

27. Ibid., p. 18.
28. Melendy and Gilbert, *The Governors of California,* pp. 247–258.
29. California State Engineer, E. A. Bailey, "Historical Summary of State Legislative Action with Results Accomplished in Reclamation of Swamp and Overflowed Lands of Sacramento Valley, California" [hereafter cited as "Bailey Report"].
30. Kelley, *Gold vs. Grain,* pp., 290–295.
31. *Grass Valley Daily Union,* Jan. 28, 1896.
32. California Commissioner of Public Works, *Report to the Governor on the Condition of the Sacramento River during the High Water of January, 1896* (Sacramento, 1896), pp. 9–11, 26–27; Commissioner of Public Works, *Annual Report* (1895–1896), pp. 15–16.
33. Ibid. (report on condition of Sacramento River), p. 14.
34. *Grass Valley Daily Union,* Feb. 16 and 20, April 6, 15, and 21, 1896; Commissioner of Public Works, *Annual Report* (1895–1896), p. 6, and *Annual Report* (1900), p. 18; CDC, *Annual Report* (1897), published as appendix XX of the *Annual Report of the Chief of Engineers for 1897* (Washington, 1897), pp. 3962–3963.
35. "Bailey Report," pp. 154–155.
36. M. A. Nurse and G. N. Randle, "Report of Engineers," Nov. 30, 1898, in Commissioner of Public Works *Report* (1898), pp. 10–11; Commissioner of Public Works, *Annual Report* (1899–1900), pp. 16–17; River Improvement and Drainage Association of California, Committee of Twenty-Four, "Report," Dec. 7, 1902 (bound as pp. 20–35 in Commissioner of Public Works, *Annual Report* [1902], p. 31); Commissioner of Public Works, *Annual Report* (1904–1906), pp. 8–10.
37. CDC, *Annual Report* (1900), published as appendix AAA, *Annual Report of the Chief of Engineers for 1900* (Washington, D.C., 1900), and as House document no. 431, 56th Congress, 1st session; same for 1901, published as appendix ZZ of *Annual Report of the Chief of Engineers for 1901* (Washington, D.C., 1901), pp. 3625–3633; same for 1902, published as appendix YY of *Annual Report of the Chief of Engineers for 1902* (Washington, D.C., 1902), pp. 2443–2449.
38. *Marysville Appeal,* June 26, 27, and 28, 1901; CDC, *Annual Report* (1901), p. 3628; same for 1902, p. 2444.

12 ~ A Policy Context Transformed: The Progressive Era and the Revival of Planning

1. For the above, see: Kleppner, *The Third Electoral System,* and his *Who Voted: The Dynamics of Electoral Turnout, 1870–1980* (New York, 1982),

and *Continuity and Change in Electoral Politics, 1893–1928* (Westport, Conn., 1987); Walter Dean Burnham, *Critical Elections and the Mainsprings of American Politics* (New York, 1970); Paul Kleppner, Walter Dean Burnham, Ronald P. Formisano, Samuel P. Hays, Richard Jensen, and William Shade, *The Evolution of American Electoral Systems* (Westport, Conn., 1981); Kelley, *The Transatlantic Persuasion,* chap. 8; J. Morgan Kousser, *The Shaping of Southern Politics: Suffrage Restriction and the Establishment of the One-Party South, 1880–1910* (New Haven, Conn., 1974); Jensen, *The Winning of the Midwest;* Samuel T. McSeveney, *The Politics of Depression: Political Behavior in the Northeast, 1892–1896* (Princeton, N.J., 1972).

2. Skowronek, *Building a New American State,* p. 4.
3. Of the large amount of literature on the Progressive Era, the following are especially valuable: David P. Thelen is excellent on LaFollette and the concept of "The People" in his *Robert M. LaFollette and the Insurgent Spirit* (Boston, 1976) and on the spread of citizen activism in his *The New Citizenship: Origins of Progressivism in Wisconsin, 1885–1900* (Madison, Wis., 1972); Otis L. Graham, Jr., *The Great Campaigns: Reform and War in America, 1900–1928* (Englewood Cliffs, N.J., 1971), provides a splendid exploration of the strong-government mystique and of the commissions; David J. Rothman, *Conscience and Convenience: The Asylum and its Alternatives in Progressive America* (Boston, 1980), describes the elite "expert" mind at work in social policy and faith in this concept; Richard Hofstadter, *The Age of Reform from Bryan to F.D.R.* (New York, 1955), is the classic study; and Wiebe's *The Search for Order, 1877–1920,* is fundamental, especially on the new middle class.
4. On conservation as a Progressive Era movement, see: Elmo R. Richardson, *The Politics of Conservation: Crusades and Controversies* (Berkeley and Los Angeles, 1962); James L. Penick, *Progressive Politics and Conservation: The Ballinger–Pinchot Affair* (Chicago, 1968); Gregory Graves, "Anti-Conservation and Forestry in the Progressive Era," doctoral dissertation, UC Santa Barbara, 1987; Smith, *The Politics of Conservation;* Samuel P. Hays' brilliant *Conservation and the Gospel of Efficiency: The Progressive Conservation Movement, 1890–1920* (Cambridge, Mass., 1959); and a valuable overview, not limited to the Progressive Era, Joseph M. Petulla, *American Environmental History: The Exploitation and Conservation of Natural Resources* (San Francisco, 1977). For a broad examination of the literature, see: Gordon B. Dodds, "Conservation and Reclamation in the Trans-Mississippi West: A Critical Bibliography," *Arizona and the West* 13 (1971), 131–171.
5. Samuel Haber, *Efficiency and Uplift: Scientific Management in the Progressive Era 1890–1920* (Chicago, 1964), p. ix.

6. Skowronek, *Building a New American State,* p. 177.
7. Hays, *Conservation and the Gospel of Efficiency,* p. 265.
8. Ibid., p. 266; see also Duane A. Smith, *Mining America,* pp. 67–104.
9. The concept of the new middle class, and its role, was first developed by Wiebe in his *The Search for Order,* chap. 5.
10. See the chap., "The Rise of the Expert," in Hofstadter's *Anti-Intellectualism in American Life* (1963). Thomas C. Cochran also gave "experts" a critical role in business history, as in his *The American Business System: A Historical Perspective, 1900–1955* (1957), pp. 68–71.
11. Wiebe, in *The Search for Order,* explores the efficiency impulse in many social groups; on Taylor, see Haber, *Efficiency and Uplift,* chaps. 1–3.
12. Hays, *Conservation and the Gospel of Efficiency,* p. 266.
13. On the growing size and attitudes of the college-educated in America in these years, see Bledstein, *The Culture of Professionalism.* Samuel P. Hays has skillfully highlighted the faith in science and technology in such works as his *Conservation and the Gospel of Efficiency* (see chap. 13), and in his brilliant introductory essay to Jerry Israel, ed., *Building the Organizational Society* (New York, 1972), pp. 1–15.
14. River Improvement and Drainage Association of California, Committee of Twenty-Four, "Report," Dec. 7, 1902 (bound as pp. 20–35 in Commissioner of Public Works, *Annual Report* [1902]), pp. 23–24.
15. R. Hal Williams, *The Democratic Party and California Politics, 1880–1896* (Stanford, 1973), p. 258.
16. Ibid., pp. 91–92; George E. Mowry, *The California Progressives* (Chicago, 1963), passim, esp. chaps. 3 and 4.
17. Described in William L. Kahrl's remarkable work, *Water and Power: The Conflict over Los Angeles' Water Supply in the Owens Valley* (Berkeley, Los Angeles, London, 1982).
18. On Californians' hopes of the canal, see McGowan, *History of the Sacramento Valley,* I, 15.
19. Sacramento *Bee,* May 6 and 7, 1902, describes the meeting and lists its officers.

    For Miller, see: *Overland,* n.s., XXVII (1896), 459–461; Guinn, *History of the State of California,* p. 906; and "A Banker's View of Reform," *Out West,* XVII (1902), 242–245.

    For McNoble, see: R. D. Hunt, *California and Californians* (San Francisco, 1926), IV, 391.

    For Poundstone, see: *Bee,* May 6, 1902; July 31, 1946, obituary.

    For Boggs, see: ibid., May 6, 1902; *Colusa Sun,* Feb. 15, 1862, and Feb. 2, 1878.

    For Glide, see: *Union* (Sacramento), *Makers of Northern California* (Sacramento, 1917), p. 59.

20. *Bee,* May 6, 1902.
21. San Francisco *Chronicle,* Nov. 27, 1920; Commonwealth Club of California, "Swamp Land Reclamation," *Transactions* IV, no. 5 (Sept. 1909), 253; *Marysville Appeal,* Jan. 25, 1906.
22. *Bee,* May 7, 1902.
23. *Chronicle,* Aug. 26, 1905; *Bee,* Feb. 24, 1938, obituary.
24. Its membership included the following:

    John Coughlan, who owned some 9000 acres in Grand Island, Colusa County (Guinn, *History of the State of California,* p. 1143);
    John Hart, one of the few Democrats, who owned a small farm near Cranmore on the Sacramento (ibid., p. 1175);
    A. C. Bingham, Marysville banker and head of the local water company (*Who's Who on the Pacific Coast, 1913,* p. 51);
    F. F. Ryer, wealthy San Franciscan whose father had developed Ryer Island in the delta, a lawyer, and active in reclamation (Lewis Publishing Company, *Bay of San Francisco: A History* [Chicago, 1892], II, 263; *Bee,* Jan. 17, 1939);
    B. Ettlinger, swampland owner on Ryer Island who lived in San Francisco, world traveler (*Chronicle,* Jan. 5, 1905; *Bee,* May 6, 1902);
    Fred W. Zeile, president of the San Francisco Mercantile Trust (San Francisco *Call,* Oct. 21, 1905);
    A. T. J. Reynolds, a swampland owner in Sacramento County, near Walnut Grove (*Bee,* May 6, 1902);
    Peter Cook, a Rio Vista banker and leading official in large reclamation companies (*Union* [Sacramento], *Makers of Northern California,* p. 35);
    R. E. Wilhoit, a Stockton banker who had held many local offices, a Republican (J. B. Detwiler, ed., *Who's Who in California: A Biographical Directory, 1928–29 . . .* [San Francisco, 1929], p. 413);
    E. W. S. Woods, worth more than a million at his death in 1922, his will being the largest estate ever filed in San Joaquin County, owned thousands of acres in delta islands, and had risen from poverty (Leigh H. Irvine et al., *A History of the New California* [Chicago, 1905], II, 928–930; George H. Tinkham, *History of San Joaquin County* [Los Angeles, 1923], p. 348).

25. For Loben Sels, see: W. J. Davis, *Illustrated History of Sacramento County* (Chicago, 1890), p. 226; for Peart, see: Guinn, *History of the State of California,* p. 641; for Tarke, see: Peter J. Delay, *History of Yuba and Sutter Counties* (Los Angeles, 1924), p. 786; Guinn, *History,* p. 962.
26. Commissioner of Public Works, *Annual Report* (1902), p. 20.
27. Ibid., pp. 5–6.

28. Committee of Twenty-four, "Report," p. 23.
29. Ibid., pp. 22–23.
30. Ibid., pp. 24, 29–30.
31. Pisani, *From the Family Farm to Agribusiness,* pp. 350–351.
32. *Who's Who in California . . . 1928–29,* p. 159; *Bee,* May 25, 1904.
33. Ibid., p. 351.
34. Commonwealth Club, "Swamp Land Reclamation," *Transactions,* IV, no. 5 (1909), 187, 199–200, 230–252, 292; Commissioner of Public Works, *Annual Report* (1905), p. 5.
35. Among sponsors from the Sacramento Valley were the California Promotion Committee, Sacramento Chamber of Commerce, Sacramento Valley Development Association, Stockton Chamber of Commerce, San Joaquin Valley Commercial Association, State Board of Trade, Oakland Board of Trade and Oakland Merchants Exchange; and the following were from San Francisco: Manufacturers and Producers Association, Chamber of Commerce, Merchants Association, Merchants Exchange, and Board of Trade.
36. *Chronicle,* May 6, 10, 12, 13, 19, and 22, 1904.
37. Commissioner of Public Works, *Annual Report* (1905), pp. 5–6; San Francisco *Bulletin,* May 23, 1904.
38. *Bee,* May 25, 1904.
39. Ibid.
40. Hunt, *California and Californians,* IV, 106–107; *Bee,* June 10, 1947.
41. *Bee,* May 25, 1904.
42. *Chronicle,* May 24, 1904; River Improvement and Drainage Association, *Bulletin No. 1,* Aug. 15, 1904, pp. 3–5. Its president was Rufus P. Jennings of the San Francisco Manufacturers' and Producers' Association. The executive committee included leaders from the earlier RIDA, notably Boggs, Ferris, Van Loben Sels, and Woods.
43. *Chronicle,* May 25, 1904.
44. RIAD, *Bulletin No. 3,* Jan. 1905, pp. 3–4.
45. RIAD, *Bulletin No. 2,* Sept. 1904, pp. 1–12.
46. T. G. Dabney, H. M. Chittenden, H. B. Richardson, and M. A. Nurse, "Report of the Commission of Engineers to the Commissioner of Public Works of California" [The Dabney Report], Dec. 15, 1904, in Commissioner of Public Works, *Annual Report* (1905), pp. 1–40.
47. Ibid.
48. A 1905 report of the U.S. Corps of Engineers denied aid on the grounds stated. See: Commonwealth Club, "Swamp Land Reclamation," *Transactions,* IV, no. 5 (1909), 283–284.
49. Samuel Hays has explored all of this at length in his *Conservation and the Gospel of Efficiency,* esp. pp. 93–125, 203–226.

50. RIDA, *Bulletin No. 4,* Feb. 1905.
51. Ch. CCCXLVIII, *California Statutes, 1905,* p. 443; Commonwealth Club, "Swamp Land Reclamation," *Transactions,* IV, no. 5 (1909), 277–280; V. S. McClatchy, "Flood Control: Its Value for Business Development," address at annual convention, California State Bankers Association, May 28, 1914.
52. *The People ex rel W. G. Chapman v. Sacramento Drainage District,* 155 Cal 373, or 103 P 207.

13 ~ The New American State Drains the Inland Sea: The Sacramento Flood Control Project Becomes Reality

1. *Marysville Appeal,* Mar. 19, 20, 21, 1907; *Colusa Sun,* Mar. 20, 1907.
2. Ibid., Mar. 22, 1907.
3. Ibid., Mar. 23, 1907.
4. *Colusa Sun,* Mar. 19–23, 1907.
5. See California Debris Commission, *Report on the Control of Floods in the River Systems of the Sacramento Valley and the Adjacent San Joaquin Valley, Cal.,* House of Representatives, 62d Congress, 1st session, document no. 81 (Washington, D.C., 1911) [hereafter referred to as "The Jackson Report"]), pp. 5, 11.
6. Ibid., p. 5.
7. Most of the Yuba's two-mile-wide bedload of mining debris was subsequently immobilized by a simple arrangement: a local gold-dredging company, in return for the gold it extracted, built high embankments for miles along both sides of the Yuba, composed of dredge tailings, which served as training walls for the stream, concentrating its flow within a reasonably narrow channel and deflecting it through the Daguerre Point sill. This isolated and fixed in place most of the mining debris. For these events, see the annual reports of the California Debris Commission from 1904 to 1910. For descriptions of damage to the barriers, see *Marysville Appeal,* Mar. 19 and 21, 1907. The 1941 *Annual Report* of the CDC stated that the project on the Yuba was completed in 1935, consisting of three training walls 85,100 feet long, in total, which formed two parallel channels for the Yuba River 500 feet wide, the work having been completed partly by the dredging companies and partly by the CDC (pp. 2125–2128, published as appendix YY, *Annual Report of the Chief of Engineers for 1941* [Washington, D.C., 1941], pp. 2124–2140).
8. "Thomas Herbert Jackson," U.S. Army Corps of Engineers, Office of History: Biographical Files; "Thomas Herbert Jackson," U.S. Army

Corps of Engineers, *Annual Report,* June 13, 1938, pp. 215–218; Michael C. Robinson, "Thomas H. Jackson," *APWA Reporter* 50 (May 1983), pp. 6–7.

9. See Jackson's 1909 remarks in Commonwealth Clubs of California, "Swamp Land Reclamation," pp. 308–309.
10. Ibid., p. 289.
11. See Frank Smith, *The Politics of Conservation,* pp. 86–125; Hays, *Conservation and the Gospel of Efficiency,* pp. 104–121, 204–227; California Debris Commission, "Report," in U.S. Government, Army Chief of Engineers, *Annual Report,* appendix EEE (Washington, D.C., 1907), pp. 226–229; "Bailey Report," p. 12; "Sacramento and San Joaquin Rivers, Calif.," House of Representatives, 69th Congress, 1st session, document no. 123, 1925, p. 53; U.S. Statutes, 1909, chap. 147, p. 249.
12. The "Jackson Report," pp. 4–5.
13. Ibid., p. 14.
14. The "Jackson Report," passim; Charles F. Curry, "Control of Floods on the Mississippi and Sacramento Rivers," *Supplemental Report on Flood Control of the Sacramento River, to accompany H.R. 14777,* extract from House Report 616, 64th Congress, (Washington, 1916), p. 134.
15. "Sacramento, Feather, and San Joaquin Rivers, California," *Hearings on a project for the relief from floods in the Sacramento Valley. . . .submitted by the California Debris Commission, February 8, 1913, and H.R. 9912 and H.R. 9913,"* Dec. 8, 1913 and Jan. 12, 1914, House of Representatives, Committee on Rivers and Harbors, 63d Congress, 2d session (Washington, D.C.), p. 46; "Flood Control," *Hearings before the Committee on Flood Control, House of Representatives, 70th Congress, 1st sess., on the control of destructive flood waters of the United States,* Dec. 12 and 13, 1927, part 2: Sacramento–San Joaquin River System (Washington, D.C.), p. 889.
16. Ibid.; Hays, *Conservation and the Gospel of Efficiency,* pp. 107–108.
17. Hays, *Conservation and the Gospel of Efficiency,* pp. 108–109, 122–124, 203–205; Reuss, "Andrew A. Humphreys and the Development of Hydraulic Engineering," pp. 24–25.
18. The "Jackson Report," pp. 1–3.
19. For the background to this decades-old, obsessive problem in California politics, see Williams, *The Democratic Party and California Politics,* passim; and Mowry, *The California Progressives,* passim.
20. "Hiram Johnson," in Melendy and Gilbert, *The Governors of California,* pp. 307–310; Spencer C. Olin, Jr., *Hiram Johnson and the Progressives 1911–1917* (Berkeley and Los Angeles, 1968), pp. 1–33; Mowry, *The California Progressives,* chap. 5.
21. Both Olin and Mowry's works, cited in note 20, are essential in learning

about Johnson's reform agenda and achievements, but it is notable that neither of them pay much attention to conservation and none at all to water issues and achievements. In this connection, read Pisani's recent rediscovery and description of the historic achievements under Johnson in water law and irrigation policy in his *From the Family Farm to Agribusiness,* chap. 11.

22. For the urgings of a Marysville leader, W. T. Ellis, see *Marysville Appeal,* Nov. 11, 1911, and his book *Memories: My Seventy-Two Years in the Romantic County of Yuba, California* (Eugene, Ore., 1939), p. 217; see also V. S. McClatchy, "Flood Control: Its Value for Business Development," address at annual convention, California State Bankers Association, May 28, 1914.
23. *Journal of the Senate* (extra session, 1911), Dec. 9, 1911, pp. 96–97; *Journal of the Assembly* (extra session, 1911), Dec. 22, 1911, p. 352.
24. "Bailey Report," pp. 163–164.
25. "An Act approving the report of the California Debris Commission. . . ," chap. 25, *The Statutes of California and Amendments to the Constitution passed at the Extra Session of the Thirty-Ninth Legislature 1911,* pp. 117–118.
26. "Bailey Report," pp. 120.
27. See McClatchy testimony [he was chairman of the Reclamation Board] in 1913–1914 congressional hearings, cited above, fn. 15, pp. 24.
28. Ibid., pp. 47–48; "Sacramento and San Joaquin Rivers, Cal.," *Hearings on the Subject of the Improvement of the Sacramento and San Joaquin Rivers, Cal.*, held on board the S.S. *Colusa,* July 23 and 24, 1915, before the House Committee on Rivers and Harbors (Washington, 1915), p. 12; V. S. McClatchy, *Hearings before the Drainage, Swamp and Overflowed Lands Committees, Senate and Assembly of the State of California* (March 29, 1915), p. 607, and "Flood Control and Reclamation in California," paper, annual meeting of National Drainage Congress, Cairo, Ill., Jan. 20, 1916.
29. "Address before Citizen's Flood Control Committee and Members of the State Legislature at Sacramento, February 24, 1925, on Senate Bill 313," p. 9.
30. State of California, Reclamation Board, *Flood Control in California* (Sacramento, 1916), pp. 26–29.
31. Hays, *Conservation and the Gospel of Efficiency,* pp. 117–125, 204–240; "Bailey Report," pp. 120–121.
32. U.S. Government, "Flood Control Act of 1917," Public Law no. 367, 64th Congress, H.R. 14777; "Bailey Report," pp. 122–123.
33. State of California Reclamation Board, *Fifth Biennial Report: 1919 and 1920* (Sacramento, 1921), pp. 24–26.

34. "Flood Control and Reclamation in California," address to National Drainage Congress, January 20, 1916.
35. State of California Reclamation Board, *Flood Control and Reclamation in California* (Sacramento, 1916), pp. 10–12.

14 ~ A Valley Transformed

1. "Sacramento and San Joaquin Rivers, Cal.," *Hearings on the Subject of the Improvement of the Sacramento and San Joaquin Rivers, Cal.*, held on board the S.S. *Colusa,* July 23 and 24, 1915, House Committee on Rivers and Harbors (Washington, D.C., 1915).
2. Commonwealth Club, "Swamp Land Reclamation," pp. 302–303.
3. On all of the following matters concerning Valley development, consult McGowan, *History of the Sacramento Valley,* for excellent and illuminating detail.
4. Curry, "Control of Floods," *Supplemental Report,* p. 138; "Jackson Report," p. 7; 1913–1914 congressional hearings (cited in chap. 13, fn. 15), pp. 40–42; Reclamation Board, *Fourth Biennial Report* (Sacramento, 1918), p. 29.
5. Reclamation Board, *Flood Control and Reclamation in California* (Sacramento, 1916), pp. 17–18.
6. California Debris Commission, *Flood Control—Sacramento and San Joaquin River Systems, California,* House of Representatives, Committee on Rivers and Harbors, 63d Congress, 1st session, document no. 5 (Washington, 1913), p. 133.
7. California Debris Commission, *Flood Control in the Sacramento and San Joaquin River Systems,* Dec. 16, 1925, Committee on Commerce, U.S. Senate, 69th Congress, 1st session, document no. 23 (Washington, D.C., 1925), p. 20; 1927 congressional hearings (cited in chap. 13, fn. 15), p. 792.
8. Charles F. Curry, "Control of Floods on the Mississippi and Sacramento Rivers," *Supplemental Report on Flood Control of the Sacramento River,* to accompany H.R. 14777. Extract from House Report No. 616, 64th Congress (Washington, D.C., 1916).
9. Curry, "Control of Floods," *Supplemental Report,* 1916.
10. Ibid., p. 65; 1913–1914 congressional hearings (cited in fn. 15, chap. 13), pp. 30–32; Major U. S. Grant, III, USCE, "Some Problems of the Sacramento River," address before river committee of Sacramento Chamber of Commerce, Nov. 20, 1923; U.S. Government, Department of the Interior, Bureau of Reclamation, *Central Valley Basin: A Comprehensive Report on the Development of the Water and Related*

Resources of the Central Valley Basin. . . . (Washington, D.C., 1949), pp. 168–169.

11. Curry, "Control of Floods," *Supplemental Report,* 1916, pp. 63–64; "Sacramento River, Calif.," *Hearings before the Committee on Rivers and Harbors,* House of Representatives, 69th Congress, 1st session, Jan. 15 and 16, 1926 (Washington, D.C., 1926), pp. 1–5.
12. McClatchy, "Flood Control," pp. 3–4.
13. See Gilbert C. Fite, *American Farmers: The New Minority* (Bloomington, Ind., 1981), pp. 17–19.
14. Kevin Starr, *Inventing the Dream: California Through the Progressive Era* (New York, 1985), p. 132.
15. Pisani, *From the Family Farm to Agribusiness,* p. 10.
16. Ibid., pp. 286–288.
17. Starr, *Inventing the Dream,* p. 134.
18. Pisani, *From the Family Farm to Agribusiness,* passim.
19. Ibid., p. 367; and for the above the whole of chap. 11, "The State Asserts Itself: Irrigation and the Law in the Progressive Period," Pisani, *From the Family Farm to Agribusiness.*
20. *Inventing the Dream,* p. 134.
21. Pisani, *From the Family Farm to Agribusiness,* pp. 378–380.
22. *Thirteenth Census . . . Vol. II: Population,* pp. 138, 150.
23. *Fourteenth Census . . . Vol. II: Population,* p. 1330.
24. *Fifteenth Census . . . Population, Vol. III, Part I,* pp. 233, 278.
25. *Twelfth Census . . . Statistics of Agriculture, Part II,* pp. 62–65, 268–269; *Thirteenth Census . . . Vol. VI: Agriculture,* pp. 148–153; *Fourteenth Census . . . Vol. VI, Part 3, Agriculture,* p. 335; *Fifteenth Census . . . Agriculture, Vol. II, Part 3,* pp. 522, 531.
26. The reports of the Reclamation Board sketch in these problems effectively. See also: Pisani, *From the Family Farm to Agribusiness,* chap. 12; State of California, State Water Problems Conference, *Report,* (Sacramento, 1916); Major U.S. Grant, III, USCE, "Some Problems of the Sacramento River," address before the river committee of the Sacramento Chamber of Commerce, Nov. 20, 1923; Stephen W. Downey, address before citizens' flood control committee and members of the state legislature at Sacramento, Feb. 24, 1925, on SB 313; *Sacramento and San Joaquin Rivers,* House of Representatives, 69th Congress, 1st session, document no. 123, Dec. 12, 1925 (Washington, D.C., 1925); California Debris Commission, *Flood Control in the Sacramento and San Joaquin River Systems,* Dec. 16, 1925, Committee on Commerce, U.S. Senate, 69th Congress, 1st session, document no. 23 (Washington, D.C., 1925); the historical reports by Bailey cited above; "Flood Control Act of 1928," 69th Congress, 1st session, Public Law 391.
27. For the California dimension of these events, see chap. 6, "The Great

Valley Systems," in William L. Kahrl, *The California Water Atlas* (Sacramento, 1979), pp. 46–57.

28. U.S. Government, War Department, Army Corps of Engineers, *Interim Survey of Sacramento River from Collinsville to Shasta Dam, Calif.*, House document no. 649, 78th Congress, 1st session (Washington, D.C., 1944), pp. 26–27; State of California, Department of Public Works, Division of Water Resources, *A Report to the State Reclamation Board on Authorization, Construction, Maintenance and Operation of Sacramento River Flood Control Project* (Sacramento, 1951), p. 51.
29. These figures are conveniently available in David Hornbeck, *California Patterns: A Geographical and Historical Atlas* (Palo Alto, Calif., 1983), appendix A, "Population of California Counties, 1850–1980," pp. 94–95.
30. For the foregoing two paragraphs, I have relied on an interview with Joseph I. Burns and Joseph D. Countryman, long-time civil engineers practicing in hydraulic engineering in the Sacramento Valley; of Murray, Burns and Kienlen, Consulting Civil Engineers, Sacramento; April 18, 1988. On the acreage protected by the project: U.S. Government, Army Corps of Engineers: Sacramento District, *Report on the February 1986 Floods: Northern California and Northwestern Nevada, January, 1987* (Sacramento, 1987), p. 68.
31. Interview, Burns and Countryman.
32. State of California, Department of Water Resources, *California High Water 1981–1982*, bulletin 69–82, August 1983, pp. 39–40.
33. Ibid., *California High Water 1983–1984*, bulletin 69–84, March 1985, p. 20.
34. For the foregoing and succeeding account of the February 1986 flood, I have drawn primarily on (1) interview, Burns and Countryman; and (2) three printed sources: Department of Water Resources, *The Floods of February 1986* (Sacramento, undated); U.S. Government, Bureau of Reclamation, Mid-Pacific Region: Sacramento, *Preventing a Crisis: The Operation of Folsom Dam during the 1986 Flood* (Sacramento, May 1986); and U.S. Army Corps of Engineers: Sacramento District, *Report on the February 1986 Floods: Northern California and Northwestern Nevada, January 1987.*
35. Department of Water Resources, *The Floods of February 1986*, pp. 27–28; letter from Joseph I. Burns to author, May 26, 1988.
36. Ibid., p. 1.
37. U.S. Army Corps of Engineers: Sacramento District, *Report on the February 1986 Floods*, "Overview," unpaged.
38. Table III–4, "Estimated Flood Damages from Overbank Flooding," in ibid., p. 43.
39. Ibid., p. 67.

40. Department of Water Resources, *The Floods of February 1986*, p. 1.
41. Ibid., p. 20.
42. U.S. Army Corps of Engineers: Sacramento District, *Report on the February 1986 Floods*, p. 62; interview, Burns and Countryman.
43. Carl Nolte, San Francisco *Chronicle*, Feb. 24, 1986, quoted in Teets and Young, *Rivers of Fear*, pp. 124–124; and Nolte quoted by Herbert Michelson in the Sacramento *Bee*, Mar. 3, 1986, as quoted in *Rivers of Fear*, pp. 33–34.

15 ~ Reflections: The Sacramento Valley as a Case Study in American Political Culture and the Policy Process

1. See Thomas R. Dye, *Understanding Public Policy*, (Englewood Cliffs, N.J., 1972), 5th ed.
2. Brewer and deLeon, *The Foundations of Policy Analysis*, p. 23.
3. Ibid., passim.
4. The following discussion of the Whigs and Republicans derives in part from Kelley, *The Cultural Pattern in American Politics*, parts II and III; and heavily from Howe's brilliant work, *The Political Culture of the American Whigs*, passim.
5. Ibid., p. 182.
6. Emory Thomas, *The Confederacy as a Revolutionary Experience* (Englewood Cliffs, N.J., 1971).
7. Martin L. Fausold, *Gifford Pinchot, Bull Moose Progressive* (Syracuse, N.Y., 1961); Gifford Pinchot, *Breaking New Ground* (Seattle, Wash., 1972).
8. Starr, *Inventing the Dream*, pp. 254–255; Olin, *Hiram Johnson and the Progressives*, passim.
9. Ibid., p. 274.
10. For the following, see Robert Kelley, "Ideology and Political Culture from Jefferson to Nixon," *The American Historical Review*, 82 (June, 1977), 531–562, *The Cultural Pattern in American Politics*, pp. 282–289, and relevant chapters in *The Shaping of the American Past*, (Englewood Cliffs, N.J., 1986).
11. For the foregoing, see: Arthur S. Link, *Woodrow Wilson and the Progressive Era 1900–1917* (New York and London, 1954), pp. 43–53; W. Elliot Brownlee, *The Dynamics of Ascent: A History of the American Economy*, 2d ed. (New York, 1979), pp. 286–300.
12. Richard E. Neustadt and Ernest R. May, *Thinking in Time: The Uses of History for Decision Makers* (New York, 1986).

≈ Bibliography ≈

~ Newspapers ~

Alta California. San Francisco.
Bee. Sacramento, Calif.
California Chronicle. San Francisco.
Call. San Francisco.
Chronicle. San Francisco.
Daily California Express. Marysville, Calif.
Daily Evening Bulletin. San Francisco.
Daily Union. Sacramento, Calif.
Grass Valley Daily Union. Grass Valley, Calif.
Herald. San Francisco.
Marysville Appeal, and *Marysville Appeal-Democrat*. Marysville, Calif.
Marysville Herald. Marysville, Calif.
Mining and Scientific Press. San Francisco, Calif.
Placer Times. Sacramento, Calif.
Sacramento Record-Union. Sacramento, Calif.
The Colusa Sun. Colusa, Calif.
The North Californian. Oroville, Calif.
Transcript. Nevada City, Calif.
Union. Sacramento, Calif.
Weekly Butte Record. Bidwell Bar, and Oroville, Calif.
Weekly Sutter Banner. Yuba City, Calif.

~ Court Cases, Transcripts ~

Edwards Woodruff v. *North Bloomfield et al.* 9 Sawyer 441 or 18 F 753. Transcript, 26 volumes, maintained in Marysville Public Library, Marysville, Calif.

James H. Keyes v. *Little York Mining Co.* 53 Cal 724.

Laux v. *Parks*. Case no. 922, Tenth District Court, Colusa County, California. (Unpublished)

Moulton v. *Laux*. 52 Cal 81. "Transcript on Appeal." State Archives file no. 3329.

Moulton v. *Parks*, 64 Cal 166. "Petition for Rehearing." State Archives file no. 6219.

The People ex rel W. G. Chapman v. *Sacramento Drainage District*, 155 Cal 373, or 103 P 207.

The People v. *Parks*, 58 Cal 626.

The People v. *The Gold Run Ditch and Mining Company*. 66 Cal 138. Microfilm of testimony maintained in Office of the Attorney General, State of California.

~ Original Sources, Unpublished ~

"Barton S. Alexander." Biographical Files. Office of History, U.S. Army Corps of Engineers. Fort Belvoir, Virginia.

Belz, Helen F. "History of Floods—Yuba City and Vicinity." Yuba City, Calif., 1956.

Colusa County, California. Swamp Land Record—Act of 1868, book A.

———. Board of Supervisors. *Minutes*, book B.

———. County Clerk Files. "Report of Plans and Specifications of Trustees of Reclamation District 124," filed Nov. 9, 1871.

Downey, Stephen W. "Address before Citizen's Flood Control Committee and Members of the State Legislature at Sacramento, February 24, 1925, on Senate Bill 313."

"Engineers and Irrigation: The Alexander Commission's Report on Irrigation in the Central Valley of California." Draft manuscript, ca. June 1987. U.S. Corps of Engineers, Office of History, Fort Belvoir, Virginia.

Grant, Major U.S., III, USCE. "Some Problems of the Sacramento River." Address before river committee of the Sacramento Chamber of Commerce, Nov. 20, 1923.

"George H. Mendell." Biographical Files. Office of History, U.S. Army Corps of Engineers. Fort Belvoir, Virginia.

McClatchy, V. S. "Flood Control: Its Value for Business Development." Address, annual convention, California State Bankers' Association. May 28, 1914.

———. "Flood Control and Reclamation in California," paper, annual meeting, National Drainage Congress, Cairo, Ill., Jan. 20, 1916.

Mendell, Col. G. H., USCE. Letter books. Bancroft Library, University of California–Berkeley.

Sutter County, California. Board of Supervisors. *Minutes*, book C and book D.

———. *Swamp Land Survey Book "A."*

"Thomas Herbert Jackson." Biographical Files. Office of History. U.S. Army Corps of Engineers. Fort Belvoir, Virginia. See also: "Thomas Herbert Jackson," *Annual Report*, U.S. Army Corps of Engineers, June 13, 1938, pp. 215–218; Michael C. Robinson, "Thomas H. Jackson," *APWA Reporter*, 50 (May 1982), 6–7.

~ Pamphlets ~

River Improvement and Drainage Association, *Bulletin No. 1*, August 15, 1904. San Francisco.

———. *Bulletin No. 2*, September 1904. San Francisco.

———. *Bulletin No. 3*. January 1905. San Francisco.

———. *Bulletin No. 4*. February 1905. San Francisco.

River Improvement and Drainage Association of California, Committee of Twenty-Four, "Report," Dec. 7, 1902 (bound as pp. 20–35 in State of California, Commissioner of Public Works, *Annual Report* (1902)—see below).

Sacramento Valley Reclamation Company. *Tule Lands* . . . (Colusa, Calif.), 1872.

~ Government Reports, Publications, Hearings ~

Belcher, Sir Edward. *Narrative of a Voyage Round the World Performed in Her Majesty's Ship Sulphur during the Years 1836–1842*. 2 vols. London, 1843.

California, State of. Commissioner of Public Works. Map, "Yolo Basin, Lower Portion . . . ."

———. ———. *Report to the Governor of California. Journals of the Senate and Assembly*. 31st session. Appendix. Vol. IV. Sacramento, 1895.

———. ———. *Report to the Governor on the Condition of the Sacramento River during the High Water of January, 1896*. Sacramento, 1896.

———. ———. *Annual Report (1895–96)*. Sacramento, 1896.

———. ———. M. A. Nurse and G. N. Randle, "Report of Engineers," Nov. 30, 1898. In *Annual Report* (1898), pp. 16–17. Sacramento, 1898.

———. ———. *Annual Report (1899–00)*. Sacramento, 1900.

———. ———. River Improvement and Drainage Association of California, Committee of Twenty-Four, "Report," Dec. 7, 1902. In *Annual Report* (1902), Sacramento, 1902.

———. ———. *Annual Report (1904–06)*. Sacramento, 1906.

———. Constitutional Convention. *Debates and Proceedings of the Constitutional Convention of the State of California, Convened at the City of Sacramento, Saturday, September 28, 1878*. 3 vols. Sacramento, 1881.

———. Department of Public Works. *A Report to the State Reclamation Board on Authorization, Construction, Maintenance and Operation of Sacramento River Flood Control Project*. Sacramento, 1951.

———. Department of Water Resources. *California High Water 1981–82*. Bulletin 69–82. August 1983.

———. ———. *California High Water 1982–83*. Bulletin 69–83. July 1984.

———. ———. *California High Water 1983–84*. Bulletin 69–84. March 1985.

———. ———. *The Floods of February 1986*. Sacramento, undated.

———. Drainage District No. 1. "Report of the Board of Directors of Drainage District No. 1." *Journals of the California Senate and Assembly*, 24th session. Sacramento, 1880.

———. Governor. "Special Message of Governor George C. Perkins." *Journals of the California Senate and Assembly*, 24th session, appendix. Sacramento, 1881.

———. Legislature. "Report of the Engineer of the Sacramento Valley Irrigation and Navigation Canal." *Journals of the California Senate and Assembly*, 17th session. Sacramento, 1868.

———. ———. "Testimony taken by Committee on Mining Debris . . . ," [Captain Wm. Corlett]. Appendix, *Journals of the California Senate and Assembly*, 22nd session, vol. IV. Sacramento, 1877.

———. ———. *Journals of the Senate and Assembly*. Passim.

———. ———. Assembly and Senate. Committees on Drainage, Swamp and Overflowed Lands. *Hearings before the Drainage, Swamp and Overflowed Lands Committees, Senate and Assembly of the State of California*. March 29, 1915. Sacramento, 1915.

———. ———. Assembly. Committee on Mining Debris. "Testimony taken by . . . as reported to the Assembly." Appendix, *Journals of the Senate and Assembly*, 22d session, vol. IV. Sacramento, 1879.

———. Reclamation Board. *Flood Control in California*. Sacramento, 1916.

———. ———. *Fourth Biennial Report*. Sacramento, 1918.

———. ———. *Fifth Biennial Report: 1919 and 1920*. Sacramento, 1921.

———. State Engineer. [William Ham. Hall.] *Report of State Engineer to the Legislature of California—Session of 1880*. Appendix, 23d session, vol. 5, document no. 1. Sacramento, 1880.

———. ———. [William Ham. Hall.] *Report of State Engineer to the Legislature of the State of California—Session of 1881*. Sacramento, 1880.

———. ———. E. A. Bailey, "Historical Summary of State Legislative

Action with Results Accomplished in Reclamation of Swamp and Overflowed Lands of Sacramento Valley, California." Appendix D. *Sacramento Flood Control Project: Revised Plans.* Sacramento, 1927.

———. State Mineralogist. H. G. Hanks, "Placer, Hydraulic and Drift Mining." *Second Report.* Sacramento, 1882.

———. State Water Problems Conference. *Report.* Sacramento, 1916.

———. *Statutes.* Passim.

———. Sutter County. County Assessor. Report. in *Weekly Sutter Banner,* Yuba City, Sept. 14, 1867.

Dabney, T. G., H. M. Chittenden, H. B. Richardson, and M. A. Nurse. "Report of the Commission of Engineers to the Commissioner of Public Works of California," Dec. 15, 1904. In Commissioner of Public Works, *Annual Report* (1905), pp. 1–40.

Ringgold, Cadwalader, USN. *A Series of Charts with Sailing Directions Embracing Surveys of the Farallones, Entrance to the Bay of San Francisco . . . .* 4th ed. Washington, 1852. [Copies maintained in California State Library]

United States. Bureau of Reclamation. Mid-Pacific Region: Sacramento. *Preventing a Crisis: The Operation of Folsom Dam during the 1986 Flood.* Sacramento, May 1986.

———. Congress. House of Representatives. "Testimony of Major U. S. Grant, III, USCE." *Hearings before the Committee on Flood Control, House of Representatives, 70th Congress, 1st Session, on the control of destructive flood waters of the United States. December 12 and 13, 1927. Part 2: Sacramento–San Joaquin River System.* Washington, D.C., 1927.

———. ———. Charles F. Curry, "Control of Floods on the Mississippi and Sacramento Rivers." *Supplemental Report on Flood Control of the Sacramento River, to Accompany H.R. 14777.* Extract from House report 616, 64th Congress. Washington, 1916.

———. ———. Committee on Flood Control. "Flood Control." *Hearings before the Committee on Flood Control, House of Representatives, 70th Congress, 1st Sess., on the control of destructive flood waters of the United States,* Dec. 12 and 13, 1927. Part 2: Sacramento–San Joaquin River System. Washington, D.C., 1927.

———. ———. Committee on Rivers and Harbors, "Sacramento, Feather, and San Joaquin Rivers, California." *Hearings on a project for the relief from floods in the Sacramento Valley . . . submitted by the California Debris Commission, February 8, 1913, and H.R. 9912 and H.R. 9913,* Dec. 8, 1913 and Jan. 12, 1914. House of Representatives, 63d Congress, 2d session. Washington, D.C., 1914.

———. ———. ———. "Sacramento and San Joaquin Rivers, Cal." *Hearings on the Subject of the Improvement of the Sacramento and San Joaquin*

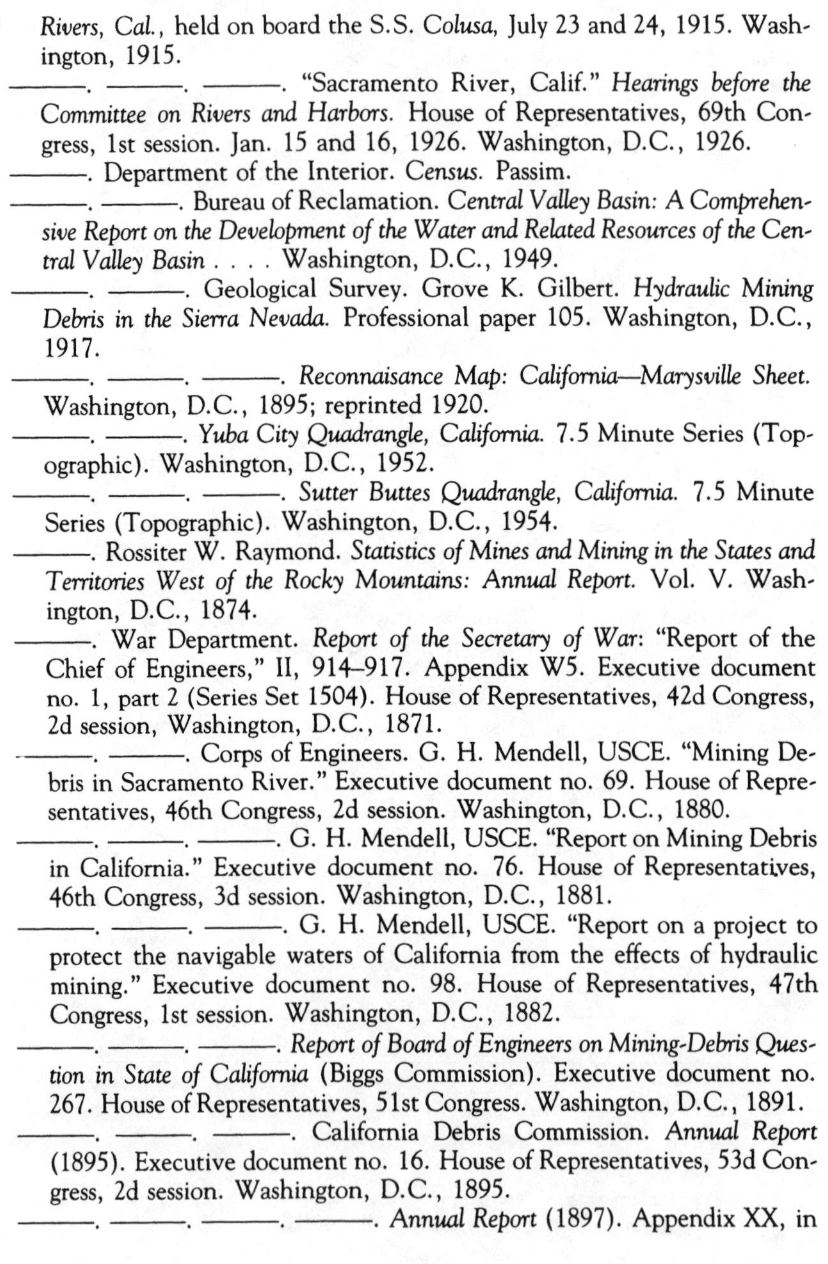

Rivers, Cal., held on board the S.S. *Colusa*, July 23 and 24, 1915. Washington, 1915.

———. ———. ———. "Sacramento River, Calif." *Hearings before the Committee on Rivers and Harbors.* House of Representatives, 69th Congress, 1st session. Jan. 15 and 16, 1926. Washington, D.C., 1926.

———. Department of the Interior. *Census.* Passim.

———. ———. Bureau of Reclamation. *Central Valley Basin: A Comprehensive Report on the Development of the Water and Related Resources of the Central Valley Basin* . . . . Washington, D.C., 1949.

———. ———. Geological Survey. Grove K. Gilbert. *Hydraulic Mining Debris in the Sierra Nevada.* Professional paper 105. Washington, D.C., 1917.

———. ———. ———. *Reconnaisance Map: California—Marysville Sheet.* Washington, D.C., 1895; reprinted 1920.

———. ———. *Yuba City Quadrangle, California.* 7.5 Minute Series (Topographic). Washington, D.C., 1952.

———. ———. ———. *Sutter Buttes Quadrangle, California.* 7.5 Minute Series (Topographic). Washington, D.C., 1954.

———. Rossiter W. Raymond. *Statistics of Mines and Mining in the States and Territories West of the Rocky Mountains: Annual Report.* Vol. V. Washington, D.C., 1874.

———. War Department. *Report of the Secretary of War*: "Report of the Chief of Engineers," II, 914–917. Appendix W5. Executive document no. 1, part 2 (Series Set 1504). House of Representatives, 42d Congress, 2d session, Washington, D.C., 1871.

———. ———. Corps of Engineers. G. H. Mendell, USCE. "Mining Debris in Sacramento River." Executive document no. 69. House of Representatives, 46th Congress, 2d session. Washington, D.C., 1880.

———. ———. ———. G. H. Mendell, USCE. "Report on Mining Debris in California." Executive document no. 76. House of Representatives, 46th Congress, 3d session. Washington, D.C., 1881.

———. ———. ———. G. H. Mendell, USCE. "Report on a project to protect the navigable waters of California from the effects of hydraulic mining." Executive document no. 98. House of Representatives, 47th Congress, 1st session. Washington, D.C., 1882.

———. ———. ———. *Report of Board of Engineers on Mining-Debris Question in State of California* (Biggs Commission). Executive document no. 267. House of Representatives, 51st Congress. Washington, D.C., 1891.

———. ———. ———. California Debris Commission. *Annual Report* (1895). Executive document no. 16. House of Representatives, 53d Congress, 2d session. Washington, D.C., 1895.

———. ———. ———. ———. *Annual Report* (1897). Appendix XX, in

Annual Report of the Chief of Engineers for 1897. Washington, D.C., 1897.

———. ———. ———. ———. *Annual Report* (1900). Appendix AAA, in *Annual Report of the Chief of Engineers for 1900.* Washington, D.C., 1900.

———. ———. ———. ———. *Annual Report* (1901). Appendix ZZ, in *Annual Report of the Chief of Engineers for 1901*. Washington, D.C., 1901.

———. ———. ———. ———. *Annual Report* (1902). Appendix YY, in *Annual Report of the Chief of Engineers for 1902*. Washington, D.C., 1902.

———. ———. ———. ———. *Annual Report* (1907). Appendix EEE, in *Annual Report of the Chief of Engineers for 1907*. Washington, D.C., 1907.

———. ———. ———. *Reports on the Control of Floods in the River Systems of the Sacramento Valley and the Adjacent San Joaquin Valley, Cal.* Document no. 81. House of Representatives, 62d Congress, 1st session. Washington, D.C., 1911 [The Jackson Report]

———. ———. ———. *Flood Control—Sacramento and San Joaquin River Systems, California.* Document no. 5. House of Representatives, Committee on Rivers and Harbors, 63d Congress, 1st session. Washington, D.C., 1913.

———. ———. ———. *Flood Control in the Sacramento and San Joaquin Rivers Systems*. Document no. 23. U.S. Senate, Committee on Commerce, 69th Congress, 1st session. Washington, D.C., 1925.

———. ———. ———. *Sacramento and San Joaquin Rivers, Calif.* Document no. 123. House of Representatives, 69th Congress, 1st session. Washington, D.C., 1925.

———. ———. ———. *Annual Report* (1941). Appendix YY, in *Annual Report of the Chief of Engineers for 1941*. Washington, D.C., 1941.

———. ———. ———. *Interim Survey of Sacramento River from Collinsville to Shasta Dam, Calif.* House document no. 649. House of Representatives, 78th Congress, 1st session. Washington, D.C., 1944.

———. ———. ———. Sacramento District. *Report on the February 1986 Floods: Northern California and Northwestern Nevada. January 1987*. Sacramento, 1987.

———. *Statutes at Large*. Passim.

Wilkes, Charles, USN. *Narrative of the United States Exploring Expedition. During the years 1838, 1839, 1840, 1841, 1842*. 5 vols. Philadelphia, 1845.

~ Secondary Works: Articles ~

Anon. "From San Francisco to Sacramento City," *Hutchings California Magazines*. IV (July 1859), 14.

Commonwealth Club of California, "Swamp Land Reclamation," *Transactions,* IV, 5 (September 1909), 235–275.

Dodds, Gordon B. "Conservation and Reclamation in the Trans-Mississippi West: A Critical Bibliography," *Arizona and the West* 13 (1971), 131–171.

Donald, David Herbert. "The Republican Party 1864–1876." In *History of U.S. Political Parties,* ed. Arthur M. Schlesinger, Jr. (New York, 1973), II, 1281–1289.

Erikson, Erik H. "Fishermen along a Salmon River." In Erickson's *Childhood and Society,* 2d ed., rev. and enl. (New York, 1963), pp. 166–180.

Ershkowitz, Herbert, and William G. Shade. "Consensus or Conflict? Political Behavior in the State Legislatures during the Jacksonian Era." *The Journal of American History* 58 (Dec. 1971), 591–621.

Frank, Richard M. "Forever Free: Navigability, Inland Waterways, and the Expanding Public Interest." *University of California, Davis, Law Review* 16 (Spring 1983), 579–629.

Gilbert, Benjamin F. "The Period of the Workingmen's Party." In Delmatier et al., *The Rumble of California Politics* (see below), pp. 70–75.

Grimstead, David. "Rioting in Its Jacksonian Setting," *The American Historical Review* 77 (Mar. 1971), 361–397.

Kelley, Robert. "Ideology and Political Culture from Jefferson to Nixon," *The American Historical Review,* 82 (June, 1977), 531–562.

Peterson, Richard H. "The Failure to Reclaim: California State Swamp Land Policy and the Sacramento Valley, 1850–1866." *Southern California Quarterly* 56 (Spring 1974), 45–60.

Pisani, Donald J. "Promotion and Regulation: Constitutionalism and the American Economy." *The Journal of American History* 74 (Dec. 1987), 740–768.

———. "Enterprise and Equity: A Critique of Western Water Law in the Nineteenth Century." *The Western Historical Quarterly* 18 (Jan. 1987), 15–37.

Reager, Frank S. "Will S. Green, 'Father of Irrigation.'" Appendix VI, in Green, *Colusa County* (see below), 1950 edition.

Reuss, Martin. "Andrew A. Humphreys and the Development of Hydraulic Engineering: Politics and Technology in the Army Corps of Engineers, 1850–1950." *Technology and Culture* 26 (Jan. 1985), 1–33.

Robinson, Michael C. "Thomas H. Jackson," *APWA Reporter* 50 (May 1983), pp. 6–7.

Scheiber, Harry N. "State Law and 'Industrial Policy' in American Development, 1790–1987," *California Law Review* 75 (Jan. 1987), 425–444.

Thompson, Kenneth. "Historic Flooding in the Sacramento Valley," *Pacific Historical Review* 20 (Sept. 1960), 349–360.

Bibliography

~ Secondary Works: Books ~

Bailyn, Bernard. *Ideological Origins of the American Revolution.* Cambridge, Mass.: Harvard University Press, 1967.

Bakker, Elna. *An Island Called California: An Ecological Introduction to Its Natural Communities.* Berkeley, Los Angeles, London: University of California Press, 1972.

Bellah, Robert N., et al. *Habits of the Heart: Individualism and Commitment in American Life.* Berkeley, Los Angeles, London: University of California Press, 1985.

Benson, Lee. *The Concept of Jacksonian Democracy: New York as a Test Case.* Princeton, N.J.: Princeton University Press, 1961.

Bledstein, Burton J. *The Culture of Professionalism: The Middle Class and the Development of Higher Education in America.* New York: Norton, 1976.

Burnham, Walter Dean. *Critical Elections and the Mainsprings of American Politics.* New York: Norton, 1970.

Brewer, Garry D., and Peter deLeon. *The Foundations of Policy Analysis.* Homewood, Ill.: The Dorsey Press, 1983.

Brownlee, W. Elliot. *Dynamics of Ascent: A History of the American Economy.* 2d ed. New York: Alfred A. Knopf, 1979.

Calhoun, Daniel Hovey. *The American Civil Engineer: Origins and Conflict.* Cambridge, Mass.: Harvard University Press, 1960.

Campbell, Ballard C., Jr. *Representative Democracy: Public Policy and Midwestern Legislatures in the Late Nineteenth Century.* Cambridge, Mass.: Harvard University Press, 1980.

Commonwealth Club of California, *Transactions.* Vol. 4. San Francisco, 1909.

Cox, Archibald. *The Court and the Constitution.* Boston: Houghton Mifflin, 1987.

Curry, Leonard P. *Blueprint for Modern America: Non-Military Legislation of the First Civil War Congress.* Nashville: Vanderbilt University Press, 1968.

Cutter, Donald C., trans. and ed. *The Diary of Ensign Gabriel Moraga's Expedition of Discovery in the Sacramento Valley, 1808.* Los Angeles: G. Dawson, 1957.

Davis, Winfield J. *History of Political Conventions in California, 1849–1892.* Sacramento: California State Library, 1893.

———. *Illustrated History of Sacramento County.* Chicago, 1890.

Delay, Peter J. *History of Yuba and Sutter Counties.* Los Angeles, 1924.

Delmatier, Royce D., Clarence F. McIntosh, Earl G. Waters, eds. *The Rumble of California Politics: 1848–1970.* New York: Wiley, 1970.

De Pue & Company. *Illustrated Atlas and History of Yolo County, Cal. . . .* San Francisco, 1870.

Detwiler, J. B., ed. *Who's Who in California: A Biographical Directory, 1928–29 . . . .* San Francisco, 1929.

Dray, William H. *Laws and Explanation in History.* London: Oxford University Press, 1957.

Dunbar, Robert G. *Forging New Rights in Western Waters.* Lincoln, Neb.: University of Nebraska Press, 1983.

Dye, Thomas R. *Understanding Public Policy.* 5th ed. Englewood Cliffs, N.J.: Prentice Hall, 1972.

Ellison, William Henry. *A Self-Governing Dominion: California, 1849–1860.* Berkeley and Los Angeles: University of California Press, 1950.

Ellis, W. T. *Memories: My Seventy-Two Years in the Romantic County of Yuba, California.* Eugene, Ore.: University of Oregon Press, 1939.

Fausold, Martin L. *Gifford Pinchot, Bull Moose Progressive.* Syracuse, N.Y.: Syracuse University Press, 1961.

Fehrenbacher, Don E. *Slavery, Law, and Politics: The Dred Scott Case in Historical Perspective.* New York: Oxford University Press, 1981.

Fite, Gilbert C. *American Farmers: The New Minority.* Bloomington, Ind., 1981.

Formisano, Ronald P. *The Birth of Mass Political Parties: Michigan 1827–1861* Princeton, N.J.: Princeton University Press, 1971.

Fredrickson, George M. *The Inner Civil War: Northern Intellectuals and the Crisis of the Union.* New York: Harper & Row, 1965.

Friedman, Lawrence M. *A History of American Law.* New York: Simon and Schuster, 1985.

Garraty, John A. *The New Commonwealth: 1877–1890.* New York: Harper and Row, 1968.

Graham, Otis L., Jr. *The Great Campaigns: Reform and War in America, 1900–1928.* Englewood Cliffs, N.J.: Prentice Hall, 1971.

———. *An Encore for Reform: The Old Progressives and the New Deal.* New York: Oxford University Press, 1967.

———. *Toward a Planned Society: From Roosevelt to Nixon.* New York: Oxford University Press, 1976.

Goodwyn, Lawrence. *The Populist Moment: A Short History of Agrarian Revolt in America.* New York: Oxford University Press, 1978.

Green, Will S. *Colusa County, California . . . With Historical Sketch of the County.* San Francisco, 1880. (The 1950 photographic reproduction includes a *Supplement* and several additional articles by Green.)

Guinn, James M. *History of the State of California and Biographical Record of the Sacramento Valley, California.* Chicago, 1906.

Haber, Samuel. *Efficiency and Uplift: Scientific Management in the Progressive Era 1890–1920.* Chicago: University of Chicago Press, 1964.

Hays, Samuel P. *Conservation and the Gospel of Efficiency: The Progressive*

Conservation Movement, 1890–1920. Cambridge, Mass.: Harvard University Press, 1959.

Himmelfarb, Gertrude. *Lord Acton: A Study in Conscience and Politics.* Chicago: University of Chicago Press, 1962.

Hofstadter, Richard. *The Age of Reform from Bryan to F.D.R.* New York: Alfred A. Knopf, Inc., 1955.

———. *Anti-Intellectualism in American Life.* New York: Alfred A. Knopf, Inc., 1963.

Hornbeck, David. *California Patterns: A Geographical and Historical Atlas.* Palo Alto, Calif.: 1983.

Howe, Daniel Walker. *The Political Culture of the American Whigs.* Chicago: University of Chicago Press. 1979.

Hunt, R. D. *California and Californians.* San Francisco, 1926.

Hyman, Harold M., and William M. Wiecek. *Equal Justice under Law: Constitutional Development 1835–1875.* New York: Harper & Row, 1982.

Irvine, Leigh H., et al. *A History of the New California.* Chicago, 1905.

Irwin, I. N., collator. *Sacramento Directory and Gazetteer, for the Years 1857 and 1858 . . . .* San Francisco, 1867.

Israel, Jerry, ed. *Building the Organizational Society.* New York: Free Press, 1972.

Jensen, Richard. *The Winning of the Midwest: Social and Political Conflict, 1888–1896.* Chicago: University of Chicago Press, 1971.

Kahrl, William L. *Water and Power: The Conflict over Los Angeles' Water Supply in the Owens Valley.* Berkeley, Los Angeles, London: University of California Press, 1982.

———, ed. *The California Water Atlas.* Sacramento: State of California, 1979.

Kelley, Robert. *The Cultural Pattern in American Politics: The First Century.* New York: Alfred A. Knopf, Inc., 1979.

———. *The Shaping of the American Past.* Englewood Cliffs, N.J.: Prentice Hall, 1986.

———. *The Transatlantic Persuasion: The Liberal-Democratic Mind in the Age of Gladstone.* New York: Alfred A. Knopf, Inc., 1969.

———. *Gold vs. Grain: The Hydraulic Mining Controversy in California's Sacramento Valley.* Glendale, Calif.: Arthur H. Clark, Co., 1959.

Kleppner, Paul. *Continuity and Change in Electoral Politics, 1893–1928.* Westport, Conn.: Greenwood Press, 1987.

———. *The Third Electoral System: Parties, Voters, and Political Cultures.* Chapel Hill, N.C.: University of North Carolina Press, 1979.

———. *Who Voted: The Dynamics of Electoral Turnout, 1870–1980.* New York: Praeger, 1982.

Kleppner, Paul, Walter Dean Burnham, Ronald P. Formisano, Samuel P.

Hays, Richard Jensen, and William Shade. *The Evolution of American Electoral Systems.* Westport, Conn.: Greenwood Press, 1981.

Kousser, J. Morgan. *The Shaping of Southern Politics: Suffrage Restriction and the Establishment of the One-Party South, 1880–1910.* New Haven, Conn.: Yale University Press, 1974.

Kroeber, Theodora. *Ishi in Two Worlds: A Biography of the Last Wild Indian in North America.* Berkeley, Los Angeles, London: University of California Press, 1971.

Lewis Publishing Company. *Bay of San Francisco: A History.* Chicago, 1892.

Link, Arthur S. *Woodrow Wilson and the Progressive Era 1900–1917.* New York and London: Harper and Row, 1954.

McComish, Charles D. *History of Colusa and Glenn Counties . . . .* Los Angeles, 1918.

McGowan, Joseph A. *History of the Sacramento Valley.* 3 vols. New York and Palm Beach: Lewis Historical Publishing Co., 1961.

McSeveney, Samuel T. *The Politics of Depression: Political Behavior in the Northeast, 1892–1896.* Princeton, N.J.: Princeton University Press, 1972.

Melendy, H. Brett, and Benjamin F. Gilbert. *The Governors of California: Peter H. Burnette to Edmund G. Brown.* Georgetown, Calif.: Talisman Press, 1965.

Merritt, Raymond H. *Engineering in American Society 1850–1875.* Lexington, Ky.: University of Kentucky Press, 1969.

Meyers, Marvin. *The Jacksonian Persuasion: Politics and Belief.* New York: Vintage, 1960.

Mohr, James. *The Radical Republicans and Reform in New York during Reconstruction.* Ithaca, N.Y.: Cornell University Press, 1973.

Mowry, George E. *The California Progressives.* Chicago: Quadrangle Books, 1963.

Nagel, Paul C. *This Sacred Trust: American Nationality 1798–1898.* New York: Oxford University Press, 1971.

Neustadt, Richard E., and Ernest R. May. *Thinking in Time: The Uses of History for Decision Makers.* New York: Free Press, 1986.

Olin, Spencer, C., Jr. *Hiram Johnson and the Progressives 1911–1917.* Berkeley and Los Angeles: University of California Press, 1968.

Penick, James L. *Progressive Politics and Conservation: The Ballinger–Pinchot Affair.* Chicago: University of Chicago Press, 1968.

Petulla, Joseph M. *American Environmental History: The Exploitation and Conservation of Natural Resources.* San Francisco: Boyd and Fraser Pub. Co., 1977.

Pinchot, Gifford. *Breaking New Ground.* Seattle, Wash.: University of Washington Press, 1972.

Pisani, Donald J. *From the Family Farm to Agribusiness: The Irrigation Crusade in California and the West, 1850–1931*. Berkeley, Los Angeles, London: University of California Press, 1984.

Richardson, Elmo R. *The Politics of Conservation: Crusades and Controversies*. Berkeley and Los Angeles: University of California Press, 1962.

Rogers, Justus H. *Colusa County* . . . . Orland, Calif., 1891.

Rothman, David J. *Conscience and Convenience: The Asylum and Its Alternatives in Progressive America*. Boston: Little, Brown, 1980.

Saxton, Alexander. *The Indispensable Enemy: Labor and the Anti-Chinese Movement in California*. Berkeley, Los Angeles, London: University of California Press, 1971.

Schlesinger, Arthur M., Jr., *The Age of Jackson*. Boston: Little, Brown, 1945.

Sellers, Charles. *James K. Polk: Continentalist 1843–1846*. Princeton, N.J.: Princeton University Press, 1966.

Sievers, Harry J. *Benjamin Harrison*. 3 vols. New York: H. Regnery, 1952–1968.

Skowronek, Stephen. *Building a New American State: The Expansion of National Administrative Capacities 1877–1920*. Cambridge, Eng.: Cambridge University Press, 1982.

Smith, Duane A. *Mining America: The Industry and the Environment*. Lawrence, Kans.: University of Kansas Press, 1987.

Smith, Frank E. *The Politics of Conservation*. New York: Pantheon Books, 1966.

Starr, Kevin. *Inventing the Dream: California through the Progressive Era*. New York: Oxford University Press, 1985.

Swisher, Carl B. *Motivation and Political Technique in the California Constitutional Convention, 1878–1879*. Claremont, Calif.: Pomona College, 1930.

Teets, Bob, and Shelby Young, compilers. *Rivers of Fear: The Great California Flood of 1986*. Terra Alta, W. Va.: C. R. Publications, 1986.

Thelen, David P. *The New Citizenship: Origins of Progressivism in Wisconsin, 1885–1900*. Madison, Wis.: University of Wisconsin Press, 1972.

———. *Robert M. LaFollette and the Insurgent Spirit*. Boston: Little, Brown, 1976.

Thomas, Emory. *The Confederacy as a Revolutionary Experience*. Englewood Cliffs, N.J.: Prentice Hall, 1971.

Thompson and West. *History of Sacramento County, California*. Oakland, Calif., 1880.

———. *History of Sutter County, California*. Oakland, Calif., 1879.

Tinkham, George H. *History of San Joaquin County*. Los Angeles, 1923.

Union, Sacramento. *Makers of Northern California*. Sacramento, 1917.

U.S. Army Corps of Engineers. *The History of the U.S. Army Corps of Engineers*. Washington, D.C., 1986.

Veysey, Laurence R. *The Emergence of the American University*. Chicago: University of Chicago Press, 1965.

Who's Who on the Pacific Coast. San Francisco, 1913.

Wiebe, Robert H. *The Search for Order, 1877–1920.* New York: Hill and Wang, 1967.

Wilkes, Charles, USN. *Western America, Including California and Oregon.* . . . Philadelphia, 1849.

Williams, R. Hal. *The Democratic Party and California Politics 1880–1896.* Stanford: Stanford University Press, 1973.

Wood, Gordon. *The Creation of the American Republic, 1776–1787*. Chapel Hill, N.C.: University of North Carolina Press, 1969.

~ Dissertations and Theses ~

Graves, Gregory. "Anti-Conservation and Federal Forestry in the Progressive Era." Doctoral dissertation, University of California, Santa Barbara, 1987.

Thompson, John. "The Settlement Geography of the Sacramento–San Joaquin Delta, California." Doctoral dissertation, Stanford University, 1957.

Hoffman, H. William. "History of Navigation of California's Feather River." Master's thesis, Sacramento State College, 1963.

~ Consultant Papers, Robert Kelley ~

[Unpublished (on deposit, Water Resources Archive, University of California–Berkeley). Fully documented.]

"The Sacramento Flood Control Project: A Documentary and Narrative History." 67 single-spaced pages. September 25, 1963. Case: *Adams et al.* v. *State of California.* Sutter Superior Court, California. Testimony given: December 1963.

"The Feather River: From Oroville to Marysville, 1848–1940." 45 single-spaced pages, with addenda. September 25, 1965. Case: *Robinson et al.* v. *State of California.* Butte Superior Court, California. Testimony given: November 1966.

"The Sacramento River: From Colusa to Butte City, 1850–1920." 26 single-spaced pages. September 10, 1966. Case: *Sacramento and San Joaquin Drainage District* v. *Zumwalt et al.* Butte Superior Court, California. Testimony given: July 1967.

"Flooding and Flood Control in the Simmerly Basin, 1853–1940." 15 single-spaced pages. Case: *Bridges et al.* v. *State of California.* Yuba Superior Court, California. Testimony given: April 1968.

Bibliography

"The Feather River: Honcut Vicinity, 1850–1940." 27 single-spaced pages. August 6, 1970. (Case did not come to trial.)

"Flooding and the Development of Flood Control Systems: Colusa Region, Sacramento River, 1850–1940." 51 single-spaced pages. June 22, 1972. Case: *Laux et al.* v. *State of California.* Colusa Superior Court, California. Testimony given: August 1972.

"Navigation on the Yuba River." 13 double-spaced pages. April 21, 1980. Cases: *State* v. *Yuba Goldfields, Inc.*; *Yuba River Investigation; Brandenburger* v. *State; Lyon* v. *State.* (No testimony.)

"The California Debris Commission (U.S. Corps of Engineers), The State of California, and the Yuba River, 1890–1910." 19 double-spaced pages. March 30, 1981. Case: same as in preceding. (No testimony.)

"The Feather River at Oroville: Navigation and the Effects of Gold Mining, 1850–1882." 35 double-spaced pages, illustrated. May 18, 1982. Case: *Water Resources* v. *Platzek.* (No testimony.)

≈ Index ≈

Note: Page numbers that are underscored signify illustrations.

Other Books By Robert Kelley

Gold vs. Grain:
The Hydraulic Mining Controversy in California's Sacramento Valley
(1959)

The Transatlantic Persuasion:
The Liberal-Democratic Mind in the Age of Gladstone
(1969)

The Cultural Pattern in American Politics:
The First Century
(1979)

The Shaping of the American Past
four editions
(1975, 1978, 1982, 1986)

[Contributor]
The California Water Atlas
William Kahrl, editor
(1979)

[Bicentennial Essayist]
The American Historical Review
"Ideology and Political Culture from Jefferson to Nixon"
Volume 82
(1977)